Kenelm Henry Digby

The broad stone of honour

the true sense and practice of chivalry

Kenelm Henry Digby

The broad stone of honour
the true sense and practice of chivalry

ISBN/EAN: 9783741135644

Manufactured in Europe, USA, Canada, Australia, Japa

Cover: Foto ©Thomas Meinert / pixelio.de

Manufactured and distributed by brebook publishing software (www.brebook.com)

Kenelm Henry Digby

The broad stone of honour

SEMPER FUIT IDEM

THE ARGUMENT.

PAGE.

I. The Interior of an ancient Castle recalls the Images of Chivalry, and prepares the Reader for resuming his Review of the heroic Character in the Middle Ages. All its Virtues proceeded from Religion 1

II. The Honour of Chivalry consistent with Piety and distinguished from the Love of Fame, and illustrated by Examples. Was not reconcileable with any Departure from the Duties of a Christian. Gave rise to Confidence, and Hatred of Suspicion, and to high Dignity . . 8

III. The Refinement and Delicacy of Sentiment which belonged to Chivalry. Examples 49

IV. Humility and Courtesy distinguished the old heroic Spirit, but peculiarly the Christian Chivalry. Its Rules and Precepts. Examples. Enforced by Religion; neglected by whose who adopted the Modern Philosophy . 57

V. The Humanity and Kindness with which the Poor were treated. Proved by the Influence of the Church. By Instances from History and Chivalrous Romances, and by the express Laws of Chivalry. Treatment of Domestics 77

VI. Humanity and Courtesy practised in War. Principles

THE ARGUMENT.

                PAGE.

of General Benevolence widely extended. The Robber Knights an Exception to Chivalry. Examples of Courtesy in War 112

VII. The Valour of Chivalry. Exerted to meet an unavoidable Evil. Instances. Distinguished from the Ferocity of Barbarous Nations. The Invention of Gunpowder. The noble Qualities which were united with Valour. Religious Heroism 140

VIII. Duelling. The Courtesy of Ancient Times allowed much Freedom. Offence not soon given. Vengeance the Spirit of the Moors. The Precepts of Chivalry opposed to Duelling. The Legislation of the Kings of Europe against it. The Judicial Combat. Instances. Condemned by the Church. Ordinary Duelling forbidden under tremendous Penalty 164

IX. Loyalty. Examples. Founded on Religion. How far limited by Theologians, and the Practice of Christian Antiquity 193

X. Friendship. Examples of heroic Friendship. Friendship was not to be sacrificed to every Conceit of public Good. The various Grounds of heroic Friendship . . . 211

XI. The Hospitality of these Ages, illustrated by Scenes from Romances. The Simplicity of its Mode. Attended by sweet Debates. The Style of Conversation . . . 277

XII. Tales of Terror. Romantic Legends 304

XIII. The Simplicity of the Chivalrous Character exemplified. In Manners, Productions of Genius, Painting, in the Customs of Life 334

XIV. Habits of Endurance required for Knighthood. Temperance, Privation, Labour, Obedience, Suffering. The Danger consequent upon such a Life no Ground of Objection. Violent Death not necessarily unprovided Death. The Chivalrous Spirit to be always ready. . 346

XV. The Amusements of these Ages. The Tournament. The Bull-Fights. The Chace. The Love of Horses. Swimming. Rowing. Chess and Tables. Painting. Mock Engagements. Walking Expeditions. The Excellence of these Games 371

Orlandus.

Esse Christianum grande est, non videri.
S. Hieron. Epist. 59, ad Marcell.

A WOLF's head, and the feet of wild boars nailed as trophies upon the wicket in front of an old tower, which was the rendezvous of hunters in the forest, announced to a tired horseman that there was exercise reserved for him in the neighbourhood of the castle, to which he was hastening. Our simple ancestors were never so happy as when in the midst of a wood; and the writings of Gaston Phœbus, Count of Foix, will shew, that they were not insensible to the poetic feeling which forest scenery is so calculated to inspire. When I was in France, young gentlemen would leave the common path and hasten to the thickest and most solitary parts, for the sole purpose of losing their way. Philip Mouske sings of Charlemagne—

> Moult volontiers de grand maniere
> Alloit en bois et en rivière
> Car nuls gens ne vont en bois
> Moult volontiers comme François.

And Englishmen are reminded of this passion as often as they pronounce the name of their Plantagenets.

"Now for the plumed helmets and neighing steeds, the sounding castle courts, the frowning battlement, and all the pomp and circumstance of chivalry!" With such words did the stranger express his delight, when, arriving at a high point which commanded a view over the forest, he beheld the crowning towers cresting the grey walls of the castle, which was about to receive him. The formalities of an arrival at an ancient baronial house, may be passed over in silence; but an incident which occurred the first night, was sufficient to awaken heroic thoughts in the most unpoetical of men. On retiring to rest, the chamber allotted him, as a younger and more familiar guest, was one which had been suffered to remain in its ancient simplicity. The walls, the ceiling, and the furniture, were as they had been some hundred years before. A little door, in a recess, but imperfectly closed, soon drew his attention. He was in a lonely part of the house, and there would be no harm in exploring. Taking up his taper, he passed on, and found himself in a great gallery, which had the appearance of having been long deserted: it had no furniture, excepting an old tapestry. The deep tarnished gilding of the ceiling indicated former magnificence; the tapestry represented graceful figures of knights and beautiful women, with hawks and pages. One part exhibited Donna Maria de

Padilla, sitting like a queen in the midst of other ladies, and the king placing on her head a crown of flowers; and in another place she sat under the shade of a wood, the king showing her a heron. It was affecting to view these scenes, now closed for ever to the figures which once animated them; to see the beautiful faces of those who once rained influence and judged the prize, which are now long since dissolved in the tomb; to reflect, in this magnificent gallery, cheered with soft music,

> How many met who never yet had met,
> To part too soon, but never to forget.

For here, no doubt, came, as to Troy at the marriage of Helen, "the spirit of a breathless calm, and the quiet beauty of wealth, the soft arrow of the eyes, the flower of love, wounding the soul."

> ——— Φρόνημα μὲν
> Νηνίμου γαλάνας, ἀκασκαῖον
> Ἄγαλμα πλούτου,
> Μαλθακὸν ὀμμάτων βέλος,
> Δηξίθυμον ἔρωτος ἄνθος.[1]

It was impossible to resist the speechless lesson of these neglected walls. "He that was yesterday an infant," says St. Jerom, "is now a boy, and will suddenly be a youth, and even perceive himself first to be an old man before he begins to admire that he is not still a boy." O miserable condition of human nature! vain is all that we live for without Christ: where is now that comely vision? Alas! the lily is withered by a southern blast, and the purple of the violet turned into paleness!

> Ἰὼ γενεαὶ βροτῶν,
> ὡς ὑμᾶς ἴσα καὶ τὸ μη-
> δὲν ζώσας ἐναριθμῶ.[2]

Passing on to the further end, he saw another door half open, but, on approaching it, a sudden

---

[1] Æschyl. Agam. 720.   [2] Sophocles, Œdip. Tyr. 1187.

gust of wind extinguished the light. After feeling
his way back, and relighting his taper, he returned
with more caution; but the wind blew so freshly
through the farther door, that he was obliged to
place the taper on the floor of the second room,
and pass on through the dark windy passage, which
he was afraid might contain one of those traps like
that into which Sir Launcelot fell, when walking
round the chamber in a strange castle, he trod on
a board which let him fall into a dungeon twelve
fathoms deep.[1] It was a winding passage which
led him into a small room, which he judged to be
in one of the towers, for it had narrow lancet
windows on three sides, and under one of them he
saw, by the light of the moon, a little iron door, off
its hinges, but leaning against the side of the opening, through which the night wind whistled. It
was like the strong tower into which the nephew of
Sir Isembarte led his unsuspecting guest, Arthur,
to sleep, shutting fast the door, which was all of
iron, and did bar it fast with four great bars, from
which Arthur escaped by bursting the window bars,
and letting himself down.[2] He removed the door,
and found himself on the battlements, looking down
upon a lake, along whose shores the trees made
solemn music. It was a scene to excite imagination and memory. Nor were the early morning
walks to which the sweet season of spring, and
the delicious groves invited him, less agreeable to
the muse. He must have been of stern mould who
could stray without rapture by the side of this
placid lake, frequented by swans, washing the green
sward, among the odoriferous shrubs and the dark
leafy recesses, opening into lawns of exquisite
beauty, on which the hares and pheasants were
peaceably feeding, or at play.

I. We have seen in Tancredus the religion of the

[1] Morte Arthur, XIX, c. 7.   [2] Arthur of Little Britain, p. 414.

Christian chivalry; in the next book, which is called Morus, we have been engaged in the melancholy review of the crimes and errors which led so many men to abandon truth; I propose, in the present sheets, to take a more detailed view of the virtues of the chivalrous character in those ages, when the Catholic faith imparted life and grace to every institution.

This opening prospect is redolent of joy and peace after the scenes through which we have lately passed. It reminds one of having traversed the scorched and desolated plains of France, where nothing remained of Citeaux to sweeten that vale of bitterness, painfully journeying till the high range of the Jura had been mounted; for then there was sudden refreshment in the mountain breeze playing round one's temples, while one gazed with rapture upon dark forests of pine and green flowering meadows, over which innumerable herds were grazing, and traced on every side the blue curling smoke to the little peaceful cottages of a pastoral and happy people.

> Never does captive with a freer heart
> Cast off his chains of bondage, and embrace
> His golden uncontrolled enfranchisement,

more than the dancing soul of youth takes leave of that parched level, with all the recollection of hot thronged cities, with "the busy hum of men," and presses on towards snow-clad mountains, with lakes and rivers rolling at their feet, to the pure sky and the beautiful land of Italy.

It must not be supposed that in concluding the last book we took final leave of the religion of chivalry. With our ancestors, the Catholic religion was still the base, the pervading spirit, the vital principle of every virtue. From it flowed the high sentiment of honour, the fervor of heroism, the contempt for riches, the zeal of loyalty, the constancy of friendship. Marcus Aurelius describes what virtues he had learnt from his father, what from his mother, what from his great-grandfather, what from his governor, what from Diognetus, Rusticus, Apollonius, Sextus, Alexander the grammarian, Fronto, Alexander the Platonist, Catullus, Maximus, and lastly, what from his adopted father, Antoninus. The Count of Stolberg beautifully remarks on these words, that "virtue is a beam of light from above, vice is shade, or the absence of light." The same beam of light spreads itself indeed into seven colours, which have each their name, but it is still one beam, one beam streaming from one all-seeing, all-enlightening, all-warming sun. The divisions and distinctions of virtue which appear in books, like the partitions of knowledge, do not exist in nature, "let them be accepted rather for lines and veins," says an English philosopher, "than for sections and separations." Wisdom, virtue, and happiness, are one, and God is the only source of all good. One virtue could not exist without all others: to be merciful according to the Christian sense, it was necessary to be liberal, poor in spirit, humble, patient, mortified; therefore he that would aspire to solid virtue was excited to the study of obtaining every grace;[1] or rather, to fulfil that short word which expressed the one great rule of life, and way of perfection; for charity was known to be the fulfilling of the law. Charity was that short word, "amo, quia amo, amo, ut amem."[2] "Charity," which the holy Columban said, "was the health of the heart,[3] drew after it every virtue."[4]

[1] P. Nieremberg Doct. Ascet. IV, 1, 5.
[2] S. Bernard, Serm. XCIII, in Cant.
[3] Instruct. XI, Bibl. Patrum.
[4] S. Bernard, Serm. LXXXIII, in Cant. Nieremberg. Doct. Ascet. I, 1, 4.

It was a short word, for it expressed all perfection,[1] therefore many religious orders had no written rules or laws in the beginning, for they grew up and were increased only by obedience to this perfect love of God engraven on the hearts of men. Such were the institutions of St. Basil, St. Augustin, St. Cœsarius, and St. Ignatius Loyola. Charity was the centre of virtues, in which all lines from the circumference met, and had their union and force.[2] Without this fixed force there could be no real virtue. It is clear that this more excellent way exceeded all human discipline, and science, and was only to be ascribed to the light of faith; but still there is ample ground to conclude with certainty, that from the moral declaimers of our age, the wise heathens would have turned in horror, who, as Pliny testifies, deemed nothing well begun, which was not commenced with prayer;[3] who ascribed virtue neither to nature nor to education, but to God alone;[4] who even believed that what the moderns would term a fortunate reply, leading to reward, or the smile of a child, which disarmed the man who was about to kill him, were prompted, as Herodotus says, θείῃ τύχῃ;[5] who thought that Jove was called Ζῆνα, as Diodorus Siculus says, διὰ τὸ δοκεῖν τοῦ καλῶς ζῆν αἴτιον γενέσθαι τοῖς ἀνθρώποις:[6] and who said that "it would be easier to found a city without a ground to stand on, than to form or preserve a state without religion."[7] For a life of virtue without religious faith, and deriving its origin from mere human principles, we must seek among such men as the

---

[1] Wolver. Abb. in cap. I, Cant. 12.
[2] Wolv. Abbas in Cant. S. Gregorii Hom. 27, in Evang.
[3] Panegyr. Aristoph. Ethic. II, c. I.
[4] Plat. Meno.
[5] Lib. III, 139; lib. V, 92.
[6] Lib. III, 60.
[7] Plutarch adversus Colotem.

Greek sophists or their French imitators in the last century. Our present purpose is to view the actions of men who were faithful Catholics in our heroic age; "but such men," as St. Augustin says, "ascribe whatever virtue they can attain in this life only to the grace of God, which is granted to those who desired, believed, and sought, and they well understand how far they fall short of that perfection of justice which reigns in the society of the angels among whom they hope to enter."[1] So that the matter and end of all these books will be found to be one, and although divers chords have been touched, it is my hope that there will result but one melody; and that as a great doctor of the middle age says in one of his divine books, "quamvis diversæ et plurimæ materiæ in diversis capitulis describantur; tamen inde nihil resonat, nisi perfectio animi ad divinum amorem."[2]

II. To begin with that high honour which set men off more than a mortal seeming.

Here was no spirit required inconsistent with the faith and discipline of Catholic chivalry, which sanctions and employs every principle that tends to spiritualize the views of men, and to free them from the yoke of earthly necessities. It is easier to feel than to explain the laws of harmony: yet it is not difficult to understand, that as one cannot be truly liberal without being provident, nor generous without being just, so one cannot have the spirit of sacrifice and humility, nor a zeal for the glory of God, without cherishing a regard to one's honour. Hence, under most circumstances, men might fearlessly repeat the noble words of Thomas Mowbray, Duke of Norfolk, to King Richard II.

---

[1] De Civitate Dei, V, 19.
[2] S. Bonaventuræ Stimulus Divini Amoris, Prolog.

> My dear, dear lord,
> The purest treasure mortal times afford
> Is—spotless reputation;—that away,
> Men are but gilded loam, or painted clay,
> A jewel in a ten-times barred-up chest,
> Is a bold spirit in a loyal breast.
> Mine honour is my life; both grow in one;
> Take honour from me, and my life is done.[1]

"Omitting to speak of spiritual things," says an old writer,[2] "which require a more high explanation, and a more arduous discourse, than I wish at present to undertake, we have nothing temporal of such value as—honour in life, and good and honourable renown after death." "Car pour acquerir et maintenir ces deux choses, nous voyons les gentilshommes, et ceulx qui sont de cœur gentil et honneste, despriser et contemner non seulement les biens meubles et immeubles, dispenser et consommer grand avoir et finance: mais aussi n'estimer rien la vie."

The mere titles of many of the old books, such as "L'Espinette du jeune Prince conquerant le royaume de bonne renommée,"[3] are characteristic of the spirit which, under various modifications, has distinguished generous men in every age. When Xenophon was accused of peculation by Heraclides, he called upon Seuthes to bear witness for him that he had not consulted his own interest in their previous communications with each other, and then he continued: "To Heraclides, indeed, everything seems trifling, excepting what tends, in any way, to gain riches; but, O Seuthes, I am of

---

[1] Act I, scene I.
[2] L'institution du Prince, livre contenant plusieurs histoires, enseignements et saiges dicts des anciens tant Grecs que Latins: faict et composé par maistre Guillaume Budé, secretaire et maistre des Requestes et conseiller du Roy, reveu, enrichy d'arguments, divisé, etc., par hault et puissant seignour, Messire Jean de Luxembourg, Abbé d'Ivry. *Paris*, 1547. Chap. V.
[3] By Simon Bourgouino. *Paris*, 1508.

opinion that there is no treasure which man can possess more honourable or excellent than virtue, and justice, and generosity."[1]

The advice of Minerva to Telemachus, in Homer, is grounded, indeed, upon a principle worthless in itself, and only worthy of a heathen. Be valiant ἵνα τίς σε καὶ ὀψιγόνων εὖ εἴπῃ.[2] This is the motive urged by Sarpedon, when he falls by the spear of Patroclus, calling out to his companion Glaucus to prevent the Greeks from carrying off his armour;[3] and that which animates the last moments of Hector, as he finds himself deserted by the figure of Deiphobus, and betrayed by Minerva.

————— νῦν αὐτί με μοῖρα κιχάνει·
Μὴ μὰν ἀσπουδεί γε καὶ ἀκλειῶς ἀπολοίμην,
'Αλλὰ μέγα ῥέξας τι καὶ ἐσσομένοισι πυθέσθαι.[4]

Yet even the ancient wisdom knew how to derive some good from its action. "Behold," says Plutarch, "how poetry is instrumental to virtue.

Τυδείδη, τί παθόντε λελάσμεθα θούριδος ἀλκῆς;
'Αλλ' ἄγε δεῦρο, πέπον, παρ' ἔμ' ἵστασο· δὴ γὰρ ἔλεγχος
Ἔσσεται, εἴκεν νῆας ἕλῃ κορυθαίολος Ἕκτωρ.

For to find a most prudent man in danger of perishing with a whole people, not sensible to the fear of death, but of shame, must have a powerful effect in exciting youth to virtue."[5] But it was reserved for our Christian chivalry, which referred all its actions to the glory of God, to be enabled to respect the esteem of posterity, without in the least assuming the pride of imaginary greatness, or becoming subject to the opinion of men.

Chaucer quotes St. Augustin, saying that "ther ben two thinges that are right necessarie and nedeful; and that is, good conscience and good los;

[1] Anab. VII, 7.   [2] Od. I, 301.   [3] Il. XVI, 497.
[4] Il. XXII, 303.   [5] De audiendis Poetis.

that is to saye, good conscience to their own persone inward, and good los for thy neighbour outward. And he that trosteth him so muchel in his good conscience that he despitheth and setteth at nought his good name or los, and recketh not though he kepe not his good name n' is but a cruel cherl." St. Bernard, abbot of St. Victor, condescends to speak of glory. "Virtus gradus ad gloriam, virtus mater gloriæ est. Fallax gloria et vana pulcritudo, quam illa non parturivit."[1] Holy men required heroic virtues,[2] and inculcated magnanimity.[3] Honour was part of religion. "Our Lord, true God, who is truth and justice, judges every one according to his intentions." It is thus that the brave Ramon Muntaner argues in his Chronicle of Arragon.[4] "Now the House of Arragon has always prospered by following faith and truth; but God confounds those who have recourse to cunning and falsehood;" and again, "every one should act loyally, for he that acts with loyalty has God with him; and he that acts otherwise will be confounded and destroyed by God." And again, "all those who do not act with sincerity and justice must expect to be thus treated by God." The highest sentiments of honour were taught by the saints and holy fathers. "Omnia tolerabilia præter turpitudinem crede," says St. Martin;[5] again he says, "observe your own actions, nec illos ideo contemnas quia latent: nam nil differt si nemo videat cum tu ipso illos videas;" and again, "magni animi hominis bonum est, non vacillare, constare sibi, et finem vitæ intrepidus expectare."[6] To live with honour was to live with charity, and the objec-

[1] Serm. I.
[2] Nieromberg, Doct. Ascet. I, II, 10.
[3] Nieramberg, IV, c. 40.
[4] Chap. CCLXXXIV, CCLXXXVI, CCXC.
[5] De quatuor virtutibus, Bib. Patrum, IV, 691.
[6] Serm. L

tions which the moderns are apt to adduce against the desire which so powerfully affected our ancestors, may be ascribed to a cause different from a love of Christian humility. Pliny says of his own age, "postquam desiimus facere laudanda, laudari quoque ineptum putamus." The honour to which our ancestors aspired was not inconsistent with their religion, nor with the remembrance that Barabbas had been preferred before their Lord; they were taught by that humiliating example to be calm when other men were preferred before them. "See, my soul," says Bishop Challoner,[1] "the Saint of saints traduced as a blasphemer, and the Author of life judged worthy of death; and learn thou henceforward not to be so much concerned about the judgment of the world; Christ was innocence itself, whereas thy sins deserve other kind of punishments than the world can condemn thee to." St. Patrick, the apostle of Ireland, has left a sentence which might serve as a motto to express the lofty sentiment of chivalry, "sufficit mihi honor, qui nondum videtur, sed corde creditur; fidelis autem qui promisit, nunquam mentitur."[2] And the holy St. Edmund expressly desires men to seek honour. "You must live," he says, "with honour, with love, and with humility; with honour before God, studying in all your thoughts, words, and works, to fulfil his will: with love, that is, to love men as in God, to love men on account of goodness, justice, or truth, for you cannot love men on account of these unless you love God, for God is goodness, and justice, and truth. So you must love the good for being good, and the evil because they might be good; lastly, you must live humbly; and there are two modes of humility: one proceeds from truth, the other from love. The first you can obtain by a

[1] Meditations, vol. I, 179.
[2] Confessio S. Patricii, c. V, Act. Sanctorum, XVII Mart.

knowledge of yourself, for no man can see you as you are in truth, if you are not humbled. The second degree you can have by remembering the humility of our sweet Lord Jesus Christ, how he humbled himself who did no sin; and this pure humility comes from love. Thus you may live with honour, with love, and with humility."[1] This desire of honour, therefore, is not to be confounded with the love of fame, which would have been an unworthy and inadequate motive; for, as St. Augustin says, " we must covet virtue, and leave to others the care of our reputation. Nobis est necessaria vita nostra, aliis fama." Men in these ages were content with having performed a great action, and indifferent about the honour which might follow from it. As when Ricciardo, the faithful squire of the King of France, fought and conquered in obedience to his orders, only that the old Count Aldobrandino might win the beautiful Lisetta, and obtain the glory. In the battle of Valencia, when the Cid defeated King Bucar and the twenty-nine kings, it happened that the Infante Diego Gonzales encountered a Moor of Africa who was of great stature, and when the Infante saw this Moor come fiercely against him, he turned his back and fled. No one beheld this but Feliz Muñoz, the nephew of the Cid, who was a squire; he set himself against the Moor, slew him, and, seizing his horse, led him to the Infante and said, "Take this horse, cousin Diego Gonzales; nobody shall ever know that it was not you who killed the Moor." This young Christian felt what Pliny so well expressed, " quanto majore animo honestatis fructus in conscientia, quam in fama reponatur."[2] Our annals realise what Cicero saw but as an imperfect vision belonging to

[1] S. Edmundi Speculum Ecclesiæ, Bibl. Patrum de la Bigne, IV, 787.
[2] Epist. lib. I, 8.

ages of remote antiquity, a period "cum homines se non jactatione populari, sed dignitate atque innocentia tuebantur:"[1] and what was once said of the few who were eminently wise became true of many; "Virtutis fructum sapiens in conscientia ponit, minus perfectus in gloria."[2] The attention with which men in our heroic age guarded this treasure produces an interesting feature in history. To give an idea of the delicate susceptibility which Calderon ascribes to the sentiment of honour, Schlegel adduces the example of the ermine, which was said to resign itself to death when pursued by the hunters, rather than cross a marsh which would sully the whiteness of its fur. When Louis IX was preparing for his expedition against the infidels, he had recourse to a stratagem. As it was usual for the kings of France to give liveries to the subjects who appeared at court on great festivals, he ordered several to be made with crosses on them, and at Christmas he gave these to the knights, who wrapping the cloak round them followed the king to his chapel, where, by the light of the tapers, they discovered to their great astonishment, first upon those who stood before them and then upon themselves, the sign of an engagement to set out for the Holy Land. Such was the character of these knights, that they all held themselves bound to answer this appeal made to their valour; and, after the divine office, they began to laugh at the dexterity of the king, and took the oath to accompany him to Asia.[3]

When Charles V desired the Marquis de Villena to lend his house to the rebel Constable de Bourbon, the reply of the Castilian was, that he could not refuse gratifying his sovereign in that request, but

[1] Pro A. Cluentio, 35.
[2] Macrobius in Somn. Scip. II, 10.
[3] Michaud, l'Hist. des Croisades, IV, p. 69.

that his majesty must not be surprised if, the moment the Constable departed, he should burn to the ground a house which, having been polluted by the presence of a traitor, became an unfit habitation for a man of honour. When Jean-sans-Peur, Duke of Burgundy, after the murder of the Duke of Orleans, had the audacity to return to Paris, where the king and princes were prevailed upon to see him, Louis de Clermont, Duc de Bourbon, was indignant at the idea of finding himself at the same court with an assassin. He rode out of Paris at the head of one hundred gentlemen of his hotel, and, forcing his way through the Burgundian troops who were about to arrest him, took the road to his domains, where he determined to spend the remainder of his days among his dear vassals.[1] While Henry V was at Southampton, waiting to embark his troops for France, walking one day without the walls he saw a banneret arrive at the head of one hundred and twenty knights, who saluted him, saying, " Seigneur King, I come to offer you this company, which I have raised at my own expense." The King, overjoyed, desired to know his name. " I am the Sir William Olendyne." " A knight, without doubt ? " " No, my lord. I had embraced the monastic state, but I have forsaken the altar for a cuirass." " Deserted the altar ! " replied the King, with anger; " you are a miscreant; begone, I do not want either you or your gifts." Olendyne embarked for France, and fought against the English at Agincourt.[2]

The cruel and unnatural Tostig offered his services to William the Conqueror when he was about to invade England, but William turned from him in horror, and would not permit him to take part in his enterprise, and Tostig departed for Norway. This delicacy never forsook the men of the heroic ages.

[1] Vies des Capit. Français du Moyen Age, V, 286.
[2] Historia Londini MS. ex Bibl. Harleian.

When William of Tyre relates the defection before Antioch, when some of the nobles withdrew from the army, his expression is, " viri nobiles et multa generositate insignes, et alii multi quorum nomina non tenemus: quia deleta de libro vitæ, præsenti operi non sunt inserenda."[1] When King Lisuarte, in Amadis, discovers the evil of his rash promise, he says, "It is better to lose my daughter than to break my word; the one evil afflicts few, the other would injure all: for, how would the people keep faith with one another, if they could not depend upon the King's truth?"[2] This answer was according to the order of knighthood, translated by Mr. Way, where the new-made knight is thus instructed:—

> Still to the truth direct thy strong desire,
> And flee the very air where dwells a liar.

King Charles III of Spain detected one of his most familiar domestics in a lie; he forbade him his presence ever after, but allowed him his pension. The old law runs thus:

> Qu'il ne soit à faux jugement
> N'en lieu ou il ait traïson
> Mais tost s'en parte à abandon
> Se le mal ne peut detourner.[3]

In Spencer when Sir Bourbon says,

> To temporize is not from truth to swerve,
> Ne for advantage term to entertain,
> When as necessity doth it constrain.
> " Fie on such forgery," said Arthegall,
> " Under one hood to shadow faces twain,
> Knights ought be true, and truth is one in all,
> Of all things to dissemble fouly may befall."

As Achilles says to Ulysses in those well-known lines,

> Ἐχθρὸς γάρ μοι κεῖνος ὁμῶς Ἀΐδαο πύλῃσιν,
> Ὅς χ' ἕτερον μὲν κεύθει ἐνὶ φρεσὶν ἄλλο δὲ βάζει.

---

[1] Gesta Dei per Francos, p. 715.   Lib. I, c. 35.
[2] L'Ordène de Chevalerie.

A remarkable instance of delicate honour is the delivery of Du Guesclin from confinement by our Black Prince. The Constable had made some remark on the fear which the English seemed to entertain of his valour, by their continuing to hold him prisoner. Upon which the Prince said hastily, "Far from it, you have only to pay 100,000 francs and you shall be free," to which, Du Guesclin, taking him at his word, made answer, " Sir, in the name of God, so be it. I wyll pay no lesse." " And when the Prince heard him say so," Froissart observes, "he wolde then gladly have repented himselfe: and also some of his counsayle came to him and sayd, ' Sir, ye have not done well, so lightly to put him to his ransome:' and so they wolde gladly have caused the Prince to have revoked that covenant; but the Prince, who was a true and noble knight, sayd, ' sythe that we have agreed thereto, we wyll not breke our promysse.'" Froissart relates how the young Earl of Saint Poule continued for a long time a prisoner in England, " in the fayre castell of Wynsore : and he had so curtesse a kepar that he might go and sport him a haukyng betwene Wynsore and Westminster : he was beleved on his faythe. The same season the Princess, mother to kyng Richarde, lay at Wynsore, and her daughter with her, my Lady Maude, the fayrest lady in all Englande : therl of Saynte Poule and this young lady were in true amours togyder eche of other, and somtyme they met togyder, at daunsynge and carollying; tyll at last it was spyed; and then the lady discovered to her mother howe she loved faithfully the young erle of Sainte Poule: then ther was a marryage spoken of betwene therle and the Lady Maude, and so therle was set to his ransome to pay six score M franks, so that when he had marryed the Lady Maude then to be rebated threescore thousande and the other threescore M to pay. And when this covynant of marryage was made bytwene therle and the lady, the kynge of Englande suffered him to repasse the sea to fetche his raunsome, on his only promyse to retourne agayne within a yere after." The King of France detained him in prison on a false charge for a long time, but at length he was delivered, and then the young Earl returned to England and wedded the lady, and so he and the countess his wife went to live in the castle of Han, on the river Eure.

At the siege of Barcelona, when the governor was on the walls in treaty with the English general, there was an alarm sounded within the city. The governor accused the general of an attempt to surprise him. The English protested their innocence, and suggested that it must arise from an incursion of their German allies, and proposed to enter the city with the governor's permission, and chase them out, after which they promised to return before the walls and finish the treaty. The governor consented. The gates were thrown open to the English, who rushed in and delivered the city from their barbarous companions, and having driven them out at an opposite gate, they proceeded to resume their former position, and to finish the treaty with the governor.

After the battle of Poictiers, the English and Gascon knights questioned their prisoners, upon their honour, as to what ransom they could pay without inconvenience; and they trusted to their statement.

The question of King Henry the Eighth's divorce from Queen Catherine, and the subsequent measures relating to the proposition of the king's spiritual supremacy, gave occasion to a display of virtue and intrepidity, not to be surpassed by any examples in the page of history. The names of Reginald Pole, of Sir Thomas More, and of Bishop

Fisher, will be dear and venerable as long as the sacrifice of worldly interest and life itself to the dictates of justice and honour shall have a claim on the reverence of mankind. But, besides these striking examples, history will sometimes afford evidence of eminent virtue which produces a new and powerful effect upon the mind, from the indirect manner in which it is brought forward. Thus by many writers the murder of the Duke of Suffolk in the reign of Henry VI has been attributed to the policy of the Duke of York, who deemed it necessary to remove so faithful a minister, before he should openly take any measures to place himself on the throne; and a similar hypothesis is certainly true in accounting for the arrest and murder of the adherents of Edward V, the Earl Rivers, the Lord Gray, Sir Thomas Vaughan, and Sir Richard Hawes, who were beheaded in Pontefract Castle, the Lords Hastings and Stanley, with the prelates of York and Ely, who were arrested at the Council in the Tower, whence Hastings was led to instant execution. I need not multiply instances which will abundantly present themselves to the recollection of the reader.

Richelieu took pains to prevail upon Gassion, a brave officer, to act as a spy towards the Count de Soissons. This would have been a step to certain advancement; but the man of honour was above the bribe. "I can give you nothing more than my life. I am ready to lose it for the service of your eminence, but it is not possible for me to sacrifice my honour."

In the time of Peter, King of Arragon, when the Spanish Admiral, Roger de Luria, a Templar, arrived at the port of Malta, where was the fleet of Marseilles; having taken the Provençals by surprise, some of his men cried out, "Now fall on." "God forbid," said he, "that I should attack them while they sleep; let the trumpet sound, and I shall wait till they are ready. Men shall not be able to say that I attacked sleeping men." They all cried out, "The Admiral has well spoken."[1] This was after the spirit of romance. When Orlando in the wood surprised Ferrau, who was engaged in a vain attempt to recover his helmet which he had dropt into a river when stooping to drink after his long contest with Rinaldo, the Count was too generous to attack an enemy under such disadvantage, and weakened, as Ferrau evidently was, by his late combat. He accordingly, after a short conference with him, rode on to join the army of Charlemagne.

Memorable is the reply of the Viscount d'Orthe, Mayor of Bayonne, to the execrable circular order of the French Court. "J'ai communiqué le commandement de votre M. à ses fidèles habitans et gens de la garnison. Je n'y ai trouvé que bons citoyens et fermes soldats mais pas un bourreau." Equally noble was the answer of Jacques de Vacquiere, who went at the head of certain magistrates to return the edicts which they could not conscientiously sign. The enraged king, Louis XI, demanded what they desired? The reply was instant: "La perte de nos charges ou même la mort plutot que de trahir nos consciences." When the Piccinini abandoned William de Montferrat, with whom they were associated by means of Francis Sforza in the siege of Monza, Jacob proposed instantly to attack William by surprise, justifying such treachery by the character of their enemy. "Was it not," said he, "by treason that Sforza directed against Milan an enemy paid by the Milanese?" Francis Piccinino, who had the command, was not to be misled by such sophisms.

[1] Chronica de Ramon Muntaner, chap. LXXXIII.

"In the noble profession of a soldier," he replied, "the sentiment of honour ought never to be subject to the subtlety of logic. Were I to judge in each war the potentates for or against whom I serve, perhaps I should never find one toward whom I might not, by similar arguments, justify perfidy. In the midst of resentment and hatred which he excites, the soldier only sleeps in quiet because he does not believe that infamous actions are possible. I do not exaggerate scruples on the laws of war, as my defection sufficiently proves; but if on the same field of battle where I have been placed by Sforza among his squadrons, and on the same day, I should employ against him the arms which he has given me, if I should abuse his confidence to massacre his soldiers who thought themselves my comrades, though I should be applauded at Milan for having betrayed a traitor, posterity would judge me, and the name of Piccinino could never be freed from this stain." This was acting according to the decision of the chivalrous manual, l'Arbre des Batailles; where the question is proposed, "If two seigneurs are at truce, and one should break it, may the other?" and the reply is "No: for if the one have sinned mortally, the other may not. Se ung homme m'avoit mis et bouté le feu en ma maison ce n'est pas pourtant a dire que je le doye aussi bouter en la sienne."[1] The Comte de Charolois, afterwards Charles the Bold, spared 26,000 of his enemies who were at his mercy, having pledged his word to grant them a day's truce, and though they broke their engagement by withdrawing to a strong post, and even scoffed at him as if he durst not attack them, still he kept his word. " Si se despita le comte durement de sa parole du matin laquelle toutefois n'osoit enfreindre; et se crucifia de quoi

[1] Chap. CVIII.

il les falloit laisser aller sans combattre et de quoi il ne seroit jamès après sans regret."[1] The son of Philippe de Valois furnished another example at the siege of Angoulême. Norwich defended the place, which was unprovided, and the inhabitants favoured France. He demanded and obtained a suspension of arms for the festival of the Purification. "Early in the morning the gates were opened and he marched out with all his warriors loaded with their effects, and passed through the French army. The Duke of Normandy, bound by his word, forbade an attack, and they withdrew in safety."[2] How admirable was the delicate honour of King John of France, which led him to return to England to die there as a substitute for the Duke of Anjou, who had broken his word by withdrawing. Otterbourne, an English author, ascribes his death to the sorrow which his son's infidelity had caused him. "Mortuus est præ dolore, quod Dux Andegaviæ unus obsidum suorum eum deceperat." After a long imprisonment in England, Arthur, the young Count of Richemont, was permitted by King Henry V to reside on the frontiers of Bretagne, at Pontorson, under guard of the Duke of Norfolk. All the chivalry of the province hastened to visit him. On Michaelmas-day the Duke of Norfolk held a fête; and Arthur, shooting with the cross-bow, carried off the prize even from the English. The Bretons transported with joy, and indignant that so noble a prince should be a prisoner, offered to fall upon his guards and rescue him; but Arthur refused to accept their service, informing them that he had pledged his honour not to pass the limits of Normandy.[3]

When La Hire had surprised the fortress of

[1] Chronique de Georges Chastellain, chap. CCLXVIII.
[2] La France sous les cinq premiers Valois, I. 492.
[3] Vies des Capitaines Français du Moyen Age, VI. 36.

Château Gaillard, seven leagues from Rouen, and after the English commandant, Kingston, had departed according to agreement, the French found the brave sire de Barbazan shut up in an iron cage, it being the ninth year since he had been taken prisoner at Melun. The bars were broken, but the knight refused to come out, because he had given his word to Kingston to be his loyal prisoner. A courier was dispatched after Kingston, who returned to deliver Barbazan.[1] In like manner René d'Anjou did not hesitate to return to his sorrowful prison in the tower of Bar, when summoned by Duke Philip, saying that he preferred any fate to the dishonour of having broken his word:[2] and after a long and cruel confinement, when Philip had consented to liberate him on exorbitant terms, which the Council of Lorraine refused to sanction, the king wrote from his tower to the regency, saying that "it deserved his esteem by refusing to agree to a dishonourable treaty, that he would never have signed it, and that he would rather remain a prisoner all his life than purchase his freedom by conditions so burdensome to his people."[3] A word once spoken was to these men holy as religion, immutable as the past. Thus Vico derives *Fas Fatum* from *Fari*. Chivalry had but one rule.

> Faith should be kept unbroken evermore,
> With one or with a thousand men united;
> As well if given in grot or forest hoar,
> Remote from town and hamlet, as if plighted
> Amid a crowd of witnesses, before
> Tribunal, and in act and deed recited:
> Nor needs the solemn sanction of an oath:
> It is sufficient that we pledge our troth.[4]

When the King of the Romans, Lewis of Bavaria, had vanquished and taken prisoner his rival, Fred-

[1] Barante, Hist. des Ducs de Bourgogne, tom. VI. p. 41.
[2] Villeneuve, Hist. de René d'Anjou, I. p. 194.
[3] Ibid.   [4] Ariosto, XXI.

erick of Austria, whom he set free on conditions
which if he could not fulfil he was bound by word
to return again to prison, Frederick finding that
this was the event, and that he could not fulfil
them, did not hesitate to place his fortune again in
the hands of his rival, rather than break his word,
and Lewis was so noble, that they became firm
friends from that hour. It is the saying of Montaigne, "On me garotte plus doucement par un
notaire que par moy-mesme—j'aymeroy bien plus
cher rompre la prison d'une muraille et des loix
que de ma parole." This was the spirit of all men
of honour,

> Saturni gentem haud vinclo nec legibus æquam
> Sponte sua veterisque Dei se more tenentem.

The Captal de Buch was taken prisoner before
Soubise, and kept in the tower of the Temple of
Paris. "The King of England and the Princes
wold gladly have had him delivered, but the French
king nor his counsayl wold not consent thereto.
Howbeit he was shewn by the prior who had him
in keeping, that if he wolde swere never to bere
arms against the crown of France, that then the
king wuld condiscend to his delyverance: the Captall answered, that he wolde never make that othe,
to dye in prison; so he abode in prison in sure
kepynge a V yere with lytill joye, for he toke his
prisonment but with lytill pacyence: and so long
he was there that at last he dyed in prison."
Henri III having resolved on the death of Henri
de Lorraine, Duc de Guise, the balafré, communicated his design to Crillon, who certainly deemed
him worthy of death as a rebel. The king proceeding to explain his intentions more clearly, for
Crillon had thought only of meeting him in battle,
the hero exclaimed, "Then let him be tried on the
charge of high treason as head of the league." The

king shewed the danger of arresting the idol of the people, and continued to explain, saying, "It is by some sudden blow, and it is you whom I expect ———." "Do not finish, Sire," cried Crillon; "permit me to withdraw from the court, where I may blush at having heard my king, for whom I would have given my life a thousand times, demand from me the sacrifice———." He was going on with the sentence, when the king stopped him, "It is enough, I pardon you, you refuse me only through your scrupulous delicacy."

Sophocles has painted a contrast similar to this last history. When Neoptolemus speaks of honour, Ulysses thinks he is jesting. The young man declares he cannot without shame retain the arms which he had been persuaded to obtain by treachery. Ulysses says in reply,

πρὸς θεῶν πότερα δὴ κερτομῶν λέγεις τάδε;[1]

The ancients had certainly some examples before them which would seem to indicate a scrupulous honour. Such was that of Themistocles, who drank bull's blood rather than survive his honour; of Camillus, who sent back the school-boys of the Valerians with that noble speech given by Plutarch; of Fabius Maximus, who so generously came to the assistance of Minutius his scornful rival, and saved him from Hannibal; of Fabricius and Æmilius, who sent despatches to their enemy Pyrrhus to acquaint him with the treacherous plot of his physician; of Sertorius, who rejected the scheme of Mithridates, saying, "A man who has any dignity of sentiment will conquer with honour, and not use any base means even to save his life;" of Cæsar, whom Cicero conjures by his right hand, which had been pledged in friendship to king Deiotarus, saying, "dexteram istam, non

[1] Philoctetes, 1219.

tam in bellis et in præliis, quam in promissis et fide firmiorem;"[1] of Curio, of whom Cæsar says that he chose to be slain in battle rather than return to appear in the presence of Cæsar, having lost the army which had been committed to his trust.[2] In cases, however, where no immediate parade and glory would attend the action, we find but few instances in the heathen annals of that scrupulous delicacy with which our Christian chivalry maintained its honour. Nicias surrendered to Gylippus, as Thucydides says, πιστεύσας μᾶλλον αὐτῷ ἢ τοῖς Συρακοσίοις.[3] When the historian relates that Nicias and Demosthenes were put to death by the Syracusans, he can only add ἄκοντος Γυλίππου.[4] Diodorus even asserts that Gylippus persuaded them in a speech of great length to execute those unfortunate generals.[5] The expression of Pliny, when lamenting the death of his friend Corellius, "amisi vitæ meæ testem," reveals at once the immense difference between the sentiments of a heathen and of a Catholic knight.

The moderns, judging of antiquity from the manners and opinions of a corrupt age, have imagined that these sentiments of honour were often reconcilable with a departure from some laws of morality, while they they were scrupulously held in observing others. But it is certain, on the contrary, that every violation of the duties of a Christian was considered as a foul dishonour. Understood according to Christian views, Plato's definition will answer for that of our chivalrous honour, τιμὴ δ' ἐστὶν ἡμῖν, ὡς τὸ ὅλον εἰπεῖν, τοῖς μὲν ἀμείνοσιν ἕπεσθαι, τὰ δὲ χείρονα γενέσθαι δὲ βελτίω δυνατὰ τοῦτ' αὐτὸ ὡς ἄριστα ἀποτελεῖν.[6] Aristotle defines honour equally well,—" Honour is the sign of being regarded with

---

[1] Cicero pro Rege Deiotar. 3. [2] Cæs. Com. de Bell. Civ. II.
[3] Lib. VII. 85. [4] Lib. VII. 86.
[5] Lib. XIII. 28. [6] De Legibus, V.

favour, and those are justly and chiefly honoured who confer the greatest benefit on others."[1] We are obliged to have recourse to the ancients for a definition of a virtue which they possessed not in an equal degree with our Christian chivalry, because, as de Sacy observes of his countrymen, "our ancestors felt rather than knew what honour was; they disfigured it by their discourse; they adorned it by their actions."[2] René d'Anjou had a list of the great families of Provence, to each of which he wrote a sentence explaining their characters. Among them we find "hospitality and kindness of Angoult; liberality of Villeneuve; wisdom of Rambauds de Simiane; simplicity of Sabran; fidelity of Boliers; constancy of Vintimille; gravity of Arcussia; valour of Blacas; preud'hommie of Cabassole; goodness of Castillon; greatness of Porcelets; loyalty of Salvaing; charity of Arces; prowesse of Terrail; wisdom of Guiffrey; friendship of Beaumont; faith of Commines; countenance of Altvillars." Every possession of virtue was a fresh title of honour, and, as in these sentences, became proverbial through a whole province. The motto of the brave Louis, husband of St. Elizabeth, was that of all chivalry, "Pie! caste! juste!" Castiglione ascribes to the man of honour, in the person of Octaviano Fregoso, piety, greatness of mind, kindness, prudence, courtesy, love of honour and merit; so that his enemies could not help commending him. The utmost purity of manners is inculcated in the old manuals of nobility.[3] What innocence and stability belonged to marriage in the middleages! No bastard even of a king could be a templar or a knight of St. John. A pure origin was as indispensable a qualification as soundness of limb. The author of le Songe du Vergier, who is disposed to

---

[1] De Rhetor. I, 5.   [2] L'Honneur François, tom. I, p. 11.
[3] L'Horloge des Princes, liv. II, c. 39.

censure the manners of his age, acknowledges that
" Ces drois sont moult favourables a ceux qui sont
mariés car trop convient garder le saint ordre de
mariage." Le Breviaire des Nobles, par Maistre
Alain Chartier, will prove the high expectations
which were entertained of all who professed honour:
they were bound to display " foy, loyaulté, droic-
ture, prouesse, amour, courtoisie, diligence, netteté,
largesse, sobrieté, perseverance." The truth of
this opinion may be further illustrated by an event
which is related by Jean Bouchet in his Mémoires
of la Trémouille. The knight without reproach
lived in the reign of Louis XI: he contracted a
friendship for a young nobleman who was lately
married to a beautiful woman, and he was frequently constrained by the importunities of his
friend to pass many days in their castle. An unhappy passion resulted from these repeated visits,
which became the horror and misery of both who
experienced it. The melancholy truth became
known to his friend, car il estoit assez mondain et
de grant esprit. Still he was confident that he
could recall his wife and friend to a sense of their
duty, and thus preserve his own honour. Acquaint-
ing them with his suspicions, he added that it was
his resolution to leave them alone in his castle, and
to depart along with his servants for one day; he
concluded with saying that he fully confided in her
virtue, and in the fidelity of his friend, who would
rather die than act dishonourably. He accordingly
left the castle, and this extraordinary measure was
crowned with success. In like manner Gyron le
Courtois, in that famous romance, was tempted to
forget his fidelity to Danayn le Roux, when he for-
tunately casts his eyes on the hilt of his sword,
where was inscribed the motto, " Loyaulté passe
tout. Faulseté honit tout, et deçoit tous hommes
dedans quels elle se herberge;" upon this he feels

such remorse for having sinned in intention that he plunges his sword into his bosom. Danayn, however, finds him, and he is recovered. In the Chronicle of Flanders we read that a certain gentleman called Fiscord having seduced the daughter of his friend and benefactor Count Arnould, shortly after conceived so extreme a horror and repentance for his disloyalty and felony, that he added to his former crime the horrible and monstrous iniquity of destroying himself. The tale of Hermonides in Ariosto is another instance of purity in faith. Philander, in his travels to Greece, was entertained at the castle of Argæus, his brother-in-arms and bosom friend. The wicked wife of the Castellan is represented as putting his fidelity to proof, but his constancy was not to be shaken. After an interval of some days, Argæus being compelled on some need to ride forth, the young knight was unwilling to remain in the castle, though wounded and requiring repose:

> Though yet he smarted with his wounds and pined,
> He dons his arms and from the tower departs,
> And wanders thence with firm and constant mind,
> Ne'er to return again unto these parts.

Meanwhile the Castellan returning to his wife, she invents a wicked tale, which fires him with indignation against his friend.

> She, by this story, made her husband hate
> The youth, than whom before was dearer none.
> Argæus credits all; without delay
> Arms him, and, breathing vengeance, posts away.
>
> In knowledge of that country not to seek,
> He overtook the knight in little space;
> For my poor brother, yet diseased and weak,
> Rode, unsuspicious, at an easy pace;
> Argæus, eager his revenge to wreak,
> Assailed him straight, in a sequestered place.
> My brother would excuse him if he might,
> But his indignant host insists on fight.

> This one was sound and full of new disdain,
>   That weak and friendly, as aye wont to be.
> My brother was ill fitted to sustain
>   His altered comrade's new-born enmity.

Philander falls his prisoner.

> "Forbid it, Heaven! I should be led astray,
>   So by just wrath and thy iniquity,
> (To him Argæus cried), as thee to slay,
>   Who loved thee once, and certes thou lov'dst me,
> Though in the end thou ill didst this display,
>   I yet desire this ample world may see
> That, measured by my deeds, I rank above
> Thyself in hate as highly as in love."

The peer gives order to lead back the half-lifeless knight, placed on a horse.

> And in a tower enclose the cavalier.
> There dooms the guiltless stripling to remain,
> And suffer prisonment's perpetual pain.
> But that ill dame, her former fantasy
>   Pursuing ever with unwearied sprite,
> Having the keys, repaired nigh every day
> To the close turret where the prisoner lay.

And evermore she offered him his liberty.

> "No, no; have thou no hope (replied the knight),
>   That my true faith shall ever change, although
> It thus should happen that, against all right,
>   I should so hard a sentence undergo.
> Let the world blame. Enough that in His sight,
>   Who sees and judges everything below,
> And in His grace divine my fame can clear—
> My innocence unsullied shall appear."

Six months passed, and no one sought the prisoner's tower. Argæus, in order to catch his old enemy Morando, gave out that he was gone to Jerusalem, hiding himself in the forest, and returning by night, so that all but his wife supposed him far away. She has recourse to a new stratagem, and relates to Philander that her husband is absent, and that a wicked enemy, Morando, has obtained

admission, and she says she has recourse now to
him, in whom is her only security. She bids him
prepare to slay Morando in her chamber that night,
and so preserve the honour of his friend, whom he
professed still to love.

> She drew my brother forth, that guilty night,
>   With his good arms in hand, and him again
> Secreted in the chamber, without light,
>   Till thither came the wretched Castellain.
> As it was ordered, all fell out aright,
>   For seldom ill design is schemed in vain.
> So fell Argæus by Philander's sword,
> Who for Morando took the castle's lord.

What more need be added of this sad history?

> Henceforth he never more was seen to smile;
>   All his discourse was sad, and still ensued
> Sobs from his breast: afflicted in the style
>   Of vext Orestes, when he in his mood
> Had slain his mother——
>   Till broken by the ceaseless grief he fed
> He sickened:

and poison administered treacherously puts an end
to his sorrows.[1]

In a famous romance, Arthur, Governar, and
Hector are entertained at a strange knight's castle.
Arthur and Governar observed that Hector was
dazzled at the beauty of the lady. "'Ah, Hector,'
quod Governar, 'a man's will ought ever to follow the order of reason.' On the next day betimes
they departed and entered into the forest; the
morning was fayr and clere and warm, for it was
then about the end of Apryl. So these lords rode
forth in great joy, till at last Governar taxed
Hector with his behaviour the last night, and said,
'Now, truly, syr, that wyll was neither good nor
honest, but like a vilayne. By the fayth that I
owe unto God, it was no honest thought: it

---

[1] Rose's translation, canto XXI.

wolde not have been wel done of a gentylman, for it were rather treason.'"[1]

Chaucer, who evinces such delicacy in the distinctions of character, and who never loses any occasion of exhibiting the peculiar manners which belonged to different ranks of society, will furnish another proof that licentiousness was considered a degradation.

> The miller is a cherl, ye know well this;
> So was the Reve, (and many other mo)
> And harlotrie they tolden bothe two.

Ramon Muntaner, a brave warrior, is continually bearing testimony, in his Chronicle, to the spotless purity of manners which distinguished the heroic princes of the House of Arragon. Mr. Coxe, in his History of the Spanish Bourbons, acknowledges that these princes were of the most virtuous and even austere habits.

These examples are sufficient to show, that men who sought the honour of chivalry aspired to the purity of a Perceval; so far were they from boasting of any dispensations to tamper with those decrees of wisdom which secure the innocence of youth and the happiness and dignity of the female sex. In opposition to the opinion of some modern writers, the lesson of chivalry was according to the wisdom of the ancients, as evinced in the law of the Athenians respecting adulterers,[2] and in the sentence of Xenophon, καὶ μὴν ὅτι γε οὐ βιάζεται, ἀλλὰ πείθει, διὰ τοῦτο μᾶλλον μισητέος. ὁ μὲν γὰρ βιαζόμενος ἑαυτὸν πονηρὸν ἀποδεικνύει· ὁ δὲ πείθων, τὴν τοῦ ἀναπειθομένου ψυχὴν διαφθείρει.[3] Men in those ages were not such sophists as to maintain that there is any

---

[1] Arthur of Little Britain, p. 64.
[2] Lysias, Orat. de Eratosthen. 32.
[3] Conviv.

connection between licentious habits and what is generous, spirited, or amiable in the human character. The baseness of those who follow the heartless and licentious Galaor was a lesson to them. On the contrary, they knew, as William de Lalain told his son, the celebrated knight, that such manners, which kill the soul, tend more immediately than any other derangement of the moral government, to destroy the imagination, to enervate the character, and to harden the heart. "Nullum denique scelus," says Cicero, "nullum malum facinus esse, ad quod sucipiendum non libido voluptatis impelleret, neque omnino in voluptatis regno virtutem posse consistere." No generous heart could endure the idea of having contributed to such misery as that which Anquetil describes in relating the death of the Duchesse de Fontanges. It is from the visions of the innocent muse, not from the courtiers of Versailles, that youth may learn the spirit of the Christian chivalry. It is the knightly Camoens who can teach them to feel the charms of honour.

> These are the raptures, these the wedded bliss;
> The glorious triumph and the laurel crown;
> The ever-blossom'd palms of fair renown,
> By time unwither'd and untaught to cloy;
> These are the transports of the Isle of Joy.[1]

Let it be observed, that the sentiment of honour was also effectual in preventing men from resting satisfied with forms, and from identifying impunity with justice. Philip of Macedon had condemned a person to pay a great fine. It appeared afterwards that he had been falsely charged. On one side was the justice of his cause, on the other the reason of judiciary forms. Philip satisfied, in some measure, both, by having the sentence recorded, and by

[1] Lusiad, IX.

rewarding the injured party with his purse. Where the modern philosophy prevails, we find that men are invariably content with attending to the judiciary form, however palpable may be the injustice of the sentence which they pronounce. The following passage from "L'Arbre des Batailles" will shew how the same honour was exercised in determining a case of conscience. Suppose the Baron should say, "Well, I gave you safe conduct to come, but not to return," would that be just? "Je vous prie regardons la intention du saufconduit." Now, assuredly, he who took it thought it would serve him in stead to return withal. "Car peu de chose seroit de aller se quand il seroit en sa presence le faisoit tuer." This would not be saufconduit but malconduit. "Item nous disons que toute promesse doit estre entendue selon l'intention de cellui a qui on la fait." Suppose I promise or swear to a king that I will go to the holy sepulchre, and I mean a little place so called near this town: you perceive this would not be according to the king's intention. If a prisoner has sworn to return in case he find not finance, and should not return through fear of death: "il pecheroit mortellement:" but if the finance be impossible, his oath was unlawful, and he must not return lest he be guilty of self-murder. The author, however, seems not quite satisfied with what he says, and so he quotes the opinion of "nostre Maistre Jehan Andrieu." Nor were the vices which disgrace the higher ranks of society in a later age deemed less derogatory to the honour of a knight. "Il doit parler plainement sans dupplicite," says Gilles de Rome, in his Miroir. Guillaume de Lalain, beginning to instruct his son, says, "De toute votre force et puissance mettez peine d'accomplir les commandements de Dieu." Then he warns him against pride, anger, envy, avarice, idleness, gluttony, and luxury.

Speaking of envy, he says, "Oncques dame d'honneur ne peut aimer homme envieux, si ce n'est en exerçant bonnes vertus, pour y etre le meilleur : comme à l'Eglise le plus devot ;—en compagnies de dames le plus gracieux et plaisant : et en armes armigeres et en armes courtoises le plus vaillant.

"Et sachez, mon fils, que de tant que etes plus noble qu'un autre, de tant devez etre plus noble de vertus : car la noblesse de bonnes mœurs vaut trop mieux que la noblesse des parents."

He then warns him against idleness; for, of the true knight, he says, "Soit pour chanter, soit pour danser, sur tous les autres il est le plus diligent et le plus joyeux à lever matin, dire ses heures, ouïr la messe dévotement, aller à la chasse, etc. Vous serez reputé à vilain si vous ne faites attemprance de vous au vin : donc par ainsi faire, mon fils, vous vivrez par cours de nature tres longuement, et serez en la grace de Dieu au regard de ce peché, aussi d'amour et de votre Dame : et aurez laissé ce très vilain et deshonnête peché de gloutonnie et vous accompagnerez avec la douce vertu d'abstinence, fleur de toutes vertus." At the court of Charles VI of France it was remarked as the greatest infamy, that many princes and lords were in the habit of not paying their debts to tradesmen. Louis de Clermont, duc de Bourbon, slain in the battle of Poitiers, while parrying a blow aimed at King John, had contracted great debts, though most distinguished for the greatness of his alms. His creditors had applied to the Pope, who, after long remonstrances, had excommunicated him. The day after the battle, when the Mayor of Poitiers came to raise up the noble dead for solemn sepulture, the bishop enforced the laws of the Church, which denied the duke's body holy rites. The young Louis, his son, only eighteen years of age, hastened to obviate the calamity; and though the laws of the State could not oblige him, he immediately paid the creditors. The excommunication was taken off; Louis conveyed the body of his father, which had been embalmed, and buried it in the church of the Franciscans at Paris, by the side of his uncle, Louis I.[1] In short, religion and honour were so inseparably united, that it was impossible to offend against the laws of the one without departing from what was required by the other. How fine is the description of a Duke of Normandy in an old romance: "Passynge ryche of goodes, and also vertuous of lyvynge, and loved and dred God above all thynge, and dyde grete almesse dedes, and exceeded all other in ryghtwysnesse and justyce, and moost chivalrouse in dedes of armes;" and when this duke made his ungracious son a knight, he told him that he must "forsake his vyces and moost hatfull lyf." But Robert said, "As for the ordre of knyghthood, I set nothynge thereby, for there is no degre shall cause me leve my condycyons nor chaunge my lyfe, for I am not in that mynde to do better than I have done hetherto, nor to amende for no man lyvynge."[2]

A noble confidence and a hatred of suspicion accompanied these sentiments of honour. Every man was taught by the Church that his mistrust ought to begin at home, according to the expression of John de Castaniza.[3] Let us take examples.

"And so Arthur rode forth all the longe daye tyll it was nere nyght; and than at the last they came to a myghtie strong toure, the which pertained to a knyght named Sir Roger the Scot. Then the vilayne sayd to Arthur, 'Syr Knyght, it is now good tyme to lodge us here, now in this castel, al thys nyght; let us goo entre in to this place; but one thynge I ensure you, the knyght that oweth this place is the

---

[1] Vies des Capitaines Français au Moyen Age, tom. V, 5.
[2] The Lyfe of Robert the Devyll, printed by Wynkyn de Worde.
[3] Spiritual Combat, 43.

most shamefullest traytor that now is lyvynge, for there is none that entreth into this place but shamefully he doth murder them whyle they be in their beddes: he is also cosyn germayne to the Duke of Bygor, and nephewe to Sir Fyrmount, who was but now of late slayne at the castell of the rock by a knyght straunger; therefore now let se what ye wyll do, whether ye wyll go lodge in this place or not.' 'Well,' sayde Arthur, 'I se well and I lie withoute, I shall be shrewdly lodged: and syth this knyght is of that lignage that ye speke of, he is my mortall enemy; how be it, as yet I cannot complayne on hym, for he dyd me never no trespasse, therefore certaynly I wyll go thyther to take my lodgyng.'"[1]

In another history, when Galaor was conducted to a castle in a forest, seated upon a rock, where the murderer Palinques dwelt, he demanded entrance, and two knights appeared upon a tower, who, winding a winch about, let down a basket by a cord, saying, "This is the way in." "Will ye promise to draw me up in safety?" said Galaor. "Yea, truly; but afterwards we will not warrant you." "Wind up, then," quoth he, "I take your word;" and he placed himself in the basket. "God protect thee, thou gentle knight," cried the damsels who had conducted him to the castle, "for thou hast a good heart." They drew him safely up, and he leapt from the basket, when the combat commenced.[2] Yet in those ages there was certainly danger of being betrayed: witness the situation of Talbot in France, or the murder of the Duke John of Burgundy, on the bridge of Montereau, in the presence of the Dauphin, in the reign of Charles VI; or the imprisonment and death of the counts of Castille, after they had been invited to the court

---

[1] Arthur of Little Britain, LVII.
[2] Amadis de Gaul, I, c. 20.

of Ordoño II, the Gothic King of Spain, in the tenth century. But confidence could not be separated from the high principles in which men were nurtured, and it extended to universal nature.

Albertus Magnus noteth, that fowlers, seeking for goshawks, found one in a vast wilderness, perched upon a tree, not offering to stir from them. They, wondering why the bird flew not away at the sight of men, perceived that she was weak, blind, lame, and wasted with decrepit age: whereupon they hid themselves, expecting the coming of other goshawks; when instantly, behold, two hastened thither laden with meat, which they pulled in pieces and thrust into the beak of the poor old one.

What confidence in the charms of nature!

In diffusing this spirit, the precepts of holy men agreed with the inclinations of chivalry. "Semper debet plura et majora de proximo credere quam valeat intueri." This is what St. Bonaventura said.[1] What deep wisdom was contained in the remark which occurs in Tirante the White, "That all the good of this world consists in faith alone." Ramon Muntaner, after taking sorrowful leave of the infante En Ferrand, who was in prison, went to the cook and gave him money, and even some of the clothes off his back, beseeching him to prevent any poison from being mixed with the prisoner's food. "I made him put his hands on the Gospel, and swear in my presence, that he would suffer his own head to be cut off before he would permit any misfortune to befall the infante arising from the food prepared for him."[2]

Georges Chastellain exclaims, after relating the confidence which King Edward placed in the promises of the Earl of Warwick, "O nature de vrai

[1] Stim. divini Amoris, pars II, c. 1.
[2] Chronica, CCXXXVIII.

noble homme, et comme par toutes terres tu es à tost et à légier deceue, et par trop estre noble et de noble entière foy, tu chiés à estre trompée et escharnie de ceulx qui te doivent faire ciel et trosne, glorifier par loenges et par graces rendues, et en contraire te procurent et gardent mort et ruine."[1] When the Duke of Ferrara disclosed to Bayard his treacherous plan, the brave knight could only express his thoughts by making the sign of the cross several times. He felt what was so affectingly described by King Henry V., when he said to the traitor Lord Scrope:—

> Oh, how hast thou with jealousy infected
> The sweetness of affiance?—Shew men dutiful?
> Why, so didst thou: seem they grave and learned?
> Why, so didst thou: come they of noble family?
> Why, so didst thou: seem they religious?
> Why, so didst thou:
> And thus thy fall hath left a kind of blot
> To mark the full-fraught men, the best endu'd,
> With some suspicion. I will weep for thee.[2]

But here was only the astonishment of the moment expressed, for had he persisted in the reproachful question, "Is this the confidence you gave me?" every man of honour would have answered in the words of the poet,

> ———— Yes, and keep it still:
> Lean on it safely; not a period
> Shall be unsaid for me:————
> ————————If this fail,
> The pillar'd firmament is rottenness,
> And earth's base built on stubble.

The knight in Ariosto who complains that none had kept faith with him, nobly adds,

> ———————————— Yet
> All with ingratitude or falsehood dyed
> I deem not, I accuse my destiny.
> Many there are, and have been more beside
> Unmeriting reproach; but if there be
> Mid hundreds, one or two of evil way,
> My fortune wills, that I should be their prey.[3]

---

[1] Chap. CCCXLI. [2] King Henry V. Act III, 2. [3] Canto XXVII.

It was "in his haste," that David said, "all men are liars." Still is there truth and virtue, honour and religion left in the world, and he that would argue from such instances against the reality of their existence, will only betray the conscious failings of his own misgiving heart. In those ages suspicion formed the religion of no man. The young took no delight in scruples and diffidence, and in having a long reach in detecting the projects of their acquaintances, believing that no one had any real affection but for himself. The young Duke of Guise indeed had recourse to a stratagem to prove whether Crillon deserved his surname of Sanspeur; but the look of the hero, when he discovered the artifice, struck the coward who had suspected him to the heart.

An historian of the civil wars, in the time of Charles I, relates a remarkable event, which shews that this confiding spirit conduced even to men's safety.—"The Lord Digby, at the commencement of the civil war, when proceeding to Holland upon the king's service, was taken by the enemy and brought prisoner with the other passengers into Hull, which was then in rebellion, under the command of Sir John Hotham. The Lord Digby being in disguise, and speaking French as a native, was considered as some wandering Frenchman, and left under a guard in some obscure corner, whilst his companion, Colonel Ashburnham, was regarded as the only prisoner of consequence, and conducted without delay to the Governor. The situation of the Lord Digby was however desperate, since he was well known to many persons in the town; and when it was considered that he was the most odious man of the kingdom to the Parliament. However, in this imminent extremity, he resolved not to give himself over, and found means to make one of his guard, in broken English, which might well have become any Frenchman, understand ' that he desired to speak privately with the governor.' He was accordingly brought before him in the presence of much company, when he gave an account of himself, as having seen much of the French service, and as having come over recommended to the king for some command. After he had entertained the company with such discourse, he applied himself to the governor, and told him, ' that if he might be admitted to privacy with him, he would discover somewhat to him which he would not repent to have known.' The governor drew him to a great window at a convenient distance from the company, and wished him to say what he thought fit. The Lord Digby asked him, in English, ' whether he knew him?' the other, surprised, told him ' no;' ' then,' said he, ' I shall try whether I know Sir John Hotham, and whether he be, in truth, the same man of honour I have always taken him to be,' and thereupon, told him who he was; and ' that he hoped he was too much of a gentleman to deliver him up a sacrifice to their rage and fury, who, he well knew, were his implacable enemies.' The other, being astonished, and fearing that the by-standers would discover him too, (for being now told who he was, he wondered he found it not out himself), he desired him ' to say no more for the present; that he should not be sorry for the trust he reposed in him, and should find him the same man he had thought him; in the mean time that he must be content to be treated as a prisoner,' and so he called the guard instantly to carry him away. He then explained to the company, with some confusion, that the fellow had told him something which the Parliament would be glad to know, and so departed to his chamber. Hotham was, by his nature and education, a rough and rude man, of great covetousness, of great pride, and great ambition; without any bowels of good nature, or the least sense or touch of generosity; his parts were not quick and sharp, but composed, and he judged well; he was a man of craft, and more like to deceive than to be cozened; yet, after all this, this young nobleman, known and abhorred by him, had so far prevailed and imposed upon his spirit, that he resolved to practise that virtue which the other had imputed to him, and not suffer him to fall into the hands of his enemies; and so he contrived to have Lord Digby privately conducted out of the town, beyond the limits of danger."

An instance where a contrary spirit produced the most unhappy consequences occurs in the History of Italy.— When the Emperor Sigismond came to Milan in 1431, by the invitation of Filippo-Maria Visconti, he was received with all honours, excepting that the suspicious Visconti could not be brought to appear before the Emperor. He shut himself up in the castle of Abbiate Grasso, and neither waited upon his guest nor would he receive a visit from him in his castle. He did not appear on the 25th of November in the church of St. Ambrose, when Sigismond received the iron crown from the hands of the Archbishop, and the Emperor departed without having seen him. It is said that by this miserable weakness he made an irreconcilable enemy of a monarch who was his natural ally, and whom he had himself invited into his territory.

The dignity which resulted from a delicate sense of honour has given rise to noble scenes. When the tables and charges of extortion were produced in open court against the Consul Metellus the whole assembly turned away their eyes, and refused to look.[1] And when Xenocrates was going to give

[1] Val. Max. II, c. 10.

his evidence, and approached the altar to swear, all the judges rose up and forbad him.

Theseus only says to Œdipus,

θάρσει τὸ τοῦδί γ' ἀνδρός· οὔ σε μὴ προδῶ.

Œdipus answers,

οὔ τοί σ' ὑφ' ὅρκου γ', ὡς κακὸν, πιστώσομαι.[1]

When Scipio was called upon to deliver up an account of the money which he had received and expended in the province of Antioch, he came into the Senate and produced the book from under his robe, which contained, he said, the exact account of the whole; but when they desired him to deliver it, he refused with dignity, saying, that he would not so dishonour himself; and with his own hands, in the presence of the Senate, he tore the book to pieces, and withdrew into voluntary exile. Livy says of him, " Major animus et natura erat, ac majori fortunæ adsuetus, quam ut reus esse sciret, et submittere se in humilitatem caussam dicentium."[2]

Pride entered largely into the virtues of a heathen; yet to be humble before the sovereign people would no doubt be an apostasy from the faith of Christians. The voice of a holy martyr might sound like Suffolk's imperial tongue.—

> Far be it we should honour such as these
> With humble suit: no, rather let my head
> Stoop to the block than these knees bow to any
> Save to the God of heaven and to my king!

Nestor declares that though Hector himself should calumniate Diomedes, and boast that he had put him to flight, neither the Trojans nor Greeks would believe it. What confidence must Themistocles have had in the patriotism of the Greeks.

[1] Soph. Œdip. Col. 649.
[2] XXXVIII, 52.

when he adopted that bold measure of obliging them to fight the common enemy at Salamis at the very time when the consideration of their belonging to separate cities, and having various interests and private animosities, seemed to forebode that they would offer but a partial and distracted resistance! Xerxes sent no messengers to Athens or Sparta when he demanded earth and water from the states of Greece. With what noble indignation did the Athenians reply to the Lacedæmonian embassy which besought them to disregard the overtures of the Persian general.—"It was human nature that the Lacedæmonians should fear lest we might make terms with the barbarian, but knowing as they did what was the mind of the Athenians, their suspicions were disgraceful: for there is no gold of the earth, nor country so gifted with beauty and excellence, the offer of which could seduce us to form alliance with the Medes to enslave Greece."[1]

Cicero celebrates it as a peculiar instance of Cato's felicity that no one ever dared to ask anything of him which was dishonourable. Not one of the Spartans chose to speak to Philopœmen about the intended present, but all excused themselves, and put it upon Timolaus, to whom he was bound by the rights of hospitality. Timolaus went to Megalopolis, and was entertained at Philopœmen's house, but when he observed the gravity of his discourse, the simplicity of his diet, and the integrity of his manners, quite impregnable to the attacks and deceits of money, he had not courage to utter a word about the present, but having assigned another cause for his visit, returned home. Froissart leaves a similar testimony to the unbending honour of the French king John, when, in recording the treason of Sir Amerey of Lumbard, who sold the

[1] Herodot. VIII, 144.

town of Calais to the Lord Geffray Charney, of
France, he concludes by observing, "I thynke he
never made the Frenche kyng of knowledge therof:
for if he had I trowe the kyng wold nat a consented therto bycause of the truse?" The honour
of Turenne was so well known that most of the
German princes treated with him without any
guarantee; his word was enough with the English,
the Swiss, the Swedes, and even the Dutch: the
Infidels themselves confided in the honour of our
Christian chivalry. Aben Alhamar, the Moor, at
the siege of Jaën, trusted his person in the hands of
his enemy Ferdinand of Castille, and became his
vassal. When the Moorish Queen of Grenada was to
be put to death on the false charge of the Zegries, in
the event of her champion failing, she had conceived
so high an idea of the Christian knights that she
sent secretly to request that Don John Chacon with
three companions would assert her innocence in
battle, and she received his promise that he would
defend her. On the last day of the conceded term,
when Musa entered her apartment in the Alhambra,
she appeared perfectly tranquil and resigned: during this dreadful day she sat on the scaffold from
eight o'clock in the morning till two in the after-
noon, and such was her confidence in the honour of
Don Juan Chacon, that she alone of all present remained without fear. At length her reliance was
rewarded by the arrival of the four knights, who
rode into the square, disguised as Turks, under
which character they had been enabled to pass the
frontier. I cannot help pausing here for a moment
to regard the force of these grave and elevated
manners in producing that commanding air, that
ceremonious dignity which characterized the ancient
knights, and which seemed to raise them above
nature. Observe how Brantome describes Antony,
the good Duke of Lorraine, " C'estoit ung tres-

homme de bien, Prince d'honneur, et de conscience—J'ai veu son pourtrait en Lorraine, et n'y avoist guères bonne maison à Nancy qui ne l'eust. Beau et honnorable visaige." As we read in Lord Surrey's elegy on the elder Sir Thomas Wyat—

> A visage sterne and milde; where both did growe,
> Vice to contemn, in virtue to rejoyce;
> Amid great stormes, whom grace assured so,
> To live upright, and smile at fortune's choyce.
> A toung that serv'd in forein realmes his king,
> Whose courteous talk to virtue did inflame
> Eche noble harte; a worthy guide to bring
> Our English youth by travail unto fame.

As Montaigne would say, his was "Un' ame à la vieille marque." Alas!

> Næ illiusmodi jam magna nobis civium
> Penuria 'st. Homo antiqua virtute ac fide.
> Quam gaudeo ubi etiam hujus generis reliquias
> Restare video. Vah, vivere etiam nunc lubet.[1]

The ideas of virtue, honour, and Christian faith were so inseparably associated in the minds of the people with the characters of such men, that whenever these qualities were named they seemed to behold them; as when it was said in an assembly of the Greeks, that a good man did not desire to seem but to be virtuous, instantly the whole multitude looked at Aristides: "these verses of Æschylus having been spoken," says Plutarch, "πάντες ἀπέβλεψαν εἰς Ἀριστείδην." When Philopœmen entered the theatre a little after his victory at Mantinea, and Pylades happened at the moment to be pronouncing the verse of Timotheus,

> The palm of liberty for Greece I won,

the people from every part turned their eyes upon Philopœmen, and caught in idea, as Plutarch says, the ancient dignity of Greece, and in their present

---

[1] Terent. Adelph. III, 4.

confidence aspired to the lofty spirit of former times. The boldness of the heroic character was the result of this spirit. Hercules, returning from Hades at the moment when his father and mother and children are about to be put to death by the Usurper, aided by the revolted citizens of Cadmus, is warned by the old man to take great care lest he should have been seen entering by some of the rebels, but Hercules replies

μέλει μὲν οὐδὲν, εἴ με πᾶσ' εἶδεν πόλις.[1]

"You have no accusation to bring against me," says Neoptolemus to Philoctetes, with a noble consciousness of honour, after he had returned him his arrows; to which the other replies:

ξύμφημι. τὴν φύσιν δ' ἔδειξας, ὦ τέκνον,
ἐξ ἧς ἔβλαστες· οὐχὶ Σισύφου πατρὸς,
ἀλλ' ἐξ Ἀχιλλέως, ὃς μετὰ ζώντων θ' ὅτ' ἦν
ἤκουσ' ἄριστα, νῦν δὲ τῶν τεθνηκότων.[2]

With our Christian chivalry this high sentiment was characterized by an indifference to the opinion of the world and to the judgment of man.

Thus the Duke of Buckingham refused to solicit mercy, which would have saved his life, when the Duke of Norfolk in tears informed him that he had been found guilty, and pronounced sentence of death: Buckingham replied with a firm voice, "My lord of Norfolk, you have said to me as a traitor should be said unto; but I was never none. Still, my lords, I nothing malign you for that you have done unto me. May the eternal God forgive you my death as I do. I shall never sue to the king for life, howbeit he is a gracious prince, and more grace may come from him than I deserve. I desire you, my lords, and all my fellows, to pray for me." He persisted in his resolution not to solicit mercy,

[1] Eurip. Hercul. Furens, 589.
[2] Sophocles, Philoctet. 1294.

and was beheaded on Tower-hill, amidst the groans and lamentations of the spectators. "God have mercy on his soul," says the reporter of his trial, "for he was a most wise and noble prince, and the mirror of all courtesy."

"It is a sad employment for innocence," says Sully upon occasion of his own disgrace, "to be obliged to bring forward and extol one's self." He might have added, it is an unworthy employment. Surely if, as he affirms, the man of virtue will experience, on a thousand occasions, that without chance and industry co-operating, virtue will not be sufficient to save him from hatred and public contempt, he may be allowed to dispense with a motive so replete with uncertainty and degradation. Still the rule of Catholic charity bound men to leave no one in ignorance through disdain of satisfying his doubts. The saints and theologians indeed have shewn how magnanimity is compatible with a humble mind, or rather how it necessarily accompanies it.[1]

"Nihil arduum humilibus," says Leo the Great.[2] Fénelon pointed out how grand and glorious a dignity belongs to the Christian. Even a heathen moralist could see the distinction, as when Cicero said of the confidence displayed by Socrates before his judges, "a magnitudine animi ductam, non a superbia."[3] So that upon these grounds there was no reason to condemn the sentence of the poet:

Σὺν τῷ δικαίῳ γὰρ μέγ' ἔξεστι φρονεῖν.[4]

The dignity which chivalry required was removed at an infinite distance from any disdain of men, or from any selfish vanity. It had no relation to

[1] Rodriguez's Christian Perfection, II, III, c. 36.
[2] Serm. V, de Epiph.
[3] Tuscul. I, 30.
[4] Soph. Ajax, 1125.

the kind of honour which Aristotle says, is the end of a political life, that by which men are made to fancy that they are good.[1] It arose from a reliance upon God: it was connected with all that is pure and holy; it was united to faith and love; it abode with him alone—

> Who in the silent hour of inward thought
> Could still suspect and still revere himself
> In lowliness of heart.[2]

III. But it still remains for us to mark that refinement and delicacy of feeling which formed so striking a characteristic of chivalry. Of this it is easy to find examples: Don Garcia Perez de Vargas was one of the most distinguished warriors who fought, at the siege of Seville, under the banners of Fernando el Santo. One day, at the beginning of the siege, Don Garcia Perez and another with him were riding by the side of the river, at some distance from the outposts, when of a sudden there came upon them a party of seven Moors on horseback. The companion of Perez was for returning immediately, but he replied, that never, even though he should lose his life for it, would he consent to the baseness of flight. With that, his companion rode off; which moment is well described in the old ballad:

> "Ha! gone?" quoth Garci Perez;—he smiled, and said no more,
> But slowly, with his esquire, rode as he rode before.

Perez armed himself, closed his visor, and put his lance in the rest. But the enemies, when they discovered that it was he, declined the combat. "The honour of the action," says Mariana, "was much increased by this circumstance, that although frequently pressed to disclose the name of the knight who had deserted him in that moment of

---

[1] Ethic. Nicomach. I, 5.   [2] Wordsworth.

danger, Garcia Perez would never consent to do so, for his modesty was equal to his courage." On returning to the camp, he was met by Ferdinand, whose first question was "What is the name of the knight who fled and deserted you?" "My liege," replied Garcia Perez, "ask anything else and it shall be done as I am commanded. This man is already sufficiently punished." Here was a reply according to the counsel of religious men. "Si fratris tui peccatum audiveris, id nemini communiceris," says a holy abbot. "Est enim mors tua."[1] The rules of a religious life prescribed another instance of this high honour, "Let men blush to say of an absent person what they could not say with charity in his presence."[2]

Froissart might supply many examples. "Then I demanded," he says, "of Sir Espaenge de Lion, 'if ever the Erle of Foix had any chyldren.' 'Yes, sir,' quod he, 'he had a faire sonne who had the father's harte, and all the countrey loved hym, for by hym all the countrey of Biern was in rest and peace.' 'Sir,' quod I, 'what became of that sonne, and it may be known?' 'Sir,' quod he, 'I shall shewe you, but nat as nowe, for the matter is ouer longe, and we are nere the towne, as ye se;' therewith I left the knight in peace." The next day, after much discourse, when they had nearly completed their journey. "'Sir,' quod I, 'if I durst I wolde fayne demaund of you one thynge, by what incydent the Erl of Foiz sonne dyed?' then the knight studyed a lytell, and sayd, 'Sir, the manner of his dethe is right pytuous, I wyll nat speke thereof; when ye come to Ortaise, ye shall fynde them that wyll shewe you if ye demaunde it.' And then I helde my peace, and we rode tyll we came to Morlens." The next day by

---

[1] B. Essaiæ Abbat. Orat. IV, Bib. Pat. XII.
[2] P. Nieremberg. Doct. Ascet. lib. V, vii, 42.

sun setting we came to Ortaise, and after Froissart
had been some time in the Earl's castle he took
occasion to inform himself of this matter. "Then I
enquired," says he, "howe Gaston the Erle's sonne
died, for Sir Espoyn of Lion wolde not shewe me
any thing thereof; and so moch I enquired that an
auncient squyer and a notable man shewed the
mater to me." The ancients were not deficient in
this delicacy. Simnias asked Socrates what was
the nature of the genius which directed him; and
Socrates remaining silent, Simnias never repeated
the question.[1] To men of this stamp a word, a look,
was sufficient to reveal deep thoughts. An ambassador, after long discourse before King Agis of
Sparta, said, "Finally," sir, "what answer do you
wish I should bear back to my countrymen?"
"That I let you speak all you wished, and for as
long a time as you wished, and that I said not a
word." This disposition prevented men from suffering their thoughts to dwell upon any ignoble
object. When Philoctetes, in Sophocles, inquires
after Thersites, Neoptolemus replies that he knows
nothing of him, excepting that he has heard that
he is still alive.[2] And Plutarch remarks that Agamemnon passed on without answering Sthenelus,
whereas he did not neglect Ulysses, but replied to
him.[3] Thus Don Juan was not able to prevail upon
the knight of La Mancha to read the book which
pretended to be a second part of his history, for he
said "that he would not encourage the scribbler's
vanity so far as to let him think that he had read
it; well knowing that we ought to avoid defiling
our thoughts and even our eyes with vile and
obscene matters." There were passions in these
ages, and therefore crimes; but men of honour
disdained to become acquainted with the detail of

[1] Plutarch de Socratis Genio.   [2] 445.
[3] De audiendis Poetis.

baseness and profligacy, and above all they avoided with the most scrupulous precision every society and every writing in which words were employed to cast the most distant reflection upon the holy faith and discipline of Catholics. A venerable abbot had said, "take heed how you speak with heretics, even for the sake of defending the faith, lest perchance their words should infuse a venom into your mind. If you find a book which is said to come from them, beware of reading it, lest it should fill your heart with deadly poison; but persevere in that doctrine which you have learned from the Church, so as neither to add to it nor to take aught from it."[1] These counsels may be censured by men of weak minds, who have neither learned the power of nature nor the principles of grace, but experience utterly disproves the maxims with which sophists would deceive them: facts prove to demonstration, that however gladly men may hear themselves styled honourable, the high and delicate sensibilities of the soul are not to be played upon with impunity. All experience bears testimony to the danger resulting from "that thirst for novelty, that restless craving for the wonders of the day," which, as Mr. Coleridge says, "in conjunction with the appetite for publicity is spreading like an efflorescence on the surface of our national character." For examples of high and genuine honour we must be content to confine our research to the number of those who scrupulously guarded their imagination from being polluted with odious images; who did not think themselves absolutely obliged to know what was said by the vilest class of mankind, who cautiously preserved their faith from the attacks of men "who denied authority, who denied the mysteries of Christianity, who de-

---

[1] B. Esaiæ Abbat. Orat. IV, Bibl. Patrum IV.

nied its morality, who denied its author, who denied God, who denied themselves, for there ends their reason;"[1] who kept their hearts unspotted by baseness, and their religion whole and unshaken, imitating the caution of the ancients, who, when they pulled down houses contiguous to temples, were careful to prop up and secure those parts which immediately joined the sanctuary.

Herodotus ascribes a most chivalrous delicacy to the Persians, saying, ἅσσα δέ σφι ποιέειν οὐκ ἔξεστι, ταῦτα οὐδὲ λέγειν ἔξεστι.[2] This was a duty strictly required in our chivalrous age, although it may be derided by those who have embraced the modern philosophy. It was inseparately connected with heroic virtues. Seuthes, King of Thrace, in relating to Xenophon the history of his father and himself, to account for his own conduct in early age, says, Ἐπεὶ δὲ νεανίσκος ἐγενόμην, οὐκ ἐδυνάμην ζῆν, εἰς ἀλλοτρίαν τράπεζαν ἀποβλέπων, ... ὥσπερ κύων.[3]

M. Hortalus, grandson of the orator Hortensius, when the house of Hortensius was reduced to poverty, would never supplicate relief from Tiberius, though he had been enabled to marry by the liberality of Augustus. As Tacitus says, "avitæ nobilitatis etiam inter angustias fortunæ retinens."[4] When at the feast given by the Phæacians, Ulysses wept upon hearing the minstrelsy of Demodocus which celebrated the contention of Ulysses and Achilles, the guests were delighted with the song, and observed him not; but Alcinous, who sat near him, perceived his grief, and instead of inquiring the cause of it, immediately addressed the company in these words:

> Ἤδη μὲν δαιτὸς κεκορήμεθα θυμὸν ἴσης,
> Φόρμιγγός θ', ἣ δαιτὶ συνήορός ἐστι θαλείῃ·
> Νῦν δ' ἐξέλθωμεν,[5] &c.

[1] De la Mennais.   [2] Lib. I, 138.   [3] Anab. VII, 2.
[4] An. II, 88.   [5] Od. VIII, 98.

The anuals of Christian chivalry abound with instances of this spirit, which gave occasion for the delicate charity of a Saint Nicholas. It was evinced in every form. We have seen in Tancredus how Claude de Beaumont killed Charles the Bold. An old writer thus ends the history of this knight:—"Lequel en mourust depuis de mélancholie quand il sceut qu'il avoit tué ung si grand prince." When David de Brechen was executed for having concealed the treason of Lord Soulis, as the people thronged to the spot they were bitterly rebuked by Sir Ingram de Umfraville, an English or Norman knight, then a follower of Robert Bruce. "Why press you," said he, "to see the dismal catastrophe of so generous a knight? I have seen ye throng as eagerly round him to share his bounty as now to behold his death." With these words he turned from the scene of blood, and repairing to the king, craved leave to sell his Scottish possessions and to retire from the country. "My heart," says Umfraville, "will not, for the wealth of the world, permit me to dwell any longer where I have seen such a knight die by the hands of the executioner!" With the king's leave he interred the body of David de Brechen, sold his lands, and left Scotland for ever. Montagu, who had been minister of King Charles V, was doomed to destruction in the reign of his successor, by the Duke of Burgundy and the King of Navarre. He was arrested suddenly as he returned from the church in the rue St. Victor: and after undergoing the torture he was beheaded. After three years had elapsed his sentence was declared to have been over hasty, and his body was taken from the gibbet. The Celestin monks of Marcoussis, whose founder he had been, buried him in their church and erected a monument. Francis I, visiting their house, expressed his surprise that a man condemned to death should have such a noble tomb. "Sire," replied one of the monks, "il n'a pas été jugé par justice, ains par commissaires." Here we observe with what delicate fidelity religious men guarded the honour of a friend.¹

The whole mind of chivalry is unfolded in Göthe's description of Hamlet. "Soft, and from a noble stem, this royal flower had sprung up under the immediate influence of majesty: the idea of moral rectitude with that of princely elevation, the feeling of the good and dignified, with the consciousness of high birth, had in him been unfolded simultaneously. He was a prince, by birth a prince, and he wished to reign only that good men might be good without obstruction. Pleasing in form, polished by nature, courteous from the heart, he was meant to be the pattern of youth and the rapture of the world."²

When Raoul d'Eu, Constable of France, had been suddenly condemned, without a trial, and beheaded in the dead of night, in the presence of a few barons, King John offered the sword of Constable to Jacques de la Marche, but he refused to accept the blood-stained spoils of Raoul, though the sword would have conferred on him the first dignity of the State; and the king afterwards did not even offer it to his best generals, Charles de Montmorenci, or the Sire de Beaujeu, or the Sire de Clermont; knowing that they would have refused it on the same grounds.³

The following scene occurs in an historian of Sienna. The ancient family of Montanini had been at war with that of Salimbeni for many generations. It arose from a dispute at a boar-chase, when a Salimbeni had been killed. At this period the noble family of Montanini had been almost destroyed, all its possessions usurped or confiscated, so that in the year 1395 there remained only a brother and sister,

¹ La France sous les cinq premiers Valois, III, 310.
² Wilhelm Meister.
³ Vies des grands Capitaines Français au Moyen Age, II, p. 144.

Charles and Angelica, who lived on a small farm in the Val di Strove. A rich churl, whose estate bordered on this spot, wanted to purchase it. He had a great influence on the plebeian government, and he was not to be offended without imminent danger. But Charles Montanini refused to sell it, resolving that his sister should have another dower besides her youth and rare beauty. The churl accused him of disaffection to the government, and he was condemned to pay 1,000 florins before fifteen days, on pain of death. Montanini, to preserve his sister from ruin, resolved to die. His maternal relations fled from him. On the morning of the fifteenth day Anselmo Salimbeni, passing on horseback before the house of Montanini, oberved some women in tears, and he learned the fate which awaited the last survivor of the hostile house. He had often seen the beauty of Angelica, but the division of their houses had prevented them from ever interchanging a word. Anselmo immediately hastened to the government, paid the fine, and set Charles at liberty. The youth returned to his sister, but no one could explain by what means he had gained his liberty. The following day he discovered the fact upon application to the authorities. In a moment of mental distraction he prevailed on his sister to believe with him that gratitude was not alone a sufficient virtue. After sunset they went to the house of Salimbeni, and Charles demanded a private interview. He stated the ruin of his family, their inability to repay his goodness in any other manner than by giving themselves up to his disposal, and trusting to his generosity and his pity. He then withdrew, leaving his sister alone with Salimbeni. This nobleman instantly left the room, and requested the chief ladies of the neighbourhood to attend upon a noble young person who was at his house. Anselmo assembled his relations, and then invited Angelica and the ladies to join them. With this company he rode to the house of Montanini, with lighted torches burning before him. "You have spoken to me in private," said he to Charles, "and I beg that you will hear my answer before this honourable company. A long time ago was I struck with the beauty, the modesty, and the virtue of your sister. You have placed at my disposal your life and your honour. I accept this precious gift, but it would be unworthy of me were I to possess it by an unlawful title. If you consent, I take, in presence of this honourable company, Angelica Montanini for my dear wife; I take her brother Charles for my brother, and I conclude, from this moment, that my goods are the common property of us both." The marriage was then celebrated with the utmost pomp.

IV. The humility and courtesy which distinguished the manners of these ages must not be passed over in silence. It is clear that the ancients were capable of admiring these dispositions. That courtesy and gentleness sometimes accompanied the old heroic spirit, may be learned from the praise bestowed by Menelaus upon Patroclus :—

> νῦν τις ἰνηείης Πατροκλῆος δειλοῖο
> μνησάσθω· πᾶσιν γὰρ ἐπίστατο μείλιχος εἶναι
> ζωὸς ἰών· νῦν δ' αὖ θάνατος καὶ Μοῖρα κιχάνει.[1]

The modesty of the ancient heroes is beautifully expressed in the reply of Memnon to Priam, in Quintus Calaber, when the old king, at the feast given to welcome his guest, had compared him to one of the immortal gods :—

> Οὐ μὲν χρὴ παρὰ δαιτὶ πελώριον εὐχετάασθαι,
> οὐδ' ἄρ' ὑποσχεσίην κατανευσέμεν, ἀλλὰ ἕκηλον
> δαίνυσθ' ἐν μεγάροισι, καὶ ἄρτια μηχανάασθαι.
> εἴτε γὰρ ἐσθλός τ' εἰμι, καὶ ἄλκιμος, εἴτε καὶ οὐχὶ,
> γνώσῃ ἐνὶ πτολέμῳ, ὁπότ' ἀνέρος τίδεται ἀλκή.[2]

---

[1] Il. XVII, 670.   [2] Lib. II, 148.

The spirit of gentleness is ascribed to Achilles when the Myrmidons lament over him:—

εἰλόμενοι περὶ νεκρὸν ἀμύμονος οἷο ἄνακτος,
ἠπίου, ὃς πάντεσσιν ἶσος πάρος ἦεν ἑταῖρος·
οὐ γὰρ ὑπερφίαλος πέλεν ἀνδράσιν———[1]

Xenophon says, in praising Cyrus, αἰδημονέστατος τῶν ἡλίκων ἐδόκει εἶναι.[2] It is a beautiful picture which Phædria, in Terence, gives of Antipho:—

> ——— Functus adolescentali est
> Officium liberalis: postquam ad judices
> Ventum 'st, non potuit cogitata proloqui:
> Ita eum tum timidum obstupefecit pudor.[3]

How amiable is that trait of ingenuous modesty in Telemachus, when he replies to Mentor, who desired him to address Nestor:—

Μέντορ, πῶς τ' ἄρ' ἴω, πῶς τ' ἄρ προσπτύξομαι αὐτόν;
Οὐδέ τί πω μύθοισι πεπείρημαι πυκινοῖσιν·
Αἰδὼς δ' αὖ νέον ἄνδρα γεραίτερον ἐξερέεσθαι.

The extreme mildness, joined with ability, which distinguished Theætetus, is beautifully eulogised in Plato: "He approached every subject with such gentleness, like the stream of the olive, which flows without any sound."[4] When Scipio paid a visit to Syphax, he met there Hasdrubal, whom he had just driven out of Spain. The king received the rival generals with hospitality, prevailed upon them to dine at the same table, and to sleep in the same bed. "Such was the courtesy of Scipio," says Livy, "and such his dexterity in accommodating his manners to all dispositions, that he conciliated not only Syphax, a barbarian unaccustomed to Roman manners, but even a most inveterate enemy."[5]

Suetonius relates an instance of Julius Cæsar's

---

[1] Quint. Calab. III, 422.
[2] Anab. I, 9.
[3] Phormio, I. 6.
[4] Plato, Theætetus.
[5] Lib. XXVIII, 19.

courtesy: "A certain person entertaining him at table, the vegetables were pickled instead of being fresh, and all the rest of the company disdained them, but Cæsar eat largely of them, ne hospitem aut negligentiæ aut rusticitatis videretur arguere." Tacitus deems it worth while to note the discourtesy of the Claudian family in Rome: "Quorum superbiam frustra per obsequium et modestiam effugeres." Courtesy was the boast of Athens; it was the virtue of the Stoics; it was deified in the Roman mythology, who borrowed it from the Greeks;[1] it was panegyrized by Cicero. Their precepts are express.

Βούλε δ' ἀρέσκειν πᾶσι, μὴ σαυτῷ μόνον.
Ἡδέως ἔχε πρὸς ἅπαντας, χρῶ δὲ τοῖς βελτίστοις.

And again, when they enter into the detail,

Τῷ μὲν τρόπῳ γίνε φιλοπροσήγορος, τῷ δὲ λόγῳ εὐπροσήγορος· Ἔστι δὲ φιλοπροσηγορίας μὲν, τὸ προσφωνεῖν τοὺς ἀπαντῶντας· εὐπροσηγορίας δὲ, τὸ τοῖς λόγοις αὐτοῖς οἰκείως ἐντυγχάνειν.

The ancients, as we learn from Athenæus, used even to study how to place and move their arms with grace.

That delicate attention to propriety which was evinced by Pisistratus, in giving the cup first to Minerva, because apparently older than Telemachus, seemed to Homer as worthy of the applause of perfect wisdom.

Χαῖρε δ' Ἀθηναίη πεπνυμένῳ ἀνδρὶ δικαίῳ,
Οὕνεκά οἱ προτέρῃ δῶκε χρύσειον ἄλεισον.

And the minister of the eleven, in consequence of his gentle courtesy to Socrates in the prison, has been immortalized by Plato.[2]

[1] There are two dissertations in two of the early volumes of the Academy of Inscriptions, one by the Abbé Gedoyn, upon the urbanity of the Romans; the other by the Abbé Massieu, upon the poetry of the ancients, in which he explains the character of the Graces; and these are both well worthy of perusal.
[2] Phædo.

Cicero, in his Orator, supplies an example, where he says, "itaque efficis, ut, cum gratiæ causa nihil facias, omnia tamen sint grata, quæ facis."

"Quid enim tam distans quam a severitate comitas? quis tamen unquam te aut sanctior est habitus, aut dulcior?"

And he fully admits its importance, saying, "Sic profecto res se habet nullum ut sit vitæ tempus in quo non deceat leporem humanitatemque versari."[1]

Lastly, he says of his own master, "Cujus et vita, et oratio consecuta mihi videtur difficillimam illam societatem gravitatis cum humanitate."

The virtue of Archedice was commemorated in Lampsacus by a pillar, which testified—

Ἡ πατρός τε καὶ ἀνδρὸς, ἀδελφῶν τ' οὖσα τυράννων,
Παίδων τ', οὐκ ἤρθη νοῦν ἐς ἀτασθαλίην.[2]

But this disposition, which appeared thus rare and heroic to the ancients, became essential to our Christian chivalry. Enumerating its ornaments, Spenser says,

> Amongst them all grows not a fairer flower
> Than is the bloom of comely courtesy;
> Which though it on a lowly stalk do bowre,
> Yet branches forth in brave nobility,
> And spreads itself through all civility.

"There was no country," says Ste. Palaye, "where chivalry did not exert its influence to promote public and private good." Nothing was little or contemptible in the eyes of a knight, when it related to doing good; and he proceeds to point out that this exercise of benevolence was extended to all classes of men, even to the person of the very lowest and most abject condition. He quotes a precept of the Chevalier de la Tour, in his book of instructions, which requires the practice of courtesy towards

---

[1] De Oratore. [2] Thucyd. lib. VI.

inferiors. "Ceux la," he says, "vous porteront plus grant louenge, et plus grant renommée, et plus grant bien que les grans: car l'honneur et la courtoisie qui est portée aux grans, n'est faite que de leur droit que l'on leur doit faire; mais celle qui est portée aux petits gentilz hommes et aux petites gentilz femmes et autres meindres, tel honneur et courtoisie vient de franc et doulx cuer, et le petit à qui on la fait s'en tient pour honoré."

Spenser devotes the whole of the sixth book to celebrate the examples and beauty of courtesy. His description of Sir Calidore is quite perfect.

> But 'mongst them all was none more courteous knight
> Than Calidore, beloved over all:
> In whom it seems that gentleness of spright
> And manners mild were planted natural,
> To which he adding comely guize withall,
> And gracious speech, did steal men's hearts away.
> Nathless thereto he was full stout and tall
> And well approv'd in battailous affray,
> That him did much renown, and far his fame display.
>
> Ne was there knight, ne was there lady found
> In Fairy Court, but him did dear embrace,
> For his fair usage and conditions sound,
> The which in all men's liking gained place,
> And with the greatest, purchas'd greatest grace;
> Which he could wisely use, and well apply
> To please the best, and th' evil to embrase,
> For he loath'd leasing and base flattery,
> And loved simple truth and stedfast honesty.

In the third canto, it is related how Sir Calepine was insulted by a proud and dastardly knight, whom he defied in these grand words:—

> "Unknightly knight, the blemish of that name,
> And blot of all that arms upon them take,
> Which is the badge of honour and of fame,
> Lo, I defie thee, and here challenge make,
> That thou for ever do these arms forsake,
> And be for ever held a recreant knight,
> Unless thou dare for thy dear Ladie's sake,
> And for thine own defence on foot alight
> To justify thy fault 'gainst me in equal fight."

The dastard that did hear himself defide,
Seem'd not to weigh his threatful words at all,
But laught them out, as if his greater pride
Did scorn the challenge of so base a thrall,
Or had no courage, or else had no gall.

Thibaud, in his Memoirs of the King of Prussia, relates the example of a Prussian prince, who severely admonished some young military pupils, at Strasburg, for treating him with insolent contempt, when they regarded him as an obscure stranger, (for he travelled in disguise). And the conduct of Henry IV of France was somewhat similar, in punishing discourteous lawyers, in the inn at Charenton, who refused to allow him, whom they mistook for a common gentleman, to have a small portion of their dinner, or to sit at the bottom of their table, there being no other provision in the house. To respect strangers was the lesson inculcated upon both occasions, in a manner which could hardly fail to make a lasting impression. The rule laid down by Demetrius, as related by Diogenes Laertius, might have been adopted as that of chivalry: τοὺς νέους ἔφη δεῖν ἐπὶ μὲν τῆς οἰκίας τοὺς γονεῖς αἰδεῖσθαι, ἐν δὲ ταῖς ὁδοῖς τοὺς ἀπαντῶντας, ἐν δὲ ταῖς ἐρημίαις ἑαυτούς.

The proverb in Catalonia said, "Oblige without regarding whom you oblige."[1] Modesty was essential to the chivalrous character. The author of the Jouvencel represents his hero in the following terms: "Il conduisoit tout soulz la main de Dieu et en son nom pour s'employer en faits notables sans vanter ou haut louer soi-meme, car louenge est reputée blame en la bouche de cellui qui se loe; mais elle exaulce celluy qui ne se attribue point de loenge, mais à Dieu. Si l'Escuyer a vaine gloire de ce qu'il a fait, il n'est pas digne d'estre chevalier, car vaine gloire est ung vice qui destruit et aneantit les

[1] Chronica de Ramon de Muntaner, CCXXXIV.

merites et les guerdons, ou benefices de chevalerie."
King Perceforest, according to these principles,
says to his knights, " Si me souvient d'une parolle
que ung Hermite me dist une fois pour moy chastier ;
car il me dist que si j'avois autant de possessions
comme avoit le roy Alexandre, et de sens comme le
sage Salomon, et de chevalerie (valeur, bravoure)
comme eut le preux Hector de Troye, seul orgueil
s'il regnoit en moy destruiroit tout."

When Sir Gareth of Orkney had at length prevailed over the prejudices of the damoysel, who had
despised him as a kitchen-boy : " ' Certes, merveille
have I,' she exclaimed, ' what manner a man ye be,
for hit may never ben otherwise but that ye be
comen of a noble blood, for soo foul ne shamefully
dyd never woman rule a knyghte as I have done
you, and ever curtoisly ye have suffred me, and that
cam never but of a gentyl blood,' as he is described
in another place ; ' Truly, Madame,' sayd Lynet
unto her syster, ' wel maye he be a kynge's sone,
for he hath many good tatches on hym, for he is
curteis and mylde and the moost sufferynge man
that ever I mette with al.' " And we are told, that
while he was page of the kitchen, " he endured alle
that twelvemonth, and never displeasyd man nor
chylde, but alweyes he was meke and mylde."

How the spirit of religion softened and refined
our nature ! ὁ δὲ παῖς, says Plato, πάντων θηρίων
ἐστὶ δυσμεταχειριστότατον—ἐπίβουλον καὶ δριμὺ καὶ
ὑβριστότατον θηρίων γίγνεται.[1] What a contrast is
this to the gentle page of chivalry, or the innocent
student, who could be guided with a silken rein !
Habits of mildness, formed in early life, accompanied men through all their age. The old historians speak of Godefroy de Bouillon as uniting
" the wisdom of Nestor, the prudence of Ulysses,

---

[1] De Legibus, VII.

the valour of Achilles, the strength of a giant, with the sweetness and humility of a monk."

St. Bernard said to Pope Eugenius, " He is truly great on whom fortune hath smiled without deceiving him." In nobility, the virtues of abstinence, humility, and devotion to God, are more illustrious. St. Jerom had said to noblemen, " Prefer not yourselves before others by reason of your nobility, and contemn not those who are not noble. Our religion hath no respect to persons : it regards not the condition of men, but their minds ; it judgeth of nobility by their manners. There is no liberty in the sight of God but not to serve sin. The height of nobility is to be illustrious in virtue."[1] In the humility thus required, there was nothing contrary to the courtesy which is most graceful in youth; for, as St. Francis de Sales says, " It never made a show of itself, nor used many humble words. Were this humility only to consult her own feelings, she would perform actions of arrogance and insolence, that she might conceal herself beneath them, and remain unknown."[2]

King Perceforest continues to instruct his knights,[3] and says, " Si me souvient d'une parolle que me dist une foys ung sainct homme, car il dist en moy chastiant que chevaliers et clercs devoient ressembler la pucelle car la pucelle doibt estre simple et coye et pou parlant, courtoise chaste et honneste en ditz, et en faitz doulce, debonnaire et piteuse envers tous bons.—Seigneurs chevaliers ainsi est il de vous, car si le gentil homme qui a receu l'ordre de chevalerie ne ressemble la pucelle en graces et en vertus, il ne doit desire nomme chevalier tant preux qu'il soit.—Seigneurs chevaliers pour ce vous ay dict ces parolles que si vous voulez seoir a la table du franc palays et recevoir honneur que vous mectez

---

[1] Epist. ad Celant. [2] Introduction to a Devout Life.
[3] Vol. II, c. 124-5.

peine a ressembler a la pucelle, car il appartient a chevalier." The Spartan education was directed to the same end. Xenophon expressly says, that a great object of Lycurgus was to instil reverence and modesty into the minds of young men.[1] It is said of the young Jacques de Lalain, when at the court of Cleves, that many loved him on account of his beauty and humility. "Jacques de Lalain, par l'humilité qui étoit en lui, eut à ce jour grand bruit en l'hotel du roi, et n'y avoit duc, comte, baron, chevalier, écuyer, dame, ni damoiselle, dont il ne fut bien accointé; en spécial des reines et princesses, desquelles il étoit volontiers vu, au-dessus de tous ceux qui la étoient."[2] The old Chronicle describes how graciously he was received when the Counts of Maine and of St. Pol led him from the jousting-ground. "Car de plus bel jeune écuyer pour lors on n'eut sçu gueres trouver; avec la beauté, qui en lui étoit, il étoit humble, courtois, et débonnaire."

Chaucer says of his knight,

> And of his sport as meeke as is a maid,
> He never yet no villanie ne said
> In all his life, unto no manner wight;
> He was a very perfite gentill knight.

The rule was, "Soyez tousjours le dernier parler dans les assemblées des gens plus agés que vous et le premier à frapper dans les combats."

> Un chevalier n'en doutez pas
> Doit ferir haut et parler bas.

Men could not praise others too much, nor speak too little of themselves. "Par especial il appartient a jeune seigneur peu parler."[3] The troubadour, Pierre Vidal, wrote a treatise on the art "de retenir sa langue." The order of "la Cosse de Geneste," instituted by St. Louis, had for the motto, "*exaltat*

[1] Xen. de Repub. Lacedæmon. III.
[2] Chastellain, Hist. de Jacques de Lalain, chap. XVI.
[3] L'Horloge des Princes.

humiles." Even the heralds contrived a distinction to dishonour the knight who was convicted of vain boasting. "He beareth Argent, *a point dexter parted, Tenné:* this diminution," says Gwillim, "is due unto him that overmuch boasteth himselfe." So essential was it to be

> Speaking in deeds, and deedless in the tongue.[1]

Tirant the White found himself unable to inform the good hermit, that it was he who had conquered in the grand tournament held by the King of England. Such was the modesty of the Douglas family, that they always spoke of the great victory of Otterbourn as the consequence of the exhausted state of the English after their march from Newcastle. Castiglione, speaking of the French, who, notwithstanding their love of freedom and familiarity, are highly pleased with modesty, takes occasion to defend the Spaniards from the charge of failing in this point, and says, "I affirm that those of the highest repute among them are generally such as are of the greatest modesty."[2] Good sense and a love of truth were often the source of this spirit. Chevert had risen from obscurity. On one occasion a person, who sought his interest, pretended to be his relation. "Are you a gentleman?" asked Chevert. "Undoubtedly! can you question it?" replied the stranger. "In that case," answered the hero, coolly, "we cannot be relations, for in me you see the first and only gentleman of my family." Examples of the most gracious courtesy present themselves in every page of our ancient annals and romances. Froissart says of the Earl of Foix, that "he was of good and easy acquayntance with every man, and amorously wolde speke to them:" and of Sir William Dancennes, that he was "ryght courtoys

---

[1] Troilus and Cress. IV, v.   [2] Courtier, book II, p. 139.

and swete of words." Christine de Pisan says of the Duke of Berri, brother of Charles V of France, "Moult est debonnaire à ses serviteurs : est prince de doulce et humaine conversacion, sanz haulteineté d'orgueil, bening en parolle et responce, joyeus en conversacion, et en toutes choses tres traictable:" and of Charles VI she adds, "humain à toutes gens, sans nul orgueil ; est plain de grant benignité, doulceur, et amour : en telle maniere, que toute personne qui le voit, soit estrangier prince ou autre est amoureux et resjoy de sa personne." I must repeat it—a religious education in youth was the foundation of all this. "It is a part of humility," says Father Eusebius Nieremberg, "to wish that no other person but one's self should want honour." [1] The sublime man Gerlacus goes so far as to say, "Omnes homines ex corde veneror." [2]

William of Tyre describes Baldwin III. "He shewed such grace and affability, that he would converse with the meanest persons who happened suddenly to salute him, and he was ever ready to speak to all men, and to listen to them; so that he was dear to the people." [3] "The Lord de la Ryver," says Froissart, "was alway swete, curtesse, meke, pacyent, and gentyll to poore men." The laws of chivalry expressly required men to practise this civility: in l'Ordene de Chevalerie it is spoken of as belonging to the purity which is signified by the bath whence the new knights were to issue, "sans nule vilennie." As the youths described by Shakspeare,

> ——— They are as gentle
> As zephyrs, blowing below the violet,
> Not wagging his sweet head; and yet as rough,
> Their royal blood enchafed, as the rudest wind,
> That by the top doth take the mountain pine
> And make him stoop to the vale.

---

[1] Doct. Ascet. lib. III, iv, 41.   [2] Solfloq. c. 34.
[3] Gesta Dei per Francos, p. 890.

Thus, in the romance of Gerard de Roussillon, we read of the knight Foulque: "he is courageous, courteous, communicative, free, good-natured, and of graceful speech."

"To say the truth," said the Countess of Foys, "Arthur is the best knyght of the worlde, and the mooste hardyest; and moreover, all the beauty of the world that can be compryed in a man is in hym. Also, he is replete wyth all grace and virtue, for he is free, meeke, and gentyl as a lambe:"[1] and the gentle Maister Stephen is described as "always free and swete of heart, with a smylyng countenaunce and a gracious clerke above all other; and also a right good valiant knyght:" and the Earl of Beaujewe is described by his valet to be "as curteys, as gentyll, as free, and as meke as a dove." Our Henry V was justly censured in France for his want of courtesy.[2] While in Paris, he asked the Maréchal de l'Ile-Adam, who spoke frankly to him on one occasion, "how he dared to look him in the face?" "Sire," replied the brave knight, "it is the custom of the French that if one man speaks to another, of whatever state or authority he may be, with eyes cast down, it is concluded that he is a bad man, since he does not dare to look in face of him with whom he speaks." "That is not our custom," muttered the King; and the Marshal had to suffer imprisonment for his chivalrous answer. The motto of the noble family of Forbin, in Provence, was "quo fortior eò mitior:" according to the lesson of George Chastellain to Charles the Bold: "Mets la haultesse et les haultes graces que tu as de Dieu en comparaison encontre leur faculté petite; car come plus haulte et glorieuse est la tienne, tant plus doibt estre humble et bening envers la leur." This amiable disposition

[1] Arthur of Little Brit. p. 85.
[2] Barante, Hist. des Ducs de Bourgogne, V, 51.

gives a charm to the most trifling incidents recorded. Porrus and Cassiel, riding in the great forest of Darnant, came about noon to a wide river, and on the banks they find a boy watching cows, whom they ask where they could pass over; and on being directed by him to a place, distant three leagues, "lors comandent le garson à Dieu," says the Romance, "and away they rode." Thus King Lisuarte courteously accosted the strange knights, whom he met in Windsor forest, "for he was the man in the world," says Vasco Lobeira, the writer of Amadis, "who with the best goodwill received all errant knights."[1] When young Arthur met some unknown ladies, the widow of the lord of the tower and her daughters, in the forest, "as soon as he saw them he lyghted downe of his hors, and ryght sweetly saluted them;" and when he meets the young varlet of the Earl of Beaujewe, his salutation is "gentyll frende, can ye tell us onye novelles?" When Rodrigo returns from his hermitage, the exercise of this courtesy is one of his first pleasures, for

> Journeying on, he greeted whom he met
> With such short interchange of benison,
> As each to other gentle travellers give;

unlike the churl's courtesy, which, Sir Philip Sydney says, "rarely comes but either for gain or falsehood."[2] When on a journey, it was common to give orders, that if any other traveller should alight at the same inn, the host might inform the first comers that they might enjoy his society at table. It was in this way that the old knight meets with Alphonso de Toledo, at the inn at Traygues, who is introduced to him as a Spanish scholar, travelling to Bologna. Incivility to strangers forfeited all knightly praise. "For them I

[1] Amadis de Gaul, I, 24.   [2] Arcadia.

would do nothing," says Beltenebros, of the knights of Leonoreta, "for they are discourteous to make knights who are travelling joust against their will." This courtesy of manner was regarded as a great indication of superior rank and chivalry; though no rules could be laid down to ensure the acquiring of it, since, as Chastellain says of Lalain, "le bon oiseau se fait de lui-meme, ainsi comme fit celui bon ecuyer." Much were the Emperor and Empress, and their court, pleased with the gracious answers of the knight of the green sword (Amadis), and thereby judged that "sure he was of high degree, for low-born men often excel in strength, but in gentle and debonair manners not, for they pertain to those of pure and generous blood. I do not affirm that all such possess them, but I say they ought to possess them, as did this knight of the green sword."[1] Shakspeare had all this feeling,

> You are well-favour'd, and your looks foreshew
> You have a gentle heart.

As Œdipus of old said to Theseus on their first meeting,

> Θησεῦ, τὸ σὸν γενναῖον ἐν σμικρῷ λόγῳ
> παρῆκεν, ὥστε βραχέα μοι δεῖσθαι φράσαι.[2]

But the answer of Olivia is finer, who repeats and comments on the page's answer,

> I am a gentleman. I'll be sworn thou art,
> Thy tongue, thy face, thy limbs, actions and spirit
> Do give thee five-fold blazon.[3]

When the old Beldam meets Marphisa at a ford, Ariosto relates her request that

> ———————— she of her grace
> Would bear her on the croupe to the other shore.

Adding,

> Marphisa, who was come of gentle race,
> The hag with her across the torrent bore.[4]

---

[1] Book III, 11.   [2] Sophocles, Œd. Col. 569.
[3] Twelfth Night, I, V.   [4] Canto XX.

The reverence, too, with which persons of exalted rank were received, had produced, no doubt, a beneficial effect in teaching them that if ever they were tempted to forget their station, other men would still remember it. Olivier de la Marche, when a young page, saw the entry of the Emperor elect, Frederick, King of the Romans, into Besançon, with the good Duke Philip of Burgundy; he says he remarked that the latter rode by his side, but in such a manner that his horse's head was only in a line with the thigh of the king. Spenser has well described the person and office of him who had to shew respect to guests—

> There fairly them receives a gentle squire,
> Of mild demeanour and rare courtesy,
> Right cleanly clad in comely sad attire;
> In word and deed that shew'd great modesty,
> And knew his good to all of each degree,
> Hight Reverence. He them with speeches meet
> Does fair entreat, no courting nicety,
> But, simple, true, and eke unfeigned sweet,
> As might become a squire so great persons to greet.[1]

When the Seneschal, in the "Lord of the Isles," has marshalled the strange guests to the princely dais, persons reprove him for having given such a place to those strangers; but he replies, that he had discharged his duty for forty years without error; adding,

> And 'gainst an oaken bough
> I'll gage my silver wand of state,
> That these two strangers oft have sate
> In higher place than now.

It was the delicate attention with which men avoided giving offence or uneasiness to others, which made courtesy of such moral importance. An instance occurs in Perceforest, which is related with amusing simplicity. As King Alexander and

[1] Faery Queen, I, 10.

Floridas were riding through the forest, they found a young man sleeping on the ground, in the shade, and a great horse grazing near him, loaded with the young man's harness: so the king calls out to Floridas, and they begin to discourse about who this may be. "Par ma foy," says the king, "sachez que je parleroye moult voulentiers à luy pour sçavoir qu'il est, mais je ne le veulx pas esveiller jusques a ce qu'il ayt dormy son somme." So they both alighted, turned their horses loose to graze, and sat down near the youth to wait, "qu'il eust dormy son somme et qu'il seveillast de son gre." In this way they waited two English hours. So at last the king could not help sneezing three times, when the stranger woke suddenly, and looking fiercely at the king, "Sire Chevalier mal avez fait qui mavez esveille et si soyez certain que si tant cussiez attendu que la collee de chevalerie me fust donnee vous lamendissiez." "Certes," said the king, "sire bachelier, 'twas not my fault, for help sneezing I could not, pray pardon me." "Sire," said the youth, who was now broad awake, "je le vous pardonne car je ne suis pas en estat de courroucer Chevaliers mais tant veulx je bien que vous sachez, que je ne fuz si joyeulx en jour de ma vie. . . . Sire, songe est et a songe mest tourné." So the king would know all his "estre;" and first his name, and in what country he was born.... "Sire," said he, "je ne suis encores pas né." "How," said the king! "Sire," said the valet, "devant n'est pas homme né jusques a ce quil se cognoist et quil est aorne de vertus." Then he must hear his dream: he was dreaming that he was just about to be made a knight, and so King Alexander, unbarring his helmet, asked him if he were not the knight he saw in his dream? and so he made him a knight on the spot.

In taking this view of the courtesy of ancient manners, it is essential to keep in mind what was shewn in the second book, that it followed naturally and of necessity from the religion which prevailed in these ages. The Church prescribed it; her ministers observed it as a part of religion; children were trained to love it; both the practice and spirit of a religious life produced it. St. Augustine, in his letter to Ecdicia, desires her to condescend to the humour of her husband, and not to wear black clothes, since that gave him offence, and tells her that "she might be humble in mind in a rich and gay dress, if her husband would insist upon her wearing such, provided it were modest."[1] As an old writer well observes, "L'ame qui loge la philosophie doit par sa santé rendre sain encore le corps: elle doit faire luire jusques au dehors, son repos, et son aise: doit former à son moule le port exterieur, et l'armer par consequent d'une gracieuse fierté, d'un maintien actif, et allaigre, et d'une countenance contente et debonnaire. La plus expresse marque de la sagesse c'est une esjouissance constante." Mdme. de Sevigné, in relating the conversion of Mdme. de Marans to a religious life, concludes with this beautiful remark, "enfin elle est bien plus aimable qu'elle n'etoit."[2] Catholic writers expressly treated upon the subject of "Christian politeness;" and who has ever conversed with a Benedictine, or partaken of a priest's hospitality without experiencing it? "We should respect in men the quality of the adorers of God," says an elegant writer, who describes the manners of good company. Excepting among those of the household of faith, where is such a sentiment to be found? The rules laid down by ascetical writers, to guide novices and monks in a cloister, might seem to have been composed for the instructions of nobles and princes; the rules of a monastery

[1] Epist. 262.   [2] Tom. III, Lett. 338.

required the same humility and modesty; the same inattention to what is served at table, the same habit of despising nothing that is offered, of complaining of nothing, of accommodating one's self to everything, of avoiding both deficiencies or excess in meals,[1] and correcting every indication of undisciplined appetite. These holy men were equally refined even in their gestures and carriage; and it cannot be doubted but that whatever refinement of manners belonged to all those ages, was derived in a great measure from an early education in the houses of the clergy. St. Bernard[2] and St. Ignatius Loyola prescribed sobriety, serenity, and cheerfulness of countenance; St. Jerome had condemned all expressions of anger and pride. St. Chrysostom says, in praise of St. Miletus, that it was the greatest pleasure to enjoy his countenance,

> Nec frons triste rigens, nimiusque in moribus horror,
> Sed simplex hilarisque fides, et mixta pudori
> Gratia.

Eusebius Nieremberg quotes Ammianus describing a wicked man, who used to walk with a frowning look, and St. Ambrose, who requires attention to courtesy, saying, "Naturam imitemur; ejus effigies formula disciplinæ, forma honestatis est."[3] Courtesy was inseparable from the religious education which was received in those ages: what beautiful fruits must that spirit of yielding and of obedience have produced? Lanspergius says, that we should obey every one in what relates to ourselves, as if we were bound to obey every one. The whole rested upon a solid base; "for God," says Nieremberg, "is no less Lord of the body than of the soul, nor ought we to serve him less with our bodily members than

---

[1] P. Nieremberg Doct. Ascet. lib. V, iv, 37.
[2] Formul. Honest. Vit.
[3] Lib. 1 de Off. 19.

with our spiritual powers."[1] Gresset sighed after this Christian politeness amidst the refinement of the literary circles of the most polished capital.

> Parmi la foule trop habile
> Des beaux diseurs du nouveau style
> Qui, par de bizarres détours,
> Quittant le ton de la nature,
> Répondent sur tous leurs discours,
> L'académique enluminure
> Et le vernis des nouveaux tours ;
> Je regrette la bonhomie
> L'air royal, l'esprit non pointu
> Du curé de sa Seigneurie.

Among those who have established a modern system of opinions, the most consistent and zealous have formally protested against it, as generating servility and pride. Some are civil, like the Roman, "Erat Quinctius," says Livy, "sicut adversantibus asper, ita, si cederes, idem placabilis."[2] Others are full of modesty in the presence of princes, and full of haughtiness and severity with those who have only virtue. Some are courteous, "but," as Fénelon says, "under pretence of courtesy, they are softened for pleasure, and hardened against virtue and honour;" others are styled the most polite and amiable of men; but in their writings they seemed to regard insolence and calumny as the perfection and end of language. If we leave the scenes of servility and dissimulation, with all the unmeaning rules of conventional correctness, where cold hearts and affected manner create an air which chills and paralyzes the frank and generous spirits of youth, there is only that morose gravity, that disdainful pride, that suspicious, ridiculous reserve, which shew that men hate and despise all but themselves. Pass from a Catholic country to one which has adopted the sensual and suspicious philosophy of the moderns, and how great is the

---

[1] Doct. Ascet. lib. V, ɪ, 39.   [2] Lib. XXXVI, 32.

contrast! To omit the mention of that refined courtesy which reigns in the palace of the popes, and which has always distinguished the high society of Christian Rome, every stranger must have been struck with the amiable familiarity descending to all ranks, which accompanies the high polish of the Roman manners. Görres says that a man of the lowest class speaks there more freely and at his ease with a cardinal, or with the Pope himself, than in other places he would with the secretary of some petty office. Religion is the cause of this; for in every person the Christian is first considered. All is natural and gracious; the master regards his servants as part of his family; he converses with them in a friendly manner, and this familiarity never leads to insolence: he is always master, and the servant always in his place. The carnival is like a holiday of children under the eyes of a father.[1] In Spain, too, the greatest affability distinguishes the nobles. The warmest partisan of the ideas styled liberal would be offended at the familiarity which prevails among all classes at the court of Madrid. The poor of Spain remember their high dignity, as belonging to the fold of Christ. In the Catholic countries of Germany and of Switzerland, the same remark is perfectly true; but pass a narrow strait, a brook, or a line of loose stones upon a mountain, and how totally do manners change! Instead of interchange of benison, each one you meet resembles him of whom the poet speaks,

Nec visu facilis, nec dictu affabilis ulli.[2]

It is not the gentle stranger so mild,

That Gawain with his old courtesy,
Though he were come again out of faerie,
Ne coude him not amenden with a word:[3]

---

[1] Rom: wie es in Wahrheit ist.
[2] Æneid, III, 621.   [3] Chaucer.

but it is one like that giant Pandafilando, surnamed of the gloomy sight; because, though his eyeballs are seated in their due place, yet he affects to squint and look askew, on purpose to fright those on whom he stares. In such lands Sir Calidore would have enough to do, and would vainly give counsel :

———— By this now may ye learn
Strangers no more so rudely to entreat,
But put away proud look, and usage stern,
The which shall nought to you but foul dishonour earn.

Every meeting in a narrow road will be liable to give rise to such discourtesy or violence, as Laius King of Thebes used to Œdipus, when they encountered each other in that fatal spot; the old man, in a haughty tone, bidding the stranger make away, as Diodorus says;[1] or his charioteer using force to turn him, as Œdipus witnesses in Sophocles,[2] when the unhappy son was provoked to direful anger, and fate pursued its way.

V. This view of the courtesy of ancient manners leads to a consideration of the humanity and kindness with which the poor were treated by the great. The general error of the moderns on this point may be resolved into their ignorance of the religion which prevailed in these ages. A Catholic knows, without consulting history, that many of their sweeping general charges must be false. An intimate acquaintance with history will prove that his confidence was just. Niebuhr, in his History of Rome, speaks of "those knights of the middle ages, whose virtues are extolled by ignorance and falsehood;" as if it had been considered highly honourable and chivalrous, to rival the Roman patricians in hating and oppressing the poor. Niebuhr does not deem it worth his notice to account for the

---

[1] Lib. IV, 64.   [2] Œdip. Tyran. 805.

prevalence of such conduct, along with the universal profession of the Catholic religion; and yet this difficulty might have suggested other thoughts, and prompted a very different sentence from the above; but he seems in this instance to have paid more attention to the general encomiums passed upon chivalry by poetical writers, than to the facts of history, which certainly render such encomiums superfluous. The moderns are willing enough to admit that men were under a monastic influence, but they do not sufficiently observe how that influence must have operated. The monks themselves related a memorable example to shew that a certain man, for having, while he was a robber, protected a holy nun from his companions, and for having spared a poor woman whom he met in a desert place, and given her money to ransom her husband, who was in prison, had attained to a perfection equal to that of a certain hermit, who had spent his life in solitude, and mortification and prayer.[1]

Without entering into any discussion as to the merits or demerits of the feudal system, there are certain obvious reflections which will lead every man of sense to conclude, that the poor and the lower classes of society were not placed by it in such a condition of misery as is generally supposed by persons who forget what an influence religion then exercised over all the actions of men, and who err also in their opinions of human nature. The cruelty of upstarts, and men who have lately acquired riches and fame, is indeed remarked by Æschylus; but he contrasts it with the mild and gentle grace of those who have inherited their possessions.[2] The same truth had been remarked by Euripides,[3] and accurately stated by Aristotle.[4] Our missionaries declared, that the greatest obstacle which they

[1] Nieromberg Doct. Ascet. I, v. 39.   [2] Agamemnon, 1015.
[3] Supp. 743.   [4] De Rhetor. II, xv.

found in Japan was the difficulty of persuading the nobles that the people were men like themselves. How completely did all the institutions and manners of Christendom in the middle ages render its nobility incapable of imagining such impiety! Marchangy ascribes a sensible remark to a knight of the fourteenth century: "People, slaves under the Romans, do you desire to know who were your liberators? consult the archives of Anjou, and there you will find this formula of enfranchisement consecrated by the feudal nobility: 'Par respect pour la Divinité et afin d'obtenir le salut eternel de notre ame, nous te déclarons libre.'" What was left of servitude in the middle ages had not been invented and introduced, but on the contrary it had been alleviated by religion under the feudal system. Thus among King Ethelstan's Laws Ecclesiastical, A.D. 925, "Let every master be compassionate and condescending to his servants, in the most indulgent manner possible. The slave and the free man are equally dear to the Lord God who bought them, and bought them all with the same price. And we are all of necessity servants to God, and he will judge us in the same manner that we on earth judged those over whom we had judicial power." Queen Blanche, mother of St. Louis, when Regent of France, ordered in many places the serfs to be made free, paying a compensation to their lords. Mathieu Sire de Monmorenci, in the same age, enfranchised those on his estates.[1] The Abbot Thomas of St. Germain des Prés, gave freedom to his own serfs. The clergy and missionaries used to purchase young heathen slaves, and baptize and make them free. Thus we read of Pope Gregory at Rome, of Amandus, Bishop of Maestricht, the apostle of the Netherlands

---

[1] Desormeaux, Hist. de la Maison de Montmorenci, I, 258.

in the seventh century.[1] Many of the slaves whom he ransomed became afterwards bishops, priests, and abbots. Bonet, Bishop of Clermont, in the seventh century purchased and sent home many slaves. St. Patrick, in Ireland, often ransomed and baptized these poor slaves. In Tancredus there are many similar examples. In general, as Vogt remarks, the condition of bond servants became much happier after Pope Gregory the Great had published that famous decree, saying, "Cum Redemptor noster totius conditor naturæ ad hoc propitiatus humanam carnem voluit assumere ut divinitatis suæ gratia, dirupto, quo tenebamur captivi, vinculo servitutis pristinæ nos libertati restitueret, salubriter agitur, si homines, quos ab initio natura liberos creavit, et jus gentium jugo substituit servitutis, in ea natura, qua nati fuerint, manumittentis beneficio libertati reddantur." Over the gate of the city of Blois was a Latin inscription to commemorate that Count Stephen and the Countess Adélaide had delivered the citizens from all taxes. It was Count Thibault who, out of compassion for the poor peasants and rustic labourers, determined the precise hour when the day commenced and ended. For ever after, as soon as the evening bell sounded, throughout all this part of France, the poor people, out of gratitude, used to cry out, "Dieu pardoint au bon Comte de Blois!"[2] On the belfry of the cathedral of Orleans, was this inscription: "Letbertus factus est liber, teste hac sancta ecclesia." The seigneurs of Tannay proclaimed the desire of the Church to give freedom to all men, with the most Christian eloquence.[3] Guizot acknowledges, that the Church derived an immense force from its respect for

---

[1] Mabillon, Acta S. II, 713.
[2] Pasquier, Recherches de la France, VIII, 52. Hist. des Français par Monteil, XIVme Siècle.
[3] Hist. des Français, par Monteil, XIVme Siècle.

equality, and for legitimate superiority. "It was," he says, "the most popular society, the most accessible, the most open to all talents, to all the noble ambitions of human nature."¹ It is remarkable to find M. Guizot condemning the system which kept the people "materially happy, but without intellectual activity."² One position may be safely affirmed, that in these ages it was never forgotten that the poor could not be injured without committing mortal sin. Phillipe V, le Long, ordered in his will that the peasants who had their farms near the forests should be indemnified, "pour les dommages que leur avoient causés les bêtes rousses et noires."³

Matthieu IV de Montmorenci, who was passionately fond of hunting, on being told by his vassals that their farms were injured by the game, not only permitted, but commanded them to kill and carry away all stags and wild boars, and other beasts, which should be found without a preserve which he retained for himself. Before his death he established a fund for clothing all the poor of his estates, after the example of many of his ancestors, whose testaments are generally filled with legacies to the church and to the poor.⁴ What a portrait does the ancient historian of Bretagne present of Jean V de Montmorenci Laval, saying, "Il fut moult prud'homme vers Dieu et les hommes, merveilleusement devot aux Eglises, et aumonier aux pauvres; aussi aima-t-il le bien du commun peuple lequel il garda et deffendit de tout son pouvoir d'oppression."⁵ It was far from being unknown in the middle ages, that to benefit the poor was the glory of the great.

---

¹ Cours d'Hist. V, 21.
² Id. I, 113.
³ La France sous les cinq premiers Valois, I, 351.
⁴ Desormeaux Hist. de la Maison de Montmorenci, I, 273.
⁵ Le Baud.

It is well observed by one who relates how Gaucher de Châtillon, Constable of France, built Halls for the market of Paris, that the history of the middle ages bears testimony to the fact of this noble ambition having been common to the superior men of those times.

When the king of Arragon was knighted in the church of St. Saviour, at Saragossa, he brandished his sword three times. The first time he defied all the enemies of the holy Catholic faith; the second, he promised to succour all orphans, wards, and widows; the third time, he promised to render justice during his whole life to great and small, strangers and subjects.[1] "The enfranchisement of the commons," would the feudal baron have said, "is a word void of sense; and you will escape from our paternal government but to fall under the dominion of royalty, when you will have worse fortune than at present under us; for now each right is mutually acknowledged, and nothing can be arbitrary in a similar contract. Henceforth you will have to perform for a king what you have been in the habit of doing for us; but your new master, being removed at a distance from you, will not trouble himself about your wants. The old bonds of connection will be dissolved. Instead of obeying sovereign nobles, you will have to obey obscure delegates of the king, seneschals, provosts, bailiffs, and other petty officers, a thousand times more despotical than their chiefs themselves." Yet, in the thirteenth and fourteenth centuries, the constitutions of many Italian and German towns were changed with mutual good will of the great and low, after the precedent set by some of the great cities. What a contrast was this to the conflict which is so often waged with ferocity, where un-

---

[1] Chronica de Ramon de Muntaner, chap. CCXCVII.

bending arrogance will not make room for the rights of the power which is coming into being, or "which even rises the higher in its pretensions the more it ought to repress itself."

Vogt says, that as the Greeks honour with gratitude the names of a Cadmus, a Cecrops, a Lycurgus, and a Solon, so do the dukes of Zähringen derive an eternal renown in the history of the Germans. By these nobles, three powerful states and republics were founded. Berthold III built Freiburg in Swabia, Berthold IV Freiburg in Breisgau, and Berthold V Berne in Switzerland; and not content with building bare walls, they gave the new citizens freedom and ability to prosper; and as this house in the olden time was illustrious, so down to our days has its honour flourished; for, as in the twelfth century, the Bertholds built Freiburg and Berne, so in later times did Charles and Friedrich found Durlach and Karlsruhe. The Abbé de Mably regards Charlemagne as a founder of liberty and a protector of the people.

The history of the counts of Spanheim alone might shew what a spirit of freedom, and what paternal care for the common people was evinced by nobles in the thirteenth century. In these days there were no perpetual taxes as at present.[1] The people of Brittany for a long time preserved the feudal independence of their nobles, through fear of the exactions suffered by the subjects of the king.[2] "I have sworne," said the Earl of Foix to Sir Gaultyer of Passac, "to minystre to my people justyce, as every lord is bounde to do to his sub-iectes; for that entente lords have theyr sygnoryes."[3] The decree of Charlemagne, in 812, says, "let no Count presume to decide causes belonging to the

[1] La France sous les cinq premiers Valois.
[2] Chronique de St. Denis.
[3] Froissart, vol. II, cap. LXXVII.

great" "sed tantum ad pauperum et minus potentium justitias faciendas sibi sciat esse vacandum."[1]

In the feudal system, the seigneur who corrupted the wife or daughter of his vassal, forfeited, according to justice, his seigneurie.[2] Antoine de la Salle, one of the most renowned poets and knights of the fifteenth century, subject of René d' Anjou, says, in his Poem La Sallade,

> Bien doïbt estre sire clamez,
> Qui de ses hommes est amez
> Et cil n'est pas sire de son pays
> Qui de ses hommes est hays,
> Nous sommes tous freres, venus d'ung cep
> Donc nous devons l'ung de l'aultre avoir mercy.

So says King Perceforest, that he must act well to all his people, "gentilz et vilains," for otherwise he would not deserve the name of king. All chivalrous books of instruction reminded men of this duty. Thus Gurnemanz von Grahars, an old knight, instructed young Perceval in his duties as a knight, and says, "Pity the wants of the poor, especially of the unhappy, who struggle with shame, and may not reveal their sorrows, and do not refuse protection to any one who shall demand it." Among the laws of knighthood given by Favin,[3] the knight is commanded to see order preserved by armed men, and to protect the people from injury. In the old German romance of Tristan, when King Mark had given the young knight his sword and spurs, he says, "nephew, meditate on the prize of chivalry: let your birth and nobility be ever before you; be humble and ingenuous; be true and courteous; be good to the poor, high-minded to the rich; adorn and make your person agreeable; honour and love all women; be mild and faithful;

---

[1] Capit. III, 812. c. 2. Balnz, lib. III, c. 77.
[2] Sismondi Hist. des François, IV, p. 25.
[3] Theatre d'Honneur et de Chevalerie.

for I pledge my honour that gold and sable agree not so well with the spear and shield as truth and mildness." These and similar instructions were, as Büsching remarks, again and again repeated. In the third book of "l'Horloge des Princes, par Don Antoine de Guevare Evesque de Guadix traduict de Castillan, par N. de Herberay Seigneur des Essars," a bishop and a feudal lord inculcate them with eloquence. They will be found in the Lusiad:

> Return the guardians of your native land;
> To tyrant power be dreadful; from the jaws
> Of fierce oppression guard the peasant's cause.[1]

"My intentions," says the Knight of La Mancha, "are all directed to virtuous ends, and to do no man wrong, but good to all the world:" so said poor Charles VI. in his sickness. It was one of the prime objects of ambition to defend the poor: and for this sacred cause did noble men devote their lives.

> Long so they travelled through wasteful waies,
> Where sorrows dwelt and perils most did wonne,
> To hunt for glory and renowmed praise;
> Full many countries they did overrun,
> From the uprising to the setting sun,
> And many hard adventures did atchieve;
> Of all the which they honour ever wonne,
> Seeking the weak oppressed to relieve,
> And to recover right for such as wrong did grieve.[2]

Even the annals of the Teutonic order furnish some striking examples of justice exercised in Prussia in defending the common people from oppression. The author of "l'Arbre des Batailles" shews the wickedness of harassing the poor people and labourers in time of war, and that "les poures Anglois" are not to suffer for the crimes of the great.[3]

He concludes, "Les vaillans hommes et saiges

---

[1] Canto IX. *Orlandus*.   [2] Faery Queen, III, i, 3.   [3] Chap. XLIX.

qui suyvent armes se doivent bien garder de faire mal aux simples gens et innocens." In time of war labourers and their servants are to be exempted from all vexation, "Car il n'y a roy, duc, conte ni personne de quelque estat ou condition que ce soit qui puisse excuser qu'ils ne soient tenus de leur garder le droit de ce privilege cy, lequel leur donna ung pape qui fut, qui par ses decretales lye et oblige tous Chrestiens du monde que seurement ils puissent labourer les terres et recueillir les biens qui viennent de leur labour par la grace de dieu dont nous vivons sur terre hommes et femmes mesmement bestes et oyseaulx."[1]

Among the statutes of the order of the Croissant, instituted by King René of Anjou in 1448, it is written, "d'avoir tousjours pitié et compassion du pauvre peuple commun,"[2] to be in deed and in word sweet, courteous and amiable to all the world, and so to live "que leur loz et fame couraige et renommée puisse etre en croissant de toujours bien en mieulx." Knights were required to love and pity the common people by one of the laws of the round table.[3] St. Remi crowned Clovis, saying, "that the kings of France would be the perpetual defenders of the Church and of the poor,"[4] for these always went together; so that if a baron or prince oppressed the poor, we find that he was also an enemy of the Church. Richard I of England would have forced a Sicilian peasant to give him up his hawk, who, however, drove off the king with sticks and stones. It indicated a proud and oppressive spirit: but he also converted a convent of monks near Messina into a magazine, which so enraged the people that they rose against him.

[1] Chap. CII.
[2] La Colombiere, Theatre d'Honneur et de Chevalerie, I, 110.
[3] Ibid. p. 132.
[4] Testament. S. Rem.

In the old romance of "Helyas, Knight of the Swan," Ydain, Duchess of Bouillon, instructs her three sons, Godfrey, Baudwin, and Eustace, saying to them, "Alwai above all thinges give laude and glorye to God in all your workes, my fayre children. Abide alway in his fear and love. Be swet, soft, and curteys to your subjects, without oppressyng or damaging them in ani wyse; yf ye be able and possible to reedifie the churches of God, and offre willingly your owne bodies in sacrifice in susteyning the holy faythe Catholyke. Keepe and defende justly your countre. Bere and sustayne the right of poore widowes and orphelins. Distribute and deele of your goddes to the nedy, comforte the sorrowful, and think for to save your soule for to have the grace of God. And I promyse you my chyldren that yf ye govern you that ye shal prospere in this worlde and have heaven at your ende. In such good and helthful doctrine did theyr good mother Ydain devoutly teach these three yong sonnes."[1] Will not these examples justify our asserting that the instruction which men received in these ages was to love and favour the common people? Did it fall short of what Cicero says? "Nihil est tam populare quam bonitas: nulla de virtutibus tuis plurimis nec admirabilior nec gratior misericordia est. Homines enim ad deos nulla re propius accedunt quam salutem hominibus dando. Nihil habet nec fortuna tua majus, quam ut possis; nec natura tua melius quam ut velis servare quamplurimos."[2] It will be said, perhaps, that the practice of men did not correspond with these instructions, but do not all the common associations with which unprejudiced persons look back upon ancient times lead to the contrary supposition? Among our old Catholic nobility what House resembled the Claudian, priding

---

[1] Chap. XLII.   [2] Pro Q. Ligario.

itself on its hatred of the people? How many, on the contrary, exceeded the Valerian in priding themselves on their hereditary love of the people? as we read of Newark's stately tower,

> Whose ponderous grate and massy bar
> Had oft rolled back the tide of war,
> But never closed the iron door
> Against the desolate and poor.[1]

How many feudal lords sought to have attendants in Heaven? as Cervantes says, by following the advice given by the Knight of La Mancha to his squire, "If thou canst keep six servants keep but three, and let what would maintain three more be laid out in charitable uses." How many noble dames felt like Penelope, that besides the religious motive, even their dignity required them to assist and comfort all in distress who should approach them;[2] not content with "writing their names in a dumb blind book, in order placidly to rely upon an invisible board of management," but conversing with these poor persons, and comforting them with looks and words as well as with their purse. King Charles V of France, in giving alms to the poor would always kiss the hands of those whom he relieved.[3] Is it unworthy of notice that the most destitute class of human beings were greeted as fellow-creatures, and treated with kindness? I confess, for my part, I can easily understand how men could feel a kind of reverence for the poor beggar. Œdipus appears as a beggar in Sophocles;[4] Robert, a prince of Flanders, and many knights were seen begging during the distress of the Crusaders.[5] Surely, at all events, it was for the advantage of humanity that this most abject condition was not regarded as utterly effacing the dignity of

[1] Lady of the Lake.   [2] Od. XIX, 325.
[3] Hist. de Charles V, par Christine de Pisan.
[4] Œd. Col. 6.   [5] Gesta Dei per Francos, 258.

man's nature, but that the beggar with his simple song could draw tears from the knightly traveller, and would always receive hospitality in the baron's hall; and that the red cross knight, when reduced to the same condition, and under disguise, could ask relief "vultu dejecto, etsi non voce," as William of Tyre says,[1] and be certain of obtaining it. How affecting was the remonstrance of St. Bonaventura, "Our Lord exercised hospitality on the cross; for there was a certain traveller who had made a long journey to a distant land, and, seeking a reception from Christ, he said, 'Memento mei, Domine, cùm veneris in regnum tuum,' and our Lord said, 'Hodie mecum eris in paradiso.' O miserable depravity of men! Our Lord received a robber into his place of refreshment, and we are unwilling to receive even good men into our earthy and muddy habitations, excusing ourselves, and saying, 'perhaps they are robbers.' Remember, miserable man, that our Lord himself received a robber; and if perchance, through poverty, thou canst not give him shelter in thy material house, at least harbour him in thy heart by having pity upon him."[2] "In the ages which are called barbarous," says the Abbé de la Mennais, "Christianity strengthened and softened power, sanctified obedience, established the true social relations, purified manners, and often supplied the place of laws. It had covered Europe with admirable institutions which, filling the immense void inseparable from political institutions, had bound to the State, by the sweet influence of a charity prodigal of benefits, the innumerable class of the unhappy. Thanks to the empire which it exercised over our ideas, man became sacred to man. Without doubt there were passions and consequently crimes, but religion knew how to derive new virtues from

---

[1] Gesta Dei per Francos, 717.
[2] Stimulus divini Amoris, cap. XIV.

them by repentance. Subject to the immutable rules, of duty, actions and thoughts tended in general to the common good; and that is the characteristic trait of the epoch. One was strong for the weak and rich for the poor. Instead of dreaming about an order of things exempt from all imperfections, the existing order was suffered to perfect itself by degrees, and each one in his own sphere endeavoured to remedy the particular evil which struck him."[1] "What monuments of alms-deeds and kindness to the poor are yet extant in the world raised by Christians in these times, who often gave not only of their abundance but spared also from their own sustenance, as also took away and alienated many things from their children and posterity to employ for charity? So many churches built, bishoprics, chauntries, and benefices endowed, so many hospitals and houses of orphans, as also for the relief of other poor impotent people; so many seminaries, schools, halls, colleges, and universities for increase of learning, open equally to the poor and the rich; so many bridges, highways, causeways, town-houses, and other public conveniences; so many monasteries, abbeys, priories, convents, nunneries, hermitages, cells, oratories, and other like for repose of virtuous poor people that would leave the world and betake themselves to the contemplations of heavenly things and exercise of a more holy and retired life."[2] And remark too, respecting the instances of injustice and cruelty, with what horror they are recorded by the old historians, which proves how much they differed from the general actions which were considered honourable among men. It is said that the Jacquerie riots were caused by the exactions of feudal lords;[3] but

[1] Essai sur l'Indifférence I, 6.
[2] Person's Christian Directory, 165.
[3] Barante des Communes et de l'Aristocratie.

it is singular if so that the barbarous agents, when asked their motives, did not ascribe their conduct to any particular cause, but, on the contrary, expressly said that they could not account for the rage which impelled them. How bitterly does Olivier de la Marche complain of the evils suffered by the poor people and merchants in time of war?[1] What sorrow and shame does Froissart exhibit when he relates the massacre at Limoges, of which the Black Prince was guilty in a moment of anger?[2] Richard Brembrow, an English knight, was ravaging Brittany in the year 1350, when the noble Beaumanoir, Chatelain of the castle of Josselin, reproached him for his conduct, expressing his astonishment that a valiant knight should make war on labourers and poor people. "In all wars," he said, "guided by chivalrous principle, true soldiers never injure the tillers of the ground."

> Mais j'ay bien de certaine noble chevalerie
> Et de toute Bretaingne la fleur de l'escurie
> Qui ne daigneroient fuir ne a mort ne a vie.

This led to the famous combat of the thirty English and thirty Bretons, in which, says the old poem, "God gave the victory to those who fought for the oppressed." Du Guesclin charged his companions, on his death-bed, to remember that neither the clergy, nor women, nor children, nor poor people, were their enemies; and Hugues du Payens would not suffer Hugues d'Amboise to be enrolled among the Templars till he had humbled himself and made reparation to the subjects of Marmoutier, whom he had vexed by exactions.[3] The ancient records give a very different idea of the conduct of the great in these ages, from that which certain modern writers would persuade us to cherish. What a testimony has Froissart left to the merit of the Earl of Foix:—

[1] Chap. IV.   [2] I, cap. 283.   [3] Hist. des Templiers, I, 15.

"Surely it is grete domage," he says, "that suche a persone sholde be olde or dye." He had his faults, "and yet for all that his people alwayes prayde to God for his longe lyfe: and I herde it reported, howe when he dyed there were in Foyze and in Byerne XM persones that sayd that they wolde gladly have dyed with hym, whereby it is to be thought that they sayd not so without it had been for grete love that they had to their lorde; and surely if they loved hym, they did but ryght and accordynge to reason, for he alwayes maynteyned them in theyr ryght and kepte ever true justyce, for all his landes and the people therein had as grete lyberte and fraunchesse, and lyved in as good peas as though they had ben in paradyse terrestre. I say not this for flattery nor for favour, nor love that I bere hym, nor for the gyftes that he hath gyven me; but I can well prove all that I have sayd, for I am sure there be a M knyghts and squyers wyll saye the same." Thus Baldwin II. Count of Flanders, son of Baldwin the iron arm, is said to have established good laws, and cleared his domain of all evil doers, seeking every possible occasion to nurture his subjects in peace and harmony, that they might enjoy all prosperity; an "office," continues the old chronicler, "truly worthy of a Christian prince, to whom nothing should be more dear than the happiness of his people—de telle sorte qu'il en soit loué de Jesus Christ, quand en conviendra rendre compte, et qu'il delaisse au monde bon bruit et honneste memoire de luy."[1] "A good lord makes good vassals," says the brave Ramon Muntaner in his chronicle;[2] "and this is seen in those of Aragon, for here the princes are not their masters but their friends: they cause justice and good faith to be observed among nobles, prelates,

---

[1] P. Oudegherst, Chronique de Flandres, 48.
[2] Chap. XX.

knights, citizens, and peasants; every one may grow rich without fear of unreasonable exactions;" he adds through his attachment to the house of Aragon, "and that is not the case with other princes." "Hence the Catalonians, and they of Aragon, have more elevated sentiments, from not being held in restraint, and no man can be a good warrior who has not elevated sentiments. Their subjects have also this advantage, that every one may speak to his lord as much as he pleases, and depend upon being always heard with kindness. On the other hand, if a rich man want to marry off his daughter, and should pray the prince to honour the ceremony with his presence, these lords are sure to attend at church, or elsewhere, and in like manner, they will assist at a funeral, or at a mass of anniversary, as if the deceased had been one of their own relations. On great festivals they invite numbers of honest people, and they accept invitations from others, whether from castles, cities, villages, or farm houses, eating what is set before them, and sleeping wherever they are invited; and if the poor people call out to them, they stop and listen to them, and relieve them, and hence their subjects love them, and fear not to die to exhalt their honour and their power, and they fear neither heat, nor cold, nor danger."

There are many pictures to be drawn from the middle ages besides these which represent the lordly towers and the chivalrous court. The painter and the true philanthropist gaze with equal delight upon those rustic villages, which are still to be seen in every Catholic country, embosomed in wood, and removed at an immense distance from the vices and misery of those towns where the "intellectual activity" is at work. There is a charm in watching the smoke curling above the thatched roofs; the flocks and herds, obedient to the night call, returning with eagerness to their accustomed stalls. Here, there is no lawyer, no rich manufacturer to stimulate the passions of a peaceable and innocent people; no great speculations ending in ruin and suicide, or in success and the license of hell. The venerable curate beholds them assembled in the church every morning and evening, and the benevolent seigneur who has passed his life among them, is proud of being considered the familiar friend of each poor cottager. In the old romance of Robert the Devil, this nobleman, after doing penance for his wicked life, is represented ending his days in the exercise of every virtue, with the view of rendering his vassals happy.

At the grand entertainment given by Louis de Clermont, duc de Bourbon, at Moulins, on returning to his duchy, in 1369, after his imprisonment of eight years in London, when he had publicly thanked his knights and vassals for their loyalty during the interval, Huguenin Chauveau, his agent, suddenly rose up and advanced through the hall, bearing an immense book, which he presented to the duke, saying that it contained the list of all persons who had refused to pay their taxes, and who had trespassed and committed injuries upon his domains during his absence. At these terrible words the whole assembly was thrown into consternation, but the duke soon dispelled all fears. "Chauveau," said he, with a severe tone, "have you also kept a list of the services which my vassals have rendered me?" With these words he seized the book and threw it upon the vast fire in the centre of the hall, where it was consumed in the flames. It was this brave Louis de Clermont who, having to choose between flying to rescue his mother, Isabelle de Valois, when the Duke of Cambridge was carrying her off, and remaining to save the poor inhabitants of Belle-Perche from the flames, devoted his first efforts to preserve his people from calamity.¹ It is said that the lowest peasant on his domains was filled with joy when he returned from the war in 1385. It was then that he founded the monastery of the Celestins, at Vichy, and the hospital of St. Nicholas, at Moulins. Every Friday he used to station himself at the gate of his palace, and distribute large alms to the poor. He was buried in the priory of Sauvigny, amidst the tears of his vassals. "Alas!" they cried, "he was our support and protector, our comfort, our duke, le plus prud'-homme, de la meilleure conscience, de la meilleure vie qu' on sçût trouver."

The knights are said, by the modern sophists, to have been men who were never weary of oppressing and hacking the poor: how different are the portraits which remain of these brave men! Witness Bayard, who went about Grenoble in the time of the plague, like a priest, visiting the poor sick people, and giving them medicines and food, supporting them at his own expense in hospitals, and visiting the neighbouring villages to relieve the distressed! When was there ever a more humane and Christian sentence than his reply to those who told him that it was throwing away his money to give money to poor people in countries ravaged by war. "Messeigneurs, je fais ce que je dois, advienne que pourra! How do you know that this poor man will not be able to save his little treasure, hiding it under a tree and finding it again when the war is over, when he will pray to God for me?"²

In the treaty concluded by Maximilian with the King of France, the emperor declares that he is moved by the desire of putting an end to the miseries which the poor people suffer whom every virtuous prince ought to pity.³ When Maximilian

¹ Vies des grands Capitaines François au Moyen Age, V, 32.
² Hist. de Bayard, Paris, 1828.
³ Chroniques de Jean Molinet, XI, 16½.

held the solemnity of the Toison d'Or in the church of St. Salvator at Bruges, in the choir were painted the arms, names, and titles of all the knights of the order, both those who died since the last festival, in the year 1473, and those who were then living. The first painting on the right hand represented the arms and titles of Duke Charles, whom God absolve! beginning, Charles, by the grace of God, Duke of Burgundy, and then was written at the end " Trespassé." The old chronicles record that many vassals, loyal servants, and subjects of the late duke burst into tears when they came to this mournful word Trespassé, for they so dearly loved him that they would hardly give credit to the account of his having been so piteously slain.

The poet Herbert, who lived in the beginning of the thirteenth century, describes a knight as follows, in his Romance of Dolopatos, King of Sicily:

> Onkes ne trouva en sa vie
> Son pareil de Chevalerie,
> Les uns par armes sorprenoit
> Les autres par dons qu'il donoit,
> Les autres par beles paroles,
> C'est un ars ki maint home afole.
> As pauvres gens qui le dontoient,
> Et qui à lui songiet estoient,
> Estoit si dous et debonere,
> Com s'il nul mal ne seust fere;
> Plus fu lor pere que lor aire,
> Ce puis-je bien par raison dire.

Büsching quotes from the Nibelungen a passage which describes the joy of the people in beholding the young squire Siegfried when he first rode to court. The poor loved and respected these men whom the moderns describe as so many wolves preying upon them. "King Edward IV. himself told me," says Philippe de Commines, "that in all battles that he had won, so soon as he had obtained the victory, he used to mount on horseback and cry out, 'save the people and kill the nobles.'"[1] Possibly, however, his private ends may have dictated this measure. Sir Thomas More could bear a better testimony to himself, saying, "Neque nobilibus eram invisus nec injucundus populo." His advice to a great man is, "let him thinke in his owne heart every poore beggar his fellow."[2] That Thierry's statement of the misery and outrages suffered by the common people is monstrously distorted, appears evident to every one who is familiar with the contemporary writers. Guillaume de Poitiers alone suffices to exculpate William from much that this writer alleges against him. Speaking of Normandy, this old author says, "All men of every class of every rank extolled the glory of Duke William, and with every kind of love wished him a long life and a happy health." Again, when William rode with such haste from Coutances against the Count of Arques that all the horses of his company died except six, it was owing to the accounts he heard of the sufferings of the people. "He was grieved to see the goods of the Church, the works of the labourer, the gain of the merchant, become the prey of armed men: he seemed to hear himself called by the deplorable groans of the poor people." He mentions his repeated and express commands against pillage: at his own expense he nourished 50,000 knights for a month at the embouchure of the Dive, while detained by winds. "The flocks could graze in the fields with as much safety as if they had been in a sanctuary; and the weak and armless man might ride on horseback singing his song, and without fear, amid troops of warriors." In England too, "he had mild attention for all, but more clemency still for common people:—and

---

[1] P. 95.   [2] On Comfort, II, 17.

he never gave anything to a Frenchman which had been unjustly taken from an Englishman." And then he repeats his assertion "that the poor unarmed man went singing on his way wherever he chose, without trembling at the sight of battalions of knights." Now certainly this author, if he does not fully exculpate William, at least exculpates religion and the opinion of the age.

The qualities of chivalry could move even the most ferocious enemies. When the Swiss, after their barbarous expedition in 1474, for which Zschokke does not attempt to justify them, had retaken Granson, and hanged up the Burgundians on the same trees from which some of their own countrymen had been suspended, it is said that the youth, the beauty, and the tears of many gentlemen moved some of the fierce conquerors, who took them under their protection.[1] In the last campaign of René d'Anjou, a general of Lorraine, proposing to burn a village of the enemy, "Capitaine," replied the Duke René II of Lorraine, "quand maulx vouldras faire enquerre conseil de moi, et pas n'en feras."[2] His sentiment might have been expressed in the very words of Socrates, πέπεισμαι ἐγὼ ἑκὼν εἶναι μηδένα ἀδικεῖν ἀνθρώπων.[3] Mark, again, what was the policy of the great in those ages. Werner I, Bishop of Strasburg, in the eleventh century, who deserves immortality for building the greatest part of that cathedral,[4] wished to have a place of security against the power of the Emperor, so he wrote to his brother, Count Ratbot, who lived in the old family castle at Altenburg, and sent him a large sum of gold and silver, with directions to employ it in building a strong castle. Time passed, and the

[1] Barante, Hist. des Ducs de Bourgogne, XI, 35.
[2] Villeneuve, Hist. de René d'Anjou, III, 122.
[3] Plat. Apolog.
[4] Begun in 1015, though not finished till the end of 300 years.

Emperor was far absent in Lombardy, and the reverend lord remembered that he, too, had worldly matters to look after, and that he ought to examine how Count Ratbot had fulfilled his directions; so with this design he ordered a troop of twenty-nine horsemen, and taking with him his chaplain and his noble pages, he set off to ride up the Rhine with great speed. About twilight he entered Basel, and still he pushed on to Augst, where he rested, and slept far into the next day, to the great joy of the pages, who were sadly knocked up with the hasty scouring of the country. The second day's journey, upon reaching the Bözberg, the Bishop pulled up, and making a spyglass of his hand, for he was not clearsighted, asked aloud whether any one could see the new castle. "Can it be that miserable crow's nest yonder, where I expected to find a noble eagle's eyry?" This was all that passed, and they rode on till about evensong, when they reached the new Habsburg, so called to express its being a place of security for the family property. Ascending the hill, the good Bishop shook his head often, and kept muttering, "no bulwark, no trench, not a wall to be seen": thus they reached the gate, which received the troop into the Count's castle. Here again the Bishop expressed his astonishment and displeasure, but the Count replied, "My most reverend Lord and brother, I have endeavoured to the best of my power to fulfil your will, and that your grace will perceive by to-morrow morning, when I shall have raised two other walls round the castle, and then you will find that I have well employed your gold and silver." The Bishop, who ever had the fear of God before his eyes, was struck to the heart by these words, as if by a dagger; "Alas, and woe is me," said he, "has my unlucky brother made a league with Satan that he can perform such a work by to-morrow morning!"

So with silent nods of the head the Bishop took leave for the night, and withdrew to his bedroom, where he lay in much trouble, till, exhausted with great fatigue, he at length fell asleep. And now at the crowing of the cock, as he lay peaceably, and two noble pages watched before the bed, lo, the whole castle suddenly resounded with such a crash of horns and trumpets that the Bishop in terror jumped from his bed, and throwing his robe round him, hurried to the battlements, whence he could see the surrounding country, but no words could describe his countenance when he saw two lines of warlike troops, infantry and cavalry, fully armed, stand around the castle, who began another flourish of trumpets. "O woe and gracious Heaven pity me!" cried the good Bishop, "Are these the two walls?" While yet speaking the Count touched him on the shoulder, and bid him fear nothing, for these were brave men, who would ensure their house of refuge: "for these," he continued, "are all our people, ready to do us honourable service, and this is better than stone walls, without hearts and arms to defend them." The Bishop, full of joy, embraced his brother, and praised him in fair words, and the Count made the noble knights and warriors come up to the castle and do homage to the Bishop, and swear to serve their race for ever; and so these were the first counts of Habsburg.[1] "These few words," says Voght, "convey the whole history of the House of Habsburg. Not by bulwarks and warlike armaments did it become great and powerful, but by the love and fidelity of its people."[2] In Switzerland, where many of the governors were cruel tyrants, such as Gesler and Landenberg, Wolfenschreff, the lords of Guardavall in the Engadine, and the Lord of Fardün, the Princes of Habsburg

---

[1] Tschudi's Chronic.   [2] II, 8.

and the Counts of Gruyere were beloved by the people; and certainly the chivalry of that country was with the mountaineers, Tell, Arnold Struthahn von Winkelried, John Waldmann of Zürich, the heroes of Morgarten, Sempach, Morat, and Nancy. Nor were the great kings who succeeded these feudal princes without their religious sentiments respecting the poor common people. The Emperor Frederick I declared, in ratifying the peace at Venice, that he considered the whole end of the imperial and royal majesty was that by its means the whole world might have peace.

Provence being afflicted by a great drought, René of Anjou exempted every city, town, and village which experienced it from all tax, and the plague having ravaged Toulon he remitted all its taxes for five years;[1] and the little village of Beauvezer being consumed by flames, René exempted the people of all tax for ten years. The death or misfortunes of these kings and feudal princes were felt as a domestic calamity in every house. When René d'Anjou lost that duchy, "who," says Bourdigné, a chronicler of the fifteenth century, "could describe the dolour of the poor Angevins, eulx voyant privez d'un si curieux et vigilant tucteur, protecteur du pays? amoureux de paix et de concorde! substantateur des povres! des dames et damoiselles honorable directeur et support! administrateur incorruptible de justice! en général, de tout son populaire très bening et miséricordieux père!"

When Prince Henry, son of Henry II, died, Bertrand de Born described the universal grief: "English and Normans," says he, "Bretons and Irish, people of Guienne, Gascony, Angers, Tours, and Mans, all have reason to weep!"[2]

---

[1] Villeneuve, Hist. de René d'Anjou, II, pp. 6, 151.
[2] Millot, Hist. des Troubadours.

When Sir Gauvain was carried dead to the castle "the mourning was so great," says the Romance, "qu'on n'y eust pas ouy Dieu tonner"; and there was such a light of tapers, "quil sembloit que le chasteau ardist,"—and all wept as if they had lost a brother, "Car Messire Gauvain estoit le meilleur chevalier du monde et le plus aime de diverses gens."[1]

The distinctions of rank were not suffered, as is now too often supposed, to prevent persons of merit from rising to their due places. The example of the Abbot Suger, the minister of Louis-le-Gros, and of his son Louis-le-Jeune, affords occasion to Sismondi for remarking "the enthusiasm which science excited in that age, and the facility with which it raised persons of the lowest class to the highest offices."[2] Alfred exhorted the nobles to choose among their vassals such youths as should appear, by their parts and inclination to piety, particularly promising to be trained up to the liberal arts. As for the rest, it was not then the custom to give the poorer sort too much of a school education, which might abate their industry and pleasure in manual labour; but he was careful to provide for the religious education of all. We have seen in Tancredus, that in the schools under Charlemagne, the peasant boys were promoted equally with the sons of nobles. In a religious point of view, it was great encouragement to the poor to hear that St. Geneviève, a simple shepherdess, was patron saint of Paris, and St. Isidore, a poor labourer, the patron of Madrid; and that Benedict, Joseph Labre, a beggar, was venerated by princes as a servant of God. In matters of chivalry too, Olivier de la Marche shews that courage was as much admired and proclaimed when shewn by the lowest

---

[1] Lancelot du Lac, tome III, f. cexxii.
[2] Hist. des François, V, p. 68.

person of the lowest condition as by the highest.[1]
In Richard the Second's time, Sir Robert Sale,
Governor of Norwich, though son of a mason, as
Froissart says, yet having the grace to be reputed
sage and valiant in arms, King Edward had made
him a knight, and Sir John Hawkwood,—who acted
so distinguished a part in the Italian wars, at the
head of an English company, after the same king's
wars in France, and who had been also knighted by
King Edward, was the son of tailor. In the Morte
d'Arthur, — that hero of romance makes a poor
man's son a knight. But I have established this
point in the first book.

In every age, there were means by which the
lower ranks could rise to nobility,[2] though Philippe-
le-Hardi may have been the first King of France
who ennobled men by letters, and Raoul l'Orfevre
the first subject so ennobled. Poverty was not an
insuperable obstacle to merit. The Emperor Frederick had a falconer, a brave man, who had a son
a year old when Conradin went to Sicily, and this
falconer being slain in battle, fighting against
Charles d'Anjou, all his estates were confiscated.
The little boy, when eight years old, used to go on
board the ships in the harbour of Brindisi, where
his mother lived in great poverty. It happened
that a servant brother of the Templars, named
Vassayl, who commanded a ship of the order called
the Falcon, which was wintering there, took a fancy
to him, seeing him, as the old Chronicle says,
mount the yards as nimbly as a little mouse. The
poor mother consented to let him sail with the
Templar, and Roger so distinguished himself, that
when he had attained the age of twenty, the grand
master of the Templars made him a serving brother,
and gave him the command of a ship. This was

[1] Hist. des François, chap. XXVIII.
[2] La France sous les cinq premiers Valois, I, 270.

the brother Roger who became so famous in the expedition of the Catalans and Aragonese against the Turks, and who became Cæsar of the empire under the Emperor of Constantinople.[1] Camoens speaks of

"The seven brave hunters murder'd by the Moor:"[2]

upon which line Castera comments: "During a truce with the Moors, six cavaliers of the Order of St. James were, while on a hunting party, surrounded and killed by a numerous body of the Moors. During the fight, in which the gentlemen sold their lives dear, a common carter, named Garcias Rodrigo, who chanced to pass that way, came generously to their assistance, and lost his life along with them. The poet, in giving all seven the same title, shews us that virtue constitutes the true nobility." Meanwhile let it be remembered, that the word vilain was no disgraceful epithet, seeing it was derived by old writers from vaillant, to express men who were companions of their Lord;[3] and that, as we read in an old Romance, "Artus fut abandonné des sa naissance aux soins des pauvres et bons vilains":[4] in which sentence, it will be well to remark the ancient phraseology of "poor and good." Be it remembered also, that there was no law like that in Rome, forbidding the right of intermarriage between high and low. There was no need of a Canuleian law to establish it; nor let that permission required in the feudal age, be deemed degrading, which the warlike nobles of every country of Europe but our own, are content now to demand for themselves. The

[1] Chronica de Ramon Muntaner, CXCIV. Moncada's Hist. of the Expedition, I, 3.
[2] Lusiad VIII.
[3] Marchangy Tristan, V, 357.
[4] Roman du Roi Artus, compiled from the Brut by Rusticien de Pise, in the thirteenth century.

distinctions of civil life were not inaccessible to the commercial classes; there was no difference between simple knights and principal citizens.[1] The counts of Toulouse and the inhabitants of Provence agreed, in 1251, that "les bourgeois honorables qui avaient coutume de vivre en chevaliers, jouissaient des memes priviléges que ces derniers."

Even Sismondi confesses that, "amidst the rocks of Lycaonia, the sandy deserts of Ascalon, or in the prisons of the Saracens, the knight and his vilain learned to estimate the just value of the chances of birth and fortune."[2] But had he been more mindful of the religion of the knight, he would have known a more secure and certain source whence this learning was derived. "Now there were shepherds," says the Gospel; and men in these ages meditated on all the sublime and affecting circumstances of its history. "How many rich men," thought they, "were stretched luxuriously, during that night, on beds covered with gold and purple! not one of them was judged worthy of being summoned by the angels, or of beholding the celestial light which surrounded them." In these ages men believed in such a thing as holy poverty, and made vows to embrace it, and revered such as did. St. Francis of Assisi, before he had embraced a religious life, would place himself among the poor before the gate of St. Peter's Church at Rome, through the love of poverty: and if the moderns would condescend to open the Lives of the Saints, they would see how many princes and feudal barons, and knights, would eat with the poor and serve them, and kneel among them in prayer, and at their deaths would carry their bodies to be put in the earth. Hence the poor loved and revered the great, for the privileges of their rank seemed to

[1] Marchangy Tristan, VI, p. 514.
[2] Hist. des François, VI, 131.

be exercised only for the common good. St. Francis prescribed a vile habit to his brethren, which was to be mended with sackcloth, and a sentiment which he had no doubt learned in his intercourse with the poor: "Quos moneo et exhortor ne despiciant neque judicent homines quos viderint mollibus vestimentis et coloratis indutos, uti cibis et potibus delicatis; sed magis unusquisque judicet et despiciat semetipsum." [1]

'What a spectacle to behold the poor in our churches! the poor who have escaped confinement in our humane institutions! to witness the meek resignation, the charitable unsuspicious eye, the profound devotion of these suffering poor, lying, very often, prostrate on the ground at the elevation, and without strength to rise again till some friendly hand is stretched out to help them: O! is it for the rich of the nineteenth century to talk of the inhumanity of the middle ages? To give alms, with them, is to encourage idleness: he is hungry, he is naked? let him work; but he is old? there are employments for all; but he is a child? do not teach him to beg; it is a mother of a large family? perhaps she does not tell the truth. We have institutions on a new system. Yes, truly, and woe to the unhappy who are doomed to receive relief from them![2] In order that the children of pleasure may not be incommoded by the sight of poverty, the poor are shut up within high walls, and condemned to confinement for the crime of being poor and miserable: thus secluded from the enjoyment of nature, an odious board of governors takes care that they should be provided with what is sufficient to support life, and then they have to endure the countenances of ferocious barbarians, who are the officers to administer this horrible humanity! Our

[1] Regula St. Francisci, cap. XI.   [2] De la Mennais.

Lord named the beggar Lazarus, and the other he only calls Dives: but now it is a shame to err, or be ignorant in naming the rich, though for the poor man it is enough if we say, "the pauper," "the vagrant," names for which we are indebted to the new philosophy. When Ulysses told Eumæus that he meant to go as a beggar to the house of Penelope, where the suitors revelled, the good man replied,

*Ὤ μοι, ξεῖνε, τίη τοι ἐνὶ φρεσὶ τοῦτο νόημα
Ἔπλετο; ἦ σύ γε πάγχυ λιλαίεαι αὐτόθ' ὀλέσθαι.*[1]

And when he came among the Phæacians, Minerva advised him to go in silence, and speak to no one, for that they detested poor strangers.[2] Is it for the proud lords who resemble such men, to pity the state of the poor in the days of Charlemagne and St. Louis?

In the middle ages arose the religious order of Knights of the Holy Trinity, founded under the sanction of Pope Innocent III, for the redemption of captives, and that of our Lady of Mercy, founded by St. Peter Nolasco, for the same object. Are those ages to be accused of being indifferent to the misery of slaves? Have the modern wars of France been marked with such humanity, as to make the deeds of ancient chivalry seem worthy of execration? Sismondi speaks of "those men of labour, whose understanding is but little elevated above that of the cattle, of whose toils they partake."[3] When men holding such language, and who can find no other designation for an agricultural and religious province, but by covering it with a black shade on their maps, complain of our ancestors for not having sufficiently respected the common people, they remind one of the tyrant accusers of Socrates,

[1] Od. XV, 325.   [2] Od. VII, 30.
[3] Hist. des François, VI, 296.

who charged him with teaching that the poor might be beaten and reviled, because he had quoted Homer,[1] describing Ulysses addressing men of eminence with respect, and useless low persons with reproach. Xenophon might have spared himself the pains of proving, on the contrary, that Socrates was a friend to the poor;[2] and with no less justice might the charges against Christian antiquity be deemed unworthy of refutation. When do we hear any of these modern sophists uttering such sentiments as those which are ascribed to Francis de Montmorenci by the historian of his house, "that he loved the people, and above all, the country peasants, while he testified the greatest respect for the clergy";[3] or such as Montaigne expresses, saying, "the class of men least to be disdained, seems to me to be that which from its simplicity holds the last rank; the manners and behaviour of the peasants I find generally more orderly, according to the prescription of true philosophy, than those of our philosophers."[4] And again, "tempests reign in the middle region, the two extremes, the philosophers [he means men very different from those who now assume this title in France], and the rustics concur in tranquillity and in happiness."[5] This was the judgment also of Aristotle, who says, Βέλτιστος δῆμος ὁ γεωργικός ἐστιν.[6] These were the sentiments of men in the ages of which I speak, and the sophists who preach the new philosophy would deem the general prevalence of them to be a destructive evil, an indication of moral darkness, and of national degradation. Nor was it only the poor and the common people who experienced this humanity. The treatment of domestics in these ages presents another striking

[1] Il. II, 188.
[2] Desormeaux, II, 384.
[3] Id. III, 10.
[4] Memorabilia, lib. I, 2.
[5] Essais, liv. II, 17.
[6] Polit. VI, 4.

example of its exercise: here again men were consistent Christians. "In the time of our ancestors," says Mr. Heber, "the interval between the domestics and the other members of a family was by no means so great, nor fenced with so harsh and impenetrable a barrier as in the present days of luxury and excessive refinement"; and speaking of some vestiges of antiquity in his university, he says, "it is easy to declaim against the indecorum and illiberality of depressing the poorer students into servants; but it would be more candid and more consistent with truth to say, that our ancestors elevated their servants to the rank of students"; they regarded them as humble friends. Gilles de Rome, in his Mirror of Chivalry, shews how a man should consider his servants as his brethren, and how in Genesis it is not said, that God gave dominion to man over man, but that servitude is in consequence of sin and the fall.

Our ancestors might have indulged an innocent pleasure in remarking, that the divine charity of religion had given rise to manners and modes of life which the muse had ascribed to the heroes of her majestic world. With what respect does Homer speak of the squires of Nestor and Diomedes, Sthenelus and Eurymedon, calling the latter a lover of virtue![1] He expressly says, that Hector loved his Eniopeus, whom Diomedes slew as he guided his lord's chariot. Men in our chivalrous times would visit their swine-herd, like Ulysses, and would rejoice on finding that they and their wives and sons were loved by this poor man. There was none of that coldness and reserve which now lies like a barrier of ice between different degrees; the swine-herd whom Homer calls δῖος ὑφορβὸς, kisses and embraces Telemachus, and the young prince calls him ἄττα, and goes into his house, as into that

[1] Π. VIII.

of a dear friend. Cervantes makes his knight with the goat-herd order his squire to sit down and eat with him in the same dish, saying, "It may be said of knight errantry as of love, that it makes all things equal." What Eumæus said of his master Ulysses, might have been repeated by the lowest servants of chivalry of their lords:

> Οὐ γὰρ ἔτ' ἄλλον
> Ἤπιον ὧδε ἄνακτα κιχήσομαι, ὁππόσ' ἐπέλθω·
> Οὐδ' εἴ κεν πατρὸς καὶ μητέρος αὖτις ἵκωμαι
> Οἶκον, ὅθι πρῶτον γενόμην, καί μ' ἔτρεφον αὐτοί,
> Οὐδέ τι τῶν ἔτι τόσσον ὀδύρομαι, ἀχνύμενός περ
> Ὀφθαλμοῖσιν ἰδέσθαι, ἰὼν ἐν πατρίδι γαίῃ·
> Ἀλλά μ' Ὀδυσσῆος πόθος αἴνυται οἰχομένοιο.[1]

Darius owed his empire to the ingenuity of his horse-page or squire Œbares.[2] Socrates gave to his divine book on the immortality of the soul, the name of a slave, Phædo, whom he instructed in philosophy. Pompylus, the slave of Theophrastus, the Peripatetic, and Persæus, the slave of Zeno the Stoic, became great philosophers.[3] Epictetus was a slave. The manners and views of our ancestors would have subjected them to no shame, when these sublime examples were brought forward: they were true to the spirit of that Apostle, whose affection for a slave was immortalized in the Epistle to Philemon. What an ancient philosopher had recommended to his familiar friend they practised, not through the pride of philosophy, but in the spirit of religion and in the simplicity of their hearts: "Non est quod amicum tantum in foro et in curia quæras: si diligenter attenderis, invenies et domi. Tu modo vive cum servo clementer. Comiter quoque et in sermonem illum, et nonnumquam in necessarium admitte consilium. Nam et majores nostri omnem dominis invidiam, omnem servis contumeliam detrahentes, dominum patrem-familias, servos

[1] Od. XIV, 139. [2] Herod. III, 85. [3] Aul. Gell. II, 18.

familiares appellaverunt."[1] When they could not keep them for friendship or for service they retained them for charity. Thus Friar Bacon is said, in the old romance, to keep his one servant, who was none of the wisest, and incapable of serving him, for charity. Nay, the custom of keeping dwarfs in kings' palaces and barons' castles was humane. These poor little creatures were thus sought after and made happy, while the incidents of life and the ceremonial of courts often drew from them simple lessons, which could make wise men weep. There was thus provision and an office for humanity in its lowest estate. Henry II, duc de Montmorenci, had such a prodigious number of domestics and retainers that the duchess represented to him the necessity of parting with some. The duke pretended to agree, and making a review of his household, whenever she named any one officer or servant as useless, he undertook his defence. "This man was of use to other people; that had been recommended to him by a friend"; at length there were only two whom he abandoned to his wife: "but," he added, "do you think that two persons would be a burden to my house; are they not sufficiently unhappy, being good for nothing, without afflicting them by a dismissal?"[2] The nobility of Spain, Rome, Naples, Genoa, and Milan, used never to dismiss a domestic, but when he was disabled by age or sickness he still enjoyed his salary. The Countess d'Aulnoy speaks of nobles in Spain who had above one hundred such useless domestics. What humanity and tenderness accompanied the grandeur of Catholic nobility! And remark well how the character of these domestics corresponded with the affection with which they were treated by their masters. They were not

[1] Macrobius Saturnal. lib. I, c. 11.
[2] Desormeaux, Hist. de la Maison de Montmorenci, III, 206.

obnoxious to the dreadful charge which Homer alleges against all who serve.¹ Nor did they resemble those insolent valets, of whom it may be said, "colluviem istam non nisi metu coercueris."² The first mention of these in our annals occurs in the description by Olivier de la Marche, of the court of Charles the Bold.³ La Colombiere complains bitterly of some modern upstarts, who prided themselves upon retaining a number of these menials, and who disdained the most noble stranger if he could not afford to display a train of them.⁴ Scipio Africanus, when on an embassy from the Senate, had only five servants, according to Polybius and Posidonius, and when Julius Cæsar passed into Britain he had but three. The grandeur and triumph of chivalry would have been but little enhanced by its multitude of retainers, if they had been only vicious instruments of ostentation, without loyalty to their master or courtesy for those who approached him; but in the domestics of our ancestors did well appear

> The constant service of the antique world,
> When service sweat for duty, not for meed.

During the pestilence which visited the army of St. Louis, Guillaume de Chartres relates, that being in the tent with an old valet de chambre of the king, named Gangelm, who was dying, this faithful servant said to him, "J'attends mon saint maitre: non, je ne mourrai point que je n'aye eu le bonheur de le voir." The king arrived at the moment, and remained with him for a considerable time, testifying the tenderest affection.

VI. The peculiar humanity which was required

---

[1] Od. XVII, 320.
[2] Tacitus Annal. XIV.
[3] L'Estat de la Maison du Duc de Bourgogne.
[4] Theatre d'Honneur et de Chevalerie, I, 131.

in war deserves a distinct consideration: the great rule was contained in that sentence in the Morte d'Arthur, "Ye shold gyve mercy unto them that aske mercy, for a knyte withoute mercy is withoute worship."

Or as the virtuous Earl of Derby, afterwards Duke of Lancaster, told the common people of Bergerac, " qui merci prie, merci doit avoir."

So when Perceforest pardoned the Knight of the Fleur de Lys, he said, " Cher chevalier, quant ung repentant requiert mercy il doit estre receu et aussi chascun doibt avoir pitie de son subject: car il nest personne vivant que nait besoing de mercy : et moy qui en ay mestier te pardonne de bon cueur." Only I require that you always receive strange knights well, and have their horses fresh shod and their arms repaired.

No plea of war or hostility exempted men from this great duty thus laid down in the Orlando:

> Let each assist the other in his need;
> Seldom good actions go without their due;
> And if their just reward should not succeed,
> At least, nor death, nor shame, nor loss ensue.
> Who wrongs another, the remembered meed
> As well shall have, and soon or later rue.
> That "mountains never meet, but that men may,
> And oft encounter," is an ancient say.[1]

It will be asked how was this compatible with the violence of war. Certainly it was not compatible with the utter recklessness of life and the cool deliberate slaughter which characterizes more recent wars; accordingly it may be affirmed that the wars of the middle ages were pursued with a far less passion for destruction, than that which prevailed in more ancient or modern times. Orderic Vitalis says, that out of nine hundred knights engaged in a certain battle there were only three slain; for besides

[1] Canto XXIII.

that they were cased in iron, they spared one another from the fear of God, and because of their habits of familiar intimacy. In the Italian wars the loss of life was so small, that it is hard to believe that the opposed armies fought seriously. In general, the bodies of the slain were not rifled; it was thought a profanation to touch what belonged to them. In 1816 an Englishman repaired to Agincourt and caused the earth to be opened in a field called La Gascogne, where tradition reported the French bodies to have been buried. There was found a quantity of gold money of the reigns of King John, Charles V., and Charles VI.

There can be no doubt but that in a multitude of instances religion softened the natures of men, and inspired a horror for shedding human blood. It was not in vain that the Church daily presented to their remembrance that for every child of man did the Saviour die upon the cross, and this fire of devotion was directed not to divide and separate but to unite all hearts, and to kindle a pure flame of love for the creatures and the redeemed of God. Religion at least was employed in furthering this end; she did not leave men to interpret the Old Testament so as to think more highly of themselves for their wars and violence. Everything in her temples spake of peace. The children of the choir had orders to take off the swords and spurs of all knights who came to the church, to the divine offices, without having laid aside their arms.[1]

Wars were not begun and conducted after the manner of the heathens. Philippe de Valois prepared for hostilities by visiting churches and hospitals, serving the poor and feeding them with his own hands, and when he had thus made the royal majesty dear to the people, he went to take

[1] Art. 15 of the Priviléges du Chapitre de Romans. Ann. 1358.

up the Oriflamme from the tomb of St. Denis.¹
The French, on defeating the Normans in the
plains of Fontenai, were alarmed at their own
victory, and endeavoured to make atonement and
express their sorrow by fasting and prayer.² But
in a former book I have shewn in what light even
a just war was regarded. In this respect the spirit
of our forefathers had no parallel among the people
of antiquity.

Diodorus ascribes a humane speech to Nicolaus,
persuading the Syracusans to spare the Athenian
prisoners;³ but Clinias the Cretan, in Plato, expresses the general opinion of heathen times, that
what most men call peace is only a name, and that
in fact war is perpetual between all nations.⁴ Even
Socrates says that the Greeks and barbarians (that
is all other nations) are enemies by nature, πολεμίους
φύσει :⁵ and the Greeks, it has been said, chiefly
esteemed the poems of Homer for being calculated
to keep up an eternal hatred of the barbarians and
a love for fighting them.⁶ On forsaking the Catholic
Church, men returned to these opinions. Fleetwood
and a vast crowd of writers, who express the sentiments of the new philosophy, seem to consider that
the glory of a country consists in its success in
injuring and destroying all other nations. For
example, they say that the words of the French
ministers, in relation to the close of a memorable
war, "that England had the glory to give peace
to Europe," were an insult to the glory of England.
But granting that peace was then advantageous to
France (on which supposition they grounded their
complaint), the spirit of Christian chivalry would
not have led men to conclude that therefore it must

---

¹ La France sous les cinq premiers Valois, I, 392.
² Annal. Fuld.   ³ Lib. XIII, 23.
⁴ De Legibus, I.   ⁵ De Repub. V, 470.
⁶ Isocratis Panegyric. 74.

needs be inglorious to England. There can be no
doubt but that the principles of universal love for
men, which appeared in some few of the eminent
sages of antiquity, were widely disseminated under
the influence of the Christian Church. Socrates, for
instance, would not be called an Athenian or a
Greek, but an inhabitant of the world; for man, as
Plato argued, is not like a plant fixed in the earth,
but a celestial being. " Our present country," says
Plutarch, " is where we enjoy fire, water, and air,
the sun, moon, and stars, under one king, God, the
beginning, middle, and end of all things."[1] And
when Anaxagoras was asked if he cared for his
country, he said, " Εὐφήμει· ἐμοὶ γὰρ καὶ σφόδρα μέλει
τῆς πατρίδος, pointing up to heaven."[2]

Antoninus Pius was called the Father of his
Country; Pausanias says that he deserved to be
named the Father of Men: so that even these
heathen sages could discern something higher than
that patriotism which instigated the nations of antiquity to commit so many atrocious injuries. Now
it is not merely reasonable to suppose, that in ages
when the Catholic religion prevailed in all countries, men who aspired to any degree of religion had
these views; but it is impossible to conceive how
they could have been devout Catholics without
entertaining them: they must have said with the
primitive Christians, " Unam omnium rempublicam
agnoscimus, mundum."[3] The evils of war were not
estimated merely with regard to a political or commercial object, but by a consideration of the obstacles which they opposed to the peace of the
Church, to the safety of the poor, and to the salvation of souls. Philip Duke of Burgundy said to
the Duke of Gloucester, in 1425, war between
Christians ought to be hateful to every Catholic

[1] Plutarch de Exilio.   [2] Diog. Laert.
[3] Apologet. adv. gentes, XXXVIII.

prince;[1] and the Emperor Charles V. expressed the same sentiments when he forbade all rejoicings in Spain for his victory. "No," said he, "a Christian people should never triumph with ostentation for the advantages which it may gain over a Christian king."

The moderns are sufficiently ready to admit the great influence which the clergy exerted over the temporal power. Let them hear how the clergy spoke of war. When the King of France was carrying fire and sword into the provinces of Count Theobald, St. Bernard wrote to the king to intercede for the people. "Too soon and lightly have you lost your good intentions. I know not what diabolical resolution has made you recommence the evil which you had begun to repair with good; for from what else but from the devil can such an intention proceed, to rage with fire and sword? The cry of the poor, the sighs of the prisoners, the blood of the slain, all rise to Him who is the father of the orphan and the protector of the widow."[2] With what feeling he describes the return of peace to the Church! "Processiones per ecclesias solenniter celebrantur, depositis armis ad audiendum verbum Domini plebes concurrunt, post multifarias egestates in brevi civitas opulenta refloret; quæ discordiæ tempore distracta fuerant, pax solidata reducit et revocat, arantur solitudines, et deserta pinguescunt." What are now considered the advantages of peace? The prosperity of commerce, the interchange of gold, or the diffusion of science; worldly motives of sufficient importance, no doubt, but certainly not more expressive of humanity than those which animated men in the middle ages in their efforts to promote peace. If we examine in detail the spirit and principles which

---

[1] Barante, Hist. des Ducs de Bourgogne, V, 194.
[2] Epist. 221.

were exercised in war, they will serve to confirm the justice of the preceding observations. To begin with a question proposed in l'Arbre des Batailles, though it may seem to have been, in this instance, a dangerous manual for hasty students; for to the question, "If the leader of an army be taken, ought we to pardon him?" the reply is, "Je preuve premierement que non." Nature gives us an example how contraries destroy each other: "si comme au feu jamais ne lui pardonnera l'eaue ne le chault au froit ne le loup au chien ne le chat au rat." Here, perhaps, the intemperate conqueror would throw aside l'Arbre des Batailles, and kill the poor captain, when he had read as far as the rat. "Mais," continues the author, "le decret est contre cette raison. Car il dit que puis que homme est en prison misericorde lui est deue." I demand now, if we have a prisoner may we require finance from him, gold and silver? There is one great law, he says, in all such cases. "Je dy vraiement que a prisonier misericorde est deue." Again, "if an English child be taken? Innocence and ignorance should be excused; and it is clear that in this child there is both, and little force: so he should be let go free without finance." But what then are we to think of those robber nests, as the Germans call them, which are still seen cresting the points of high rocks, and along the shores of the Rhine, and amidst savage forests? That they are the vestiges of wicked men who lived by violence, and who set the laws of chivalry and the opinion of the age at open defiance, but not as evidence to prove that those laws and that opinion were favourable to the oppression of the weak. After the battle of Wakefield, the Lord Clifford murdered his prisoner, the young Earl of Rutland, son of the Duke of York, as he knelt upon his knees. But how was this action regarded? "By this act," says Hall, "the Lord Clifford was accounted a tyrant and no gentleman." The robber knights boasted of their exploits. Froissart gives the words of Marcel, who had occupied a strong castle in Auvergne for the space of ten years, whose depredations brought in a revenue of 20,000 florins, and who was tempted to sell his fortress to one of the king's generals. "What a joy was it when we rode forth at adventure, and sometyme found by the way a riche priour or marchaunt, or a route of mulettes of Montpellyer, of Narbone, of Lymons, of Fongans, of Tholous, or of Carcassone, laden with cloths of Brusselles, or peltre-ware comynge from the fayres, or laden with spycery from Bruges, from Damas, or from Alysander! Whatsoever we met, all was ours, or else raunsomed at our pleasures. Dayly we gate newe money; and the vyllaynes of Auvergne and of Lymosyn dayly provyded and brought to our castle whete mele, bread ready baken, otes for our horses and lytter, good wyne, beffes and fatte mottons, pullayne and wylde foule. We were ever furnyshed as though we had been kings. When we rode forth, all the country trembled for fear. All was ours, goynge or comyng. How took we Carlaste! I and the Bourge of Compayne; and I and Perot of Bernoys took Caluset. How did we scale, with little aid, the strong castle of Marquell, perteyning to the Erle Dolphyn! I kept it nat past fyve dayes, but receyed for it, on a fayre table, fyve thousand franks, and forgave one thousand for the love of the Erle Dolphyn's children. By my faith, this was a fayre and a good life!" Yet living by the saddle must have had its vexations. A chief who infested the country near Basle, on one occasion when he came to examine his spoil left by the terrified merchants, found it to consist of 400 bales of saffron. In the old tower of Walter Scott, of Harden, it was the custom, when provisions were exhausted, for the lady to place a dish on

the table, which on being uncovered was found to
contain a pair of spurs, a hint to the riders that
they must shift for their next meal. But if there
were men in the middle ages like the old inhabitants
of Greece described by Thucydides,[1] there were also
heroes like Hercules, when he became the servant
of Omphale, and cleared the country of such plunderers.[2] Ludwig the strong, Count Palatine, in one
day cut off the heads of fifty of the robber knights.
Governar used to be able to track Arthur by the
carcases of such men that he found on the roads.
"He walked," says the romance, "till he saw ten
robbers lying slain; then Governar said to Jaquet,
'My lord has been here.'"[3] The cruel giants in
England used to call their castles, "la douloureuse
tour, le chasteau tenebreux, le val sans retour, le
val des faux amans, le pont perdu, or le pont sous
l'eau; la salle perilleuse; Maupas; le chasteau de
la douloureuse garde; le lit advantureux; le chasteau du trespas; la forest perilleuse": the knights
of the round table were employed in conquering
them, and giving them to knights of honour and
courtesy, who changed the name of these castles
into "la tour de la belle prise, chasteau de la joyeuse
garde, le chasteau des dames; le pont trouvé," in
the same manner as the Axine became the Euxine
Sea, when the savage manners of the borderers
were softened. Thus Blanckenau, on a high rock
rising over a black flowing river, three leagues from
Fulda, had been a robber's nest, and the terror of
the neighbourhood, but in the year 1265 it was converted into a convent of Cistercian nuns, so that the
trumpet was exchanged for the vesper bell. The
emperor, Frederic I, destroyed many of the castles of the robber knights in Lombardy and on
the Rhine.[4] Pope Urban V excommunicated all the

[1] Lib. I, c. 5.
[2] Diodor. Sicul. IV, 31.
[3] Arthur of Little Britain.
[4] Raumer, II, 103.

free companies of robber knights who infested France in the reign of King John. Rodolph of Habsburg, before and after his rise to the throne, was an inveterate foe to these robber nests. The Colmar Chronicle relates how in a short time he made himself master of seventy of these castles, taking many by stratagem. At Maintz he denounced war without mercy against them. "Be not troubled on their account," said he to the nobles, "they are not gentle or noble men who afflict the poor people and disturb peace. Your true nobility is chivalrous and gentle. It protects against injustice, and commits it not." Yet, while thus defending the poor, an incident which occurred to him will show with what little justice the great were sometimes accused of oppression. "One morning, in the winter of 1288," says the Colmar Chronicle, quoted by Voght, "Rodolph being at Maintz with his troops, went out in plain clothes, and, as it was very cold, entered a baker's house to warm himself. The baker's wife, not knowing him, muttered between her teeth, 'Methinks soldiers might very well keep out of the way of poor folks!' Upon which the emperor said, 'O, my good woman, do not envy me this little fire, I am an old soldier who have spent my all in serving the avaricious Rodolph, who only allows me common necessaries.' 'That serves you very right,' said the baker's wife; 'what makes you serve men who lord it over all, and grind us poor bakers in Maintz to the ground?'" Rodolph was going on to defend himself, when she hastily threw water on the fire, and made such a thick smoke in the house that the emperor was glad when he got out of the door. At dinner that day he told the merry tale, and sent a boar's head and a flask of wine to the woman, who came back trembling when she heard that the soldier was the kaiser himself, and begged for pardon. Rodolph granted it upon condition that she would relate all that passed before the company, and not leave out how she scolded him, which made all the court to laugh heartily, so he sent her away.

At the pacification of Kenilworth, some of the barons and their adherents refused to be comprehended in its articles, and betook themselves to a course of open robbery for their subsistence. This was when Edward I. was a young prince. Amongst them was a knight, celebrated for his strength and intrepidity, named Sir Adam de Gardon, who, lurking in the woods, with a few hardy followers, infested the high road between Winchester and Farnham, robbing all passengers and plundering the neighbouring estates, especially of those whom he knew to be of the royal party. He had hitherto braved or eluded all the force that had been sent against him, when Prince Edward undertook the task of freeing the country from this its greatest terror. He accordingly proceeded with a few armed followers to the forest which Gardon most frequented, when, gaining sight of him, our heroical prince commanded his attendants to keep their distance, and rushed forward to measure swords with the daring outlaw, hand to hand. The combat was long, the parties being nearly matched in strength and valour, which qualities Edward admiring in his adversary, promised him his life and fortune if he would yield himself his prisoner. Gardon, who was well assured of the prince's honour, threw down his arms, and Edward took him into his immediate service, and that very night sent him with a letter to his mother, informing her of his safety from the danger to which he had exposed himself.[1] Henry I, of Hesse, the Child of Brabant, in the thirteenth century, was celebrated for destroying the castles of

---

[1] Milner, Hist. of Winchester, vol. I, p. 266.

robbers, and for protecting the people from wicked outlaws. He built a hospital and a church in Frankenberg, a monastery in Marburg, and the chapel and hall of the castle; for, as is continually shewn, respect for the clergy always accompanied humanity for the people.

The examples of humanity and courtesy in war abound in our ancient annals. With what zeal and eloquence the flower of King Edward's chivalry, Sir Walter Manny, Sir John Chandos, Sir James Audley, Sir Eustace Dambreticourt, interposed to save the citizens of Calais, is known to every reader of Froissart. During the siege of Gaeta, 1435, the garrison, pressed by famine, drove out a number of women, children, and old people, who the counsellors of Alphonso represented ought to be forced back: but Alphonso the Magnanimous deserved this day the title by which he is distinguished in history. "I had rather," said he, "not take the city, than fail in humanity." He caused provisions to be distributed among them, and gave them leave to retire whither they chose.

When the governor of Calais perceived the intention of the English to reduce him to famine, "he constrayned," says Froissart, "all poore and meane peple to yssue out of the town: and on a Wednysday, there yssued out of men, women, and chyldren, mo than XVIIC. and as they passed through the hoost, they were demanded why they departed, and they answered and sayde, bycause they had nothyng to lyve on: than the kyng dyd them that grace that he suffred them to passe through hys host without danger, and gave them mete and drinke to dyner, and every person iid. sterlyng in almes, for the which dyners many of them prayed for the kynges prosperyte."

After the great battle of Navaret, which restored Peter to the throne of Castile, the Black Prince said to him, "'Sir Kyng, I requyre you, in the name of love and lygnage, that ye will graunt me a gyfte and a request.' The Kyng, who in no wyse wolde deny his request, sayde, 'Good cosyn, all that I have is yours; therefore I am content, whatsoever ye desire, to graunt it.' Then the Prince sayd, 'Sir, I requyre you to give pardon to all your people in your realme, such as hath rebelled agaynst you, by the which courtessy ye shall abyde in the better rest and peace in your realme.'" Thus, again, Froissart relates of the Scotch, upon their victory near Otterbourne: "When the Scottes sawe the Englysshmen recule and yelde themselfe, than the Scottes were curtes and sette theym to their raunsome, and every man sayd to his prysoners: 'Syrs, go and unarme you, and take your ease, I am your mayster': and so made their prysoners as good chere as though they had been brethren, without doing to them any damage." Sir Mathew Reedman was taken prisoner by Sir James Lynsay, who suffered him to go to Newcastle on his faith, to return in three weeks: but no sooner was he gone, than Sir James Lynsay lost his way; for it was dark, and a mist, and he fell into the hands of the Bishop of Durham; and so he was brought prisoner to Newcastle, and there he found Sir Mathew Reedman, who made him dine with him, and then they were exchanged for each other.

After the battle of Poitiers, when the Lord Berkeley was sore wounded by a sword through both the thighs by the French squire, Jehan of Helenes, whom he had followed for the space of a league, the squire demanded if he wolde yeeld hym or not; the knight then demanded his name. "'Sir,' sayd he, 'I hyght Jehan of Helenes, but what is your name?' 'Certenly,' sayd the knyght, 'my name is Thomas, and I am Lord of Berkeley, a fayr castell on the ryver of Severn, in the marches of Wales.' 'Well, Sir,' quoth the squyer, 'then ye shall be my prisonere, and I shall bring you in savegard, and I shall see that you shall be healed of your hurt.' 'Well,' sayd the knyght, 'I am content to be your prisoner, for ye have by lawe of armes wonne me': then he swar to be his prisoner, rescue or no rescue. Then the squyer drewe forth the sworde out of the knyght's thyes, and the wounde was opyn; then he wrapped and bounde the wounde, and sette hym on his horse, and so brought hym fayre and easely to Chaterlerant, and there taryed more than fifteen days for his sake, and dyde gette hym remedy for his hurt; and when he was somewhat amended, then he gotte hym a lytter, and so brought hym at his ease to his house in Picardy. There he was more than a yere tyll he was perfectly hole."

A beautiful instance of the courtesy which distinguished the English and French when opposed in war was the reception of Du Guesclin in the English camp, when he sought redress from the Duke of Lancaster for the injury committed by Sir Thomas of Canterbury, in treacherously surprising his young brother Oliver when riding unarmed before the gate of Dinan, and making him prisoner in defiance of the truce. Du Guesclin found the Duke in his tent playing chess with Jean de Chandos, while Jean de Monfort, the Earl of Pembroke, and Robert Knole stood looking on. The English nobles received him with the greatest kindness, and upon hearing his accusation Sir Thomas was instantly ordered to make his appearance: at the same time Du Guesclin was refreshed with wine. A challenge was the result, and Jean de Chandos lent Du Guesclin his best horse: at the request of the French the battle took place in Dinan, to which the Duke of Lancaster and his nobles repaired. Du Guesclin vanquished his enemy, sparing his life, but the Duke commanded that Sir Thomas should pay the sum of 1,000 florins as an additional punishment for his villainy, deliver his horse and armour to Du Guesclin, and be for ever prohibited from appearing at the English court.

The English praised the French for their gallantry at Creci. "Les ennemitz se porterent mult noblement: mais loiez soit Dieux, illesques fusrent noz ennemiz desconfitz."[1] When Charles VI of France knighted the sons of the Duc d'Anjou at St. Denis, the knights and ladies of England were invited to the feast by couriers sent expressly, though the French and English were at war. This courtesy did not forsake them on the field. In the battle of Poitiers, Sir John Chandos seeing that the French barons had not their horses, alighted, and gave his own horse to his esquire, and continued to fight on foot;[2] and in 1632, at the bridge of the Fresquel, when Henri II, Duc de Montmorenci, was wounded, and his horse fallen to the ground, the officers of the king's army opposed to him pretended not to see him, that his friends might have time to come up and rescue their noble chief,[3] which however was not attempted by them.

The courtesy of the Black Prince to his prisoners has extorted the admiration of all men. "The same day of the batayle at night the prince made a supper in his lodginge to the French kyng, and to the most part of the great lordes that were prisoners; the prince made the kyng and and his son, the Lord James of Bourbone, the Lord John d'Artois, the Erle of Tankervylle, the Erle d'Estampes, the Erle Dampmartyne, the Erle of Gravyll, and the Lord of Pertenay, to syt all at one borde,

[1] La France sous les cinq premiers Valois, I, 503.
[2] James Clifton, Hist. de Chandos.
[3] Desormeaux, Hist. de la Maison de Montmorenci, III, 392.

and other lords, knyghtes, and squires, at other tables; and always the prince served before the kyng as humbly as he coude, and wolde nat syt at the kynges borde for any desyre that the kyng coulde make; but he said he was nat suffycient to syt at the table with so great a prince as the kyng was; but then he sayd to the kyng, 'Sir, for Goddes sake make non yvell nor hevy chere, though God this day dyd nat consent to folowe your wyll; for, Sir, surely the kyng, my father, shall bear you as moche honour and amyte as he may do, and shall accord with you so reasonably that ye shall ever be frendes toguyder after; and, Sir, methynke ye ought to rejoyce, though the journey be nat as ye wolde have had it, for this day ye have wonne the hygh renome of prowes, and have past this day in valyantnesse all other of pour partie; Sir, I say natte this to mocke you, for all that be on our partie that sawe every mannes dedes are playnly acorded by true sentence to gyve you the price and chapelette." Thus, again, on his entrance into London. "The Frenche kyng rode through London on a whyte courser, well aparelled, and the prince on a lyttell blacke hobbey by hym."

When Francis I was the prisoner of Charles V, Erasmus advised the Emperor to practise this chivalrous humanity:—"If I were Emperor," he wrote to him, "thus would I address the King of France. 'My brother! some evil genius has kindled war between us: Fortune has made you my prisoner, she may make me yours. Your misfortune has led me to reflect on the evils incident to humanity. The war between us has continued too long; let us begin another contest; I give you your liberty, give me your friendship; let the past be wholly forgotten. I desire no ransom: let our only rivalry be which of us shall excel the other in good offices.'"

A traditionary sense of religion induced the heathens in early times to erect no lasting memorials of conquest over their enemies. Nicolaus, in his speech to the Syracusans, reminded them that the forefathers of all Greeks never erected their trophies of stone but always of wood, ὅπως ὀλίγον χρόνον διαμένοντα, ταχέως ἀφανίζηται τὰ τῆς ἔχθρας ὑπομνήματα:[1] they felt the uncertainty of all human affairs, and the need of respecting a fortune which might be their own. Our Christian ancestors equally refrained from erecting such monuments, but from the higher motives of religion and mercy. To commemorate victory by an obelisk, a bridge, or triumphal arch, was the custom of the heathen nations only in the most inhuman and atrocious age of their history. Our ancestors erected a cross or a chapel out of regard for their enemies: thus Jean Molinet says on the death of Charles the Bold that the Duke of Lorraine "fist eslever une croix de pierre lez un petit ruisseau, en la place ou son corps feut trouvé, afin que les passans eussent memoire de son ame."[2] But when the religious innovators had inspired men with a contempt for the wisdom of their fathers, they naturally returned to the worst practices of heathen antiquity. The chapels and crosses at Morat and Ploermel have been replaced by obelisks. In 1805 it was proposed to erect an obelisk on the plain of Bouvines to be a monument of the glory of the French arms in 1214. The project being abandoned, the venerable priest of Bouvines purchased a piece of land at his own expense, which formed part of the field of battle, and built a simple chapel, with two pictures representing the event, and every year on the 27th of July he celebrates the divine office.

But to return to the humanity which was ex-

[1] Diodorus, XIII, 24.
[2] Chroniques de Jean Molinet, chap. XXXV.

ercised in war. After the battle of Poitiers "the prisoners were put to ransom, and they found the Englyssemen and Gascoyns right courtesse: ther were many that day putte to ransom and lette go, all only on their promyse of fayth and trouth to return agayn bytwene that and Christmas to Bordeaux with their ransom. Then that nyght they lay in the field besyde where as the battayle had been: some unarmed them, but not all, and unarmed all their prisoners, and every man made good chere to his prisoner, and they ransomed them but easily, for they sayd they wolde sette no knyghtes ransome so hygh but that he myghte pay at his ease and maynteyne styll his degree." "Modesty," says St° Palaye, "induced the conquerors to bestow particular attention in comforting the vanquished, and in assuaging their grief. 'To-day the fortune and lot of arms have given me the advantage,' they used to observe on these occasions: 'I owe nothing to my valour; to-morrow, perhaps, I shall fall under the blow of an enemy less formidable than you.'" Thus Sir Calidore addresses the knight whom he had overthrown:

"All flesh is frail and full of fickleness,
Subject to fortune's chance, still changing new;
What haps to-day to me, to-morrow may to you."

"When two noble men encountre," says King Arthur, "nedes must the one have the werse, lyke as God wil suffre at that tyme." So, in Perceforest, when the strange knight had been overthrown in the forest, Gallafar said to him, "Sire, ce n'est pas par ma bonne chevalerie ains par ma fortune qui a ce coup fait pour moy."[1]

Thus the fifth of the twelve knights who made vows at the coronation of Gadifer, King of Scotland, after swearing that, in the tournament he

[1] Perceforest, vol. IV.

would make the king quit his saddle three times, and that he would present his three horses to the fair Codrilla, added "non pas que l'excellent prince ne soit plus preux à cent doubles que je ne suis, mais ainsi le vouldra fortune." Well might a poet exclaim,

> "O goodly usage of those antique times!
> Then honour was the meed of victory,
> And yet the vanquished had no despight." [1]

One of the first deeds of the Emperor Frederick I was to liberate his prisoner, Count Conrad von Dachau, without ransom. The honour of his victory was enough for him; though Raumer, a modern writer, gives another turn to the event, saying, "he knew that men often become richer by disdaining than by taking money."

When any prisoners were led to René d'Anjou, says an old historian, "il fesoit acte vrayment héroïque et signe de la royauté, qui sentoit son honneur et la noblesse jointe à une grande bonté, car il les recevoit très débonnairement, leur faisoit de grands présents, et les renvoyait en leur pays, se souvenant qu' il avoit esté prisonnier comme eulx." Even the glory of an enemy was admired. In Perceforest, when Marones, Norgal, and their companions, had been overthrown by Passelion, and were riding slowly on, says Marones, "It troubles me much that I do not know his name, for I should be worth more ever after while I lived." "How!" cries Norgal, "worth more to know him who has done us such dishonour, so that you can never speak of this adventure but to our shame and his honour." "Norgal," said Marones, "ou vous n'estes si gentil de cueur que fut vostre pere, ou ignorance vous destourne a cognoistre la verite. Car sachez de vray que l'homme qui dit bien

[1] Spenser.

d'autruy exaulce son honneur et en faitz d'armes le preux chevalier doibt tousjours celer ses prouesses et recorder celles d'aultruy. Et sil est porte par terre dung preux chevalier il doit estre tres desirant de le cognoistre parquoy il puisse icelluy nommer et reciter ses prouesses devant dames damoiselles et chevaliers; car tous vaillans hommes sont tenus de ramener a memoire en temps et en lieu les faitz des vaillans chevaliers et les prouesses qui sont faictes sur eulx et leur est honneur d'autruy exaulcer. Si recordez doresnavant les faicts d'aultruy, et vous y acquerrez honneur."[1]

After the battle of Dorylæum, the Crusaders did justice to the valour of the Turks, saying, "if the Turks did not want the true faith, they would be the first warriors of the world. The Franks and the Turks are by nature warlike, and born for battle and heroic exercise."[2]

Vinisauf relates that in the middle of a great battle which Richard fought against the Turks, after raising the siege of Joppa, Saladin's brother Saphadinus, a liberal and magnificent man, and to be compared with the best if he had not spurned at the faith of Christ, destined two noble Arabian horses for the king, entreating him that he would accept them as a present and mount them, and if by divine favour he should escape from the battle, that he would remember his courtesy, which the king took and gave ample remuneration afterwards.[3]

Even in the savage wars of the German reformation, when Götz von Berlichingen lost his arm, not only those on his side and his friends, but even the enemy lamented his wound.

Thus Giontes, nephew of King Lisuarte, when

---

[1] Vol. V.
[2] Tudebod, apud Duchesne, Hist. Franc. Script. 782-83. Orderic Vital. 730.   [3] Lib. VI, 22.

overthrown by Amadis, whom he did not know, cries out "Be he whom he may, God prosper him wherever he goes! for he won our horses like a good knight, and like a good knight restored them."[1]

Froissart says, upon the death of Sir John Chandos, "for his dethe his frendes and also some of his enemies, were right souroufull; the Englysshmen loved him, bycause all noblenesse was found in hym, (in a hundred year after there was nat a more curtesse, nor more fuller of noble virtues and good condycions amonge the Englysshmen than he was); the Frenchmen hated him bycause they douted hym: yet I herde his dethe greatly complayned among right noble and valiant knyghtes of France, sayenge that it was a great dommage of his dethe: for they sayd, better it had ben that he had ben taken alyve."[2] The misfortune of no great man was a matter of indifference on the ground of his being a stranger or an enemy.

The readers of the Palmerin of England will remember how the loss of the Prince Dom Duardos was blazed in the courts of divers noble princes, as in the court of Arnedos, King of France; of Recindos, King of Spain; in the court of Belagriz, the Soldan of Niquea; with the noble Mayortes, the great Khan; and many princes more, to whom the loss of the English prince was as grievous as to Palmerin himself. For proof whereof, the employed pains of divers noble men might remain as witness, who walked the forests and unknown passages in many countries. That martial behaviour was never more esteemed than it was during the search of the strayed prince. Nay, to the stranger and the enemy a still more exact courtesy was considered due.

At a martial game held in Smithfield during

---

[1] Amadis de Gaule, II, 13. [2] CCLXX.

the reign of Richard II, the queen proposed a crown of gold as the reward of the best jouster, if he should be a stranger; but if an English knight had the praise then a rich bracelet was to be his reward. The same polite preference of strangers influenced the chivalry of England, and they promised to give to the conqueror, if he were a foreign knight, a fair horse with his trappings; but if he were one of their own land, then only a falcon should reward him.[1]

Virtuous kings and barons were loved, not only by their own subjects, but by strangers also, as Beltenebroso says to Don Quadragante, in Amadis de Gaule, "I am not this king's vassal, nor am I of his land, but for his goodness my heart is disposed to serve him."

There is something very affecting in the respect which men in these ages shewed to the virtues of their enemies. When the flower of the chivalry of England, Edward Prince of Wales and of Aquitaine, passed out of this world, "King Charles of France dyd his obsequy," says Froissart, "reverently in the holy chapell of the paleys in Paris; and there were many of the prelates and nobles of the realm of Fraunce.... And as soon as the French kyng knew of the deth of his father, King Edward III, he sayd, how ryght nobly and valiantly he hadde reygned, and well he ought to be putte newly in remembraunce among the nombre of the worthyes; than he assembled a great nombre of the nobles and prelates of his realme, and dyd his obsequy in the holy chapell in his palys at Paris." In the account of the battle of the thirty English and thirty Bretons, one remarks how "glory and honour are ascribed to the brave of both sides; both were noble

---

[1] Mill's Hist. of Chivalry, vol. I, p. 268.

combatants, but God gave the victory to those who fought for the oppressed."

Perdiras and Lionel, in quest of Perceforest, riding through the forest of Darnant, about vespers, see coming "deux jeunes damoiseaux sur deux roussins moult las de course et les damoiseaux moult las et moult suans et leurs draps tous deschirez des branches des arbres si que la chair leur apparoissoit nue en plusieurs lieux": four knights were following them, whom Perdiras and Lionel immediately attacked, and the youths being preserved, knelt down to thank them, and they all rode to a monastery, where the good monks gave them lodging. Now inquired the knights who these young fair squires might be. They were of the lineage of Darnant the enchanter, and were to have been sent in quest to seek out his murderer; but such was their admiration for Perceforest, they they two had privately set out in quest of him, that they might be made knights by his hand; but these four strangers came suddenly upon them. Perdiras and Lionel then sent them to the castle of a noble lady, to wait there for Perceforest.

The fortress of Chateau-neuf-de-Randon was surrendered to the French almost out of respect to the memory of Du Guesclin, whose valour had animated the besiegers, and who died of a fever before the day which had been fixed upon by both parties for the surrender of the English garrison. During the illness of the constable, and as soon as the physician had declared that his life was in danger, the besieged, that is the English, whose fate had been determined by his life, when they were informed of his situation, instantly proclaimed public prayers, and implored God that he would restore an enemy so formidable indeed to them, but so full of virtue, so good, so generous in victory, that they would consider it a glory if it was to him they must surrender. These are passages of history which alternately gratify and astonish. Far less pleasing, let it be confessed, is the perusal of the annals of modern warfare. Such sentiments are no longer expected or admired. The savage wars of the "Reformation," and of the last Revolution, when men professed to be the champions of humanity without religion, revived the scenes of heathen fury. We hear of heroes who make drinking-cups of the skulls of the slain, and who would glory in wearing a mantle, like that of the cruel King Ryon, which was made of the beards of kings whom he had killed. The commander is extolled who teaches his men to hate their enemies. One example from the religious wars of France will illustrate this remark. The Huguenots joined with foreigners, English and German, had obliged the venerable and religious hero, Anne de Montmorenci, Constable of France, to lead the Catholic army. He was afflicted with a cruel disorder, the gravel, and on the eve of the battle of Dreux, it was thought that he could not rise from his bed; but no sooner had he learnt that the battle was unavoidable, than he rose, armed, and mounted on horseback. The Duc de Guise, astonished at his appearance, asked him how he felt himself. "Well," replied the generous old man, "the battle which is about to be fought for God and the king, is a remedy which has cured all my evils."[1] When his troops were put into disorder by the Protestant army at St. Denis he was surrounded on all sides, but still he fought desperately, when Robert Steward, presenting a pistol to his throat, desired him to surrender. "Surrender!" cried the constable, "do you not know me?" The aspect of this renowned hero in his 70th year, made no impression upon the Scotch fanatic. "It is because I know you," he

---

[1] Desormeaux, Hist. de la Maison de Montmorenci, II, 333.

said, "that I give you that," and discharged his pistol, which mortally wounded the constable, who still fought till he fainted, and fell to the ground.[1]

In heathen history there are, it is true, some few instances of generosity in the conduct of war. After the defeat of Asdrubal, Scipio determined to set the Spanish captives at liberty, and to sell the Africans for slaves. In executing this order the quæstor discovered among the latter a youth who was reported to be of royal origin. Upon being brought before Scipio the boy related the circumstances of his family and of his own capture, having engaged in the battle contrary to the orders of Masinissa, his uncle, and being taken in consequence of his horse falling. Scipio gave him a gold ring, a tunic with a Spanish jacket, ornamented with gold clasps, and a horse, dismissing him, escorted by a troop of cavalry, which had orders to follow him as long as he pleased.[2] Sophocles makes Ulysses order that the dead body of Ajax, his enemy, should be buried with honour; and upon Agamemnon reminding him that it was the body of his enemy, Ulysses replies,

ὅδ' ἐχθρὸς ἀνήρ, ἀλλὰ γενναῖός ποτ' ἦν.
νικᾷ γὰρ ἀρετή με τῆς ἔχθρας πολύ.[3]

Eurystheus expresses a similar sentiment when he praises his enemy, in the Heraclidæ of Euripides: [4] and even in Homer the brave son of Menœtius reproves his companion for reviling the enemy, and says,

Μηριόνη, τί σὺ ταῦτα, καὶ ἐσθλὸς ἰὼν, ἀγορεύεις;
ὦ πέπον, οὔτι Τρῶες ὀνειδείοις ἐπέεσσιν
νεκροῦ χωρήσουσι, πάρος τινὰ γαῖα καθέξει.
ἐν γὰρ χερσὶ τέλος πολέμου, ἐπέων δ', ἐνὶ βουλῇ.[5]

---

[1] Desormeaux, Hist. de la Maison de Montmorenci, II, 374.
[2] Livy, XXVII, cap. 19.   [3] Ajax, 1386.
[4] 999.   [5] Il. XVI, 627.

And again, in the Odyssey, Ulysses reproves the exultation of Telemachus over the slain.

οὐχ ὁσίη, κταμένοισιν ἐπ' ἀνδράσιν εὐχετάασθαι.[1]

a sentiment which occurs also in Euripides.[2]

The Roman war with Porsenna has instances of a chivalrous intercourse between the contending armies; a truce had been concluded, and it happened that some games were celebrated just at the same time: on this the Tuscan general came into the city, won the crown, and received it. But these are examples which are striking from their singularity. When Darius resolved upon retreating from Scythia, he expressed no scruples or concern in leaving the sick and wounded behind, to be slaughtered the next morning by the Scythians.[3] Tacitus, in the first book of his Annals, relates, with the utmost coolness, instances of barbarities committed by the Romans, which are sufficient alone to cover the name of that people with eternal infamy. The barbarous speech of Agamemnon, in Homer, to Menelaus, reproving him for hesitating to kill his wretched prisoner, Adrastus, who begged for mercy and promised ransom, and at the same time declaring, that not even the child in its mother's womb should be spared;[4] the conduct of Ulysses and Diomedes to Dolon, their prisoner, first promising him life to gain intelligence, and then their savage reply to his renewed entreaties for mercy;[5] the relentless fury of Agamemnon in killing the two poor sons of Antimachus, Periander and Hippolochus;[6] the brutal taunts of Idomeneus over his fallen enemy, Othryoneus, who deserved the praise and pity of a generous foe;[7] the joy of Achilles when he finds Lycaon disarmed, and

[1] XXII, 412. [2] Electra, 902. Suppl. 534. Phœniss. 1663.
[3] Herodot. lib. IV, 135. [4] Il. VI, 55.
[5] Il. X, 446. [6] Il. XI, 122. [7] Il. XIII, 374.

mercilessly slays him;[1] the Μή με, κύον, γούνων γουνάζεο of Achilles to dying Hector, though he too had insulted the fallen Patroclus; the dastardly cruelty of the Greeks when they flocked round his dead body, οὐ δ' ἄρα οἵ τις ἀνουτητί γε παρέστη, exemplifying what Teucer says in Sophocles, when anxious to secure the dead body of Ajax,

$$\text{------------ τοῖς θανοῦσί τοι}$$
$$\text{φιλοῦσι πάντες κειμένοις ἐπεγγελᾶν,}[2]$$

are instances, out of a multitude, to shew that feelings of humanity were in general unknown to the heathen warriors. An historian would be guilty of great injustice were he not to proclaim that it was totally a different spirit which inspired the heroes of the middle ages. There breaks forth light from every page of its annals to cheer the lover of humanity. Even the passions of men, and the confusion consequent upon the fall of empires, are made subservient to virtue and to peace. A procession of illustrious heroes passes on before us, each of whom might have truly said with the sage of Greece, "I should wish neither to be injured nor to injure, but if it were necessary either to injure or to be injured, ἑλοίμην ἂν μᾶλλον ἀδικεῖσθαι ἢ ἀδικεῖν.[3] In the midst of conflicting interests, surrounded with troops of warlike youth, we behold men, whose valour had led them on to deathless renown, now resembling the Roman whom Cicero observed during the days of general confusion, "nihil nisi de pace et concordia civium cogitantem."[4] The union of warlike spirit with the most tender love for men, is one of the most striking contrasts which the history of the middle ages presents. One cannot picture to one's self, without astonishment, young and bold knights returned from victorious

[1] Il. XXI, 49. [2] Ajax, 961.
[3] Plato, Gorgias, 49. [4] Philip. X.

battle, hanging up their swords in their hall, and hastening to minister to sick pilgrims with the gentlest attention, discharging all the duties of a nurse with the most careful delicacy. Yet such were the knights of St. John. The world can afford no sight more grateful than the union of power with beneficence, of valour with love for the creatures of God.

In Tancredus I have endeavoured to trace the horrors of the storming of Jerusalem to their true source. An old writer, who describes the slaughter of the Saracens in Acre, adds, that it was a miserable spectacle to the Christians themselves who had a right heart, susceptible of compassion.[1]

The brave Spaniard, Muntaner, relates with sorrow the massacre of the Greeks at Rodosto by the Catalonians, and Moncada, in describing the same event, says that "the knights and officers in vain endeavoured to put a stop to the horrible cruelties committed by their enraged soldiers, for that these indulging their fury had lost the fear of God, and the respect which they owed to their chiefs and to themselves": words which sufficiently shew that such inhumanity was not considered consistent with honourable warfare.

It was not for the men of later times to censure Christian antiquity for having neglected the great duties and interests of humanity. Such complaints were ridiculous from the lips of men who were continually possessed with the spirit of war, not through the passions of nature, but through the desire of vain glory, or from the principles of commercial avarice; men who avowedly acted upon the system of force being justice, and who had been joined in arms with mercenary soldiers; wretches to whom the weeping female would kneel in vain; whose

[1] Chron. Trsp.

uplifted arm the smile of a helpless infant, the age of the wounded warrior, would never stay. Besides, it is not on the field alone that the spirit of inhumanity can be exercised. The manners of an age are not to be estimated solely by a reference to the conduct of war; and our ancestors did not seem of opinion that an unfeeling heart and an undoubting confidence are the sole qualifications for a perfect legislator. They did not sacrifice to political arrangement all the kind sensibilities which would indulge even the fancies of the poor. With them, legal order was not the watchword of inhumanity and intolerance. The cross was over their tribunals of judgment, to remind those who pursued an adversary, of the passion of Christ; of Him who forgave His enemies. A nation was moved more by the principle of an unbounded love, than by the fear of a human judge, though the judge were the administrator of laws enacted by a Confessor.

VII. It cannot be necessary to use many words in proof of the brave spirit which accompanied this mildness and humanity, though it must not be passed over in silence, lest one might seem to infer that manhood had been melted into courtesies, valour into compliment, and that men were only turned into tongue. So much certainly is true, that his spirit was held but in little esteem who deemed himself as valiant as Hercules, when he " only told a lie and swore it." [1]

> Ever their noble chivalry and courage will I sing,
> How their blades cut many a helm, and many an iron ring;
> How they struck from hawberks sparks of fire on high,
> How the dust in clouds arose, darkening all the sky.[2]

Yet nothing hitherto advanced need be unsaid here. Valour and adventurous chivalry were but exerted

[1] Shakspeare's Much Ado about Nothing, IV, 2.
[2] The Book of Heroes, or the Exploits of Wolfdietrich, III, 13.

to meet a necessary evil. "Je demande tout premierement," says the author of l'Arbre des Batailles, "si c'est chose possible que cestuy monde soit sans bataille. Et je respons vrayement que non." "The just," says a Platonic philosopher, "make war only through necessity: they would prefer that the necessity were removed, and with it their virtue in arms, rather than that it should continue to make their virtue necessary; as physicians, if good and humane, would rejoice to see their science at an end with the diseases which had required it."[1] Hence St. Augustine shews how Christians may lawfully become soldiers; "non benefacere prohibet militia, sed malitia": but then war was to be held as a dreadful evil, and as an old director of knightly men says, the great and powerful should seek peace and preserve it, and carefully avoid the occasion of war.[2] Andromache tells Hector that in one day her seven brothers fell in battle by the hand of Achilles. Chivalry was not that cursed thing to be the cause of such mighty woe, or to pursue it as good.

——— οἱ δ' ἐχάρησαν Ἀχαιοί τε Τρῶές τε,
ἐλπόμενοι παύσεσθαι ὀϊζυροῦ πολέμοιο.[3]

If the heroes of Homer deemed it no shame to rejoice in hope of the termination of war, do we imagine that the Christian warriors of the middle age, who heard the unceasing thunders of the Church against all lovers of blood,[4] had less humanity? With them the words of Nestor might have been engraven on every shield, as they expressed the sentiment of every noble heart:

Ἀφρήτωρ, ἀθέμιστος, ἀνέστιός ἐστιν ἐκεῖνος
Ὃς πολέμου ἔραται ἐπιδημίου ὀκρυόεντος.[5]

---

[1] Maximus Tyr. XXX, 2.
[2] L'Horloge des Princes, liv. III, c. 12.   [3] Il. III, 111.
[4] Levesque. La France sous les cinq premiers Valois, t. I, p. 140.   [5] Il. IX, 63.

"War," says the brave Spaniard Moncada, "is a calamity for all men, and often the name only distinguishes the conquerors from the conquered."[1] It is true, the spirit of Theseus, who refused to go by sea when he could fight his way by land, was still regarded as an indication of something noble. In the pursuit of an enterprise "a knight was never to shun bad and perilous passes, never to leave the direct road through fear of meeting bold knights, or monsters, or wild beasts, or any obstacles which the power or courage of a single man might overcome":[2] but what greater glory than to devote one's life to protect the weak and innocent; to fight for justice, for the altars and the domestic hearths of our fathers? If Æschylus, perceiving the approach of death, found no exultation in the remembrance of his poems, but in being able to record on his tomb that he was an Athenian, and that the Persians could bear witness to his valour at Marathon,[3] surely there was nothing barbarous in the raptures with which our forefathers recorded their valiant deeds in defence of their religion and of their country. Even a modern French critic[4] acknowledges that there is in the records ascribed to Turpin a foundation of interest that nothing can efface. The prodigious efforts of Roland, Olivier, and the other Paladins, surprised in the defiles of Roncevaux, to resist, at the head of 20,000 men, the successive attacks of three bodies of an army, of 100,000 each, the calm and unconquerable courage of these intrepid knights, their glorious death, that above all of Roland, who consents not till the last moment to sound his terrible horn as a signal of distress, who expires surrounded with a pile of

---

[1] Expedition of the Catalonians, &c. 380.
[2] Favin, Theatre d'Honneur et de Chevalerie.
[3] Pausanias, Attic. lib. I, 14.
[4] Ginguené, Hist. lit. d'Italie.

enemies that he has killed, and after breaking his sword, Durandal, against the rocks, that it may not fall into the hands of the infidels, even his farewell address to this formidable sword, the companion and instrument of so many exploits,—all these circumstances, and many others of this grand and celebrated scene, in whatever manner they may be related, are always sure of their effect.

How memorable were the exploits of the Norman knights, who merely by dint of personal valour were enabled to found kingdoms! In the middle ages, a crowd of states thus created were spread over the continent, and the islands of Europe and Asia; giving rise to the kings of Sicily and Jerusalem, the princes of the Morea, the dukes of Athens, of Thebes, and the lords of Negropont. The expedition from Catalonia and Arragon against the Turks, described by Muntaner and Moncada, in which a band of adventurers left their country trusting only to their courage, executed a series of most brilliant deeds of arms, exhibited the most sublime devotion; and effected a long and difficult retreat, in spite of almost insurmountable obstacles, may be compared with the expedition of Cyrus and the retreat of the ten thousand. How heroic were the deeds of the Almogavares, who combated the Moors in Spain for so many ages! What an instance of the power of individual valour was furnished by the four brothers, called Petralippes, sons of Pierre d'Aulps, of the house of Blacas, in Provence, who, after serving under Robert Guiscard, were enlisted successively in the armies of the emperors Alexis and Manuel, when at the siege of Corfu they scaled the formidable rock in face of the enemy! What feats of valour were performed by Mathieu de Montmorenci at the battle of Bouvines, where with his own hand he captured twelve imperial banners, to commemorate which Philip Augustus desired that twelve eagles should be borne on the shield of Montmorenci.[1] What a spectacle did Richard Cœur de Lion present on one occasion as he returned from battle with his armour stuck full of arrows, and many sticking in the harness of his horse! Saladin accused him to the Bishop of Salisbury as being too prodigal of his life. After Saladin's great defeat by Richard, his Saracens excused themselves by urging the matchless force of the enemy, particularly of one man, whom they called Melek Ric, whom they said no one could resist. When the caravan of provisions for the Christian army was attacked by the Turks, near Ramula, Baldwin Carron was thrown from his horse, but immediately brandishing his sword, and redoubling his strokes, he made himself inaccessible, says Vinisauf. When the Mareschal de Boucicaut, the Comte de Nevers, and the other French knights were treacherously caught in ambush by the Saracens, who had laid chevaux-de-frise across the only way by which they could have escaped, having been deserted by the Hungarians, in whose army they had entered as volunteers, like wild boars, more furious when surrounded, these brave men, by dint of marvellous strength, conquered all those obstacles, and cut their way through the enemy.

"Ha, noble contrée de François," exclaims the ancient historian, with a most laudable pride in the virtue of his country, when he has conducted his heroes out of this perilous condition, "ce n'est mie de maintenant que tes vaillains champions se monstrent hardis et fiers entre toutes les nations du monde." The chivalry of Hercules seemed revived when the knight of St. John slew the dragon, and when Count Conrad fought with lions.

[1] Desormeaux, Hist. de la Maison de Montmorenci, I, 35.

When the unfortunate Henry II, duc de Montmorenci, was examined before the commissioners of the Parliament at Toulouse, he said, smiling to Saint Preuil, "Look there at poor Guitant, how afflicted he is; you will see that he will weep when he is called upon to speak." And so it was, for the evidence of this gentleman was interrupted with tears and sobs. "The smoke which enveloped him," said he, speaking of the fatal moment when the duke was taken, "prevented me at first from recognising him: but seeing a man who had broken through six of our ranks, and killed some soldiers in the seventh, I knew that it could only be M. de Montmorenci: I was convinced of it when I saw him on the ground with his horse dead."[1] Bayard alone guarded a bridge over the river Garigliano for the space of half an hour, against two hundred of the enemy. Froissart says of the battle of Poitiers, "kynge John was that day a full right good knyght: if the fourth part of his menn hadde done their devoyers as well as he dydde, the journey hadde ben his by all lykelyhode." As in the chivalrous age of Rome, single families, like the Fabii, supported a war—

Una domus vires et onus susceperat urbis.

Seven brothers of one house of the Digbys were slain at Towton, fighting for king Henry VI.

*Una dies Fabios ad bellum miserat omnes;
Ad bellum missos perdidit una dies.*[2]

What Ramon Muntaner says of the heroes of Aragon might have been affirmed of most noble houses, that "one might make a fine book of their prowess and deeds of chivalry." Romantic history furnishes innumerable candidates for Merlin's siege

---

[1] Desormeaux, Hist. de la Maison de Montmorenci, III, 418.
[2] Ovid. Fast. 11.

perilous. "Tell me," said king Lisuarte, to the ambassador of Famongomad, giant of the boiling lake, and others, "where I may send a knight to carry my answer." "To the boiling lake," replied he, "which is in the isle of Mongasa." "I know not the manner of these giants," quoth Lisuarte, whether a knight can go amongst them safely?" "That," replied he, "doubt not: when don Quadragante is present no wrong can be committed: I will be his warrant." The king found two knights ready to carry his reply,[1] who no doubt resembled Charles the Bold, " qui n'avoit oncques eu la paour au visaige," as an old chronicle says, "et duquel on disoit partout, qu'il ne craignoit rien en ce monde, fors la chute du ciel." This invincible spirit attracts the most admiration when it is presented in contrast with the dejection of those who have experience of defeat; such as the Athenian sailors the night after their fleet was driven back by the Syracusans, when neither Nicias nor Demosthenes could prevail on them to renew the battle, διὰ τὸ καταπεπλῆχθαι τῇ ἥσσῃ καὶ μὴ ἂν ἔτι οἴεσθαι κρατῆσαι.[2] However, it must be confessed that there would be but little to please in these records if we were only to imagine ferocious warriors, like Aristomenes, of whom tradition says that he thrice sacrificed the Hecatomphonia, the offering prescribed by the Greeks for those who had slain in battle a hundred enemies with their own hand, or men whose only renown consisted in having fought as often as Siccius Dentatus, the Roman Achilles, who had been engaged in 120 battles,[3] even though we were to be told that each was a threefold combat, such as that between the Pæones and the Perinthians, as Herodotus relates, ἄνδρα ἀνδρὶ, καὶ ἵππον ἵππῳ καὶ κύνα κυνί.[4] It is a

[1] Amadis de Gaule, II, 12.   [2] Thucydid. lib. VII, 72.
[3] Aul. Gell. II, 11.   [4] Lib. V, 1.

savage sound to hear Wolfdietrich reply to the queen of King Marsilius of Messina, in the Book of Heroes;

"For the love of bloody battles around the world I rove."

And it must have been a barbarous spectacle to behold, as described by Froissart, Messire Yewains Charuel, who sat at the table of king Charles of France, after the battle in which the thirty Bretons had conquered the thirty English in Brittany, "qui avoit le viaire si detaillé et découpé qu'il montroit bien que la besogne fut bien combattue"; or Messire Enguerrant Duedins, a knight of Picardy, who had been in the same battle, "et qui montroit bien qu'il y avoit été." In the Teutonic romances, it is true, one is struck with the praises bestowed upon the most ferocious warriors:[1] and, without doubt, the German chivalry was prepared on many grounds for adopting the new system, which was so favourable to the views of men who desired to emancipate their passions from all restraint. "When you see a man with a gallinacious gladiatorial air, a fierce countenance, a rustic voice, an austere language, a ferocious manner, you know him to be a German," says Cornelius Agrippa.[2] A very different character belonged to the chivalry of England, France, and Spain. Men who were animated by the true spirit of Christian knighthood had other virtues in addition to valour, and even their valour was something far nobler than the mere courage of nature.

When Anne de Montmorenci could not prevail upon the Swiss to defer battle, he said to his friends around him, "Let us march, and perform from a sense of duty what they do through fero-

[1] On the Ancient Teutonic Poetry and Romances, illustrations of Northern Antiquities.
[2] De Vanitate Scientiarum.

city."[1] There was nothing of barbarous threatening in such valour. "Crests made no wounds," as Livy says, nor did a ferocious aspect cause dismay. The noble reply of Eteocles to the messengers, describing the formidable appearance of the invading warriors,[2] expressed the sentiment of our Christian chivalry. Its valour arose from other motives than the mere instinct of ferocity.

"If the Moors of Spain," says a writer rather prejudiced in their favour, "loved courage and strength, it was only because with courage and strength they could command the weak; if they loved victory, it was because victory destroyed the enemy and yielded rich booty."[3]

The inference which Plutarch derives from a passage in Homer, as illustrating the difference between Greek and barbarian valour, might be employed also in reference to that of our chivalrous ancestors. "Dolon," he says, "is liberal of promises:

Τόφρα γὰρ ἐς στρατὸν εἶμι διαμπερὲς, ὄφρ' ἂν ἵκωμαι
Νῆ' Ἀγαμεμνονέην·

"but Diomedes promised nothing; he only said that he would have less fear if he had a companion; for prudence is Grecian, βαρβαρικὸν δὲ καὶ φαῦλον ἡ θρασύτης. Many Trojans," he continues, "fell into the hands of the Greeks, but no Greeks into those of the Trojans; and many Trojans came as suppliants to Greeks, as Adrastus, the sons of Antimachus, Lycaon, and even Hector, begging for burial, but not so the Greeks. ὡς βαρβαρικοῦ τοῦ ἱκετεύειν καὶ ὑποπίπτειν ἐν τοῖς ἀγῶσιν ὄντος· Ἑλληνικοῦ δὲ τοῦ νικᾶν μαχόμενον, ἢ ἀποθνήσκειν."[4]

[1] Hist. des Hommes illustres de la France, II, 261.
[2] Æschyl. Sept. cont. Theb. 393.
[3] Hist. de la Domination des Arabes et des Maures en Espagne, par Conde, vol. II, p. 253.
[4] De Audiendis Poetis.

Of such valour our annals are rich in examples. One very memorable was that of John, King of Bohemia, the most distinguished among the slain in the battle of Creci, in whom age had not chilled the fire of youth; for though blind, he placed himself in the first division of the French, and as the issue grew dubious, ordered the four knights, his attendants, to lead him into the hottest of the battle, "that I too," said he, "may have a stroke at the English." Placing him in the midst of them, and interlacing their bridles, they spurred forward their horses, and were almost immediately slain. However, it is true the desperate heroism of Philippe-le-Hardi, the fourth son of King John of France, in the battle of Poitiers, was extolled and rewarded above the prudence of the Dauphin and his two brothers, on that memorable day.

The occasion for individual valour, during the wars of the Middle Ages, was met with all the spirit of the ancient heroism, like that of the Athenian king Codrus. Every distinguished hero was recognized as a power, and spoken of almost as an army. Each man felt the advantages to which the gifts of nature entitled him, and his personal importance was the foundation of his dignity.

The Prior of the Chartreuse, shewing to Francis I the enormous cleft in the skull of Jean-sans-peur, as it lay in the ducal vault at Dijon, said to him, "Sire, c'est par là que les Anglois sont entrés en France."

In the fourteenth century the Castilians, after their defeat, on the banks of the Ebro, by Gaston II, Comte de Foix, owed their safety to the valour of the Captain Ruydiaz de Gaona, inhabitant of Logroño, seconded by that of three other brave men, who stopped, at the head of a bridge, the advance of a victorious army, and gave time to the vanquished to put themselves in a state of defence. If we can hardly believe that Vortemir, the British chieftain, who commanded against the Saxons, pulled up a tree by the roots, and with the club killed Horsa and defeated the Saxons,[1] we must at least admit that the Swiss themselves acknowledged, that they owed their victory of Morat to René II of Lorraine, the hero who had before fought in their ranks at Granson; to whom they accordingly yielded the treasures of the Duke of Burgundy.

It would lead us too far from the object of these sheets, if we were to consider all the advantages and opportunities of heroic virtue and of public good which the system of the Middle Ages afforded in the mode of raising and directing a military force.[2] Muratori confesses that he feels a kind of repugnance in beginning to treat upon standing armies.[3] And Sismondi, who cannot be accused of too much partiality to the old manners and opinions of Europe, speaks on one occasion as if he were a knight of the Middle Ages. "The invention of firearms has had consequences for the human race far more disastrous than plague or famine; it has subjected the power of man to calculation, it has reduced the soldier to the rank of a machine, it has deprived valour of its most noble part; of everything which made it personal. It has increased the power of despots, and diminished that of nations; it has destroyed the security of towns, and ramparts can no longer inspire confidence."[4] The chivalrous spirit has always evinced a horror and contempt for similar inventions. Archidamus, the son of Agesilaus, beholding the dart of a catapult, then for the first time brought from Sicily, cried out, Ὦ Ἡράκλεις,

---

[1] Nenn. c. 45.
[2] See Marchangy, la Gaule Poétique, III, 60.
[3] On Public Happiness.
[4] Hist. des Repub. Ital. tom. VI, p. 5.

ἀπόλωλεν ἀνδρὸς ἀρετά. And Lycus, in the play, blames Hercules for using a bow, calling it κάκιστον ὅπλον, though it seemed to Amphitryon, on the contrary, as πάνσοφον εὕρημα.¹ The poisoned shirt seems to have been a punishment on Hercules for his having used arrows which had been dipt in the blood of the Hydra.² It was the Saracens who introduced the custom of poisoned poniards, though the Swiss, after the battle of Granson, found poisoned arrows of English steel in the camp of the Burgundians.³ Ulysses is represented going in his Greek ship to Ilas, at Corinth, to procure poison for his arrows; but this prince, like a worthy knight, refused to give it.

———————— ἀλλ' ὁ μὲν οὔ οἱ
Δῶκεν, ἐπεί ῥα θεοὺς νεμεσίζετο αἰὲν ἐόντας.⁴

Virgil's knight may have only employed it against wild beasts.⁵ Ælian mentions the custom to condemn it.⁶

In 1139, Pope Innocent II, and afterwards the Emperor Conrad, forbade the use of the crossbow, which was then generally used in Italy. The French held it as too murderous an instrument for generous warfare. Mr. Meyrick shews that it was an error to ascribe its invention to Richard I of England.⁷ Richard was killed by the shot from an arcubalist, a machine which he often worked skilfully with his own hands. So that Guillaume le Briton, in his Latin poem, called Philippeis, introduces Atropos making a decree that Richard should die by no other means than by a wound from this destructive instrument, the use of which he had revived and introduced among the French, in the crusade, after

---

¹ Euripidis Hercul. Furens, 185.   ² Diodorus Sic. IV, 11.
³ Barante, Hist. des Ducs de Bourgogne, tom. XI, 33.
⁴ Od. I, 262.   ⁵ Æneid, IX, 773.
⁶ De Animal. V, 16.   ⁷ Treatise on Ancient Armour, I, 81.

it had been interdicted by the Pope. But it was the employment of fire which excited the greatest horror, for it seemed to deprive valour of all advantage over cowardice. So when the Greek fire spread terror in the Christian camp, "Biau Sire Dieu Jesus Christ," cried the brave Louis IX, "garde moi et toute ma gent." The use of gunpowder was first introduced into Europe by the Arabs.

In 1340, at the battle of Wadacelito, and in 1342, at the siege of Algeciras, the Moors made use of cannon, those mighty engines which have given so terrible a truth to the term, μάχης καυστειρῆς. Their own historians affirm that they used them as early as 1257, at the siege of Niebla. Bayard would never spare any enemy whom he found armed with a harquebusse. In the year 1524, when these instruments were coming into use, the contempt which Fernando of Alva expressed for them, before a gentleman of Burgos, who boasted, in the presence of a lady, that he was a good shot, gave rise to a celebrated duel between these knights, which was discovered by the unintentional exchange of mantles, which had been thrown on the ground.

Orland, having vanquished the wicked King of Friesland, and seized his horrid engine, the gun, after steering his vessel out of sight of land,

> He seized the tube, and said: "That cavalier
> May never vail through thee his knightly pride,
> Nor base be rated with a better foe.
> Down with thee to the darkest deeps below!
> O loathed, O cursed piece of enginery,
> Cast in Tartarean bottom, by the hand
> Of Beelzebub, whose foul malignity
> The ruin of this world through thee has planned!
> To hell, from whence thou came, I render thee."[1]

---

[1] Orland. Fur. cant. IX.

The hatred of "the smutty grain," and of those instruments the invention of which Milton ascribes to Satan, is again finely expressed by Ariosto:

> How, foul and pestilent discovery,
> Didst thou find place within the human heart?
> Through thee no more shall gallantry, no more
> Shall valour prove their prowess as of yore.[1]

And the complaint of the Knight of La Mancha is familiar to all: "Blessed be those happy ages that were strangers to the dreadful fury of these devilish instruments of artillery, whose inventor, I am satisfied, is now in hell, receiving the reward of his cursed invention, which is the cause that very often a cowardly base hand takes away the life of the bravest gentleman; and that in the midst of that vigour and resolution which animates and inflames the bold, a chance bullet (shot, perhaps, by one that fled, and was frighted at the very flash the mischievous piece gave when it went off), coming, nobody knows how, or from whence, in a moment puts a period to the brave designs and the life of one that deserved to have survived many years."

But what gives a peculiar interest to the valour of these ages, is the union which it maintained with high and generous qualities of soul. The heathen heroes, indeed, seem to have regarded valour alone as a sufficient virtue for one mortal. Witness the words of Æneas to Ajax in the tragedy of Rhesus, and of Polydamas to Hector in the Iliad:[2] but with our Christian chivalry to be without reproach was more essential than to be without fear. In l'Arbre des Batailles, the object of one chapter is to consider "Lesquels sont les plus fors en bataille les justes ou les pecheurs." First the author says, "les pecheurs sont les plus fors." He quotes the instance of Alexander, "loquel fut moult grant

[1] Cant. XI.   [2] Il. XIII, 727.

pecheur et occist presque tous les roys du monde :" also those of Sennacherib, Jonathan, and Holofernes, great sinners and strong in arms : " Mais faisons aucun argument pour la partie contraire. David petit homme en comparation du grant Golias par sa bonte vainquit icellui Golias grant en bataille." But the fact of the English and Bretons being " mal resistables en bataille," while the brave and virtuous Saint Louis suffers loss, seems to him as proving that victory depends not upon the virtue or wickedness of men, but solely on the inscrutable will of God. Hence the peculiar devotion of the brave, who were always ready to evince their humility and dependence upon Heaven. The Chevalier Bayard went on foot, with staff in hand, as a common pilgrim to St. James of Compostella. " Il ne convient pas que chascun soit aussi preux que fut Hector de Troye, ne le roy Alexandre, mais de necessite il convient qu'il soit preudhomme." This is what Perceforest says. Even when men could not boast of much intellectual ability, valour was accompanied by a generosity, a faithful friendship, and a desire to employ personal force and courage for a good end, which indicated a great nobleness of soul. As when Sir Thomas Malory relates, that " after the feste and journeye, Kynge Arthur drewe hym unto London, and soo by the counceil of Merlyn, the kyng lete calle his barons to counceil, for Merlyn had told the kynge that the sixe kynges that made warre upon hym wold in al haste be awroke on hym and on his landys, wherfor the kyng asked counceil at hem al, they coude no counceil gyve, but said they were bygge ynough " ;[1] or as in the battle under the walls of Tangiers, during the expedition of Alfonso V of Portugal against the Moors, when Gonçalo Vaz Coutinho, being sur-

[1] Chap. X.

rounded by the Moors and on the point of perishing, Martin de Tavora, his mortal enemy, ran to his assistance and rescued him; or as when Sir Walter Mauny cried, "a man should peril his body to save the lives of two such valiant knights." Well might Shakspeare say,

> He that is truly dedicate to war
> Hath no self-love; nor he that loves himself
> Hath not essentially, but by circumstance,
> The name of valour.[1]

As exhibiting a noble spirit of perseverance too, it demanded respect:

> "When first I took this venturous quest,
> I swore upon the rood
> Neither to stop, nor turn, nor rest,
> For evil or for good."

And it is difficult to refrain from admiring the skill and self-devotion displayed, even in the most extravagant exploits, as when Orlando meets Rodomont on the bridge near Montpelier, who disputes the passage; when Orlando advances, takes the formidable Saracen in his arms, jumps with him into the river, and escapes by swimming to shore.[2] How glorious is the description which Ovid gives of the Fabii:

> Quosque vident, sternunt; nec metus alter inest.
> Quo ruitis, generosa domus? male creditur hosti;
> Simplex nobilitas, perfida tela cave;
> Fraude perit virtus.

But further, I would suggest to such of my readers as it may more immediately concern—

> This thought which ever bribes the beauteous kind,

that the motive which induced our brave ancestors to be so careless of each other's blood, was fre-

[1] Hen. VI, II, v. 2.   [2] Canto XXIX, 40.

quently the result of a disposition which, in its legitimate sphere, is allied to honour, to humanity, and to goodness. They did not make war against peaceful convents, holy altars, and the venerable institutions of piety:

>———————— They neither came
>For pride of empire nor desire of fame.
>Kings fight for kingdoms, madmen for applause,
>But love for love alone; that crowns the lover's cause.

Like Othryoneus in Homer, the young Thracian from Cabesus, who came as a volunteer to defend Troy, out of love for the fairest daughter of Priam, whom he woo'd; and he sought no portion with her; but he promised to accomplish a great work.

>ἐκ Τροίης ἀέκοντας ἀπωσέμεν υἷας Ἀχαιῶν.[1]

The valour which sought to merit love, was a noble self-devotion to a great end, not an affectation of boldness and a show of cruelty, after the manner of those who, as Tacitus saith, "Militiam in lasciviam vertunt."[2] When King Perceforest was told of the necromancers who occupied the forest, he grew melancholy, and falling asleep, a dwarf appeared to him, and called him "roy recreant" for suffering such an evil so near to him. At the word "roy recreant," he started up, and called two squires who guarded the chamber, and said, "Va tost, et fais seeller mon grant cheval et deux fors roucins pour vous deux et si le faiz si coyement et secretement que la royne ma femme ne le sache et puis fais les amener derrière ma tente. Sire dist l'escuyer je feray vostre commandement." And the King ordered the other to bring him his armour, and so he armed himself, and came out, and found the horse, and mounted without putting his foot in the stirrup, "et incontinent apres monterent ses deux

[1] Il. XIII, 367.   [2] De Vit. Agricol.

escuyers"; and one carried his shield, and the other his sword, and so they galloped off to the forest.[1] In such examples, one is not so much struck with the display of courage as the heroic virtue which made men devote themselves to whatever cause seemed noble and just; and to feel that death was far preferable to the sense of having consented to dishonour. This was the spirit to which Pericles alluded in those glorious words, where he says, "Our fathers indeed resisting the Medes, and abandoning their houses and estates, γνώμῃ τε πλείονι ἢ τύχῃ καὶ τόλμῃ μείζονι ἢ δυνάμει τόν τε βάρβαρον ἀπεώσαντο."[2] Who does not admire the fixed resolve and the faithful constancy with which men met death in a sacred cause, rather than abandon it, and survive their friends? As Livy describes Decius unable to rally his flying soldiers, "patrem P. Decium nomine compellans," and saying, "quid ultra moror familiare fatum? Datum hoc nostro generi est, ut luendis periculis publicis piacula simus"; and then rushing on to death:[3] or, as Sallust relates of Catiline, "postquam fusas copias, seque cum paucis relictum videt Catilina, memor generis, atque pristinæ dignitatis, in confertissimos hostes incurrit, ibique pugnans confoditur."

After the dreadful battle with the Parthians, when the two Greeks advised young Crassus, already wounded, to retire with them and escape to Ischnæ, he replied, "There was no death, however terrible, the fear of which could make him leave so many brave men dying for his sake." He then embraced and dismissed them: for all that remained for himself was to die.[4]

—————— Ceoiditque in strage suorum
Impiger ad letum et fortis virtute coacta.[5]

---

[1] I. c. 34.   [2] Thucydid. I, 144.   [3] Lib. X, 28.
[4] Plutarch, Life of Crassus.   [5] Lucan, IV.

Æneas apologizes for having escaped from Troy.[1] The same feeling animated Priam and Anchises, and Crœsus, who would gladly have been slain on the fall of Sardis.[2] By the Christian rule, indeed, men were not to seek destruction, or to think of propitiating the gods by voluntary death; but it was still sweet and honourable to die for one's country; and it was still permitted men to feel that there may be moments when, to desire life any longer, would indicate a base and selfish heart.

Sebastian I, King of Portugal, after having three horses killed under him, in the fatal battle with the Moors, was entreated by some one, seeing that all hopes of the day were at an end, to surrender himself a prisoner, and save his life; but he replied fiercely, "When a king has lost his liberty he ought to die": and so, refusing quarter from the Moors, who recognized him, this young king was slain fighting to the last. He felt like that generous king Arthur, who, when "he loked abonte hym, and was ware of al hys hoost and of al hys good knyghtes how they were layed to the colde erthe, sayd, 'Jhesu mercy where are al my noble knyghtes becomen? Allas that ever I shold see thys dolefull day, for now I am come to myn ende. Now gyve me my speere,' and albeit Syr Lucan did remember hym of his night's dreame and what the spryte of Syr Gauwayn told him; 'tyde me deth betyde me lyf,' sayth the king, and so rushed against the enemy, and dyd full nobly as a noble kyng shold." And so, also, after the dreadful slaughter of the Saxons at Thetford, when Ingwar and his Danes approached the royal residence, and sent the king his haughty summons, one of the bishops advised Edmund to fly; but the king replied, "I desire not to survive my dear and faithful subjects.

---

[1] Æneid, II, 431.   [2] Herodot. I, 85.

Why do you suggest to me the shame of abandoning my fellow-soldiers? I have always shunned the disgrace of reproach, and especially of cowardly abandoning my knights, because I feel it nobler to die for my country than to forsake it: and shall I now be a voluntary recreant, when the loss of those whom I loved makes even the light of heaven tedious to me?" Terrible moments these; but moments when the heart of man, exalted by faith, is stronger than all the power of the material world, and listens to no necessity but the dictate of right and justice.

Lefebvre, when the French had forced their way, after dreadful carnage, into the very centre of Zaragoza, believing that he had effected his purpose, required Palafox to surrender, in a note containing only these words: "Head quarters, St. Engracia: Capitulation!" The heroic Spaniard immediately returned this reply: "Head quarters, Zaragoza: War at the knife's point!" And so, when King Edward II had retreated from the fatal battle of Bannock-Burn, he was accompanied by Sir Gilles de Argentine, till he had gained the summit of a hill, and there this noble knight took leave of his sovereign, and returned to the fight:—

"Speed hence, my liege, for on your trace
The fiery Douglas takes the chace,
  I know his banner well.
God send my sovereign joy and bliss,
And many a happier field than this!—
  Once more, my liege, farewell."——

Again he faced the battle-field,—
Wildly they fly, are slain, or yield.
"Now, then," he said, and couch'd his spear,
"My course is run, the goal is near;
One effort more, one brave career,
  Must close this race of mine."
Then in his stirrups rising high,
He shouted loud his battle cry,
  "Saint James for Argentine.
    *   *   *   *

He fell, while the generous Bruce hastens to save him, but only arrives to receive his last words.

> "Lord Earl, the day is thine!
> My sovereign's charge and adverse fate,
> Have made our meeting all too late;
>   Yet this may Argentine,
> As boon from ancient comrade, crave—
> A Christian's mass, a soldier's grave."
>
> Bruce press'd his dying hand,—its grasp,
> Kindly replied; but in his clasp,
>   It stiffen'd and grew cold,—
> And, "O, farewell!" the victor cried,
> "Of chivalry the flower and pride,
>   The arm in battle bold,
> The courteous mien, the noble race,
> The stainless faith, the manly face."
>
> Bid Ninian's convent light their shrine
> For late-wake of de Argentine.
> O'er better knight, on death-bier laid,
> Torch never gleam'd nor mass was said.[1]

In Tancredus it was impossible to speak of the devotion of the Crusaders, without making mention of their valour; so that there remains little for this place. The old tombs of religious warriors, in various churches and monasteries of Europe, are objects which remind us continually of that religious heroism which distinguished the Middle Ages. In the church of the Cistercian monastery of Leubus, in Silesia, is the monument of a knight, who died in 1240. The inscription, so beautiful for its simplicity, has been almost effaced by the Hussites:

> Bello, consilio, virtuteque claruit iste
> Martinus Buswoy, cujus sis gloria Christe.

The old chivalry of Germany was proud of its Gero, in the tenth century, the first Margrave of Lausitz, the friend and champion of Otho the Great, renowned equally for his valour in war, as for his

[1] Sir Walter Scott.

wisdom and justice and piety. Immense was the number of his religious foundations. In one convent, which he founded, he is thus commemorated:

> Henrici I fortissima prælia gessit
> Magnique Ottonis gloria magna fuit.
> Virginibus miseris certum construxit asylum
> Ut laudes Christi virgo pudica canat.

In order that all the passions of nature might be consecrated to religion, men were anxious to devote their courageous spirit to some sacred cause, to the defence of Christian people, or to the removal of obstacles opposed to the happiness of the human race. Their zeal may have been in some instances extravagant, but it cannot be denied that, even when it needed correction, it evinced a spirit the most contrary to everything selfish and ungenerous. Men were indeed more ready to admire than to criticise, when they heard how—

> Many a time hath banished Norfolk fought
> For Jesu Christ; in glorious Christian field,
> Streaming the ensign of the Christian cross,
> Against black pagans, Turks, and Saracens;
> And, toil'd with works of war, retired himself
> To Italy; and there, at Venice, gave
> His body to that pleasant country's earth,
> And his pure soul unto his Captain Christ,
> Under whose colours he had fought so long.[1]

It was a monk, named Diego Velasquez, in the monastery of Santa Maria de Fitero, in Navarro, who accepted the offer of King Alphonso to defend Calatrava; thus giving rise to that famous order of the Knights of Calatrava, which became a noble bulwark of Christendom. At the siege of Rhodes, d'Aubusson had received five wounds, but when the knights pressed him to retire, he replied, "Here is my post; I cannot die with more renown than

---
[1] Richard II, IV, 1.

in the field of battle, for the defence of our holy religion."

Odo de St. Amand was one of the most renowned grand-masters of the Temple. He had been married before his admission to the order; he was one of the handsomest men of the age; his accomplished manners gained him the love of all men, and his high virtue made him the object of general respect. His wife having retired to a convent where she took the veil, he assumed the red cross. His services were soon rewarded by the highest dignity, according to the desire of Amalrich, King of Jerusalem. In a fatal battle, being struck to the ground, he was made prisoner by the Saracens, and sent to Damascus. Saladin's nephew was a prisoner at the same time, in the hands of the Templars, and the Sultan desired the grand-master to procure him in exchange for himself. "God forbid," said the noble knight, "that I should give so bad an example to the Templar knights, and leave them ground to hope that they could be ransomed whenever they suffered themselves to be made prisoners. Only his belt and his dagger can a Templar dare to redeem, and his motto must be for ever 'Victory or death.'" This great man therefore died in prison. All the Templars or Knights Hospitallers, whom Saladin took prisoners, he slew without any respect for humanity.[1] He resolved to exterminate the Templars, "quos in bello noverat prævalere."[2] Their rule forbade any Knight Templar to fly before three enemies.[3]

Enough, however, has been shewn in Tancredus relative to the spirit of the Templars. The other religious orders of knighthood employed for the benefit of religion and humanity, had equal claims to the praise of undaunted heroism. In 1211,

[1] Chronic. Gervas. [2] Hist. Hieros. 1153.
[3] Raumer, I, 495.

Hermann von Salza was grand-master of the Hospitallers; his heroic deeds against the infidels, and his high honour, were celebrated through the world. Humble in prosperity; never cast down at a reverse of fortune, Hermann, as a statesman, a ruler, and a soldier, is equally great, and corresponds with the ideal of a perfect man. Such was his personal character, that Pope Honorius III, and the Emperor Frederick II, chose him to be an arbitrator between them; and both shewed him equal respect and friendship. It was Salza who sent brother Hermann Balch, with one hundred knights, against the whole people of the Prussian infidels, three millions of bold warriors. He is described as an Achilles in bravery, and a Ulysses in prudence. He conquered everywhere, and founded towns. Like a lion in war, he was a mild and gracious ruler over his new people; he gave them instructors, took care of the sick, defended the priests, and gained the hearts of all.

Between 1230 and 1238, the Teutonic order under him flourished in its greatest splendour. After all its wars, Prussia, it is said, became, within forty or fifty years, the most flourishing and the best governed land in Europe. It has been said also that, in consequence of the institutions of the knights, the people of Prussia, in the thirteenth and fourteenth and the first half of the fifteenth centuries, enjoyed more freedom than any German state now possesses. It is certain that the knights in Prussia, like the Benedictine monks in other parts, tilled the land, planted vines, reclaimed waste fens, erected magnificent structures: the towns were enclosed with thick walls and towers, and more than one thousand churches and convents built in less than seventy years, facts which can hardly be reconciled with the justice of the acccusations brought against them by many writers, supported as they are by vague popular tradition among the Lithuanian peasants. But however this may be, enough has been seen to prove that the valour of chivalry was not that of ferocious barbarians, but the spirit of generous and devout men, who were humane and lovers of their country, and the disinterested benefactors of the human race.

VIII. But the lover of humanity, after having seen how courtesy and valour belonged to the character of men in these ages, will naturally pursue his inquiries, and demand an explanation of the custom of duelling, which is commonly said to have been derived from these ages; and although I would gladly escape from all hateful and ungracious subjects, it will be impossible to refuse his invitation, to answer the objection which he may so reasonably adduce, founded on the practice of our age, and this opinion which traces it to that of the heroic times. In the first place, when we ascribe courtesy to the manners of these ages, we must be careful to remember that it was a disposition which does not necessarily correspond with the idea which the moderns may sometimes entertain of it. "I should like to know," says Montaigne, " en quel temps print commencement cette coustume de si exactement poiser et mesurer les parolles et d'y attacher nostre honneur." It is clear that it did not exist among the Greeks nor among the Romans. " On appelle Cæsar, tantost voleur, tantost yvrongne à sa barbe." We see the liberty of invective mutually used between the greatest warriors of these nations, when words were only followed by words, without, drawing any other consequence.—So far Montaigne. That this custom prevailed among the Greek and Trojan heroes is known to every reader of the Iliad. It may be strikingly observed in the language of Agamemnon, when exciting the Greek warriors to battle, who, so far from evincing displeasure at his reproaches, always obey his command, and sometimes even applaud his solicitude. In the Odyssey one of these scenes is described by Nestor—

"Ὃς τὼ μὲν χαλεποῖσιν ἀμειβομένω ἐπέεσσιν
Ἕστασαν.[1]

Antiochus did not feel himself called upon to fight with Ulysses for preventing him from speaking, though in doing so he applied his hand to his mouth.

———— ἀλλ' Ὀδυσεὺς ἐπὶ μάσταχα χερσὶ πίεζε
Νωλεμέως κρατερῇσι, σάωσε δὲ πάντας Ἀχαιούς.[2]

Another instance is when Ulysses declines taking a part in the games, and Euryalus calls him merchant, a lover of pelf, like to him who navigates—

Ἀρχὸς ναυτάων, οἵτε πρηκτῆρες ἔασιν,
Φόρτου τε μνήμων, καὶ ἐπίσκοπος ᾖσιν ὁδαίων
Κερδέων θ' ἁρπαλέων.[3]

Ulysses, indeed, answers with spirit, but he only tells his accuser that he is the fairest in person and the silliest in mind, that his words were insolent and indecent; and he contents himself with disproving his charge by engaging in the games, and after the triumph of Ulysses, Euryalus, by desire of the king, is reconciled to him, making him a present of a sword, and saying,

Χαῖρε, πάτερ ὦ ξεῖνε· ἔπος δ' εἴπερ τι βέβακται
Δεινόν, ἄφαρ τὸ φέροιεν ἀναρπάξασαι ἄελλαι.[4]

The noble speech of Agamemnon to Nestor, who reproved him for having robbed Achilles of his prize, will shew that the Homeric heroes would condescend to ask pardon of one whom they had

[1] Od. III, 148. [2] Od. IV, 287.
[3] Od. VIII, 163. [4] Ibid. 408.

injured.¹ They also laboured to appease enmities. Ajax and Idomeneus revile each other at the games, and are appeased by Achilles.² The reply of Themistocles to Eurybiades, who moved to strike him, is celebrated; and Socrates made a similar insult offered to himself the occasion of a jest, the same Socrates of whom Laches said, that if all the rest had acted like him in the battle of Delia the Athenians would not have lost the day. Philopœmen, hurried away by his impetuous temper, publicly reproached Lycortas, one of the most distinguished warriors of Megalopolis, with having suffered himself to be made prisoner. A more decided insult could not now be offered to a soldier; yet here it only served to inspire the injured hero with the greater magnanimity. Lycortas shortly after accepted a commission from him, and on the tragical death of Philopœmen he immediately marched to Messena, and exercised justice upon all who were concerned in the murder.³ The Romans also approved of the reply of Augustus to the challenge sent him by Antony: they despised the false courage of all such champions; and Livy relates examples of the kind only to condemn them. Marius sent no other answer to the challenge of the Teutonic bravo than that he might strangle himself if he was tired of life. The Romans knew how to respect true bravery, yet nothing was more contemptible in their eyes than the profession of a gladiator.

That contempt for life which Diodorus attributes to the barbarous people of Gaul, which led them to delight in single combats, could gain them no higher praise among the heroic nations of antiquity than is expressed in these words, βάρβαρόν τινα μεγαλοψυχίαν ἐπιδεικνύμενοι.⁴

[1] Il. IX, 115—158. [2] Il. XXIII.
[3] Pausanias, lib. VIII, 51. [4] Diodorus Siculus, lib. V, 28.

But what will, perhaps, surprise many persons much more, is the fact that this liberty of speech was practised by the knights and barons of the middle ages with the same effect. When Joinville had given his opinion in favour of the King remaining in Palestine, the other great officers of the army were highly displeased, and indulged themselves in ridiculing Joinville, calling him *poulain*, to which he used to reply, "il aimoit mieux etre poulain que chevalier recreux," that is, recreant knight. Poulain signified degeneracy, from the union of a Syrian man with a French woman, whose son was supposed to be of a base and degenerate nature. Both expressions were therefore, as we should think, highly insulting; "on ne voit pas néanmoins," says Ducange, "que cette affaire ait eu aucune suite: ce qui prouve qu'on n'étoit point si delicat qu'aujourdhui sur le point d'honneur, ou du moins, qu'avec la meme bravoure, on sçavoit mieux entendre raillerie dans l'occasion." Upon all occasions of this kind they seem to have adopted, by mutual consent, the custom of the Greek and Trojan heroes, as described in the words of Achilles to Æneas:

Ὁπποῖόν κ' ἄιπῃσθα ἔπος, τοῖόν κ' ἐπακούσαις,

which was even sanctioned by the advice of Minerva to Achilles, when she restrains him from drawing his sword against Agamemnon:

ἀλλ' ἤτοι ἔπεσιν μὲν ὀνείδισον, ὡς ἔσεται περ.[1]

Sismondi observes, that the mutual attention with which a refined civilization inspires us for one another was then but little practised. The delicacy of the point of honour was not easily offended; and when reproach was repaid with reproach, one

[1] Il. I, 211.

held that all injury was repaired. He refers to a "tenson" between the Marquis Albert Malespina and Raimbaud de Vaqueiras, two of the greatest seigneurs, and most valiant captains, "at the commencement of the thirteenth century, in which they mutually reproach one another." To give the lie was not an occasion for combat;[1] the dishonour rested with him who was convicted of falsehood.[2] The first duel that was fought for such an offence was during the miserable reign of Henry II of France, between two courtiers, La Chastegneraye and Jarnac. No polished nation has ever defended the modern practice on the ground of its being necessary for the maintenance of courtesy: the manners of Europe were courteous before it commenced, and those of some nations are still gross and barbarous in the extreme after it has prevailed with them for a long period. The truth is, that this liberty of speech, within the bounds of gentleness and religion did not offend while men were innocent, and it was absolutely unavoidable while frankness, good humour, and high spirits were united in fellowship. Our ancestors loved that feeling expressed by Montaigne, so full of truth and honesty, of benevolence and good sense, " Je souffriroy estre rudement heurté par mes amis ; tu es un sot, tu resues : j'ayme entre les galans hommes, qu'on s'exprime courageusement, que les mots aillent ou va la pensée. Il nous faut fortifier l'ouie et la durcir contre cette tendreur du son ceremonieux des paroles. J'ayme une societé et familiarité forte et virile : une amitié qui se flatte en l'aspreté et vigueur de son commerce."

Henry IV of France, recapitulating, before all the court, the names of the most distinguished

---

[1] D'Audiguier, le vray et ancien Usage des Duels, p. 46.
[2] Gerdil, Traité des Combats singuliers, 164.

warriors, placed his hand upon Crillon's shoulder, and said, "Messieurs, voici le premier capitaine du monde.—Vous en avez menti, Sire, c'est vous," replied Crillon.

Εὐτραπελία, πεπαιδευμένη ὕβρις ἐστί. This is Aristotle's definition, which is adopted also by Cicero.[1] "Being cheerful, the young, says Aristotle, are of gracious and polished manners; for elegance of manner is only insolence refined." So that the boy of whom Aulus Gellius tells us that he would give every one a box on the ear; or Hugh Capet, so called from his custom, when a little boy, of taking off, sans façon, the caps of his companions,[2] might have been courteous in the sense of Aristotle and Cicero, and of our chivalrous ancestors. La Colombiere, indeed, would call this, if pushed too far, "jeu de vilain," yet he sanctions the opinion, when he says, "The stomachs which can digest nothing but the most delicate food are weak. Rough and depraved souls can endure no words but such as seem to them as of an agreeable tone; on the contrary, good stomachs which can digest the hardest meat, are compared to those strong and generous spirits which despise words of insult, and which obtain renown by deeds of virtue."[3] Among the laws of knighthood, it was expressly forbidden to quarrel with one's companion, even though he should be in the wrong;[4] and thus Gilles de Rome, in his "Miroir," says, "c'est chose muliebre, femenine, estre furieux et ardant en ire.—Et n'est chose plus glorieuse en prince qui est de grant couraige que entendre les injures et les souffrir en souveraine patience et que se il est blesse qu'il le passe sans vengeance ou punition." Men scorned

[1] Orat. pro M. Cælio.
[2] Nicole Gilles, Chroniques de France.
[3] Theatre d'Honneur et de Chevalerie.
[4] Favin, Theatre d'Honneur et de Chevalerie.

the absurd vanity of the Earl of Oxford, who would not drink because the squire of the Black Prince had obeyed his lord's orders and carried the cup first to Sir John Chandos before he presented it to him.

The following circumstance was related only to prove the previous discontent and fiery temper of Robert, son of William the Conqueror. Being in the castle of L'Aigle, in Normandy, with his two brothers, William Rufus and Henry, these two youths, out of gaiety, had thrown some water upon him, as he was crossing the court to go to his apartment, along with the son of Hugues de Grentemenil, whom William had lately deprived of his possessions in England, for having left that kingdom. Robert suffered himself to be instigated by this young man so far as to rush upstairs with his sword drawn. The two princes drew theirs and made ready to receive him. In an instant the castle was in an uproar. The king presented himself, and with difficulty prevented a combat. But Robert could not overcome his resentment, and the same evening he left the castle, and entered upon that war which involved his father in so much misery, and was near depriving him of life before the castle of Gerberoy. The frank and honest courtesy of these ages encouraged a manly intercourse, and the warm and affectionate attachments of men were often expressed by the language and manifestation of the opposite feeling. What men admired was not the unamiable temper condemned by Horace;[1] nor was it that craft or mystery, the τὸ βλέπειν ἐναντίον, which the old comic poet represents as the qualification of the man who conquers Cleon in impudence.[2] It was not the swaggering of the upstart, or of vain carpet knights,

---

[1] Ep. I, xviii, 15.   [2] Aristoph. Equites, 1238.

―――― οὔπω μάλα εἰδότι θύριδος ἀλκῆς,

still less that " mystère du corps, inventé pour cacher les defauts de l'esprit," which Castiglione so well exposes in banishing those persons from his court " who seem like women, who, in their gait, posture, and every gesture, appear so tender and languid, as if their limbs were disjointed the one from the other; and who pronounce every sentence with that soft and languishing air, as if they were on the point of expiring, and who, the more they converse with persons of quality and distinction, the more they are addicted to these ridiculous fooleries." But it was the sweet gentleness of the Christian youth, that amiable, yielding, affectionate spirit, which delighted in obedience, and in making every one happy. It was that which the Roman orator deemed worthy of the highest praise, "retinens veterem illum officii morem, non infuscata malevolentia, non assueta mendaciis, non fucata, non fallax, non erudita artificio simulationis vel suburbano, vel etiam urbano."[1]

Once more then let us ask, with Montaigne, at what period was this custom introduced, which obliges men to measure with such delicacy the phrases of their conversation? which gave occasion for holy men, like Nieremberg, to say, that "in this matter of honour, men have invented such laws, such punctilios, such impertinent formalities, that if they were all truly and really mad, they could not have done more absurdly; and that if David cursed the mountains of Gelboe, because Saul and Jonathan died upon them, with much more reason would the high mountains of honour be cursed upon which so many souls have been seen to perish." The answer

[1] Pro Plancio.

will delight those who know how to love the virtues,
while they detest the abuse and the perversion of
chivalry. "The opinions on the point of honour,"
says Sismondi, "which have had such an influence
not only upon chivalry, but upon all our modern
system of civilization, have come to us from the
Arabians, to whom they belong, and not to the Germanic nations. It is from them that we have derived
this religion of vengeance, this so delicate appreciation of offence and affronts, which makes them
to sacrifice their lives, and those of their family, to
wipe away a stain upon their honour, which in
1568 caused all the Alpuxarra of Granada to revolt,
when 50,000 Moors perished to revenge the blow of
a cane given by Don Juan de Mendoza to Don
Juan de Malec, descendant of the Aben Humeya."
One of the caliphs sacrificed a flourishing city,
containing 200,000 souls, and the property of
millions, to a similar feeling. About the year 895,
the rage for duels prevailed in the greatest degree
among the Moors of Spain, instances of which are
related by Condé in his History.

Hence we may look for the traces of Spanish
origin in such a code of duelling as Maffei's treatise Della Scienza Cavalleresca, in which insults
are classed and subdivided, and the proper quantum of revenge laid down. If we would exhibit
a true Christian knight, we must not produce
one whom no history records with praise, such
as a Vincent de la Rosa, who used to say that he
had fought more duels than Gante, Luna, Diego,
Garcia de Paredez, or others; or a Marcellus, who
never refused a challenge to single combat, nor failed
of killing the challenger; but some renowned hero,
like Godefroy de Bouillon, of whom William of
Tyre testifies that he was always unwilling to engage
in a single combat, or the Emperor Frederick Barbarossa, "Vir Christianissimus, infimis familiaris,

quibuslibet victis clementissimus, obliviosus injuriæ."[1]

If we seek to learn the real sentiments of the Christian chivalry in this respect, they may be found in the lives of the great knights of the middle age, or in the professed treatises on chivalry. I have given instances, in Tancredus, of the forgiveness of injuries, as practised by the heroes of Christendom. They might be multiplied without end. John King of Bohemia, son of the Emperor Henry VII, was one of the most accomplished young knights of the fourteenth ceutury. To him the words of Cicero were applicable, "Semper in animo ejus esse placidissimam pacem."[2] His grand object of ambition was to be the arbiter and the pacificator of Europe, as he was the bravest and most gallant knight. Always on horseback, he traversed the continent to reconcile the divisions of Christian princes. In 1330 his personal exertions appeased Martino della Scala, and restored Brescia to peace and prosperity. Judiciary forms would not have required a blow to be endured, if it had been deemed in any case a stain requiring blood to wash it out. When Humfred was granting a charter to the convent of Pradelles, in Normandy, he gave more than the usual blow to one of the three witnesses, who were his son, Richard de Lillebonne, and Hugues, son of the Count Waleran. The second of these asked why he had been struck so violently? "Because you are the youngest," replied Humfred, "and perhaps you may live long, and lest you should forget the transaction."[3] The diabolical custom of seconds to encourage and inflame enmity, was utterly unknown. Scarcely could Tancred prevent the strife between his men and those of Raymond from

---

[1] Jacobi de Vitriaco Hist. Orientalis, lib. III, apud Martene in Thesauro Anecdot. 111.
[2] Tuscul. V.   [3] Sismondi, Hist. des Français, IV, 203.

leading to bloodshed: "Sed occurrit viro ratio," says the historian, "quæ sanguinem vetat fundi Christianum."[1] The same sentiment occurs perpetually in the old chivalrous romances. Thus in Arthur of Little Britain, when Governar had reproached Hector with having had the designs of a villain and a traitor, and when Hector began to be sore chafed, and they fell to blows, Arthur interferes, and prevails upon them to make it up.[2] Nay, the very Moors themselves caught so much of the Christian spirit in Spain, as to furnish instances of similar interference; at least, Christian writers ascribe such sentiments to them. Thus in the civil wars of Granada, when the two Moorish knights, Albayaldos and Alabez, were going to engage in a duel with the Master of Calatrava and Don Manuel Ponce de Leon, the flower of all Christian knights, as the four knights met at the fountain in the forest by break of day, suddenly the Master's horse began to neigh, and looking towards the Granada road, they saw a knight galloping in full speed towards them. The Moors recognized the valiant Muza, who hearing that they had left the city in consequence of a challenge, made all possible haste to prevent the combat. "So, gentlemen," cried he, as he advanced, "you intended to enjoy the battle to yourselves; as Alla lives, I spurred my horse bravely to join you, and, if possible, prevail on knights of such tried valour to drop their design, as there is no such great urgency for fighting. Will it be any advantage to slaughter each other? Your lives are too precious to be thrown away so lightly. It would grieve me to the heart to see a misfortune happen to any of you; let me not, therefore, entreat in vain." The Master replied that he was ready to waive the battle, and left it

[1] Gesta Tancredi, XCVIII. [2] Page 64.

to Señor Albayaldos. The Moor had designs of vengeance, and refused; the battle began, and the Moor was mortally wounded. In his agony he expressed a wish to be baptized. The knight, overjoyed, carried him to a fountain, and baptized him, and shortly after he died, calling upon God, and saying,

> Friendship's voice had I but followed,
> This had never been my state,
> Tho' my body's doomed to perish,
> Be not such, my soul, thy fate!
>
> Into thy dear hands I trust it,
> Who redeem'dst me on the cross,
> Hear my prayers, and let thy mercy
> Save me from eternal loss.
>
> All I ask thee, noble Muza,
> All the comfort thou canst give,
> Is beneath this pine to lay me,
> Soon as I shall cease to live.
>
> When thou seest the king, thy brother,
> Tell him I fell like a man;
> That I died a faithful Christian,
> And forswore the Alcoran.

Again, when Muza meets the hopeless knight, and the Knight of the Sun, who are hastening to encounter each other in mortal combat, for the love of Lindaraxa, the gallant knight, Muza, shews them the folly of such a duel, and says, "It looks not well to see these quarrels between friends. Had Albayaldos followed my advice, we should have been now returning happily to Granada. I was once in your situation, but I tranquillized my bosom, and I did not make Alhamin atone for the ingratitude of a woman. No! it would have been a crime. Away, then, with this rancour, and let us return home." Nor would Muza leave them, but still he followed them, in hopes of effecting a reconciliation.

The precepts of chivalry, as well as the laws of every kingdom, expressly required men to cherish such sentiments, and differed widely from that opinion, sanctioned and enforced, though in open contradiction to the law, which renders the military service of some nations in this age obnoxious to that reproof of the Grecian orator, τί ἂν ἔτι ταύτην εἴποι τις εἶναι τὴν πολιτείαν ἐν ᾗ ταὐτὰ προστάττουσιν οἱ νόμοι ποιεῖν καὶ μὴ ποιεῖν;[1] La Colombiere, in his Theatre of Honour and Chivalry, says, that he feels called upon, as a Christian and a lover of his country, to write against the execrable practice of duels.[2] "There is a remedy for all things but death," he says, "and there is no insult so great but one can find an equivalent satisfaction for it, to save the honour and reputation of him who has been insulted."[3] "To say the truth," he adds, "since we are Christians, the laws of honour ought not to be laws of blood." The knights of the Holy Sepulchre took an oath that they would avoid duels. Noble writers employed themselves in teaching men how to escape all occasions which might lead to combat. Thus there is the "Traité du point d'honneur et des regles pour converser et se conduire sagement avec les incivils et les facheux."[4] Marc de la Beraudiere, treating on the proper method of avoiding quarrels, says, "I shall begin with piety. Piety belongs to him who is cheerfully courteous, humane, charitable, peaceable, devout, saturated as it were with every good quality which a virtuous man ought to possess. Now he who is compassionate, and full of kindness, is furnished with much friendship; those who are possessed of this piety are peaceable, hating dissensions and quarrels, not wishing to

---

[1] Æschines cont. Ctesiphon. 38.   [2] Tom. II, p. 2.
[3] Colombiere, II. p. 536.   [4] Paris, 1675.

offend any one, fearing to have any dispute with any one whatsoever, tant ils sont pleins de preud'hommie et de bonté."[1] The Sieur d'Audiguier makes the same reflection, and adds, "Besides this, in every age men who were truly great have shunned the manners, and actions, and opinions of the vulgar, so that to conform to them is to abandon all pretensions to magnanimity."[2]

This was the spirit evinced by the illustrious Turenne, after his conversion to the Catholic church. Ramsay relates that he never had a quarrel with any person, though often in situations which seemed to render it almost unavoidable. He was insulted in the theatre by some strangers, who threw his hat into the pit; but he only took occasion to make them blush for the barbarity of their own conduct.

Gonsalvo, the great captain, being asked in what circumstances of his life he took most pride, replied, that it was his having never drawn his sword excepting for the glory of God and the service of his master; and the Marquis of Pescara used to say that the honour of a gentleman did not consist in fighting duels, but in knowing how to avoid the engagement to fight. King Richard I was challenged, in terms the most insulting, by Leopold, Duke of Austria, before the Emperor Henry. Richard acting, not as a king, but as a Christian knight, refused to draw his sword against him, and d'Audiguier says that he was more esteemed for refusing to fight this duel, than for having conquered Saladin.[3]

Chancellor Bacon observes that the spirit of duelling had often distinguished the vilest populace: certainly the language and actions and society which lead to duels belong peculiarly to

[1] Le Combat de seul à seul en champ clos, par M. Marc de la Beraudiere. Paris, 1608.
[2] Le vray et ancien Usage des Duels, p. 37. [3] Ibid. p. 124.

men of the basest character. "How often does it happen," says M. Gerdil, preceptor of the Prince of Piedmont, in his Traité des Combats Singuliers,[1] "that indiscreet observations, on the subject of some little difference between two persons, or some hasty word passed by one of them, occasion their pursuing, at the point of the sword, an affair which they would otherwise have forgotten, and thus sacrificing their lives to avoid being exposed to some scandalous rumour. Thoughtless and unjust men, you take little heed of those arrows of the tongue, which have carried death into the bosom of your brother. You are the author of his death. The earth, moistened with his blood, cries for vengeance against you, and requires that the punishment should fall on your head. The fatal security in which you live after the mournful results of your imprudence, excuses you not before God." Of those who fight duels through fear of public opinion, he says, "A man who has no other courage would be a coward when he is out of sight. There is no one perfectly safe but the man who derives his courage from principles which nothing can shake, and with whom the exact fulfilment of his duty is everything."[2]

The third part of this excellent and learned treatise may be consulted with great advantage.

"A duel," says Gerdil, and the remark contains the aggregated wisdom of all ages, "is contrary to the maxims of religion, therefore it cannot but extinguish or weaken real courage. Without a sense of religion, there can be no real courage; none that can be depended upon, none universal, unconquerable, beyond the fear of death." "Il n'y a rien que de monstrueux," says Sully, "dans la démarche de deux petits-maîtres qui s'en vont furtivement sur le pré tremper dans le sang l'un

---

[1] Turin, p. 300.   [2] Vide Cicero de Off. II, 19.

de l'autre des mains poussées par un instinct tout pareil à celui des betes carnassieres."

These sentiments of chivalry were supported by the laws of every kingdom, as they were no doubt inspired by the injunctions of the church. Towards the end of the reign of John IV, King of Portugal, the practice of duelling became prevalent in that kingdom. Andrea d'Albuquerque, the Portuguese general, issued an order, declaring that it was only by combating the enemy with the greatest valour that any injury or affront could be repaired. The succeeding monarch, Dom Pedro, in the first year of his reign, published a severe law against all who fought duels. By the laws of Aragon, duels were strictly forbidden. A knight, who killed another in a duel, had his head cut off without mercy.

The legislation of the French monarchs presents a continued effort to repress the practice of duelling. St. Louis substituted evidence and written proofs, instead of judiciary combat; his ordonnance was confirmed, in 1303, by Philippe-le-Bel. Charles IX declared it high treason. Henry IV, whose conversation with Sully, as related in the memoirs of this minister, is so interesting, made it death, and he appointed the Mareschals of France to decide upon particular cases. This was confirmed, in 1626, by Louis XIII, in whose reign the Counts Montmorenci de Bouteville and Deschapelles were found guilty, and executed by a sentence of the Parliament. Yet the Countess of Bouteville, in supplicating the king to pardon her husband, concluded her affecting petition by saying, "such is the character of my husband, that if he knew he could put an end, by his death, to the rage for duels, he would come forward and offer himself as a victim."[1]

[1] Desormeaux, Hist. de la Maison de Montmorenci, III, 287.

The unhappy spirit of that particular age had irresistibly drawn him on to the crime. In the reign of Louis XIV the law punished with death and forfeiture of nobility, both the principal and seconds. This was confirmed by Louis XV.

Puffendorf approved of the plan of requiring all gentlemen to swear that they would neither send nor receive a challenge, which was sanctioned by the Mareschals of France, in the beginning of the reign of Louis XIV, and by an edict in 1651, but it does not appear to have been carried into effect. The princes of the house of Savoy have likewise endeavoured to suppress duels. Charles Emanuel I forbade them expressly, both as grand-master of the order of St. Maurice, and as sovereign, in 1619. Charles Emanuel II required all gentlemen to take an oath not to fight duels, and succeeding princes have repeated these decrees. If we take a long period of time, duelling has prevailed more in England than in France, yet in the latter country, from the reign of Henry IV to 1757, there were twelve ordonnances, and at least eight acts of regulation, each of which is introduced by a confession that the act preceding it had been ineffectual. M. de Lomenie, Secretary of State, in 1607, calculated how many French gentlemen had perished in duels, from the accession of Henry IV to that period, and he found that the number, in about eighteen years, was four thousand. During the minority of Louis XIV, three hundred of the first nobility perished in the same manner. In vain did edicts follow and confirm edicts, while a sense of religion declined.

It remains to discover, if possible, how men came to suppose that a practice, so contrary to the religion and the spirit of the middle ages, was derived from them. Without doubt, the ancient duel having been an act of law, in consequence of the circumstances of these ages, was sanctioned by the practice and opinions of some truly heroic men. Where no human judgment could decide, it was an appeal to Heaven, and the Almighty was supposed to interfere in pronouncing upon the guilty. The motto was "Dieu defend le droit," which is often true in metaphysical strictness, and to the outward eye, since, as a king exclaims,

> What stronger breast-plate than a heart untainted!
> Thrice is he arm'd that hath his quarrel just;
> And he but naked, though lock'd up in steel,
> Whose conscience with injustice is corrupted.[1]

It was an appeal to Heaven when the Marquis of Mantua, as described in the famous ballad, takes an oath, in the hermit's cell, upon the death of his nephew Baldwin, not to use a razor or change his clothes, not to enter town or city, or be unarmed, or eat on a table-cloth, or occupy a seat at a board,

> Till I see Carlotto punish'd
> Or by justice, or in fight,
> Till he dies when I accuse him,
> Pleading in the cause of right.

Let not men be over hasty in drawing a conclusion from this, favourable to the opinions of those who hold to the superior wisdom or humanity of later times. "When the judicial combat was abolished," says Sismondi, "the torture was substituted, and free men were not exempted from it. Between these two modes of seeking the truth, it is difficult to say which is the more absurd; but that of the ages which we call civilized is beyond doubt the more cruel."[2] It seems hardly fair to say that the judicial combat and the torture were equally

---

[1] Shakspeare, Henry VI, Second Part, Act III, ii.
[2] Hist. des Français, I, 214.

absurd; at least, the following examples will show that there were redeeming features in the former, which should have screened it from so odious a comparison.

When the Chevalier Boucicaut was travelling from Brussels into Prussia, being arrived at Königsberg, where were many strange knights, who had come from different countries to take part in the war, which was about to commence between the Teutonic order and the Paynims of Lithuania, he heard that a valiant Scottish knight, Messire William Douglas, had been treacherously slain by certain Englishmen. Although he had no personal acquaintance with Douglas, yet feeling that a deed of such atrocity ought not to be endured, and finding that no knight or squire had taken up the quarrel, notwithstanding the number of Scottish gentlemen there assembled, he caused proclamation to be made to all the Englihsmen: " Que s'il y avoit nul d'eulx qui voulust dire que le dict chevalier n'eust esté par eulx tué faulsement et traistreusement, que il disoit et vouloit soustenir la querelle du chevalier occis."

In the reign of Louis the Stammerer, the Countess of Gastinois was accused of having poisoned her husband. Gontran, her accuser, cousin-german of her husband, passed for so redoubted a warrior, that she was abandoned by all her relations and friends. Ingelger, a youth of seventeen, son of Tertulle, a gentleman of Brittany, presented himself as her champion, killed Gontran, and was made by the countess her heir. The Archbishop of Tours gave him in marriage the fair Adelinde, his niece, with the castles of Amboise, Buzençay, and Chatillon. From him were descended the Counts of Anjou, who mounted the throne of England. Similar to this was the combat of Sir Hugh-le-Blond, in the old ballad, where he defends the honour of the queen.[1] If it were the idea of such trials which made Chaucer's knight exclaim

> To fight for a lady ! a benedicite !
> It were a lusty sight for to see,

—surely the expression merits pardon.

There cannot be a more affecting instance of the virtue and glory belonging to the hero of these days, than that which occurs in the History of Gallien Restauré, when the brave Gallien hastens to defend the cause of his innocent mother, the beautiful Jacqueline, who was falsely accused by his wicked uncles, and about to suffer a cruel death. The first thing he heard upon his arrival, was the lamentation of the poor. "La meilleure demoiselle de ce pais," they cried, "sera aujourdhuy exilée à grand tort, les pauvres étoient soutenus par elle : maudit soit celui qui est cause que nous la perdrons." And now the awful hour arrived, when Jacqueline was conducted forth to hear the fatal sentence. Alas ! in vain did she call upon her faithful Olivier, who was slain at Roncevaux. Burgaland was the foe who defied her friends. She implored one of her relations to accept the challenge, but he replied, "Je n'entreprendrai pas cela, de combattre contre Burgaland." When Gallien saw his mother thus forsaken, and that no person dared to defend her, he advanced, took her by the hand, and said, "Madame, faites bonne chere, car jusqu'à la mort je prendrai votre cause en main et vous défendrai pour justifier votre innocence." Then the challenge was accepted, and the lists cleared. Jacqueline knew not her son : "Si elle l'eut connu," says the writer of this history, "elle eut aimé mieux être bruslée que de le laisser combattre contre Burga-

---

[1] Scott's Minstrelsy of the Border, vol. III, p. 51.

land." The combatants prepare for action; Gallien, raising his hand, and making the sign of the cross upon his forehead. Burgaland defied him in bitter terms, while Gallien, we are told, " reclama le nom de Jesus, en le priant qu'il lui voulust être en aide." The battle commenced, and Gallien seemed to sink under the blows of his adversary: " Quand la pauvre Jacqueline vit ce coup, elle se jetta la face contre terre, et se prit à pleurer en disant; vrai Dieu, vous sçavez que je suis accusée à tort, n'etant coupable aucunement de la mort de mon pere; protegez, s'il vous plait, le chevalier qui combat pour moi." But Gallien recovered himself, and replied to the taunts of Burgaland, saying, " Jesus Christ a toujours été le protecteur des innocens, j'ai esperance en lui." Burgaland foamed with rage; the people cry out for pity: " Helas! il est trop jeune, si ce n'etoit son courage il seroit deja mort." Gallien pronounced the high name of our Saviour. " Car celui," says the writer, " qui le nommera ne perira le jour qu'il les aura prononcez, s'il n'est faux ou parjure et qu'il n'ait tort en ce qu'il veut disputer." Once more all hope of Gallien seemed to be at an end, but our Lord had mercy on the child, and he gave his adversary a mortal wound, who fell dead on the spot. The historian goes on to relate, after some delay, how Jacqueline discovers him to be her son: " Quand Jacqueline l'entendit parler elle fit un cry, puis tomba pasmée; quand elle fut revenue elle commença à pleurer, vint vers Gallien et l'embrassa et dit: Loué soit Dieu, quand il m'a fait la grace de revoir mon fils, et que je le vois en santé devant moi. De tout le mal que j'ay souffert et enduré il ne m'importe, puisque j'ay recouvert mon enfant."

Another instance of single combat, according to the spirit of the middle ages, was that between Guy and Colbrand, the Danish giant, under the walls of Winchester, in the reign of King Athelstan.[1] The Danish king having landed with 50,000 men, and laid siege to Winchester, prepared to settle the question by single combat, between one of his men, Colbrand the giant, and any English warrior Athelstan might fix upon. The English king was in great distress, ashamed to own that he had not a Christian hero who was a match for this Goliah of the Pagans, while he sighed in vain for his brave Guy, Earl of Warwick, who was then absent on a pilgrimage to the Holy Land. In this extremity, he was admonished, in a nocturnal vision, to choose for his champion a poor pilgrim, whom he should find next morning at the eastern gate of the city, dressed in a manner that was then made known to him. Being early upon the watch, he accordingly sees the pilgrim described, entering the city from Portsmouth. This proved to be Guy himself, who had landed the day before at the above-mentioned haven, though greatly emaciated and disfigured by his toils and austerities. It required little persuasion to induce so good a man to resume his arms, and to risk his life in defence of his king and country. In short, the challenge is now accepted of. They meet in the vale of Chilcomb, and Colbrand is slain, after a long and doubtful combat. The shield of Florence still bears witness to the iron mace, studded with balls, with which Mugello the giant struck the shield of Everardo de' Medici, in the famous combat near the walls of that city, leaving marks of blood corresponding with the projecting balls of the club. Even in the combat between man and beast, as a trial of innocence, one almost is tempted to overlook the extravagance in the gratification which is inspired by observing how men confided in the force of

---

[1] Knighton, de Event. Angl. I, 1.

justice. Macaire, a nobleman and archer in the body-guard of King Charles V of France, in 1371, envied another nobleman of the same guard, Aubry de Montdidier. Having watched his opportunity, he at length found him in the wood of Bondy, with no other companion but his hound. Here he murdered and buried him, and returned to the court. The hound lay on the grave till hunger forced him to enter the city; and after appearing at court, and being caressed and fed by the friends of his late master, he went back to the wood; and this visit he repeated so often, and he was so dejected and miserable, making extraordinary howlings, that it drew attention, and he was watched and followed to the wood, when he was seen to lie down upon a spot, where the earth seemed to have been lately disturbed. Upon opening the ground, the body of the murdered knight was found; the dog was taken home, and on being introduced into the assembly of the nobles, he searched about, and at length, singling out the murderer, sprang at his throat, and would have strangled him, if he had not been beaten and driven back. The king was informed of the circumstance, and the dog being brought before him, in presence of the court, again flew at the knight, and seemed, by his pitiful cries, to call out for justice and revenge. The nobleman stoutly denied the charge; and the king was in the end persuaded to give orders that the nobleman and the dog should fight together on a certain day. The king and the whole court attended in the island of Notre Dame, at Paris. The nobleman was armed with a club, the dog was allowed a tub for shelter. The moment he was let loose he flew at his enemy, and though struck to the earth, he at last succeeded in seizing hold of the club, and throwing the nobleman on the ground, who then called out aloud, and promised to discover the truth, if he was delivered from the savage animal. He then confessed the murder in the presence of the king.[1] But this extravagant institution, however legally established, cannot be defended. The uniform judgment of the church condemned it. One example of its enormity is sufficient to excite horror. Le Gris and Carrouge, two gentlemen of Normandy in the reign of Charles VI, had been friends from childhood. Carrouge had followed the expedition to Scotland; on returning home, his wife, whom he tenderly loved, confessed, with shuddering, that Le Gris, his false friend, had outraged his honour. Carrouge demanded justice of the king, who referred him to the parliament. Le Gris proved, by the testimony of the Count d'Alençon, that he was twenty-three leagues distant from the castle of Carrouge at the hour when he was said to have committed the crime. The vehemence of the accuser prevailed; and it was decided that there should be gage de bataille. The combatants fought near the walls of St. Martin-des-Champs. Carrouge vanquished his enemy, who continued to deny the charge; but he was hung upon the gibbet. In course of time, a criminal, who resembled him, confessed that it was he who had committed the crime. Carrouge was in Africa, where he died: his wife, overwhelmed with remorse, enclosed herself within a walled-up cell, and spent the rest of her life in that sorrowful penance.[2]

Single combats, for a public cause and by public authority, were known to antiquity; and Strabo says of them, κατὰ ἔθος τι παλαιὸν τῶν Ἑλλήνων. Such was that of Hector and Ajax, Diomedes and Æneas, Menelaus and Paris, Æneas and Turnus; and in real history, that of Hyllus and Echemus, for the government of the Peloponnesus;[3] Hype-

[1] La Colombiere, Theatre d'Honneur et de Chevalerie, II, p. 300.
[2] La France sous les cinq premiers Valois, III, 61.
[3] Herodot. lib. IX, 26.

rochus, King of the Acheans, and Phemius, King of the Enians,[1] for the countries near the river Inachus; Pyræchmes the Etolian, and Degmenos the Eleian,[2] and that which Cyrus would have fought with the Abyssinian king; and that related by Livy,[3] between Corbis and Orsua, Spanish princes, who fought before Scipio for the principality; and that between Pyrrhus and Pantauchus, before the army. These ancient combatants made use of nets, or of any artifice by which they might overcome the enemy. Judicial combats were practised by the Pagan Saxons.[4] In the Gombette law, framed by Gondebald, King of Burgundy, the first mention occurs of duels, to which men were commanded to refer the contests which they refused to determine by oath. The Lombard laws in Italy authorized such combats, but only when fought "cum fustibus et clypeo." This mode of purgation was confirmed in England by the Conqueror; and it continued later than the reign of Henry III, though always condemned at Rome. The Salic code excluded judicial combats, which led Montesquieu to frame some very extravagant conjectures. That duels did not take place among the Goths appears from the letter of Cassiodorus, secretary to Theodoric, addressed in the name of this king to the people of Pannonia. "Be subject to justice, which gives peace to the world. Why have you recourse to single combats, when you have judges to terminate your disputes? Imitate the magnanimity of the Goths, as remarkable for moderation at home as for the terror of their arms when abroad." Gerdil ascribes this character to their intercourse with the Greeks, on the banks of the Danube. Andrew Alciat, the celebrated jurisconsult and one of the restorers of jurisprudence, main-

[1] Plutarch, Quæst. Græc. c. III.   [2] Strabo, I, 8.
[3] XXVIII, 21.   [4] Turner's Hist. of the Anglo-Saxons, I, 224.

tained that single combats for a public cause were
lawful; and he approved of the example of Charles
of Anjou, brother of St. Louis, and Peter of Aragon, who, he says (according to the common
mistake), were agreed through means of Pope
Martin, and the College of Cardinals (who, on
the contrary, used their utmost efforts to prevent
the duel, the Pope actually writing to King
Edward to put a stop to it), to meet at Bordeaux, and decide their difference by single combat, under the sanction of Edward I of England,
to whom the city belonged.[1] Grotius approved of
them,[2] as did also Puffendorf.[3] Dante maintained
the justice of the Romans' claim to empire, on the
ground of its having been given to them in duel,
when the Horatii and Curiatii fought, and afterwards in the wars with the Sabines and Samnites.[4]
Hence he seems to have deemed high qualities
necessary for those who engage in such combats:
"Scilicet, ut non odio, non amore, sed solo justitiæ zelo, de communi assensu agonistæ seu duelliones palæstram ingrediantur."[5] Gerdil, however,
following the Catholic doctors, Cajetan, Valentia,
Azovius, Sylvius, and others, maintains that such
combats were unlawful. As the old Manual of
Chivalry says, "Trial by battle was reproved by
holy church, yet allowed by royal custom and corporal seigneurie."[6] Its author utterly condemns trial
by battle as tempting God, contrary to Holy Scripture.—" Est une chose bien oultrageuse et plaine de
grande folie de vouloir veoir si clerement par visible
experience la droicturiere puissance de Dieu et soy
combattre ainsi corps a corps en estat de peche
mortel.—Si est une moult grande folie.—For if God
wished he could do it without the blow of a mortal

[1] Des Duels, c. III.   [2] Law of War and Peace, II, 23, 10.
[3] VIII, 8, 5.   [4] De Monarchia, lib. II.
[5] De Monarchia, lib. II.   [6] L'Arbre des Batailles.

sword." To the same effect argues the Clerk in the dispute with the Knight in le Songe du Vergier. Judicial combats were always condemned by the popes and councils. St. Louis suppressed them as a tempting of God. Agobard, Bishop of Lyon, in the eighth century, represented to Louis le Debonnaire, their evil as sanctioned by the Burgundian law; he wrote a treatise against superstitious trials, and shewed that duels were opposed to the Scripture. The third council of Valence, in 855, condemned them; and declared that he who killed another in a duel should be deprived of the prayers of the church. Pope Nicholas I, in a letter addressed to Charles the Bald, 867, declared strongly against making the example of David and Goliah a precedent to sanction duels. Pope Stephen V, in 888, rejected the proofs of hot iron and boiling water as superstitious inventions. Atto II, Bishop of Vercelli, in the tenth century, declared publicly that it was tempting God to seek the truth by combats. Yves, the learned Bishop of Chartres, in the end of the eleventh century, proclaimed his horror at this cruel superstition. St. Bernard, in 1146, addressed a letter to the clergy and people of the East of France, as likewise one to the Abbat Suger, in 1149, remonstrating against the barbarous practice of duels as destructive of salvation. The third council of Lateran, under Alexander III, in 1179, and the fourth, under Innocent III, in 1215, condemned superstitious trials and such combats; and lastly, St. Raymond in the thirteenth century condemned them without any exceptions, which sentence was formally approved of by St. Antony, Bishop of Florence, in the fifteenth.

As for duelling, in the proper sense of the term, that is, without obtaining permission from the highest judicial power, the church fulminated her thunder against those who practise it, in accents sufficient, as D'Audiguier says, "to make the hair stand up straight from one's head." By the ancient discipline, they who fell were deprived of Christian burial. In 1477, a council of Toledo, under Sixtus IV, renewed the ancient prohibitions, and refused burial, even though the sacrament of Penitence had been received. The first bull of Julius II, "Regis Pacifici," 1509, prohibits duelling on pain of excommunication ipso facto. The second of Leo X, "Quam Deo," 1519, orders the same penalty for the witnesses and aiders: these are confirmed by the third of Clement VII. Pius V extends the prohibition to all Christendom, and entreats the powers of the earth to assist him in suppressing such disorders. The Council of Trent pronounces excommunication and loss of Christian burial upon all duellists who fall, and calls a duel "an invention of the Devil to ruin souls by the bloody death of the body";[1] and as some doctors thought that the decree of the Council only regarded public and solemn combats, Gregory XIII, by the bull 1582, "ad tollendum," declares the penalty to be incurred by private duellists. Clement VIII, confirming all the old decrees, extends the pain to all concerned in duels, all who even have intention to fight, all seconds, advisers, and witnesses, ex industria, and all who do not use their influence to prevent them: and finally, Benedict XIV, in his Constitution "Detestabilem" of 1752, denies Christian burial to those who die off the field of their wounds, though after having received absolution. In 1654, at the general assembly of the clergy of France, the decree had been extended to all who were voluntary witnesses of a duel, and absolution from the sentence of excommunication was reserved for the bishop. Any philosopher who proposed to encou-

[1] Seas. 25.

rage the development of the whole greatness of man's nature must agree to the justice of these decisions; for to countenance an act of impiety is to corrupt honour and virtue at their source. Pope Innocent XI, Alexander VII, and Benedict XIV, have condemned the usual propositions defended by the moderns in support of duelling. It is certain that these propositions are at utter variance with the principles of the Christian religion; it is certain that with our ancestors a recklessness of life and a thirst for blood were never admitted to form a part of the character of an honourable combatant; the names of duellists are not found in history, unless for detestation.[1]

The custom of duelling without defensive armour, which began about the reign of Henry III of France, was considered as an innovation upon the law of arms; and Sir Walter Scott speaks of a book in two huge volumes, written by a French gentleman, to support the venerable institutions of chivalry against this unceremonious mode of combat. Still it is true

> Some sins do bear their privilege on earth.[2]

Pride, revenge, an ambitious spirit, a horror of following our Saviour in bearing reproach, may be among these sins, but the poet wisely says on earth, where a veil is cast over their native deformity: yet the heroic spirit of our fathers was kindled and cherished by celestial fire; and it was the steady light of faith which directed their steps. Richardson's hero, relating his answer to a challenge which he had received in Italy, and in which he had expressed his unwillingness to risk the final perdition

[1] Le vray et ancien Usage des Duels, 28.
[2] Shakspeare's King John I.

of his adversary or of himself, concludes with observing, that "this hint of a still superior consideration was likely to have more force in that Roman Catholic country, than, I am sorry to say, it would in this Protestant one." Even the profane writers, who wrote treatises on the duel, spoke with horror of the peril in which it involved the soul.[1] Men were not left ignorant of their duty in these ages: St. Romuald was of the family of the Dukes of Ravenna: having been present at a duel by his father's orders, in which his father killed his adversary, he retired shocked and humbled to the Benedictine monastery of Classis, to do penance for the crime of having been accessory to the death; and he afterwards became founder of Camaldoli, in Tuscany: there he was able to find that peace for which his gentle spirit sighed; "nam Christi jugum suave est, et onus leve; nempe mansuetudo, castitas, lenitas, bonitas, gaudium spiritus, abstinentia ab omnibus vitiis, charitas erga omnes, sancta discretio, fides immobilis, affectionum toleratio, à mundo sejunctio, cupiditas à corpore discedendi et occurrendi Domino Jesu Christo."[2]

VIII. Loyalty to their king, descending through all ranks of society, from the highest class of subjects to the lowest vassal, who was proud of his dependence upon a generous chieftain, was the essential virtue of those ages, nobly expressed by Humphrey, Duke of Gloucester, in Henry VI.[3]

> And may that thought when I imagine ill
> Against my king———
> Be my last breathing in this mortal world.

This was in obedience to one of the first laws of

---

[1] Le Sieur d'Audiguier, le vray et ancien Usage des Duels, 3.
[2] B. Esaiæ Abbat. Orat. 28, Bibl. Pat. XII.
[3] Second Part, I, 2.

knighthood;[1] but it does not follow that it was the result of any policy or contrivance on the part of the great, as Sismondi would infer, who says that men in power have always sought to make men reconcile honour with submission, and to inspire them with a fancy that there was something chivalrous in forgetting their own interest to obey the will of another. The true explanation of the facts of history can only be found by classing loyalty among the virtues which nature intended men to exercise. It is certainly a disposition which has been displayed by the generous part of mankind in every period and country of the world. Thus, when Menelaus threatens with death the messenger of Agamemnon if he does not deliver up the letters with which he was entrusted, this faithful servant triumphantly exclaims,

'Αλλ' εὐκλεής τοι δεσποτῶν θνήσκειν ὕπερ.[2]

Herodotus relates that when Xerxes was returning to Asia in a Phœnician vessel, a dreadful storm arose, so that the pilot declared the only chance of safety depended upon lightening the ship. Xerxes hearing this opinion, had the baseness to cry out, "Ἄνδρες Πέρσαι, νῦν τις διαδεξάτω ὑμέων Βασιλέος κηδόμενος· ἐν ὑμῖν γὰρ οἶκε εἶναι ἐμοὶ ἡ σωτηρίη. This appeal to the generous feelings of human nature was successful, and several of the Persians leaped into the sea.[3] The apparent incredibility of this relation will be removed on recollecting the fact, that when the Duke of York, afterwards James II, had entered the boat which was reserved for his escape from the sinking vessel, the crew who remained on board saluted him with cheers as they went down. During the massacre in the second triumvirate,

[1] Favin, Theatre d'Honneur et de Chevalerie.
[2] Euripid. Iph. in Aulid. 301. [3] Lib. VIII.

when freedom was given to slaves who dispatched their masters, one of these faithful men suffered himself to be slain sitting in the litter, that his master might escape as one of the bearers. The famous anecdote of Lucilius will remind us of an event in the history of Italy, which might be selected as a fine example of chivalrous loyalty. On the descent of Ferdinand upon the coast of Calabria, against the French, who were then in possession of Naples, the Spaniards were defeated, and Ferdinand returned to Messina, after owing his life to the generosity of his page, Giovanni di Capua, brother to the Duke of Termini. The king's horse had slipped and fallen upon him; his feet were held in the stirrup, and he was on the point of being made prisoner by the enemy, when this young man gave him his own horse, made him fly, and remained himself on foot to await the death which would have otherwise overtaken his master A noble instance of this generous spirit is related by Joinville : the Sultan requiring the person of St. Louis as a hostage from the French army, the words were hardly pronounced when "le bon chevalier Messire Geoffroy de Sargines," exclaimed with a furious voice, " on doit assez connoitre les François, pour les croire prets à souffrir mille morts plutot que de livrer leur prince entre les mains de ses ennemis. Ils aimeroient beaucoup mieux que les Turcs les eussent tous tués, qu'il leur fust reproché qu'ils eussent baillé leur roi en gaige." The king desired to be given up, but the army was resolute in its determination to refuse him. This was the only occasion when the king was disobeyed. Here again the world presented a field for exercising the spirit which a religious education had imparted in the cloister. To obey with simpleness and generosity was a virtue for temporal chivalry as well as for a religious life.

Raoul Tesson had been drawn into a conspiracy by Néel and the Comte Regnault, against William, Duke of Normandy, the Conqueror. Raoul had sworn to strike the duke the first in the battle; but when he saw the banner of Normandy, with the arms of the duke, he was seized with remorse, and communicated his scruples to some of his officers, who reminded him of his prior obligation to serve the duke; and advised him to evade his seditious oath as unlawful: "Quoi qu'il en soit, vous acquitterez votre serment envers Néel et ses complices, en frappant doucement de votre gantelet la personne du duc, et ce fait, vous tiendrez votre part." Accordingly Raoul, separating himself from the others, rode up to the duke, who was then near the king, and, without speaking, he drew off his gauntlet, and struck him on the shoulder, and then he said, "Monseigneur, ne prenez à déplaisir si je vous frappe, cela n'aye fait pour mal que je vous veuille; ainsi faire me convient pour acquitter mon serment. Je vous servirai aujourd'hui loyaument comme mon seigneur." The duke answered him, "Raoul, grand mercy; or, pensez de bien faire, je vous prie": and then the warrior flew to the head of his squadron. The manner in which William was preserved from assassination, presents a fine instance of the loyalty of those ages. It was Guy de Bourgogne who had formed the conspiracy against his friend and benefactor. He was joined by a seigneur of Coutances, Grimault du Plessis, whom the history affirms to have been of the lineage of Ganelon, and by the Comte of Bayeux, and the Vicomte du Coutentin. William set out on a journey to Valognes, doubting of nothing, and this expedition was the signal for the conspirators who assembled at Bayeux, who resolved to kill him at Valognes. A certain fool, named Galet, or Gilles, to whom the young duke used to give old clothes, in passing, remarking the sudden arrival of these different lords, began to suspect their object. Relying upon his character, he went to play off his buffooneries before them, who were enjoying themselves at table, speaking with freedom; "car pour sa folie ils ne se méfioient de lui." His suspicions were thus confirmed. "Et si print un baton sur son col," after the manner of idiots, "et ne cessa de cheminer tant, qu'il vint à Valognes devant minuit. Il heurta lourdement de son baton à la porte du logis où etoit le duc Guillaume," saying, "qu'il vouloit parler à lui, et pour chose qu'on lui sut demander, ne voulut dire ce qui l' amenoit avant qu'il ne lui eut parlé." As soon as he was admitted to the duke, he told him "qu'il etoit en grand danger d'etre pris et tué"; and so gave him the names and object of the conspirators. William refused at first to credit the account. "Mais voyant que Galet ne cessoit de brailler et crier: fuyez, fuyez, ou vous etes mort. Si saillit promptement de son lit, print ses brayes, et pour se déguiser, s'affubla d'un manteau seulement, descendit à l'étable, print un cheval, monta suz, et s'en partit chevauchant grand erre, vers les Vés St. Clement." He soon heard a great noise of horses and the clinking of arms, and judging that this was the troop of his ferocious enemies, he left the road, and hid himself in a wood, till the men had all passed on towards Valognes. Then fearing to approach Bayeux, which was the head-quarters of the conspirators, he took a road to the left, towards the sea, and at break of day arrived at a village named Ryes. As God would have it, the Seigneur of the village was risen, sitting at his door, ready to go out on his affairs, when Duke William came up, whose horse was so tired, that he was obliged to beat it with a stick: the duke saluted him to ask the road to Falaise; the Seigneur de Ryes, who recognized him, instantly cried out, "Sainte-Marie, Monseigneur, qui vous mène ainsi et en si pauvre équipage ? Qui etes vous, dit Guillaume, que me cognoissez ? Par ma foi, répondit le gentilhomme, on m'appelle Hubert de Ryes, et tiens de vous ce village sous le Comte de Bessin. Découvrez moi votre affaire hardiment, et ne me célez rien ; car, en verité je vous sauverai comme moi-meme." The duke related his story, how he was threatened and obliged to fly: the Seigneur, having heard it, made him enter his house, and then called his three sons, and said to them, "Beaux écuyers, velci votre droit seigneur ; montez à cheval, et suz toute l'obéissance que vous devez à lui et à moi, je vous commande que vous le conduisiez a Falaise, et vous gardiez d'entrer en ville, en bourg ou en village, ni en grand chemin." And after taking leave, " chevauchèrent grand erre, passèrent la rivière de Foupendant, à gué, et vindrent arriver à Falaise, où ils furent reçuz à grand joie. Quand Hubert de Ryes eut mis le duc à chemin, il demeura en sa maison, sans parfaire aucuns voyages, pensant bien que le bruit seroit bientot répandu de la fuite et poursuite de Guillaume, et que grande parole seroit de la chose. Et si, comme il etoit encore séant à sa porte, velecy venir une grande troupe de chevaucheurs, qui venoient, la bride avallée, de devers Cotentin, et le vont assermenter, s'il avoit vu Guillaume le Batard. Par foi, dit il, velecy aller, et ne peut etre loin ; car son cheval est moult travaillé. Attendez-moi, j'irai avec vous et nous le ratteindrons. Lors monta à cheval, et les mena le dit Hubert tout le contraire du chemin de Guillaume." The duke, to perpetuate the memory of the road which he took from Ryes to Falaise, caused the ground to be raised a great height at the expense of his enemies ; and this Chemin Haussé, as it is called, exists still in a few places. I have myself followed its course from the village of Cintheaux, in the direction of Fresney le Puceux.

What an interesting scene was that, after the battle of Creci, when Philippe, who had fled and wandered for a long time, at length arrived, about midnight, at the castle of La Broye, two leagues from Creci, belonging to Robert de Grandcamp, who was devoted to his service. Philippe knocked loudly at the great gate, while the old châtelain, fearful as to the fortune of the day, was on the battlements. "Hommes d'armes, qui êtes-vous?" he asked. "Si vous ne servez monseigneur de Valois vous n'entrerez oncques dans mon chastel."— "Ouvrez, ouvrez, châtelain," replied Philippe, "c'est l'infortuné roi de France." Recognizing the voice of the king, the châtelain immediately came down, let fall the bridge of the portcullis, and received the king and his suite.

A young German page had endeavoured to defend the Duke of Orleans from the murderers, and was slain in the attempt. When the assassins had fled, he was found by the duke's side in the rue du Temple, and he expired in a few minutes, with the words, "Ah mon maître! haro monseigneur, mon maître." Richard Cœur de Lion being attacked on a hunting party by a body of Saracens, when four of his companions out of six were killed, William de Porcellet cried out, in the Saracen tongue, "I am the king"; thus enabling Richard to escape, who gave in exchange for his friend the ten most powerful ameers that were among his prisoners.[1] The origin of the name of Porcellet was to be seen before the revolution in France, represented in sculpture on the portals of a house in Arles, and of another at Burgos, in Spain, belonging to the family. This William lived afterwards in Provence, honoured and beloved

[1] Vinisanf.

by the surrounding people. It was his grandson who, in the next century, was spared by the indignant multitude, in the Sicilian Vespers, in consideration of his distinguished virtue.[1]

In 1167, when all Italy had risen against the Emperor Frederick I, and he was retreating across the Alps, being at Susa, a plot was made to murder or carry him off as he lay in bed. It was discovered, and Herman von Siebeneichen, a true knight, lay down in the emperor's bed, while Frederick disguised himself, and fled away with only five attendants, favoured by the darkness.[2]

The ancient loyalty was finely evinced by the Duke of Lorraine, who, in spite of his recent and perfect alliance with René, Duke of Bar, did not the less send troops against him, to defend the Count de Ligny, to whom he had promised assistance.[3] In those distracted times when the Emperor, Henry IV, fled to Worms in his distress, the loyal conduct of the citizens there became the object of praise and imitation to the other states of the Rhine. "Celebre apud omnes erat nomen Wormatiensium pro eo quod regi fidem in adversis servassent," says Lambert von Aschaffenburg. Our age has to boast of having produced the army of La Vendée, which had Lescure and La Rochejaquelein for its heroes; whose chivalrous loyalty in defence of their king has been the subject of the memoirs of the Marchioness of La Rochejaquelein, which an illustrious German has pronounced to be the epic poem of modern times.

Let not the declamations of false patriotism, and of a base philosophy deprive this virtue of its high value, and of its ever honourable renown. Sismondi talks of "le fanatisme de loyauté."[4] Every-

[1] Papon, Hist. générale de Provence, tom. II, p. 395.
[2] Raumer, Geschichte der Hohenstaufen, II, p. 212.
[3] Hist. de René d'Anjou, tom. I, p. 43.
[4] Hist. des Repub. Ital. III, 133.

thing is fanaticism with these gentlemen, which cannot be expressed by x and y. "In a moral view," says Mr. Hallam,[1] "loyalty has scarcely perhaps less tendency to refine and elevate the heart than patriotism itself; and it holds a middle place in the scale of human motives, as they ascend from the grosser inducements of self-interest to the furtherance of general happiness, and conformity to the purposes of infinite wisdom." The language of Burke is nobler when he speaks of "that generous loyalty to rank and sex, that proud submission, that dignified obedience, that subordination of the heart which kept alive, even in servitude itself, the spirit of an exalted freedom, the unbought grace of life, the cheap defence of nations, the nurse of manly sentiment and heroic enterprise." It must be remembered, however, that the loyalty of which we speak was essentially the result of the religion which prevailed in the middle ages. With Catholics it formed part of their religion. When poor Joanna, Queen of Naples, embarked for Provence, all the people who had accompanied her to the shore, wept bitterly as she departed, and as long as her three galleys could be discerned, even as a small speck on the sea, they were watched by the anxious crowd; and, when they could no longer distinguish the frail bark which was to bear their young queen, in the depth of winter, through a passage which the nautical ignorance of the age rendered dangerous, they repaired to the churches, and surrounding the altars, besought the Almighty to grant her a safe and happy voyage. The poorest peasant thought it his duty to pray devoutly for the soul of his prince. Flatterers are loyal in the presence of princes, and in their harangues to the world: these men were loyal in the presence of their God, and in the silence of meditation and prayer: forgetting their own

[1] History of the Middle Ages.

wrongs and the ingratitude of princes, forgetting the injuries offered to their religion, resolved to believe that their king could do no evil, that he never could wish to oppress and insult them, when prostrated before the adorable victim, their solemn song was "Domine, salvum fac Regem," as if the safety of their king was the only specific object among temporal blessings for which a prayer should mount to heaven. This was certainly one of the great triumphs of the Church. "The Christian religion," says Montaigne, "has all the signs of extreme justice and utility; but none more apparent than its positive recommendation to obey magistrates." "If," says Jean de la Haye, baron des Coutaux, "princes, great, courageous, powerful lords, and the people wearied with taxes, be not restrained by the fear of God, a great state cannot endure long. If it be not supported by the reverence instilled by the prelates of the Church, excellent in manners and doctrine, it is not possible that one king can restrain them, car la force luy sera ennemie et le plus fort voudra estre roy."[1] But if loyalty was thus a part of religion, it followed of necessity that it could not be the spirit of universal passive obedience, which some French orators, in the reign of Louis XIV, appeared to inculcate, and which certain political factions in England have maintained when they ascribed to their king the supremacy of spiritual and temporal power; an obedience which belonged to Turks and Moors, but not to the sons of Christian chivalry, who feared God while they honoured their king. The fear of God was a secure and invariable foundation for this virtue to rest upon: had it depended upon sentiment alone, there would have been too many occasions presented by the cruelty or weakness of princes to prompt

---

[1] L'Origine des Poictevins, 47.

generous men to renounce it; for, sooth to say, rulers not unfrequently seem to take pains to prevent sentiment from being the source of their subjects' loyalty. The base spirit generated by a despot, which prompted men to counterfeit Alexander's wry neck, the Sicilian tyrant's dim sight, and the Æthiopian king's deformity,[1] may be discerned in the writings of the later Romans, not excepting Seneca and Pliny, the latter of whom says to Trajan, "ambulas inter nos, non quasi contingas."[2] Chivalry breathed nothing dastardly and servile. Its own feelings would have directed men to say with Achilles,

'Εγὼ δ' ἐν ἀνδρὸς εὐσιβεστάτου τραφεὶς,
Χείρωνος, ἔμαθον τοὺς τρόπους ἁπλοῦς ἔχειν,
Καὶ τοῖς 'Ατρείδαις, ἦν μὲν ἡγῶνται καλῶς,
Πεισόμεθ'· ὅταν δὲ μὴ καλῶς, οὐ πείσομαι.

I have said that the loyalty of these ages was a religious duty. It is well to inquire, therefore, what religion taught respecting submission to princes. In general, the doctrine of the holy fathers, of the schools, and of the whole Church, according to the divine command, was the duty of obedience in all temporal concerns to the civil ruler, or to whatever government was once established. It is curious to observe that the Jesuits, who have been calumniated as the inventors of the doctrine of tyrannicide, have been the most constant in their labours to promote submission to rulers, and the most faithful to practise that submission. No sooner had the unguarded sentence of Mariana appeared, than they procured its formal condemnation eleven years before the parliament of Paris considered it. Castro-Palas, Suarez, Emmanuel Sa, Valentia, Escobar, Heissius, Bécan, limit the

---

[1] Diodor. Sicul. III, 7.   [2] Panegyr.

right of subjects, in extraordinary cases, to the legal deposition of a tyrant. Father Lallemand,[1] Theophile Raynaud,[2] Julien Hayneure, and Bourdaloue, have exhausted all that can be said to enforce loyal submission, according to the divine law. However, without alluding to the frightful spectacles which the fancy of the religious innovators and the sophists of France have given to the world, in the putting to death kings, not by a legal judgment, but contrary to all laws human and divine, it is obvious to the common sense of mankind, that this was but the general duty, which could only be enforced in general terms, and that there might be cases in which kings would lose the power of commanding, when it would be the will of God that subjects should transfer their allegiance, and perhaps of necessity without premeditation. Accordingly the doctors of the Church in their writings, which were destined exclusively for the learned, and intended to be consulted by men only when they were placed in the most difficult circumstances, were obliged to meet these delicate questions, and to solve them in such a manner as might be most agreeable to justice and the divine will. The learned writer of the historical documents in defence of the Company of Jesus, has shown in an elaborate treatise,[3] that the universal doctrine was, that no man on his own authority could kill a tyrant of an established government; but that the State might in a general assembly adopt such legal measures as were absolutely necessary to put an end to intolerable tyranny. St. Thomas, the Angel of the school, and Almain, so revered in the University of Paris, both decided that a tyrant usurper might be treated

---

[1] Reflexions morales sur le Nouveau Testament, t. II, vi, p. 318.
[2] De Virtutibus et Vitiis, IV, 606.
[3] De la Doctrine du Tyrannicide.

as an outlaw,[1] and that the subjects who rose against
a legitimate tyrant would not be unfaithful.[2] Such
was the doctrine of Cajetan the Dominican,[3]
Dominique Soto,[4] Sylvestre de Prieras, Menschius,
Gonzales Salcedo, St. Bernard, the last father of
the Church, St. Bonaventure, St. Antonin of
Florence, St. Raimond de Segnafort, and Yves de
Chartres. That the tyrant, "who loaded his people
with taxes, and who opposed religious associations
and learning," might be resisted by his subjects,
was the doctrine of the famous Gerson, of the
University of Paris, taught by the Sorbonne and by
all the universities of Europe. The most celebrated
jurisconsults of all nations held the same doctrine;
such as Luca de Pena, Bartholus, Antony Rampinus,
Lewis Carreri, Anthony Massa, Hector Capicius,
Fernand Vasquez, Thomas Actius, Cataldinus de
Boncompagno, Paul Voet, Andrew Lanfranc, Conrad
Brunn, Charles Dumoulin, Paul de Castro, De Placa
de Moraca, Prosper Farinacius. Moreover, the
history of Christendom will shew that this was the
recognized and universal doctrine. It is needless to
point out the well-known instances in the early
ages of England, when it was acted upon. The
history of Italy, Germany, and Spain will prove
the unity of opinion upon this subject, which prevailed in these nations. Charlemagne, that famous
warrior, that great legislator, that restorer of the
Western empire, was told by his vassals, that if he
wished them to be faithful, he must see the laws
maintained;[5] and his laws not only permitted, but
enjoined the faithful to warn kings of their faults,

[1] St. Thom. lib. II. Sent. dist. 44, 9, 2, art. 2. Aurea Doct.
de Suprema Potestate Laica, 38.
[2] S. Thom. Opusc. 39, lib. I, cap. 6.
[3] Summa, 2, c. 2, 9, 42, art. 2.
[4] De Justitia et Jure, V, 9, 11.
[5] Petitio Populi Worm. an. 803.

and to correct them.[1] Towards the end of the reign of Philippe-le-Bel, when this prince loaded his subjects with taxes, and exercised arbitrary power, Joinville openly opposed him, and the troubles in consequence were not appeased till after the king's death, in 1315, by Louis Hutin, who sent commissioners to examine and remove the grievances occasioned by his father. Joinville, in his letter to Louis Hutin, preserved by Du Cange, directs it, "a son bon amey seigneur le roy de France et de Navarre"; and at the end of the letter he says, "Sire, ne vous desplaise de ce que je au premier parleir ne vous ay apalley que bon signeur, quar autrement ne l'ai-je fait à mes signeurs les autres roys qui ont estey devant vous, cuy Dex absoyle." Had it not been for his subsequent crime, the murder of the Duke of Orleans, the name of John Duke of Burgundy would have stood high in history, from his interference to save his vassals from the cruel tax which was proposed in 1405. And it seems hard to condemn the party of the Duke of Orleans, when, being denied common justice, they rose in arms to drive a murderer, such as the Duke of Burgundy, from near the throne. In the old ballad, we have the cry of the chivalry of Spain, when they marched under Bernardo del Carpio to oppose Charlemagne,

> Free were we born, ('tis thus they cry,) though to our king we owe
> The honour and the fealty behind his crest to go.

Bernardo goes farther than religion would allow.

> The king that swerveth from his word hath stained his purple black,
> No Spanish lord will draw the sword behind a liar's back.
> But noble vengeance shall be mine, an open hate I'll show;
> The king hath injured Carpio's line, and Bernard is his foe.

---

[1] Capit. Car. Calv. tit. 29, c. 10.

In the Chronicle of the Cid, we read how that warrior refused to kiss the king's hand. "And when King Don Alfonso saw that the Cid did not do homage, and kiss his hand, as all the other chief persons, and prelates, and council had done, he said, Since now ye have all received me for your lord, and given me authority over ye, I would know of the Cid Ruydiez why he will not kiss my hand, and acknowledge me; for I would do something for him, as I promised unto my father, King Don Fernando, when he commended him to me and to my brethren. And the Cid arose and said, Sir, all whom you see here present, suspect that by your counsel the King Don Sancho, your brother, came to his death; and therefore I say unto you, that unless you clear yourself of this, as by right you should do, I will never kiss your hand, nor receive you for my lord."[1] Again, when the King Don Alfonso took the Cid into his favour, and said unto him that he might return with him into Castille, my Cid, says the Chronicle, "thanked him for his bounty, but he said he never would accept his favour, unless the king granted what he should request; and the king bade him make his demand. And my Cid demanded, that when any hidalgo should be banished, in time to come, he should have the thirty days, which were his right, allowed him, and not nine only, as had been his case; and that neither hidalgo nor citizen should be proceeded against till they had been fairly and lawfully heard: also, that the king should not go against the privileges, and charters, and good customs of any town, or other place, nor impose taxes upon them against their right; and if he did, that it should be lawful for the land to rise against him, till he had amended the misdeed. And to all this the king accorded."

[1] Book III, p. 87.

When Prince Arthur was kept in prison at Falaise by his uncle King John, Holinshed says, "There were divers of his captaynes which uttered in plaine wordes that he should not find knyghtes to keep his castells, if he dealt so cruelly unto his nephew."[1] The letter of Eudes II, Count of Champagne, to King Robert of France, is a noble specimen of chivalrous boldness. The king, without having heard the cause, had judged him unworthy of his fiefs. It is not the attack upon his estates that he deplores, but that upon his honour. "How could I refrain from defending my own honour? God can bear witness, in my soul, that I had rather die with honour than live with shame."

In these ages, were not wanting men of brave spirits, who would advise their king, as the Portuguese nobles did Affonso the Brave in the Council at Lisbon. "It is true," says Ramon Muntaner, in his chronicle, "that every one, whether great or small, is bound to advise his lord whenever he can be of service to him: and if it should be a man who cannot speak personally to the king, he ought to address himself to some one who can mention it to him; or at least he ought to communicate it by writing. And if the king should be wise enough to perceive the excellence of the advice, he ought to follow it; and if he should not, at least he who gave it will have a clear conscience, and have performed his duty. It was with this view that I composed a discourse, which I sent by a secretary to the king and the infante, to Barcelona; for I was not able to mount on horseback to go myself." Then follows the discourse in Catalan verse.[2] Castiglione decides, that a gentleman ought to quit the service of a prince, if it should reflect dishonour upon him: "for such as attend upon the bad must

[1] 555. [2] Chap. CCLXXI.

be bad."[1] He says, that to direct and persuade
his prince to good, and dissuade him from evil, is
the true fruit of the courtier's art.[2] A number
of French nobles, who had vainly interposed to
save Conrad, immediately left the court of Charles
d'Anjou in disgust, when the young prince was
put to death. Among them, Robert de Béthune,
before leaving Naples, killed, with his own hand,
Pietro di Bari, who had pronounced the iniquitous
sentence; and he made his servants execute justice
upon the wretch whose hand had fulfilled it. In
like manner Gaucher de Châtillon, Constable of
France, after vainly endeavouring to save Jacques de
Molay, the grand master of the Templars, left the
Court of Philippe-le-Bel, in 1313. The great then
were not mere courtiers, who required to be insulted
to learn that they ceased to please. A word, a look,
was sufficient for them; and they hastened from the
court to the vassals whom they protected, and to
the castles amidst the woods and rivers which were
so dear to them. When Edward the Black Prince,
in his last years, began to impose heavy taxes, and
to act with injustice, the virtuous Sir John Chandos,
whose zeal and fidelity had been so well proved,
withdrew from court to his estate in Normandy,
where he remained till summoned once more by the
prince to assist him in his last danger.[3] Sir
Walter Mauny was travelling through France with
a safe-conduct from the Duke of Normandy. When
he came to Orleans, for all his letter, he was arrested, and brought to Paris, and there put in
prison. When the Duke of Normandy knew
thereof, he went to the king his father, and
shewed him how Sir Gaultier of Mauny had his safe-conduct; wherefore he requires the king, as much

---

[1] Courtier, lib. II, 141.   [2] Lib. III, 360.
[3] La France sous les cinq premiers Valois, II, 271.

as he might, to deliver him. The king answered and said, how he should be put to death, for he reputed him for his greatest enemy. "Then," said the duke, "Sir, if ye do so, surely I will never bear armour against the King of England, nor all such as I may let": and at his departing, he said, "that he wolde never enter agayn into the kynge's host." Finally, Sir Walter was liberated, and honoured by the king, who dismissed him with presents.

I shall quote but one example more, and that from an early age of our Christian chivalry. When Theodoric, in his old age, became tyrannical, and promoted covetous ministers, who loaded the people with intolerable burdens, and practised many crimes, Boëthius undertook to lay before the king in private the tears of his subjects; but finding no redress, he publicly addressed him in the full senate-house. He professed the most steady allegiance in his own name, and that of the other senators; but they desired the liberty, which was their inheritance, of laying open their grievances. He reminded him, that there is no tribute comparable to the precious advantage which a prince derives from the love of his subjects; he entreated him to re-assume that spirit which made him reign in their hearts; to listen to those whose loyalty had been approved by the successes of his prosperous reign; to bear his subjects in his bosom, not to trample them under his feet, and to remember that kings are given by Heaven for the happiness of the people; not to govern by the utmost exertion and extent of their power, but by the rule of their obligations; to be the fathers of children, not the masters of slaves, and to reign over men, not as tyrants at will, but so that the laws themselves only govern. This generous speech was deemed by the king an act of rebellion, and Boëthius was banished by a decree of the mercenary, ungrateful senate.

After which sentence, by the king's order, he and his father-in-law, Symmachus, were carried prisoners to the strong fortress of Pavia, in 523. Trigilla and Conigast unjustly accused them of high treason, and Symmachus was beheaded. Boëthius was tortured and put to death in a castle situated in a desert place, midway from Pavia to Rome, in the 55th year of his age, 23rd of October, 525. He had zealously seconded the Pope, St. John, in defending the faith; he fell a martyr to the liberty of the people, to the dignity of the Roman senate, and in part to the Catholic faith.

IX. From the loyalty of those ages, we pass to a consideration of the friendship which often accompanied it, and which belonged essentially to the chivalrous spirit. Alexander honoured Craterus, and loved Hephæstion, because he knew that the former loved the king, the latter Alexander.[1]

Vinisauf will furnish many instances in which heroic friendship was displayed. Shortly after the feast of All Saints, a party being sent out to forage, preceded by a troop of Templars, the Turks rushed suddenly upon them in great multitudes. The Templars jumped down from their horses, and standing back to back, prepared to fight to the last, and already three of them were slain. A most obstinate battle ensued, when lo! Andrew de Chamgui, with a fresh force, came to the assistance of the Templars; but the Turks, still pouring on in greater numbers, were again too strong for the Christians, when King Richard, hearing the tumult, dispatched the Counts of St. Paul and of Leycester, with William of Cageu and Otho de Pransinges, and immediately after, armed himself and followed. In the mean time the counts, as well as the Templars, were engaged with an overwhelming force of the enemy. King

---

[1] Plutarch's Apophthegms.

Richard came up, and his escort immediately represented the madness of encountering such a host. "Oh, king," they said, "we ought not to begin what we shall not be able to finish; we do not deem it right with so few to combat such a multitude of the enemy, whom you cannot resist; and let not the hope of Christianity perish; it is a wiser counsel that you should be safe, when we can decline the danger." To which reasoning and persuasion the king replied, his colour changing with his boiling blood: "Sith I have sent dear comrades to battle, with a promise of following to assist them, if, as I have engaged, I do not defend them with all my strength, but being absent and wanting, which Heaven forbid, they should meet death, I will never again usurp the name of king." So with no more words, rushing into the midst of the Turks, like a thunderbolt, he pierced through and cut them down, and dispersed them, killing, amongst others, a famous ameer called Avalchais; and then, with many prisoners and his friends delivered, he returned to the camp.[1] There is extant a sirvente, dictated by Richard while in prison, of which one of the stanzas is to the following effect: "Let my English, Norman, Gascon, and Poitevin barons be assured, that I never had a companion so vile, that I would not pay for his deliverance."[2] This was no uncommon virtue.

The first thought of René d'Anjou, when cast a prisoner into the Tower of Bar, in Dijon, was to procure a ransom for his companions in misfortune, that they might return home to Lorraine, while he should be left alone in the Tower of Bar.[3]

When praising the Marquis of Montferrat, Rambaud de Vaqueiras reminds him of their common

---

[1] Lib. IV, 30.   [2] Hist. des Troubadours, I, 59.
[3] Hist. do René d'Anjou, I, p. 163.

adventures. "You remember, my lord, when we were about attacking Azaistrigo, 400 knights pursued you as hard as they could spur. With ten companions only, you faced about upon them, and they feared you more than the crane does the falcon. I came up when you had great need of me. We raised up the Marquis Albert, who had been disarmed. I have been in hard prisons for having well served you in your wars; many are the good strokes I have made for you. At Messina I covered you with my mantle; I came very à-propos to the battle, at the moment when lances, arrows, swords, and knives were at your face and breast; and when you took Rondasso, Paterno, Palermo, and Calatagirone, &c., I was the first under your banner."

"The Cid," says the Chronicle, "sent for all his friends, and his kinsmen, and vassals, and told them how King Don Alfonso had banished him from the land, and asked of them who would follow him into banishment, and who would remain at home. Then Alvar Fañez, who was his cousin-german, came forward and said, 'Cid, we will all go with you, through desert and through peopled country, and never fail you. In your service will we spend our mules and horses, our wealth and our garments, and ever while we live be unto you loyal friends and vassals.' And they all confirmed what Alvar Fañez had said, and the Cid thanked them for their love, and said that there might come a time in which he should guerdon them."[1]

This resembled the friendship which actuated the kinsmen and comrades of Sir Launcelot of the Lake. What a display is there of "the braveries of the princely friendship" in that generous reply of Sir Bors, when he is informed of the hero's misfortunes! "Sir," said Sir Bors, "alle is welcome that

---

[1] Lib. III, 97.

God sendeth us, and we have had moche wele with you and moche worshyp, and therfor we wille take the wo with you, as we have taken the wele." These are the sentiments of Theseus when he consoles Hercules, whom he finds sitting with his head covered through shame and horror for having slain his own wife and children in his madness.

$$\chi\acute{\alpha}\rho\iota\nu\ \delta\grave{\epsilon}\ \gamma\eta\rho\acute{\alpha}\sigma\kappa o \upsilon\sigma\alpha\nu\ \grave{\iota}\chi\theta\alpha\acute{\iota}\rho\omega\ \phi\acute{\iota}\lambda\omega\nu,$$
$$\kappa\alpha\grave{\iota}\ \tau\tilde{\omega}\nu\ \kappa\alpha\lambda\tilde{\omega}\nu\ \mu\grave{\epsilon}\nu\ \ddot{o}\sigma\tau\iota\varsigma\ \grave{\alpha}\pi o\lambda\alpha\acute{\upsilon}\epsilon\iota\nu\ \theta\acute{\epsilon}\lambda\epsilon\iota,$$
$$\sigma\upsilon\mu\pi\lambda\epsilon\tilde{\iota}\nu\ \delta\grave{\epsilon}\ \tau o\tilde{\iota}\varsigma\ \phi\acute{\iota}\lambda o \iota\sigma\iota\nu\ \delta\upsilon\sigma\tau\upsilon\chi o\tilde{\upsilon}\sigma\iota\nu\ o\check{\upsilon}.[1]$$

To be as faithful as the lion was to Geoffroi de la Tour, is a promise repeatedly occurring in the old annals. Geoffroi was one of the boldest knights in the first crusade. One day, as he passed near a wood at the head of his troop, he heard the roar of a lion, and his companions were unable to dissuade him from going to seek the adventure. He saw a lion, round which a horrible serpent was entwined, and with great dexterity he killed the serpent with his sword, without hurting the lion. The grateful animal lay down at his feet, and followed him ever after when he went to hunt or to battle. When Geoffroi embarked to return to France, the captain of the vessel, refusing to take his companion on board, the lion threw itself into the sea, and swam after the ship till its strength failed, and it sank in the midst of the waters.

Of the princely friendship, old romances present repeated instances, each in more lively colours than the other. When Arthur heard how his Knight Governar was kept in the castel of Brosse, to be exposed to the "mervaillous and right horrible monster the foulest figure that ever was seen or heard of—'Wel, maister,' said Arthur, 'sith it is thus as ye saye, as God helpe me, there is nothing shal holde

[1] Eurip. Hercul. Fur. 1223.

me, but I wyl go thither and put my body in jeopardy for his, for it were a great shame for me thus to leese my knyght; therefore, Bawdewyn, frend, make redy al my gere, for I wyl remeve tomorrow betymes, for certaynly I wyll abyde no lenger for al the worlde': and whan the maister herd him, he knew wel that there was none myght let hym of hys enterpryse: how be it, he sayde: 'Sir, he ought not to be reputed neither for sage nor wise that wyl take on hym suche a thyng that he cannot acheve, and to go there as perill is without remedi: it is no hardines thus to do, but a ful gret foly: therefore, syr, for Goddes sake, abyde.' 'Maister,' quod Arthur, 'speke no more to me thereof, for sureli, sir, I wyl go thyder and loke ones on that foule monster, though he be the devyl of hell.'"[1] And, in the same romance, after the defeat and slaughter of the emperor's troops, "when he was in prison, sore syck, and herd the great sorow that was made in the castel on their bringing in the body of the Kyng of Mormalles, who was slain by Kyng Florypes—'Ye!' sayd the emperor, 'and how doth Kyng Florypes? I charge you, tell me the trouth.' 'Syr, for Goddes sake, enquyre noo more of that matter tyl ye be perfite hole.' 'I wyl not,' sayd the emperor, 'I wyl know it.' 'Syr, sith it please you, I shal tell you the playne troth: it is so, indeed al your people are destroyed, and your brother, King Florypes, and al your other kynges, are al slayn.' And when the emperor herd that, he had so gret sorows, that he closed his tethe togyder, and cast his handes abrode, and therwith his heart did ryve asonder, and so dyed for sorowe."[2]

Another example occurs in the dark page of Angevin history. When that wicked man, Bertrand

[1] Arthur of Little Britayne, p. 161. [2] Ib. p. 516.

de Born, fell at last into the hands of his enemy, Henry II, king of England, the latter wished to indulge his vengeance before sending him to death; and, having called him into his tent, and rallied him on his former boasts, concluded by saying, "I believe, indeed, that you have lost your senses." "Yes, seigneur," replied Bertrand, with a melancholy tone, "I lost them the day when the valiant young king, your son, died: that day I lost my senses, my genius, my understanding." At the name of his unnatural son, which he did not expect to hear pronounced, the king burst into tears and fainted away. On coming to himself he was quite changed: his plans of vengeance were gone, and he beheld in the man who was in his power, only the ancient friend of the son whom he regretted. Instead of reproaches, sentence of death, or ruin, "Sire Bertrand, Sire Bertrand," said he, "it is right and well that you lost your senses for my son, for he wished your welfare more than any man living; and, for the love of him, I give you life, your goods, and your castle: I give you my friendship and my grace, and I grant you five hundred marcs of silver, to repair the losses you have sustained."

On some occasions, this spirit of loyal friendship gave rise to vows and engagements. Thus Thiebaut V, Count of Blamont, founded the order of Fidelity, in 1416, at Bar, in which city, forty knights of Lorraine were solemnly associated, engaging to "love and aid each other in good as well as in bad fortune." Their decoration was a hound with a collar, on which was engraved, "Tout ung."[1] In like manner René d'Anjou, King of Naples, created a fraternity of knights, entitled of the Crescent, with

[1] Hist. de René d' Anjou, par le Victe. de Villeneuve, tome I, p. 19.

engagements similar to those which existed between St. Louis and Hugues, duc de Bourgogne, Clisson and Duguesclin. If one of the knights should be in prison, or should have fallen sick in a far country, and any one or many of his companions should pass within ten leagues of the place where he lay, these were under obligation to visit him, or, at least, to send some other knight, in case they could not trust their own persons.[1]

Boucicaut, returning from Jerusalem, heard that Philippe d'Artois, Comte d'Eu, as he returned from the Holy Land, had been arrested by the Sultan, and conducted to Damascus. Boucicaut hastened thither, and finding all his efforts to liberate his friend fruitless, he remained with him a voluntary prisoner for four months, at the bottom of an infected dungeon. A knight felt himself bound to assist a brother in arms, even before attending to the wants of a lady. It was a still stronger obligation than that which held him to defend women.[2]

In the year 1438, Annibale Bentivoglio was treacherously arrested by Francisco Piccinino, governor of Bologna, and kept in chains in the fortress of Varrano, in the neighbourhood of Parma. Five young friends of Annibale set out secretly from Bologna to deliver him. These were Galeazzo and Saddeo, sons of Mess. Lodovico di Marescotti de Calvi, Zenese Parolaro, Jacobo di ser Giorgio de Malavolti Strazzaruolo, and Michele di Martino da Bologna. On the night of the ninth of June, they arrived at the fortress of Varrano. They were provided with a ladder of ropes, but at the foot of the wall they found a wooden ladder, which had been left there by accident. Galeazzo raised this to the wall of the fortress, and fastened to it the ladder of

[1] Hist. de René d'Anjou, par le Victe. de Villeneuve, tome II, p. 42.
[2] Hist. de la Chevalerie Française, par Gassier, p. 18.

ropes, which being lifted up by a long lance, he threw round the corner of a battlement, and so mounted first upon the wall. Having tied it firmly, he said to his comrades, "Venite su." When all were on the top, they drew up the ladder, and during this time, a violent thunderstorm, with rain, burst over the place. Galeazzo said to Zenese, "Where is Annibale?" for Zenese being a relation of the governor, had been frequently admitted into the fortress, and was able to point out the spot where their friend was confined. Upon arriving at the door of his prison, they found it locked and barred. It was near two hours before daybreak. Then Zenese said, "Let us wait for daylight, when the guard will come to open the door of the tower." At sunrise the governor called one of his servants, named Marchese, and ordered him to open the doors. The sentinel, upon going to the tower, was seized by Galeazzo. The governor heard the noise, and asked what was the matter. "You are betrayed," was the reply; but the governor heard it not. Galeazzo said to Michele and Jacobo, "Hold him fast, and if he speak a word dispatch him." Then Galeazzo, with Saddeo, his brother, ran into the tower to seize the other guard, who had mounted to sound the bell, and they caught him, crying, "Traitor! if you sound it you are a dead man." They took him prisoner, and upon descending, they found Marchese dead, for he had persisted in crying out, and so Michele di Martino had been obliged to kill him. They then locked the apartment of the governor's wife, and desired the servant, upon pain of death, to go with them to the door of the governor's room, and demand entrance. The governor opened his door, and was immediately seized by Galeazzo. Upon discovering Annibale, they liberated him by means of hammers and punches, which they had provided to disengage his feet from the irons. They remained in the castle all that day, fearing the people of the village, and were careful to ring the Ave-Maria and the bell at change of guard, and to observe the usual customs of the castle, which Zenese knew; and so the people below remained in ignorance of what had occurred. At one hour after midnight, they left the castle, having taken out the tongue of the bell, and thrown it into the ditch; and getting down the wall, they destroyed the ladder. Then they had said to the governor's wife, "We are going in the name of God, and we shall take your husband with us, and if you raise the least alarm, we will put him to death." They then tied the governor, and after carrying him for ten miles, they set him free. Finally they arrived at Bologna with Annibale Bentivoglio, where they succeeded in expelling Piccinino, and restoring their friend to his former prosperity.[1]

The dark history of the wars of Italy is relieved with many such instances. Against Conrad, the last of the Hohenstaufen, were the formidable party of the Gwelfs and the might of the French; but for him were youth, and heroic courage, and the hearts of men and women. Conrad and his friend Frederic, conducted to Naples by Charles of Anjou, were condemned as high traitors. They were playing at chess when the messenger arrived, who declared the sentence of death. They heard it calmly, and played on. As in their lives, so in their deaths, were they united, and died, an eternal model of heroic courage and friendship.

When the Mareschal de Boucicaut, between whom and Saintré the friendship was proverbial, had at length obtained his freedom, having paid his ransom to Bajazet, he refused to avail himself

[1] Muratori, Rer. Ital. Script. tom. XVIII, 607.

of his liberty while his friend and companion, the Comte de Nevers, who had been taken prisoner with him in the same battle, should continue a captive in the hands of the Turks. Upon his return to prison, the count said to him, "Ha Mareschal, de quel couraige venez vous vous mettre derechef en ceste dure et maudite prison, quand vous vous en pouvez aller franchement en France?" to which Boucicaut replied, "Monseigneur, ja à Dieu ne plaise que je vous laisse en ceste contrée. Ce ne sera mie tant que j'auray au corps la vie: à grand honte et à grand mauvaistié me debvroit tourner de vous laisser emprisonné en lieu si divers, pour m'en aller aisier en France." After a considerable time, the Mareschal succeeded in obtaining the deliverance of his friend, and then they both together returned to France, after burying, with all the honours in their power, the body of the noble Comte d'Eu, who had died in the same prison.

In the Palmerin of England, we read how the noble Primaleon, upon hearing of the misfortunes which had befallen his dear friend, Don Duardos, "departed as covertly as he might from Constantinople, renouncing father, mother, wife, children, lands, living, and all, that the loyalty he bore to his friend might declare, he preferred his safety before his own solace. And that his deeds might be answerable to his good intent, he vowed to travail the course of his life, to search in every desolate and unfrequented place, but he would find his dear friend, Don Duardos, whose welfare he as heartily desired as his own life."

This duty of searching after lost friends, is called into constant exercise by the writers of old romance. When a knight perished in a distant country, his friends were sure to complain like Achilles, when he heard of the death of Patroclus—

―――――― ὁ μὲν μάλα τηλόθι πάτρης
'Εφθιτ'· ἡμεῖο δὲ δῆσεν, ἀρῆς ἀλετῆρα γενέσθαι.

Thus the strange knight accosted the Greek knight, (Amadis, who was returning to Great Britain after his long absence,) saying, "We would enquire a thing for which we have undergone great toil, and will yet go through more. Know you any tidings of a knight called Amadis of Gaul, in quest of whom his friends are perishing, and wandering all over the world? When the Greek knight heard this, the tears ran down his cheeks for pure joy, to think how true his friends and kinsmen were to him";[1] and the scenes which generally ensued upon meeting, may be exemplified in that passage of the same Romance,[2] when Don Brian of Monjaste meets his friends unexpectedly, "that good knight who would have been everywhere beloved for his own worth, even though he had not been son to King Ladasin of Spain. When he saw the troops of his friends unexpectedly, he alighted and went towards them with open arms, saying, I would embrace you all at once, for I regard you all as one." We have seen in Tancredus, that some went to the Crusade, "that they might not leave their friends." A similar instance is furnished by Rambaud de Vaqueiras, where he says to the Marquis de Montferrat, "Then when you went to the Crusade, I had no wish, God pardon me, to pass beyond sea. But to comply with your entreaties, I took the cross and made my confession, and went under your standard." And as far back as in the time of Homer we have a similar example; for Minerva discloses to Nestor that all the other companions of his guest are but youths from Ithaca, who followed him for friendship's sake—

[1] Book III, 15.   [2] IV, 5.

οἱ δ'ἄλλοι φιλότητι νεώτεροι ἄνδρες ἔπονται
πάντες ὁμηλικίῃ μεγαθύμου Τηλεμάχοιο.[1]

Homer says, that Achilles came to the siege of Troy only through regard for the Atridæ, which Pausanias remarks will justify the hero for remaining aloof on being injured. Xenophon only followed the war as a volunteer, for he went with Cyrus that he might enjoy the friendship and conversation of Proxenus. We have a similar example in the old tragedy. Orestes says, speaking of his young friend Pylades, "I indeed go on this voyage on account of these calamities,

οὗτος δὲ συμπλεῖ τῶν ἐμῶν μόχθων χάριν."

And when Orestes refuses to fly, if Pylades must be sacrificed in his place, the latter refuses to survive in the event of Orestes being made the victim, saying,

κοινῇ τ' ἔπλευσα, δεῖ με καὶ κοινῇ θανεῖν.

Orestes still perseveres; shews him how much more reasonable and fit it is that he, Orestes, a wretched exile, should die, and not Pylades, who is innocent and happy: finally he desires him to return home, and to marry his sister, and to cherish her for his sake; so he concludes,

καὶ χαῖρ'· ἐμῶν γὰρ φίλτατόν σ' εὗρον φίλων.
ὦ συγκυναγὲ καὶ συνεκτραφεὶς ἐμοί,
ὦ πόλλ' ἐνεγκὼν τῶν ἐμῶν ἄχθη κακῶν.[2]

Euryalus displays such friendship for Nisus, when the latter had disclosed his intention of making a night-expedition.[3] The scene in the forest, when Nisus endeavours to deliver his friend, and they

---

[1] Odyssey, III, 363. [2] Eurip. Iph. in Taur. 600, 675, 708.
[3] Æneid, IX.

both perish, must only be described by Virgil. When the companions of Ulysses were tempted by Circe to enter her fatal dwelling, Eurylochus held back διϊσάμενος δόλον εἶναι, and saw them depart to destruction, and only wept; and then he returned to Ulysses, and related the event. Ulysses, without saying a word, takes up his sword and his bows, and then bids him lead on the same way back. The cowardly traitor endeavours to dissuade him. There is nothing finer in chivalrous record than the spirit which breathes in the answer of Ulysses:

> Εὐρύλοχ', ἦτοι μὲν σὺ μέν' αὐτοῦ τῷδ' ἐνὶ χώρῳ,
> Ἔσθων καὶ πίνων, κοίλῃ παρὰ νηὶ μελαίνῃ·
> Αὐτὰρ ἐγὼν εἶμι· κρατερὴ δέ μοι ἔπλετ' ἀνάγκη.[1]

It was this same Eurylochus who was such an enemy to night-adventures, the advocate of comfort and prudence.[2] When Amadis, Galaor, and Sir Balays came to the cross-road, where the dead knight was lying on a bed, they were all greatly amazed. Then said Galaor, "I swear by my faith of knighthood not to leave the place till I know who this knight was, and why he was slain, and to revenge him if justice demand it." "Brother," answered Amadis, "this vow somewhat displeaseth me; I fear it will detain you long." It was, indeed, a rash vow; and he who made it was guilty of much extravagance. In addition, Amadis thought of Oriana, from whose sight he would not willingly be hindered; nevertheless Galaor replied, "I have sworn." And he alighted, and seated himself by the bed, and his comrades did the same, for they would not leave him alone.[3] The squire of the Knight of La Mancha, resolving on one awful occasion to follow his lord, the author of that history infers, that he must

[1] Odyss. X.   [2] See his Speech, Od. XII, 279.
[3] Vol. I, c. 23.

have been of noble descent, or at least the offspring of the old Christians. St. Augustine commemorates the friendship which Nebridius, a young African, evinced for him; who forsook his own country near Carthage, and Carthage itself, so familiar to him, his paternal farm, his house and his mother, and for no other cause came to Milan, unless that he might live with him.[1] When Sir John of Hainault went into England, to accompany the Queen Isabel, though the adventure was one of great pain and peril, yet, we read, "there were great plentye, what of one countrey and other, that were content to go with hym, for his love."

> Men through all fortunes faithful to their lord,
> And, to that old and tried fidelity,
> By personal love and honour held in ties,
> Strong as religious bonds.

In our heroic history, the greatest emperor was as faithful in his friendship as the poorest squire. When Charlemagne heard of the death of Pope Adrian, who was his bosom friend, Eginhard says, that he wept and lamented, as if he had lost his brother or his son. Erat enim in amicitiis optime temperatus, ut eas et facile admitteret et constantissime retineret; colebatque sanctissime quoscunque hac affinitate sibi conjunxerat. Such was the friendship of the King of France for his constable, Oliver de Clysson. Froissart speaks of the night when Sir Oliver de Clysson so narrowly escaped death, from the hands of Sir Peter of Craon and his company, when struck in the head by falling from his horse right against a baker's door, who was up, and busy to bake bread, and had left his door half open, so that he fell in at the door, (God shewing great grace to the constable; for if the

---
[1] Confess. VI, 10.

door had been shut, he would have been slain without remedy.) Speaking of that night, he says, "tidings came to the kyng's lodging, and it was told to the kyng, as he was goynge to his bedde"; the constable had left the palace long after midnight, "and while riding with his company, and his torches besyde him, and talking with a squire of his, saying, tomorrowe I must have to dyner with me the Duke of Thourayne, the Lord Coucy, Sir Johan of Vyen, Sir Charles Dangers, the Baron of Ivry, and divers others, wherfore speke to my stewarde that they lacke nothing; and saying of these wordes, issuing out of the street of St. Powle, and coming into the hygh streate, Sir Peter of Craon and his company, who had made good spyall on him that night, came upon him, and strucke out the torche, and the constable thought it was the Duke of Thourayne that followed and sported with him, and sayd, Ah, Sir, it is yvell done; but I pardon you, ye are young, and full of play and sporte; but soon he was undeceived, and well nigh murdered, as is well known." So when it was said to the king, "Ah, Sir, we cannot hyde fro you the great myschief that is now sodenly fallen in Paris. What myschiefe is that? quod the kyng. Sir, quod they, your constable, Sir Olyver of Clisson, is slayne. Slayne, quod the kynge; and howe so, and who hath done that deed? Sir, quod they, we cannot tell, but this myschiefe is fallen on hym, hereby in the streat of St. Kateryn. Well, quod the kyng, light up your torches; I wyll go and se hym. Torches anone were lighted up. The kyng put on a cloke, and his slyppers on his fete: then such as kept watch the same nyght went forth with the kyng; and such as were abed, and heard of these tydynges, rose up in hast and followed the kyng, who was gone forth with a small company, for the kyng tarried for no man, but went forth with them of his chamber with torches, and came to the baker's house and entered, and certayn torches taryed without. Then the kyng found his constable nere dead, but not fully dead, and his men had taken off all his gear to see his woundes; and the fyrst worde that the kyng said was, Constable, howe is it with you? Dear Sir, quod he, ryght febly. Who hath brought you in this case? quod the kyng. Syr, quod he, Peter of Craon and his company, traytoursly and without defense. Constable, quod the kyng, there was never dede so derely bought as this shall be. And the surgeons gave good hopes, and the constable thanked the king for his noble vysytacyon; and the kyng departed, and by that time it was clere daylight."

The friendship of the last Darius was admirable. When all advised him to break down the bridge of the Cydnus, to retard the enemy's pursuit, he answered, "I will never purchase safety for myself at the expense of so many thousands of my subjects, as must by these means be lost": and his last words are a most affecting evidence. When Polystratus brought him some cold water, as he lay in his last moments, when he had drunk, he said, "Friend, this fills up the measure of my misfortunes, to think that I am not able to reward thee for this act of kindness. But Alexander will not let thee go without a recompense, and the gods will reward Alexander for his humanity to my mother, to my wife, and children. Tell him I gave him my hand, for I give it thee in his stead." So saying, he took the hand of Polystratus, and immediately expired.

When there were such kings, it is not strange that there should have been subjects ready to die for them, as for the friend of their heart. When Chnodomar, King of the Alamanni, was taken by the Romans, two hundred of his companions, and three of his intimate friends, delivered themselves up voluntarily, resolved either to share his captivity, or to die with him.[1] Jean de Troyes bears testimony to the love which was borne to Charles VII by his pages, for, in relating the funeral of this monarch, he says, that six of his pages were next the body, mounted on horses covered with black velvet: "Et Dieu sçait le douloureux et piteux deuil qu'ils faisoient pour leur dit maistre. Et disoit on lors que l'un de dits pages avoit esté par quatre jours entiers sans boire et sans manger, pour cause de la dite mort."[2]

The favour of kings was not deemed a compensation for the loss of a friend. Henry IV of France was so inconsistent as to complain of the Comte d'Aubigné, for continuing his friendship to the Seigneur de la Trémouille, who was exiled from court: "Sire," replied the count, "Monsieur de la Trémouille is sufficiently unhappy in having lost the favour of his master; I have deemed it my duty not to abandon him at the time when he stands most in need of my friendship."

"The Spaniards," says the Countess d'Aulnoy, "never forsake their friend in sickness; their cares and concern are far greater in time of affliction, and they make it a point to visit their friend three or four times a day, though, on other occasions, they nay not meet four times in the year." The spirit of religion here breaks out. St. Jerome said, speaking of the charity of the ancient monks, that the sick person used to be tended with such attention, "that he wanted neither the delights of a city, nor the affection of a mother." Thus the green knight, in Tristan, came to ransom his friend, who expresses his wonder how a younger son could find so much money, "Ne vous mettez pas en peine," he replied; "en grande nécessité voit-on les grands amis et selon le proverbe besoin fait trotter la vieille."

[1] Ammian. Marcellin. XVI, 13. [2] P. 18.

It is admirable to contemplate the power of friendship in heroic times. In vain had a multitude of heroes displayed prodigies of valour before the walls of Troy; in vain had the gods themselves taken part in the combat. Achilles alone can put an end to the bloody strife, and when at length he issues forth from his tent, it is to revenge his friend; one, he declares, as dear to him as his own father.[1] Plato, for the sake of a friend, poor and in exile, exposed himself to the fury of a tyrant, travelled through many lands, passed over the sea, and shunned no danger, when it was in his power to have remained contemplating in the Academy, and nourishing his mind with the study of truth.[2]

Alcinous supposes that the tears which Ulysses sheds, on hearing Demodocus sing the fall of Troy, proceed from the love of some companion whom he lost there in battle, and concludes with a general position, saying,

——— οὐ μὲν τι κασιγνήτοιο χερείων
Γίγνεται, ὅς κεν, ἑταῖρος ἰὼν, πεπνυμένα εἰδῇ.[3]

Æschylus ascribes the virtue of friendship to the gods. Thus Vulcan, being contrained by Jupiter to chain down Prometheus, expresses his horror and reluctance:

τὸ ξυγγενές τοι δεινὸν, ἥ θ' ὁμιλία.

The chorus, when threatened with the vengeance of Jupiter, refuses to leave Prometheus alone, Mercury warns them, that Prometheus is about to be visited with dreadful thunder. The chorus is immovable.

μετὰ τοῦδ', ὅ τι χρὴ, πάσχειν ἐθέλω·
τοὺς προδότας γὰρ μισεῖν ἔμαθον.

---

[1] Il. XIX, 321.   [2] Max. Tyr. Dissert. XXI, 9.
[3] Odyss. VIII, 585.

Prometheus and the chorus disappear together, amidst thunder and darkness.

According to another account, "Hercules, seeing Prometheus so cruelly punished for his benevolence to men, took up his bow, and shot the vulture which preyed upon his liver; and persuading Jupiter to relent, preserved the common benefactor."[1]

To pass over the extravagant and cruel act to which friendship led Amys and Amylion, our old romances present instances of the most perfect friendship. Vainly did the devil tempt the good king Don Rodrigo to refrain from fulfilling the last request of the old hermit. "And the king marvelled at this; nevertheless, though his reason concluded that this false hermit was a servant of God, he left not for that to bury the good hermit, who there lay without life; and he began by himself to carry him to the grave which he had made, and then he saw that the false hermit went away over the mountain at a great rate." This old friendship is expressed by Sir Amylion when he says to Sir Amys,

> From this day forward ever mo,
> Neither fail, either for weal or wo,
> To help other at need,
> Brother, be now true to me,
> And I shall be as true to thee.

They loved each other, "à tort et à travers," as Henri IV said to Crillon. François Auguste de Thou, eldest son of the celebrated president, was beheaded at Lyon in 1642, in the 35th year of his age, for not having betrayed his friend by disclosing the secret of a conspiracy with which Cinq Mars had entrusted him.

When Perceforest heard the news of the death of

---

[1] Diodorus Sicul. IV, 17.

his friend Alexander, he sunk his head on his horse's neck, and so rode with his company for two leagues in silence. "Si n'estoit homme vivant qui osast parler à luy." At length the queen took his little son Betides by the hand, whom the king loved above all other creatures, and led him before the king, and said, "Sire, voicy Betides vostre cher fils qui vous faict feste." The king replied, "Dame, si l'enfant avoit sens il n'auroit talent de faire feste quant celui que tous les gentilshommes du monde tenoit en joye est mort." After a long time the knights and barons came and made a long oration, to induce him to abandon his sorrow, and saying all possible things to denote their love and admiration for the departed king. Perceforest, however, made them this short reply, "Seigneurs, allez vostre voye car à ce que je voy de vous, assez tost avez oublie ung homme quel quil soit puis quil est mort."[1]

How affecting is the account of Sir Launcelot, when he hears the tidings of Sir Gawayn's death. "'Fayr Sirs,' sayd Syr Launcelot, 'shewe me the tombe of Sir Gawayn, and than certeyn peple of the towne brougt hym into the castel of Dover, and shewed him the tombe. Than Syr Launcelot knelyd down, and wepte, and prayed hertelye for his soule, and Syr Launcelot laye two nyghtes on his tombe in prayers and wepyng"; and again, when we see him deprived of those who were all his "erthely joye," "Syr Launcelot swouned and laye longe stylle whyle the heremyte came and awakyd him, and sayd, 'ye be to blame, for ye dyspleyse God wyth suche manere of sorrowe makynge. Truely,' sayde Syre Launcelot, 'I truste I doo not dyspleyse God, for he knoweth myn entent. For my sorowe was not, nor is not for ony rejoycing of synne, but

[1] Vol. IV, c. vi.

my sorowe may never have ende. For whan I remembre and call to mynde her beaute, bountee, and noblesse, that was as wel wyth her kyng my lord Arthur, as wyth her. And also whanne I saw the corses of that noble kynge and noble quene so lye togyder in that cold grave made of erthe, that somtyme were so hyghly sette in moost honourable places, truly myn herte wolde not serve me to susteyne my wretchyd and carefull body.'"

King Perceforest, instructing his son Betides, says, " entre plusieurs amys ayez ung amy especial esprouvé." Your brother in affection, as Orestes replies to Iphigenia;[1] or as those who had once sat together at King Arthur's table, in Winchester. With the ancients, it was the praise of a man to say that he had but few friends:[2] for they that were friends to many, could be friends to no one.[3] It was a Pythagorean maxim μὴ πολλοῖς ἐμβάλλειν δεξιάν. Castiglione says, "nor would I that more than two enter into this so strict a league; there may be danger in a greater number; as in music three instruments are not so easily made to agree together as two."[4]

In the collegiate church of Avesnes, in the Ardennes, there was the following epitaph on two young Spaniards, whose mutual friendship was so warm, that one of them expired upon hearing that his companion was killed at the siege of La Capelle:

>   Laurentii et Francisci
>   Mortale quod fuit,
>   Hic conditur.
>   Immortale quod superest
>   Votis juva, viator,
>   Et mirare:

---

[1] Eurip. Iph. in Taur. 484.   [2] Eurip. Supp. 867.
[3] Aristotle, Ethic. IV; Plutarch de Amicorum Multitud.
[4] The Courtier, II, p. 152.

> Laurentio dum funus amico
> Pius parat Franciscus
>   En ipse cadit.
> Ille globo, hic mœrore;
> Ille Regi, hic amico,
>   Uterque Deo.
> Nunc bonos Belgica tellus tegit.
> Vitam dedit Hispana
>   Capella mortem.

The annals of ancient chivalry are rich in examples of friendship. Who has not on his tongue the friendship of Pylades and Orestes, of Pelopidas and Epaminondas, those two illustrious Thebans, the first delighting more in the exercise of the body; the latter in the improvement of the mind. The friendship of Theseus and Pirithöus, and a thousand other instances. In all history there is nothing more affecting than the picture which Plutarch gives of Philopœmen grieving for his friends, in his dungeon, the night after his defeat. When Dinocrates sent a villain, by night, to give him poison, he received the cup, and only asked the man "whether he had heard anything of his cavalry, and particularly of Lycortas. The executioner answering that they had almost all escaped, he nodded his head, in sign of satisfaction, and, looking kindly upon him, said, thou bringest good tidings, and we are not in all respects unhappy." Without uttering another word, or breathing the least sigh, he drank off the poison.

Thus, again, when Marcus Coriolanus refused the pecuniary reward offered to him, after his great victory over the Volscians, he added: "One favour only, I desire. I have a friend among the Volscians, bound with me in the sacred rites of hospitality, and a man of honour. He is now among the prisoners, and I request his freedom." It was then that Cominius gave him the title of Coriolanus. Socrates said, looking upon Menexenus, standing with Lysis, "O son of Demophon, which of you is the eldest?" "We are not sure," he replied. "Well then, which is of the best blood; you will not of course doubt?" "Yes, assuredly, we are in doubt." "As well as which of you is the fairest?" he proceeded. Here they both smiled. "Certes, then, I will not ask you which is the richest, for you are friends, are you not?" "We are, indeed," they replied. "But it is said all things are common between friends; so that, in this respect, you do not differ, if it be true what is always said of friendship!" They assented.[1] At the same time it must not be forgotten that the divine charity which influenced Christians prevented them from contracting any alliance which would have been opposed to its extension.

Particular friendships, in religious communities, were even condemned,[2] and, without doubt, the sentiments of human affection were less strong than those which induced men to love the greatest stranger, on the ground of his belonging to the House of Faith. Even in temporal chivalry, the bonds which connected two or three persons, were not to end in sedition and division, to the ruin of that love, which is the great mark and privilege of those who are Catholic disciples of Christ. There would have been a case of vicious friendship if men, by means of a particular alliance, had lost this sentiment for those persons who were not agreeable to the palate of their minds, through want of refinement, of natural or of artificial accomplishments; there would have been an end of Christianity. Therefore, all familiarity was not chivalrous friendship with our ancestors, for it could only exist along with fidelity to God and loyalty of faith, which implied divine charity. Perhaps, indeed, the very

---

[1] Platonis Lysis.   [2] Niereuberg. Duct. Ascet. VI, 11, 17.

want of familiarity was favourable to love. Under such circumstances, one had nothing to lament, nothing to forget, nothing to forgive; one had only to believe that every grace and good rested with the amiable stranger. Still, however, these religious bonds were not incompatible with ordinary friendship; they only preserved it from abuse. As of old, the interchange of right hands continued to be considered as a holy pledge. Who does not admire that sentiment of the Arcadian king:

> Quam petitis, juncta est mihi fœdere dextra.

And that of Scipio, when Syphax was brought captive into his presence; for Livy remarks, "movit et Scipionem, quum fortuna pristina viri præsenti fortunæ conlata, tum recordatio hospitii dextræque datæ." [1]

When Cyrus, too, in the presence of Orontas, was shewing the treachery of that man to the Greeks, he gives the breach of this pledge as an example of his black ingratitude and impiety, saying, καὶ δεξιὰν ἔλαβον καὶ ἔδωκα.[2]

When Lord Marmion, upon leaving the castle of Tantallon, offers his hand to the Earl of Douglas, the conduct and reply of that chieftain present a striking instance of the dignified caution which these notions tended to generate. For

> Douglas round him drew his cloak,
> Folded his arms, and thus he spoke:—
> "My manors, halls, and bowers, shall still
> Be open, at my sovereign's will,
> To each one whom he lists, howe'er
> Unmeet to be the owner's peer.
> My castles are my king's alone,
> From turret to foundation stone—
> The hand of Douglas is his own;
> And never shall in friendly grasp
> The hand of such as Marmion clasp."

---

[1] XXX, 13. [2] Xen. Anab. VI.

As Goetz von Berlichingen and Franz von Sickingen were at Heidelberg, during the festivities of Ludwig, the Count Palatine, they happened one day to meet certain nobles, who received them with stretched-out hands. Goetz, surprised at this reception from one of the party, said aloud, "He has given me his hand, he cannot have known me." The other answered, "Truly, I did not know you when I gave you my hand." Immediately Goetz went up and caught hold of his hand, and said aloud, "You did not know me when you gave me your hand, to whom you would not have offered it had you known me; there, take it back again"; and so saying, he turned aside.

The friendship of chivalry, like all the other virtues which were intimately connected with a religious feeling, was marked with a character of modesty and reserve; differing from that of those men who "are ever good at sudden commendations." Nature even dictated this feeling. Eumæus says of his absent master and friend,

Τὸν μὲν ἐγὼν, ὦ ξεῖνε, καὶ οὐ παρεόντ' ὀνομάζειν
Αἰδέομαι·

And Pliny says of his young friend, "hoc ipsum amantis est, non onerare eum laudibus." [1]

> Brave Percy; fare thee well, great heart,
> ——————— this earth that bears thee dead
> Bears not alive so stout a gentleman.
> If thou wert sensible of courtesy,
> I should not make so dear a show of zeal.

These are the words of Prince Henry. The modesty of the chivalrous character preserved our ancestors from that spirit of ridicule and disdain which their descendants have so generally adopted in reference to their companions and brethren. It was

---

[1] Lib. I, Epist. 14.

a fine and honest boast of Hippolytus, which might have been repeated by every knight who practised the principles of his order.

> Οὐκ ἐγγελαστὴς τῶν ὁμιλούντων, πάτερ,
> Ἀλλ' αὐτὸς οὐ παροῦσι κἀγγὺς ὢν φίλοις.

Few are capable of loving him whom they are accustomed to make the subject of their mirth. Even in the event of an unavoidable separation, in consequence of the guilt of one, the other found in the charity of the Catholic religion a means of preserving his faith. "If a friend," says Caussin, "chance to fail, whether it be by evil life, or through manifest contempt of you, or out of other evil dispositions, yet must you, on the decayed trunk, honour the last characters of love: you must keep the secrets which he hath at other times committed to you, and not publish his defects. Friendship is so venerable, that we must honour even its shadows, and imitate the Pythagoreans, who celebrated the obsequies of such as forsook their society, to bury them with honour." How triumphantly, then, did the doctrine and practice of these ages disprove the melancholy lines of the tragedian, where Œdipus reminds Theseus that time conquers all things, and thus concludes,

> Θνήσκει δὲ πίστις, βλαστάνει δ' ἀπιστία,
> Καὶ πνεῦμα ταὐτὸν οὔποτ' οὔτ' ἐν ἀνδράσι
> Φίλοις βέβηκεν, οὔτε πρὸς πόλιν πόλει.[1]

We are now prepared to remark the confidence which was inspired by friendship. The precept of the Greeks was general.

> Χρηστοῦ πρὸς ἀνδρὸς μηδὲν ὑπονόει κακόν.

---

[1] Sophocles, Œdip. Colon. 611.

Our Christian chivalry adopted it in every sense. The words of Henry IV of France, when he presented the mareschal Biron to the deputies of the Parliament, were admirable. "Behold a man whom I present alike both to my friends and to my enemies." Happy the man whom this feeling has never disappointed: to the last he can repeat that magnificent sentence of Shakespeare's hero:

> ——————— Countrymen!
> My heart doth joy, that yet, in all my life
> I found no man, but he was true to me.[1]

Happy the man who has nourished this feeling, though he should live to experience that it may deceive. "I had not foreseen domestic treason," said the emperor Henry IV, "I was not on my guard against it. Heaven bestowed on me the blessing of not imagining that there could be such madness in my friends, or such impiety in my children." Enguerrand de Marigny had a dear friend in Raoul de Presle, one of the most learned and eloquent men of his age. When Marigny was accused, his cruel and cowardly enemies dreaded the influence of his friend Raoul, and accordingly, without the least pretence, they brought a charge also against him of conspiring against the king, and he suffered arrest and imprisonment. What a testimony was here! and what confidence in the virtue of a friend. Observe, too, how Alexander treated the friends of Philotas and Parmenion; Dionysius those of Dion; Nero those of Plautus; Tiberius those of Sejanus; Henry II those of St. Thomas of Canterbury. How well must Robert Bruce have known the fidelity of the gentle knight, Sir William Douglas, when he called him to the side of his death-bed, and having made known his

[1] Jul. Cæsar, V, v.

desire to have his heart taken to Jerusalem, to be presented to the holy sepulchre, concluded his affecting address with these words: "Bycause I knowe not in all my realme no knyght more valyant than ye be, nor of body so well furnyshed to accomplysshe myn avowe in stede of myselfe, therefore I require you, myn own dere aspeciall freade, that ye wyll take on you this voiage, for the love of me, and to acquite my soule agaynst my lorde God; for I trust so moche in your nobleness and trouth, that and ye wyll take on you I doubt not but that ye shall achyve it."[1] Poor Sarpedon, in his agony, comforted himself with thinking that Glaucus would not suffer his dead body to be stripped by Patroclus:[2] and his last words express a noble reliance upon his friend.

What confidence is evinced in that fine address of Jason to his brave companions after they had successfully achieved the adventure of the Cyanean Rocks!

'Ω φίλοι, ὑμιτέρῃ ἀρετῇ ἰνι θάρσος αἴξω.
Τούνικα νῦν οὐδ' εἶκε δι' ἀΐδαο βιρέθρων
Στιλλοίμην, ἔτι τάρβος ἀνάψομαι, εὖτε πέλισθι
Ἐμπέδοι ἀργαλέοις ἐνὶ δείμασιν.[3]

Perhaps some reader will repeat these lines with rapture, and apply them to the brave companions of his youth, with whom he may have spent his happiest hours. It may have been with him as with our German forefathers. "Hæc dignitas, hæ vires, magno semper electorum juvenum globo circumdari, in pace decus, in bello præsidium."[4] Alas! my dear comrades! he will be ready to exclaim

οὐ γάρ οἱ πάρα νῆες ἐπήρετμοι καὶ ἑταῖροι—

---

[1] Froissart, I, 20. [2] Il. XVI, 494.
[3] Apollon. II, 643. [4] Tacitus, de Mor. Ger. 13.

partners of many a course through Lincoln Washes and the dark wintry seas which encompass Tattershal's lofty towers and Ely's Isle, and are ye gone, and will these alternate scenes of pain and joy no more return, when towards the close of a laborious day we have come to our harbour in gay triumph, and then refreshed our hearts with no Centaurean banquet, hearing the mutual encouragement

———————— O fortes, pejoraque passi
Mecum sæpe viri, nunc vino pellite curas;
Cras ingens iterabimus æquor.

Hector well knew what friends belonged to Diomedes when he vowed upon the morrow that it should be known whether this fierce warrior would venture to await him, and added,

————————ἀλλ' ἐν πρώτοισιν ὀΐω
κείσεται οὐτηθείς, πολέες δ' ἀμφ' αὐτὸν ἑταῖροι.[1]

And equally fine is the testimony borne to the loyalty of his own companion in the sentence which closed Diomedes' noble reply to Agamemnon, when the king had advised the Greeks to sail home, and their heroic champion spurned the counsel and desired him to fly, for the Greeks would remain; then adding,

———————— εἰ δὲ καὶ αὐτοί,
φευγόντων σὺν νηυσὶ φίλην ἐς πατρίδα γαῖαν.
νῶϊ δ', ἐγὼ Σθένελός τε, μαχησόμεθ', εἰσόκε τέκμωρ
Ἰλίου εὕρωμεν· σὺν γὰρ Θεῷ εἰλήλουθμεν.[2]

Homer, in this last sentence, teaches the grounds, the security, and the rule of heroic friendship.

Another instance is, where Meriones appeals to Idomeneus, and says, "Others, indeed, may not know what I am in battle; but you, I think, can bear witness": to which Idomeneus replies,

[1] Il. VIII, 536. [2] Il. IX, 46.

οἶδ' ἀρετὴν οἷός ἐσσι· τί σε χρὴ ταῦτα λέγεσθαι;[1]

What Hegio says in the play of the friend of his youth is very beautiful:

> Cognatus mihi erat: una a pueris parvoli
> Sumus educati: una semper militiæ et domi
> Fuimus: paupertatem una pertulimus gravem
> Quapropter nitar, faciam, experiar, denique
> Animum relinquam potius quam illas deseram.[2]

The same poet, whose pictures of youthful friendship are most engaging, makes the old Chremes take example from the friendship of young men for each other, to practise the same virtue towards his equal in age.

> ————— quod potero, adjutabo senem.
> Ita ut filium meum amico atque æquali suo
> Video inservire, et socium esse in negotiis:
> Nos quoque senes est æquom senibus obsequi.[3]

That princely friendship inspired a confidence and a knowledge of what passed in the heart of a companion, which is finely illustrated by Southey in the passage where the old man relates to Roderick the resolution of his friend Pelayo, and adds,

> None better knew his kinsman's noble heart,
> None loved him better, none bewailed him more;
> And as he felt, like me, for his reproach
> A deeper grief than for his death, even so
> He cherished in his heart the constant thought
> Something was yet untold, which, being known,
> Would palliate his offence, and make the fall
> Of one till then so excellently good,
> Less monstrous, less revolting to belief,
> More to be pitied, more to be forgiven.

Such being the friendship of chivalry, it is not strange that it should have been a virtue highly

---

[1] Il. XIII, 272. [2] Terence, Adelph. III, iv.
[3] Heaut. III, i.

prized in heroic times. "To cast away a good friend," says Creon, in the Tragedy, "is the same as to deprive one's self of life."[1] The friendship of a brave man was a gift that used to be offered to kings.

At the supper of Seuthes, King of Thrace, when the guests in succession rose up and drank to the royal host, they, according to custom, made him presents, one of a horse, another of a slave, another of splendid garments, another of a silver vase and tapestry, worth ten minæ; but Xenophon was in doubt what he should do, for he happened to be placed in the most honourable seat next the king: when the wine-bearer brought him the horn, Xenophon however rose up with boldness, and taking the horn, said, Ἐγὼ δέ σοι, ὦ Σεύθη, δίδωμι ἐμαυτὸν καὶ τοὺς ἐμοὺς τούτους ἑταίρους, φίλους εἶναι πιστούς.[2] When Abradatas had received back his wife from the generous Cyrus, he hastened to the king, and taking him by the right hand, said, Ἀνθ' ὧν σὺ εὖ πεποίηκας ἡμᾶς ὦ Κῦρε, οὐκ ἔχω τί μεῖζον εἴπω, ἢ ὅτι φίλον σοι ἐμαυτὸν δίδωμι καὶ θεράποντα καὶ σύμμαχον.[3] When the Chevalier Bayard took leave of the hospitable family of Brescia, to shew his gratitude, he said to the lady, "I give you my word, that as long as I live you will possess in me a gentleman for your servant and your friend."

It is important to observe that the sentiments of chivalry were opposed to the opinion of those who would sacrifice private friendship to every conceit and phantom of public good; a doctrine which Socrates condemned as impious,[4] which Aristophanes held up to the ridicule of the Athenians, when he made Cleon appeal to them for the truth of his assertion:

---

[1] Sophocles, Œdip. Tyr. 610.
[2] Xen. Anab. VII, III.
[3] Xen. Cyrop. VI, 1.
[4] Plato, Euthyphro.

οὐ φροντίζων τῶν ἰδιωτῶν οὐδινὸς, εἰ σοι χαρισοίμην.¹

One which Sophocles puts in the mouth of a tyrant who will not permit a sister to bury her own brother, saying,

καὶ μεῖζον' ὅστις ἀντὶ τῆς αὑτοῦ πάτρας
φίλον νομίζει, τοῦτον οὐδαμοῦ λέγω.²

One which renders Ulysses, who adopted it, an object of horror, when he says, alluding to the father who was unwilling to sacrifice his daughter,

―――――――― Ego mite parentis
Ingenium verbis ad publica commoda verti.³

And one which Camoens has associated with the Machiavelian cruelty of Affonso IV of Portugal, that undutiful son, unnatural brother, and cruel father, who made a journey to Coimbra that he might see the beautiful Inez when the prince his son was absent on a hunting party, and then unmoved by her tears, consigned her to the daggers of his three counsellors, Alvaro Gonzalez, Diogo Lopez Pacheco, and Pedro Coelho, who persuaded him that her death was beneficial to the state.

> In tears she utter'd—as the frozen snow,
> Touch'd by the Spring's mild ray, begins to flow,
> So just began to melt his stubborn soul
> As mild-ray'd pity o'er the tyrant stole;
> But destiny forbade; with eager zeal,
> Again pretended for the public weal,
> Her fierce accusers urged her speedy doom;
> Again dark rage diffused its horrid gloom
> O'er stern Alonzo's brow: swift at the sign
> Their swords unsheath'd, around her brandish'd, shine.
> O foul disgrace, of knighthood lasting stain,
> By men of arms an helpless lady slain!⁴

"Carneades," says an old writer, "made an eloquent oration at Rome against justice, but I

―――――

¹ Equites, 786. ² Antigone, 182.
³ Ovid. Met. XIII, 1. ⁴ Lusiad, III.

never read that any man was witty against friendship." Yet what becomes of friendship when subservient to the maxims of this new philosophy? Montaigne forgets himself so far as to speak of the "generous murder of a friend" when he alludes to Brutus, though indeed he can convince no reader that he himself believed in such a character: but in our age the act of the Pazzis and the Salviatis has been extolled by a writer of eminence, who supports the principle which was condemned by Gerson and the Council of Constance as heretical, and tending to foster treason and falsehood, after it had been proclaimed by the famous Jean Petit in defending the murder of the Duke of Orleans in 1408. It was, however, principally to the fanaticism and hypocrisy of the religious innovators of the sixteenth century, and to the sentiments which they succeeded in establishing, that we may ascribe the diffusion of those maxims which are opposed to the security of friendship. Cavendish relates, in his Life of Cardinal Wolsey, that after the mild and eloquent discourse of the aged Cardinal Campeggius, the Duke of Suffolk stept forth from the king, by his commandment, and spake with an haught countenance these words :—"'It was never merry in Englande,' quoth he, 'while we had any cardinalls amongst us,' which wordes were set forthe both with countenaunce and vehemency, that all men marvailed what he intended; to whom no man made answer. Then the duke spake againe in great despight: to the which my Lord Cardinal perceiving his vehemency, soberly made answer, and said, 'Sir, of all men within this realme, ye have least cause to dispraise cardinals; for, if I, poor cardinal, had not been, you should have had at this present no head upon your shoulders, wherewith you might make any such bragge in despight of us, who intend you no manner of damage; neither have we given you any cause to be with such despight offended. Therefore hold your peace, my Lord, and pacify yourself, and speak like a man of honour and wisdom, and speak not so quickly or reproachfully to your friends; for you know best what friendship I have shewed you, which I never yet revealed to any person alive before now, neither to my glory nor to your dishonour.' And therewith the duke gave over the matter without any further words or answer, and went his way."

The whole legislation of the unhappy period which succeeded these wretched times was directed to encourage private treason; to excite brethren to rise up against brethren, and children against their parents; making friendship yield to faction and party spirit, as in the worst times of Greece, when, as Thucydides says, τὸ ξυγγενὲς τοῦ ἑταιρικοῦ ἀλλοτριώτερον ἐγένετο. The dearest friends were changed into enemies. In Germany, the Count of Solms Greifenstein joined the innovators, and the Count of Hohensolms remained faithful to the Church: the two relations became foes; they fought under the castle of Greifenstein, and the latter noble count was slain. The spot where he fell is still pointed out. When the English council forbade the Lady Mary to have mass said in her house, these men summoned her servants aud commanded them, on their allegiance, to insult her and disobey her orders, and, upon their generous refusal, they were sent to the Tower. Strype, who was thoroughly imbued with the sentiments of the reformers, after saying of Sir Thomas Eliot, " this was one of the learnedest and wisest men of this time, who promoted true wisdom and virtue among his countrymen,"[1] gives the letter which this knight sent to Cromwell, requesting a grant of some of the church lands, and

---

[1] Ecclesiastical Mem. I, c. 31, p. 342.

assuring him that he "joys at the king's godly proceedings." The letter concludes thus: "I beseech your good lordship now to lay apart the remembrance of the amity betwixt me and Sir Thomas More" (who had been lately martyred), "which was but usque ad aras, considering that I was never so much addicted unto him as I was unto truth; and natural shamefastness more reigneth in me than is necessary; so I most humbly desire you, my special good lord, that it may like his highness to reward me with some convenient portion of the suppressed lands; and whatsoever portion of land that I shall attain, I promise to give your lordship the first year's fruits."[1]

But to leave these wretched men and return to the admirers of Brutus. Dante was not in their number when he described the punishment inflicted upon those who had betrayed their benefactors, and then said

>———————— That upper spirit
> Who hath worst punishment—
> Is Judas; he that hath his head within
> And plies his feet without. Of th' other two,
> Whose heads are under, from the murky jaw
> Who hangs, is Brutus. Lo! how he doth writhe
> And speaks not. The other, Cassius, that appears
> So wide of limb.[2]

Brutus was said to have affirmed,[3] that for the cause which induced him to kill his dear friend and benefactor, he would have murdered his own father! O what a contrast to the mind of Hector, when he mourns over the prospect of his country's fate, and yet confesses to his wife—

---

[1] Vol. I, p. 421. [2] Hell, Cant. XXXIV.
[3] Epist. ad Brut. 16, which is considered not genuine.

ἀλλ' οὔ μοι Τρώων τόσσον μέλει ἄλγος ὀπίσσω,
οὔτ' αὐτῆς Ἑκάβης, οὔτε Πριάμοιο ἄνακτος,
οὔτε κασιγνήτων, οἵ κεν πολέες τε καὶ ἐσθλοὶ
ἐν κονίῃσι πέσοιεν ὑπ' ἀνδράσι δυσμενέεσσιν,
ὅσσον σεῖ', ὅτε κέν τις Ἀχαιῶν χαλκοχιτώνων
δακρυόεσσαν ἄγηται, ἐλεύθερον ἦμαρ ἀπούρας·

But Hector was worthy of the dark ages! Machiavel would have found it hard to persuade him that Romulus murdering his brother and consenting to the assassination of Tatius, his colleague, was completely justified by the consideration of promoting the public good.

Antonius, the consul, on the eve of the battle with Catiline, when the ruin of this conspirator was inevitable, happened to be seized with a fit of the gout, so he could not personally engage in the destruction of an old friend: the command devolved upon Petreius. The Roman senate understood him well, and, to their eternal honour, it appears that they were satisfied with his conduct.

Blosius, of Cumæ, was carried before the consuls and interrogated about the sedition; he answered that he loved Tiberius Gracchus so dearly, that he thought fit to follow him whithersoever he led, and begged pardon upon that account. They who were his judges, says an old writer, were so noble, that though they knew it no fair excuse, yet, for the honour of friendship, they did not directly reject his motion, but put him to death because he did not follow, but led on Gracchus, and brought his friend into the snare; for so they preserved the honours of friendship on either hand, by neither suffering it to be sullied by a foul excuse, nor yet rejected in any fair pretence."

Notwithstanding the base Ciceronian sentence, "immemor beneficiorum, memor patriæ,"[1] it may

[1] Philipp. II, 2.

be affirmed that the great consul would never have been guilty of an action conformable to it. He refrained from even mentioning to his intimate friend, Q. Metellus, his detestation of that senator's brother, the tribune, who was his own personal enemy, and a hater of the republic; nay, for the relief of this very man, the enemy of his country, did Cicero procure a decree, because he was his friend's brother, unlike the poet, whose impartiality consigns his kinsman to a place in Hell.[1] "Addam illud etiam," says Cicero, "quod jam ego curare non debui, sed tamen fieri non moleste tuli, atque etiam, ut ita fieret, pro mea parte adjuvi, ut senatus-consulto meus inimicus, quia tuus frater erat, sublevaretur."[2] On the banishment of this tribune from the city, when almost personally threatened, in a letter from Metellus, Cicero says to him in reply, "I not only forgive, but highly applaud your grief." It was his personal affection for Pompey which made him embrace his cause, and it was his gratitude for past favours that made him resolve to run all his hazards. "Ingrati animi crimen horreo."[3] And again he says, "nec mehercule hoc facio reipub. causa, quam funditus deletam puto, sed ne quis me putet ingratum in eum, qui me levavit eis incommodis quibus ipse affecerat."[4] When at Formiæ, amongst the political theses which he formed for the amusement of his solitary hours, one was, in civil war, whether we ought to act with our benefactors and friends, though they do not, in our opinion, take right measures for the public interest;[5] and one may almost conclude, with respect to his real opinion, from observing his conduct to his brother Quintus, whose company he was so far from

---

[1] Dante places Geri of Bello, his kinsman, son of his grandfather's brother, in the eighth circle of Hell, canto XXIX.
[2] Epist. Fam. I, 2.   [3] Ibid. X, 9, 255.
[4] Ibid. IX, 19.   [5] Ad Att. IX, 4.

desiring in his flight to Greece, that he pressed him to stay in Italy, on account of his personal obligations to Cæsar, and the relation which he had borne to him.[1] He expresses his astonishment on finding young Brutus in Pompey's camp, because the young man had always before professed an irreconcilable hatred to Pompey, who was the murderer of his father,[2] and this from a principle which the wisest counsellors of antiquity admitted, as may be instanced in the reply of Phœnix to Achilles;[3] nay, many of the most distinguished Romans avowed their abhorrence of the contrary sentiment with as much zeal as could be expressed by any Knight of the Round Table. "They accuse me of a crime," says Matius, in his beautiful letter to Cicero,[4] "because I generously lament the death of one who was necessary to me; because I feel indignant that my friend has perished; for they say that one's country is to be preferred to friendship; but I will not act deceitfully. I confess that I have not arrived at this degree of wisdom. Nevertheless, I do not believe that these men, who dislike me on account of my constancy to Cæsar, would rather have their own friends like themselves than like me." It is certain that he spoke the sentiments of the ancient brave. When the last hour of Galba had arrived, the army deserted his cause, rejected his promises, and all turned away from him, "excepta Germanicorum vexillatione," says Suetonius. "Hi ob recens meritum quod so ægros et invalidos magnopere fovisset, in auxilium advolavere." The same historian relates a circumstance respecting the death of Nero, which merits great admiration. After describing the public joy, so natural on that occasion, he adds, "and yet there were not wanting per-

---

[1] Ad Att. IX, 16.   [2] Ad Att. XI, 4.
[3] Il. IX.   [4] Epist. Fam. XI, 28.

sons who, for a long time, used to scatter spring and summer flowers upon his grave." Upon the whole, then, we may conclude that the feelings and judgment, if not the theories and doctrines of antiquity, led men to hold the rule of chivalry with respect to the conduct of friendship; the heart taught them what cannot be better expressed than in the words of Æschines, in which he alluded to his great rival, saying " he who is a bad father can never be a good public leader; nor can he ever love the people who does not love those who are near and precious to him. He who is a bad man in private life, can never be good in public."[1]

To the honour however of Demosthenes, we must remember that sentence in his oration against Meidias : μετρία γὰρ δίκη παρὰ τῶν φίλων ἐστὶν, ἄν τι δοκῶσι πεποιηκέναι δεινόν, μηκέτι τῆς λοιπῆς φιλίας κοινωνεῖν. τὸ δὲ τιμωρεῖσθαι καὶ ἐπεξιέναι τοῖς πεπονθόσι καὶ τοῖς ἐχθροῖς καταλείπεται. As for the conduct of the first Brutus to his sons, Plutarch says that "it was an action not easy to praise or condemn with propriety; for either the excess of virtue raised his soul above the influence of the passions, or else the excess of resentment depressed it into insensibility. Neither the one nor the other was natural or suitable to the human faculties, but was either divine or brutal." The Christian philosophy secured the interests of friendship and the delicacy of sentiment without leading men to speak like Themistocles, who went so far as to express a wish that he might never be seen sitting on a tribunal where his friends could find no favour; or like Agesilaus, who, though renowned for justice, held that when a man's friends were concerned, a rigid regard to justice was a mere pretence. Plutarch gives us an instance in a short letter of his to

[1] Cont. Ctesiphon. 78.

Hidrieus the Carian, which is written in the spirit of honest Davy, where he beseeches Justice Shallow to countenance William Visor of Wincot against Clement Perkes of the hill.[1] Timoleon mourned during twenty years for the deed he had been tempted to commit through a false principle of patriotism, in opposition to friendship. Epaminondas would not kill a tyrant without the forms of justice, though to give freedom to his country; and he counted him a wicked man, however good a patriot, who would not spare his former friend and host if he met him in battle. "Hence," says Montaigne, "let us not be ashamed to believe que l'interest commun ne doit pas tout requerir de tous contre l'interest privé; et que toutes choses ne sont pas loisibles à un homme de bien pour le service de son Roy, ny de la cause generale et des loix. C'est une instruction propre au temps. Si c'est grandeur de courage et l'effect d'une vertu rare et singuliere de mespriser l'amitié, les obligations privées, sa parole, et la parenté, pour le bien commun et obeïssance du magistrat, c'est assez vrayement pour nous en excuser, que c'est une grandeur qui ne peut loger en la grandeur du courage d'Epaminondas."[2]

Muratori relates that a commissary of war thought to pay his court to Francis II, Duke of Modena, by particularly harassing his own country, Varrano, making a greater levy of soldiers there than in any other place, and that he had for his reward, to be deprived of his office by this wise prince.

When the Milanese were defeated at Corte Nuova, in 1237, by the imperial troops of Frederick II, numbers of their army would have perished from the hostility of the Bergamese, to whose territory

[1] Shakspeare's Hen. IV, 2d Part, Act V, scene 1.
[2] Essais, III, i.

they had fled, if Pagano della Torre, Lord of Valsassina, had not secured their escape and reception, by conducting them into his own fiefs. This gave rise to the exaltation of the House della Torre. The people of Milan were so grateful that they even compromised their own liberty rather than appear ungrateful to that noble family.

Nevertheless, the Christian chivalry was far from induciug men to believe that private friendship or enmity would justify any proceeding which was criminal, or opposed to the safety of one's country. The knights of the Crescent, instituted by René d'Anjou, swore to be religious, to love all other knights as their own brothers, to defend their honour, conceal their faults, shame, or dishonour, but to warn them as often as there should be occasion, that they might amend. Marino Faliero died unpitied: and the horror with which the gentlemen of Spain have always regarded the memory of Count Julian and his daughter will be a sufficient proof of their judgment, which agreed with that of Pericles, when he replied to a friend who asked him if he would perjure himself for his sake,—$\Delta\epsilon\tilde{\iota}$ $\mu\epsilon$ $\sigma\upsilon\mu\pi\rho\acute{\alpha}\tau\tau\epsilon\iota\nu$ $\tauο\tilde{\iota}\varsigma$ $\phi\acute{\iota}\lambda\omicron\iota\varsigma$, $\grave{\alpha}\lambda\lambda\grave{\alpha}$ $\mu\acute{\epsilon}\chi\rho\iota$ $\theta\epsilon\tilde{\omega}\nu$.[1] Without doubt it was held highly honourable to extend, as far as was consistent with innocence, the influence of private affection. "I was in his court," says Sir John Froissart, alluding to Richard II, "more than a quarter of a yere togeder, and he made me good chere bycause that in my youth I was clerk and servaunt to the noble Kynge Edwarde the Third, his grauntfather, and with my Lady Philyp of Heynault, Quene of Englande, his grandame, and whan I departed fro hym it was at Wynsore, and at my departynge the kyng sent me by a knight of his called Sir John Golofer a goblet of silver and

---

[1] A. Gell. Noct. Attic. I, 3.

gylt weyeng two mark of sylver, and within it a C nobles, by the which I am as yet the better, and shall be as long as I lyve; wherefore I am bounde to pray to God for his soule, and with moche sorrow I write of his death."

Goethe says, on the invasion of Frederick of Prussia, that the public mind was divided, his grandfather and his father taking different sides: to the former Maria Theresa had given as a present, a chain of gold, and her portrait; accordingly he was for Austria. In like manner, the young Lord Grandison did not hesitate to declare publicly that his obligation of gratitude to Charles I on the behalf of his house, had determined him to offer the sacrifice of his life. The brave Mareschal de Boucicaut gave, as his second reason for resolving to assist the King of Hungary against the Saracens, "pour la bonne chere que le roy de Hongrie luy avoit faicte en son pays," a ground which the modern bard of chivalry has deemed sufficient to support a claim of assistance, when he describes the gallant Ferraught rushing into Rokeby Hall with young Redmond in his arms, end delivering the salutation and charge of O'Neale his father:

> He bids thee breed him as thy son,
> For Turlough's days of joy are done;
> And other lords have seized his land,
> And faint and feeble is his hand,
> And all the glory of Tyrone
> Is like a morning vapour flown.
> To bind the duty on thy soul,
> He bids thee think of Erin's bowl!
> Now is my master's message by,
> And Ferraught will contented die.

Without doubt friendship is admirable even where it seems to rest upon doubtful grounds, as in that description of the guard of O'Neal, who "were for

the most part beardless boys without shirts, who in
the frost wade as familiarly through rivers as water-
spaniels. With what charm such a master makes
them love him, I know not," says the writer of
'Nugæ Antiquæ,' "but if he bid come, they come;
if go, they do go; if he say do this, they do it."
Better such friends than the calculating, arguing
sophists, to whom we might apply what the Jester
said of the lords of Milan, warning his master,
Count Tano Alberti, against such allies, "You
might sound the horn of Roland for a year together
without bringing five of them to your assistance."
The Black Prince expressed himself to the following
effect in rendering a reason to his counsellors for
assisting King Peter of Castille: "Also, besyde that,
the kyng my father and this kyng Daupeter hath a
great season ben alyed togyder by great confedera-
cyons, wherfor we are bounde to ayde him in case
that he requyre and desyre us so to do."

When the deputation was sent to Kenilworth
Castle to Edward II, urging him to resign the
crown, it was intended that it should consist of
representatives from every order in the State; and
so bishops went, and earls went, and so did abbots,
and knights and burgesses and justices, and citizens
of London; "but," says Holinshed, "none of the
Friar Minors went, bycause they woulde not bee
the bringers of so heavie tydings, sithe he had ever
borne them great good will."

When King Louis IX had taken prisoner the
Count of La Marche's son and forty knights who had
joined the count in rebellion, some advised the king
to hang them as rebels, but this counsel he rejected
with horror, saying, the son had been obliged to
obey his father.

One has never heard an objection raised to that
beautiful passage in the Lay of the Last Minstrel,
where the young Lady Margaret of Branksome

escapes to the "green wood at dawn of light," and,

> The watchman's bugle is not blown,
> For he was her foster father's son.

There were no doubt grave reasons to justify the conduct of Sir John Savage, Sir Bryan Sandforde, and Sir Simon Digby, who left King Richard III on the eve of the battle of Bosworth, and thereby materially aided the cause and spirit of his adversary; and yet it is impossible not to feel admiration for that gallant gentleman, John Duke of Norfolk, slain at Bosworth, who, being warned by divers to refrain from the field, insomuch that the night before he should set forward towards the king, one wrote on his gate,

> Jack of Norfolk be not too bolde,
> For Dyken thy mayster is bought and solde.

"Yet al this notwithstanding," says Hall, "he regarded more his othe, his honour, and promise made to King Richard, lyke a gentleman and a faythul subject to his prince, absented not hym self from his mayster, but as he faythefully lived under him, so he manfully dyed with him, to his great fame and lawde." Nay, one must admire Richard Nevill, Earl of Warwick, though fighting for Edward IV against poor King Henry, for on the alarm at Ferrybridge, when the Lord Fitzwalter and the Bastard of Salisbury were slain, "his brother the Erle of Warwycke," says Hall, "being mounted on his hackeney, came blowing to Kyng Edward, saying, 'Syr, I praye God have mercy of their soules which in the beginning of your enterprize hath lost their lyfes, and because I se no succors of this world, I remit the vengeance of punishment to God our Creator and Redeemer,' and with that lighted downe and slew his horse wyth his sword, saying, 'Let him fly that wyl, for surely I wil tarry with him that wyl tarry with me,' and kissed the cross of his sword."

It remains for us to consider what were the ordinary grounds of friendship. In those ages of simplicity, friendships not being a metaphysical nothing, created for contemplation, and ending in dialogues of news and prettinesses; it was essential that a friend should be either qualified for counsel or for service. "If he could no counsel give," he must be "bygge enough," as King Arthur's knights said. If he knew not letters, he must have been able to swim, according to the Roman maxim. Titus was a worthy friend, for, when his father Vespasian was surrounded by the Britons, and in extreme danger, he rushed upon the enemy and rescued him.[1] Socrates was a worthy friend, for in the battle of Delos, when the Athenians fled, and Xenophon, having fallen from his horse, was lying on the ground, the philosopher took him upon his shoulders, and saved him.[2] Diomede defending Nestor when Hector was upon him, and Ulysses fled,[3] of which baseness Ajax took care to remind him, in a famous scene,[4] Ajax with Mecisteus and Alastor, coming to help Teucer, and carrying him off wounded to the ships;[5] Menelaus coming with Ajax, like a wintry torrent from the mountains, to the assistance of Ulysses, when he fought the Trojans single-handed, and being left alone, and having no horn like that of Rolando, he shouted three times to his friends, three times as loud as the mouth of man could shout, and still defended himself:

Αἴας δ' ἐγγύθεν ἦλθε, φέρων σάκος, ἠΰτε πύργον,
Στῆ δὲ παρὲξ·[6]

or Epaminondas delivering Pelopidas in the

[1] Dion. Cassius.
[2] Il. VIII, 90.
[3] Il. VIII, 330.
[4] Strabo, IX, 27, p. 403.
[5] Ovid. Met. XIII, 1.
[6] Il. XI, 485.

battle with the Arcadians, proved themselves worthy of that friendship which was so needful for the safety of heroic men. What would have become of Duke Godfrey of Bouillon, left without a horse, if Count Raymond had not come to his assistance, and given him one; for the heroic Godfrey had no money, in consequence, says the historian, of his liberal alms, and of the bounty with which he had relieved the poor and exhausted soldiers.[1] Edward Clifford was a worthy friend, when he stoutly bestrode his nephew, Sir Johan Chandos, who had fallen to the earth in battle, "for the Frenchmen wolde fayne have had him, and defended him so valyantly, and gave round about him such strokes that none durst aproche nere to him; also Sir John Chambo, and Sir Bertram of Case, seemed like men out of their myndes when they saw their maister lye on the erth"; and when the most part of the English "were discomfyted and taken, alwayes Edwarde Clifforde wolde not departe from his nephue there as he lay." Then after the battle, "the barons and knights of Poictou were sore disconforted, when they saw their seneschall, Sir John Chandos, lye on the erthe, and coude nat speke: then they lamentably complayned and sayd, A, Sir Johan Chandos, the floure of all chivalry, unhappily was that glayve forged that thus hath wounded you, and brought you in parell of dethe; they wept pyteously that were about hym, and he herde and understoode them well, but he could speke no worde; they wronge their handes and tare their hceres, and made many a pytefull complaynt, and specially suche as were of his own house; then his servants unarmed him, and layde him on pavesses, and so bare him softely to Mortimer, the next fortress to them; aud this noble knight

---

[1] Gesta Dei per Francos, p. 258.

lived not after his hurte past a day and a night, but so dyed; God have mercy on his soule."

Vinisauf, the historian, relating the return of a caravan of provisions for the Christian army, which was attacked by the Turks near Ramula, while escorted by Manasserius de Insula, Richard de Erques, Theodoric Philip, and some companions, Baldwin de Carron, Otho, and many squires, and kinsmen and friends, says, that their friendship was proved in necessity, "for the Turks attacked them suddenly in great force. Richard of Erques and Theodoric, being dismounted, Baldwin fought bravely until the men brought up horses and remounted them. There you would see a fierce contention, horses and the riders on the ground, and the fire flashing from the swords. Baldwin himself is thrown, and immediately commands one of his squires to get off his horse and give it to him. Baldwin was no sooner mounted, than he saw the head of the poor boy who had carried himself bravely while on horseback, cut off with one blow. Philip, his companion, is taken prisoner with his squire, and Baldwin and the others labour to rescue him. From a third horse, Baldwin is thrown, and now the blood flows from every limb, and his sword is blunted with hacking, and in his despair he calls out to the brave soldier, Manasserins de Insula, saying, 'O Manasserius, do you desert me?' which Manasserius hearing, he flew to the assistance of his friend; and these two heroes fought a multitude of the Turks, when Manasserius is thrown to the ground, and trampled upon by his horse's hoofs, and one of his legs torn off, and meanwhile none of their friends knew of their situation, when lo! God sent them a deliverer in the noble Count of Leicester, who came up and hurled from his horse the first Turk who opposed him, whose head Ausconus, companion of Stephen de Long Champs, cut off. Stephen fought bravely, and the Christians coming up in greater numbers, at length the Turks were put to flight, and the band of heroic brothers delivered gloriously."[1] In the great battle with the Turks, after the delivery of Joppa, Vinisauf relates that King Richard happened to see the noble Count of Leicester thrown from his horse in the midst of the enemy, and that he cut his way through and delivered him, helping him to mount another horse; and shortly after, in the same battle, he rescued Radulfus de Malo Leone, who was actually prisoner in the hands of the infidels. Well might each of these Paladins say of his companion, what Diomedes pronounced of Ulysses, when he chose him to be his comrade in the night expedition to the Trojan camp:—

Τούτου γ' ἑσπομένοιο καὶ ἐκ πυρὸς αἰθομένοιο
Ἄμφω νοστήσαιμεν, ἐπεὶ περίοιδε νοῆσαι.[2]

In the romance of the Round Table there is another fine example. Sir Launcelot, riding in a forest, exhausted with the heat of a scorching day, arrives at dark at a forester's house. The forester received him well, and gave him a bed in an upper room. The knight undressed and lay down, but the night was as sultry as the day had been. He rose quickly, and looked out of the iron-grated window; the moon shining clearly, enabled him to see the way stretching far through the forest. Presently he was aware of a knight, mounted on a foaming steed, who came up to the door of the house, and beat violently at it with his spear. Presently came galloping up two other horsemen, who commenced to fence at him: "Do you know me?" asked the strange knight. "We do," answered one of the assailants, "as the foulest and falsest seneschal living." When Sir Launcelot heard that, he knew that it was his own friend, the seneschal of King

[1] Lib. V, c. 52. [2] Hom. Il. X, 246.

Arthur's court. Incontinent he seized his sword, burst open the cross-bars, leaped out of the window, fought with the strange assailants, defeated them, saved his friend, and bound by oath his two enemies to appear at King Arthur's court by the next day of Pentecost.[1] It is not strange that such friends were prized. When Sir Boost and Hector met at King Arthur's court, they embraced, " Si commencerent à plourer du dueil quils avoient que Lancelot nestoit avec eulx." "Dieu le nous amaine," said Boost to Arthur, who told him Launcelot might soon arrive, " car je ne seray jamais joyeux devant que je le voye."

But if friendship were thus needful in arms and battle, it was no less so in council and retirement. Henri IV of France being opposed by Sully, parted from him in anger, but the next day he called to visit him, and expressed his wish that Sully would forget what had passed, and concluded, saying, " As soon as you cease to contradict me in matters which I know do not please you, I shall conclude that you no longer love me." On one occasion, Sully said to the king, "I perceive that your Majesty is more pleased with me now than you were a fortnight ago." "What! have you not forgotten that?" exclaimed Henry. " Do you not know that our little quarrels ought never to last beyond twenty-four hours?" Nor were men in these ages neglectful in their friendships of less important qualities. The "omnium horarum homo" of Tacitus, like that Mummius, of whom Cicero says, " Cuivis tempori hominem esse,"[2] was never without his tribute of affection. That amiable fellowship between Pisistratus and Telemachus, on their journey, was ascribed by the latter to early habits of intimacy, to similarity of age and pursuits. It was enough sometimes when hearts responded to

[1] Vol. III of Lancelot du Lac.   [2] De Oratore, II.

> That mysterious sense by which mankind
> To fix their friendships and their loves are led.

αἰεί τοι τὸν ὁμοῖον ἄγει θεὸς ὡς τὸν ὁμοῖον.

This was the friendship which the shade of Darius remembers, when he says to the chorus of old Persians,

> Ὦ πιστὰ πιστῶν, ἥλικές θ' ἥβης ἐμῆς
> Πέρσαι γεραιοί.[1]

Lucan, describing how the Romans in the contending armies recognized each other, says,

> Admonet hunc studiis consors puerilibus ætas.

But St. Augustine gives the most affecting description of the same friendship. "I had found a friend too dear to me, through society of studies. Of the same age as myself, like me, in the flower of youth; he had grown up along with me from a boy, and we used to accompany each other to school, and we used to play together." This was the youth whose death so sensibly affected him, "Ecce abstulisti hominem de hac vita... suavis mihi supra omnes suavitates illius vitæ meæ."[2]

Quinctilian reckons among the advantages of a public education, the firm friendships which last for life, "religiosa quadam necessitudine imbutæ. Neque enim est sanctius, sacris iisdem, quam studiis initiari."[3] In the middle ages the system of education, whether in cloisters or castles, was fruitful in this beautiful plant of friendship. "The connection," says Büsching, "which a long intercourse necessarily produced, knit together by the double bonds of benefit and gratitude, became indissoluble. Hence chivalry produced so many bonds for life and death, and for ever. Children were to repay the benefits conferred upon their fathers, and so they stood by their benefactor or by whoever

---

[1] Æschyl. Persæ, 667. [2] Confess. IV, 4. [3] I, 11.

succeeded him."[1] Neither rank nor riches interfered with the cultivation of generous friendship. This deserves especial notice. There were young men, born in the lower walks of life, who, as Cicero remarks, "sive felicitate quadam," (a remarkable expression, of which the Christian moralist may avail himself,) "sive bonitate naturæ, sive parentium disciplina, rectam vitæ secuti sunt viam": who, by education and character, by virtue and religion, and by all the delicate and elevated qualities of the soul, were, in the highest sense of the term, gentlemen.

> Ingenui vultus puer, ingenuique pudoris,
> Quales esse decet, quos ardens purpura vestit.

Formed, as it were, by the hand of nature, to win the affections of men, since

> Gratior et pulchro veniens in corpore virtus,

education and habit had confirmed and extended the advantage, by uniting it with graceful, unaffected, and engaging manners. Possessing a taste and an ability for the higher branches of intellectual cultivation, their hearts glowed with those generous feelings which enabled them to reap for themselves, and to dispense to others, the real benefits of learning. Sincere in their attachment to the institutions of their country, zealous in their religion, they discharged all the duties of social life from the highest and purest principles, ἱκανῶ γὰρ τῶ φύλακε κωλύοντε, δέος τε καὶ αἰδώς.[2] Modest and humble, as men of the noblest blood, they exhibited, in addition, a peculiar sensibility to the blessings and happiness of life, and a gratitude towards the Providence whence they flow: gentle to their inferiors, free and generous to their companions,

---

[1] Ritterzeit und Ritterwesen, p. 18. [2] Plato de Repub.

submissive and respectful to those who were placed in a superior station: above all, that which gave rise and stability to these virtues, they united all the gaiety of youth and of an unburdened conscience, with a reverence for the duties and the ordinances of religion, and with the most profound piety towards God. To befriend youth of this character was the pride of men possessing rank and affluence; to obtain their friendship, losing sight of the difference of rank which might divide them, and thereby removing the air of patronage, was found to be their interest and their happiness. I need not point out, in this place, the degradation which was believed to follow from cultivating an acquaintance with what is familiarly termed low company, but I must desire your attention to this axiom in the honour of those ages,—that, both in youth and in manhood, it was as much the praise of a gentleman to forget the adventitious circumstances of birth and rank in the formation of virtuous friendship, as it was his disgrace and infamy, in every period of life, to be the companion of vulgar vice, from a similarity of principle and disposition.

"Esto comis etiam erga tenuis fortunæ sodales," said Erasmus; and it was a wise precept, for its observance could hardly fail to secure men one of the most valuable and permanent of human enjoyments. The friendships of the world, founded upon base passions, upon interest, vanity, and pride, what are they?

> Hunc, quem cœna tibi, quem mensa paravit amicum,
> Esse putas fidæ pectus amicitiæ?
> —— bene si cœnem, noster amicus erit.[1]

---

[1] Martial.

Or, as Ovid remarks,

> Donec eris felix, multos numerabis amicos,
> Tempora si fuerint nubila, solus eris.[1]

Such was the fate of Wolsey,

> Where'er he turns he meets a stranger's eye,
> His suppliants scorn him, and his followers fly.
> Now drops at once the pride of awful state,
> The golden canopy, the glittering plate,
> The regal palace, the luxurious board,
> The liv'ried army and the menial lord.
> With age, with cares, with maladies opprest,
> He seeks the refuge of monastic rest.
> Grief aids disease, remember'd folly stings,
> And his last sighs reproach the faith of kings.

But from a consideration of such events men did not conclude, as some moderns would teach, that poverty and obscurity, of themselves, furnish men with the virtues which gave rise to real and permanent friendship. An allusion to either poverty or riches, as affecting its use and stability, is equally indicative of the false estimate which we have formed of its nature. "Quamobrem, hoc quidem constat," says Cicero, "bonis inter bonos quasi necessariam benevolentiam esse: quæ est amicitiæ fons à natura constitutus." And again, "Digni autem sunt amicitiæ quibus in ipsis inest causa, cur diligantur." And again, "Virtus, virtus inquam, et conciliat amicitias et conservat. In ea est enim convenientia rerum, in ea stabilitas, in ea constantia." Hence appears the great advantage which attended an education in those monasteries, and universities, and castles, where a facility was afforded to youth of high family, towards forming acquaintance with their contemporaries, who might otherwise have been condemned, by the obscurity

[1] Tristia.

of their birth, to remain, for life, unknown and undistinguished by those who had it in their power to reward merit, and consequently unable to employ the talents which they might eminently possess in aiding the institutions of their country, and in promoting the instruction and the happiness of mankind. Where the ancient religion has been abandoned, men of low origin, who have risen without personal merit, to riches and a certain degree of rank in the world, will generally despise all intimacy and connection with persons of this description. They resemble the foolish father, of whom Juvenal speaks,

>Qui miratur opes, qui nulla exempla beati
>Pauperis esse putat.————————

They take the converse of a great moral precept, and say to their children,

>Μᾶλλον ἀποδίχου πλοῦτον ἄδικον ἢ δίκαιαν πενίαν.

These persons are well prepared to quit the season of life's prime, and of man's best virtue, they are ready to move in that eccentric and wretched circle of human existence,

>Where man himself is but a tool,
>Where interest sways our hopes and fears,
>And all must love and hate by rule.

"As it is the humour of these creatures," says Castiglione, "to take no notice but of princes, let it be ours to take none of them." Where the Catholic religion was the guide of chivalry, such feelings and prejudices excited contempt; they were held to be absolutely unworthy men of birth and character, inconsistent with honour, with freedom and independence, with generosity of spirit, with all the elevated feelings which belong to men of true nobility, as well as with the faith and the first duties of a Christian.

This leads me to the great source of friendship in our heroic age—the religion of chivalry, which was the foundation and strength of its friendship. What security resulted from the Catholic spirit of mortification, which was ever ready to bear another's burden![1] In all ages men seem to have been aware of the advantage of contracting friendship with persons who are dear to Heaven. It was on this ground that Diomedes chose Ulysses as his companion on the expedition by night to the camp of the Trojans.[2] Whoso desires fellowship with a man of light, sceptical, or worldly mind, should never reckon upon its continuation.

> Yea, he deserves to find himself deceived,
> Who seeks a heart in the unthinking man.
> Like shadows on a stream, the forms of life
> Impress their characters on the smooth forehead,
> Nought sinks into the bosom's silent depth:
> Quick sensibility of pain and pleasure
> Moves the light fluids lightly; but no soul
> Warmeth the inner frame.[3]

Our Christian knights were not without such reflections. Even those whose pursuits were most foreign from the sanctuary, evince a soundness of judgment in the choice of friends. Pierre Vidal, the troubadour, thus advises a companion. "Prefer among young men those who have feeling: they are always desirous of honour, and are naturally magnificent. Keep company with such as are of manly age, provided they think with nobleness: they love grave men, such as praise virtue and combat vice, and have an inclination to whatever is good. Shun those whose manners are corrupt, and

---

[1] Nieremberg, Doct. Ascet. VI, xi, 10.   [2] Il. X, 245.
[3] Schiller's Wallenstein, by Coleridge.

whose tastes are low. In them you will find a sovereign contempt for poets. Still, some few of these characters repent after a long time, and amend their lives, and it is better to associate with them than with proud, stupid, rich people, who are daily more and more puffed up with wind. Shun those who join a revolting brutality to some talent, and who delight in low company. You will find other barons who think of nothing besides drinking, eating, and sleeping. Shame is all that can be gained in their company."[1] The maxim of Godfrey of Bouillon,

Who fears no God, he loves no friend,[2]

was repeated in every instruction to youth. The same sentiment occurs in the Toison d'Or, " s'il n'est feable et loyal à Dieu il ne peult être aux hommes." " Non est fidus amicus nisi in Deo, et qui sua non quærit."[3] Hence friendship required and promoted virtue. It was too dignified to admit within its circle that trifling and worldly character which accommodates itself to all opinions and manners. " Proteus like, to read with the studious, to engage in the arena with the lovers of the games, to hunt with hunters, to drink with drunkards, to frequent the bar with civilians, ἰδίαν ἤθους ἑστίαν οὐκ ἔχοντος, is miserable and contrary to friendship, which requires a certain stable and unchangeable disposition,—retaining the same custom." It is Plutarch who says this.[4] "A flatterer," he says, "thinks that he ought to do all things that may be agreeable; but a friend, always doing what is right, is often agreeable, but often the contrary, not wishing this, but neither avoiding it if it is proper for him to be

---

[1] Hist. des Troubadours, II, p. 29.
[2] Jerusalem Delivered, IV.
[3] Thomas à Kempis, lib. de Recogn. 3.
[4] De Amicor. Multitud.

so."[1] "To love another," says Aristotle, "is to wish well to him, and to do him good for his sake, and not for one's own."[2] Not to study his advantage, but merely to contribute to his pleasure in society while we are with him, is to wish well to ourself and to do him good for our own sake. Solon admonished Crœsus in his prosperity; so did Socrates, Alcibiades; Cyrus, Cyaxares, and Plato Dion; but Euctus and Eulæus, the companions of Perseus, flattered him in his success and reproached him in his fall, after the battle of Pydna, when vanquished by the Romans.

"Friendship is of use to young men," says Aristotle, "in preserving them from vice," (καὶ νέοις δὲ πρὸς τὸ ἀναμάρτητον.[3]) It was the same reflection which made Plato require fear as one of the two essential qualifications in a candidate for victory, δύο γὰρ οὖν ἐστὸν τὰ τὴν νίκην ἀπεργαζόμενα, θάρρος μὲν πολεμίων, φίλων δὲ φόβος αἰσχύνης πέρι κακῆς. Ἄφοβον ἡμῶν ἄρα δεῖ γίγνεσθαι καὶ φοβερὸν ἕκαστον.[4] Friendship, however, with our Catholic ancestors, was not confined to be a mere remedy for evils or an instrument of good. It was itself an emanation from the highest good, and it terminated in the fountain of all friendship and of all love. Τὸ ἄρα φίλον ἡμῖν ἐκεῖνο εἰς ὃ ἐτελεύτα πάντα τἆλλα, ἃ ἕνεκα ἑτέρου φίλου φίλα ἔφαμεν εἶναι (ἐκεῖνα) οὐδὲν δὴ τούτοις ἔοικε."[5] "Your friend," says Thomas à Kempis,[6] "is he who loves you in God, and who bears with your faults on account of God; he is your friend who loves the safety of your soul, who laments for you and prays for you, who rejoices with you and loves you in charity."

As men did not love themselves in their friends,

---

[1] De Adulat. et Amici discr. [2] De Rhetor. II, 14.
[3] Ethic. VIII, 1. [4] Plato de Legibus, I.
[5] Platonis Lysis. [6] Lib. de Recog. Prop. Frag. 3.

but God, it was unavoidable that they should
shrink from a friendship which was independent of
religion. The Catholic spirit, like that of love,
though strong as death, was to the highest degree
delicate and susceptible. It was essentially the
spirit of submission to the great laws by which
the Almighty governs the moral world; it was
incapable of seeking to resist or alter them; it
could neither enlarge nor diminish the sphere of
its own action. Hence, the words of St. Augustine were most justly expressive of its influence,
when he said "beware of those who praise you
ill, and say euge, euge. They praise falsely. You
are a great man, a good man, accomplished,
learned; but why a Christian?" why a Catholic?
"They praise you on those points on which you are
unwilling to be praised; they condemn that which
is the source of your joy; and if perchance you
should reply, 'Why dost thou praise me, O man,
for being good? If thou thinkest that I am
good, it is Christ who hath made me good; praise
him.' But the other will add, 'For shame! be not
unjust to yourself, you have made yourself what
you are.'" "Confundantur qui dicunt mihi, euge,
euge."[1] "Friendship," says St. Chrysostom,
is a plant of Heaven;"[2] it grows with the spiritual growth of men; it is strengthened by the
silence of meditation; everything that belongs to
religion and genius feeds and strengthens it; the
music of evening choirs; the peaceful aspirations
of the soul; the adorable sacrament of the altar.
"Amicitia quæ desinere potest," says St. Jerome,
"vera nunquam fuit."[3] Founded on what is divine
and eternal, it can never fail. The golden words,
"Know thyself," apply here also, for through the

[1] In Ps. XXXIX, § 26.   [2] Hom. II, in 1 Thessal.
[3] Ep. ad Rufin. 3.

bond of charity, thy friend is like thyself, and thou knowest him as thine own soul. Such was the friendship of St. Augustine and Alypius, of St. Basil of Cæsarea and St. Gregory Nazianzen; of innumerable holy monks, who inhabited those romantic abbeys, whose ruins now inspire every feeling breast with profound sadness; of innumerable students, who were trained within their walls to learning; and, doubtless, also, of many devout souls, concealed to the eye of the world, under the steel panoply of temporal warfare. Among the epistles of St. Boniface, there is one from an attendant priest to Balthardus. "My soul is weary of my life (it is thus he writes) on account of my love for you; for I am left alone and without help from relations. Pater meus et mater mea dereliquerant me, dominus autem suscepit me. The great ocean is between thee and me, and yet we are joined in love, for true charity is never dissolved by distance of place. Nevertheless, to say the truth, sadness never departs from my soul, nor can sleep give rest to my spirit, for love is strong as death. Now then, dearest brother, I beseech you come to me, that I may behold you before I die, for the love of you never forsakes me. I pray for you as for myself, day and night, each hour and moment, that you may always have health with Christ. May you be happy and holy. May we live to our Lord for ever. I beseech Him humbly, with tears falling to the ground, to bear assistance, that we may be worthy of that glory, where the joyful songs of angels resound for ever."[1]

"A faithful friend," says St. Chrysostom, "is the medicine of life; for what can not be effected by means of a true friend; or what pleasure, what utility, what security does he not afford?

[1] Epist. 63.

what pleasure has friendship! the mere beholding him diffuses an unspeakable joy, and at the bare memory of him the mind is elevated. I have known one who used to beg holy men to pray first for his friend and then for him. Such is friendship, that through him we love places and seasons; for as bright bodies emit rays to a distance, and flowers drop their sweet leaves on the ground around them, so friends impart favour even to the places where they dwell, and when we return to these places without these friends, we weep and lament, remembering the days which we spent in their society. With friends even poverty is pleasant. Words cannot express the joy which a friend imparts: they only can know who have experienced it. A friend is dearer than the light of heaven; for it would be better for us that the sun were extinguished than that we should be without friends. Many who behold the sun are still in darkness. He who loves does not wish to command nor to have authority, but has greater pleasure in obedience and receiving commands, and he had rather confer a benefit than receive it, and still appear to be a debtor, and not a benefactor. I know that many cannot understand this; and the reason is, because I speak about what is in heaven. Were I to speak of some Indian plant to one who had never been in that region, he would have no idea of it after all my description, and this plant grows in heaven, having branches, not loaded with pearls, but bearing life, which is the sweetest of all fruits."[1]

Buoncompagno, a Florentine, wrote a treatise on friendship, and distinguished between twenty-six different kinds of friends. The spirit of those ages, with the simplicity of truth, knew of no such

[1] In 1 Thessal. Hom. XI.

distinctions. Charondas, the Thurian legislator, perceiving that good men were injured by the friendship of evil men, forbade persons to form such friendship, and imposed a heavy penalty on the transgressors.[1] The divine legislator of Christians taught them by his example to treat no man with disdain, but to embrace all in the exercise of charity.

Aristotle[2] and Plutarch[3] both say that whom your friend loves you must love, and whom he hates you must hate. The friendship of Christian chivalry would participate in the love, but not until it had overcome the hatred. The moderns think they evince friendship when they gain any promotion for another in the affairs of this world. Our ancestors thought they evinced friendship as often when they opposed as when they promoted advancement. Count Theobald requested St. Bernard to use his interest with Pope Eugenius to procure for his son William, who was but a boy, some ecclesiastical dignity. St. Bernard replied, " Heartily do I wish our little William all good; but above all things that he may stand well with God. For this reason, I must never procure for him an office, his accepting of which would be opposed to the will of God, and by which he might lose God."[4] Even the ancients had regard in friendship to the instruction of others. Pliny concludes his letter to Caninius with observing, that " as friends they ought mutually to excite each other to the love of immortality."[5] With our ancestors the desire to instruct a friend and lead him in the way of heaven was a motive which induced them to devote themselves to the study of religion, and to prostrate themselves in prayer to God. Hear St. Augustine.

---

[1] Diodorus Sicul. XII, 12. [2] De Rhetor. II.
[3] Apophthegm. [4] Epist. 271. [5] Lib. III, 7.

"A friend comes to you from a journey, that is, from the journey of this life, in which all are passing like travellers, and no one can remain at rest as if the ground were his, but to every man it is said, 'You are refreshed, now pass on, proceed on your way, give place to the new guest.' Perhaps some one who is your friend may come to you from an unfortunate journey, that is, from an evil life, wearied, unable to find truth, by hearing and receiving which he might be happy; but fatigued with all the desires and poverty of the world, he comes to you as to a Christian, and he says, Give me a reason, make me a Christian; and, perchance, this which he asks you are not able to give him, through the simplicity of your faith, and you have not wherewithal to appease his thirst. Simple faith may, indeed, suffice to you; to him it cannot suffice. Is he, therefore, to be deserted, is he to be dismissed from under your roof? You must have recourse to God; knock and pray, seek and persevere; learn and teach. Disce et doce."[1]

In all circumstances of life, friends discharged a religious service. When Louis de Clermont, Duc de Bourbon, heard of the calamity which had befallen King Charles VI, he immediately went to the monastery of St. Julian, and there shut himself up for two days, to implore Heaven for his nephew! Lastly, the friendship of these ages extended beyond the grave. Here was one of the grand triumphs of the Catholic religion, by which it proved itself suitable to the wants of mortal men, and worthy of the beneficence of God. With heathens, the loss of a friend was a calamity which admitted of no consolation; the bond was severed for ever; and when the body was once committed to the flames, there was an end of service, and no longer an object

[1] Serm. 105.

for fidelity. True it was a consolation to Pompey's freedman to have touched the body, and assisted at the funeral, of the greatest and noblest soldier Rome ever produced;[1] and the friendship of the two youths, Cloridan and Medor, for Dardinel, was still exercised in rescuing his body, that it might not lie among the other slain, giving rise, in this heroic adventure, to that beautiful episode in Ariosto; but how soon did this poor shadow of friendship vanish for ever! It was in vain that Thetis reminded her son of the success of his prayers for the punishment of Agamemnon: deeply groaning, Achilles replied to her: "My mother, Heaven, indeed, has fulfilled my desires:"

Ἀλλὰ τί μοι τῶν ἧδος, ἐπεὶ φίλος ὤλεθ' ἑταῖρος,
Πάτροκλος; τὸν ἐγὼ περὶ πάντων τῖον ἑταίρων
Ἴσον ἐμῇ κεφαλῇ, τὸν ἀπώλεσα.[2]

The best consolation that poetry could devise for the friends of Diomedes, on the death of that hero, was to suppose them changed into swans, who should be always distinguished from others by their propensity to approach Greeks. These were the birds of Diomedes. What irremediable sorrow does Homer ascribe to Achilles on the night when the ghost of Patroclus appeared to him! The Greeks were retired to sleep after their banquet,

Πηλείδης δ' ἐπὶ θινὶ πολυφλοίσβοιο θαλάσσης
Κεῖτο βαρυστενάχων, πολέσιν μετὰ Μυρμιδόνεσσιν,
Ἐν καθαρῷ, ὅθι κύματ' ἐπ' ἠϊόνος κλύζεσκον.[3]

And again, after celebrating his funeral, when the other Greeks were retired to sweet sleep,

—————— αὐτὰρ Ἀχιλλεὺς
Κλαῖε, φίλου ἑτάρου μεμνημένος, οὐδέ μιν ὕπνος
Ἥρει πανδαμάτωρ, ἀλλ' ἐστρέφετ' ἔνθα καὶ ἔνθα,
Πατρόκλου ποθέων ἀδροτῆτά τε καὶ μένος ἠΰ·

---

[1] Plutarch.   [2] Il. XVIII, 80.   [3] Il. XXIII, 59.

'Ηδ' ὁπόσα τολύπευσε σὺν αὐτῷ, καὶ πάθεν ἄλγεα,
'Ανδρῶν τε πτολέμους, ἀλεγεινά τε κύματα πείρων·
Τῶν μιμνησκόμενος, θαλερὸν κατὰ δάκρυον εἶβεν,
Ἄλλοτ' ἐπὶ πλευρὰς κατακείμενος, ἄλλοτε δ' αὖτε
Ὕπτιος, ἄλλοτε δὲ πρηνής· τότε δ' ὀρθὸς ἀναστὰς
Δινεύεσκ' ἀλύων παρὰ θῖν' ἁλός.[1]

To cherish, indeed, a fond memory of a friend, as of an object never again to be approached or served, was permitted them. "Alike loving the present and the absent," says Aristotle, of friends, "and therefore equally the dead."[2] Men deceived their hearts with words,

————— Τοῦ δ' οὐκ ἐπιλήσομαι, ὄφρ' ἂν ἔγωγε
Ζωοῖσιν μετέω, καί μοι φίλα γούνατ' ὀρώρῃ·
Εἰ δὲ θανόντων περ καταλήθοντ' εἰν ἀΐδαο,
Αὐτὰρ ἐγὼ καὶ κεῖθι φίλου μεμνήσομ' ἑταίρου.[3]

This is the consolation of Achilles, when he prepared to honour the dead body of Patroclus. Such thoughts were honourable to human nature, but most ineffectual to give it peace. Our Christian chivalry had other views; it had to lament only temporary absence from a departed friend, not an eternal separation, and the end of his existence. "Illum dilige sepultum ut viventem dilexisti," says Petrarch to one who had lost his brother, "illum coge saepius ad te reverti commemoratione pia et frequenti."[4] Bossuet never passed through Nanteuil without stopping to pray devoutly on the tomb of the Mareschal de Schomberg, his early friend and benefactor; and the Cardinal de Pavia, in his account of the death of Pope Pius II., describes an affecting scene. "We stood weeping round the venerable old man, who, looking on me, made signs that I should approach. Then, with a faint voice he said, 'Pray for me, my son, for I am

---

[1] Il. XXIV, 3.   [2] De Rhetor. II, 4.
[3] Il. XXII, 387.   [4] Epist. lib. II, 1.

a sinner'; and then turning his eyes to the cross, which was placed before him, he repeated, with tears, 'Miserere mei Deus, miserere mei.' When I in vain endeavoured to reply, 'be mindful of me, my son, he said, 'and offer prayer to God for me.' These were his last words."[1] Those of Bayard were the same, as he took affectionate leave of his dear friends, and said, "Remember my poor soul." The grateful piety of the children of St. Bruno inscribed him in their ritual. The prior general of the Carthusians instituted in all monasteries of the order throughout the world a perpetual anniversary obit for the repose of his soul.[2] By the rule of the hermits of the fountain of Avalon, on the death of a brother, every member of the community observed a fast for seven days; and if any novice or stranger should have been surprised by death, as soon as the hermits were apprised of the event, they took upon themselves to perform his penance. Happy men, who freely devoted themselves not only to serve the living, but also to follow after the dead! They had well marked our Saviour's words, that some kind of evil cannot be by one man removed from another without prayer and fasting; that as in the natural world the evil and guilt of one man are suffered to descend upon another, so the charity and faith of one can serve many; "For though," as Sir Thomas More says, "man's penance, with all the good workes that he can doe, be not able to satisfie of them selfe for the least sinne that we doe; yet the liberal godenes of God, through the merite of Christes bitter passion, without which all our workes could neither satisfie nor deserve, nor yet in dede neither merite nor satisfie so muche as a sponefull to a great vessel full, in comparison of

[1] Comment. Jacobi Piccol. Card. Papiensis, I, 360.
[2] Vie de Bayart, par Alfred de Terrebasse.

the merite and satisfaction that Christ hath merited and satisfied for us himselfe: this liberal goodnes of God, I say, shall yet at our faithful instance and request cause our penance and tribulation, paciently taken in this worlde, to serve us in the other world, both for release and reward, tempered after such rate as his high goodness and wisdom shall see convenient for us, whereof our blind mortalitie could not here imagine nor devise the stint."[1] The weak service of a mortal nature can never satisfy even the affectionate heart: as Goethe says, "Did man undertake gratefully to acquit himself always for all that he owes to God, to his ancestors, and his parents, to his friends and his companions, time and sensibility would both fail him"; but by rendering the assistance of devout suffrage at the divine altars, his service partook not of the shortness of his time, or of the infirmity of his nature. The third, seventh, tenth, and thirtieth day after the decease, and the anniversary for ever, beheld the great propitiatory sacrifice of the altar, and heard the sublime memento, for those who were gone before with the sign of faith, and who slept in the sleep of peace. The genius of Tacitus has transmitted the life of Agricola, graven in immortal characters, to be the praise and admiration of all ages: the ability of Clarendon has enabled him to erect a temple to an unhappy king, a monument of awful and instructive events, where age may remember, and youth may learn the lessons of disinterested patriotism, and of constant though unrecompensed fidelity; but the piety of Joinville induced him to have a chapel in his house, a sanctuary to friendship; an altar where he might continually beseech God to absolve the soul of Louis, and to receive it into his eternal rest.

---

[1] Book on Comfort, chap. XL.

This was more grateful to the heart than either an epitaph or a history; and this was the consolation of Christian friendship.

X. The hospitality of these ages is a subject not unworthy of the muse. One of the most picturesque poets of antiquity furnishes some festive scenes of great beauty: such as the feast of Jason and his companions on the evening before their departure from Greece;[1] or that in the palace of Phineas at Salmydessus on the Euxine, after the Argonauts had delivered that prince from the dreadful harpies,[2] when Jason makes a generous speech to his blind host, who furnishes an instance in his reply of what Berkley recommends in his Siris; the giving men a glimpse of another world superior to the sensible; "so that while they are thinking only of cherishing the animal life, they may be led to a remembrance of the intellectual." Another instance is the entertainment given to the Argonauts in the castle of Lycus, the chief of the Mariandyni, when Jason relates his adventures to their admiring host. Prior objects to the heroes of Homer their passion for an equal feast. Virgil makes King Evander[3] reason like Belarius in Shakespeare:

——— Fair youth, come in :
Discourse is heavy fasting ; when we've supped
We'll mannerly demand thee of thy story.[4]

Axylus of Arisba, near Abydos, whom Diomede slew, resembled in one respect the Christian baron on his estates:

Ἀφνειὸς βιότοιο, φίλος δ' ἦν ἀνθρώποισιν·
Πάντας γὰρ φιλέεσκεν, ὁδῷ ἔπι οἰκία ναίων.[5]

Such was also the hospitality and munificence of Cimon, who kept a public table, and used to give

[1] Apollon. Rhod. I, 457. [2] Id. II, 305.
[3] Æneid, VIII, 197. [4] Cymbeline. [5] Il. VI, 14.

money to poor guests; and of Gellias of Agrigentum, who used to station servants at his gates, to invite all strangers to enter, and partake of hospitality. Many of the other Agrigentines had the same custom, as Diodorus adds, ἀρχαϊκῶς καὶ φιλανθρώπως ὁμιλοῦντες; so that Empedocles said of them,

Ξείνων αἰδοῖοι λιμένες, κακότητος ἄπειροι.

On one occasion Gellias received 500 horsemen coming in the winter time from Gela; and he gave to every man a habit and a cloak.[1] When Nestor entreats Telemachus to sleep in his house, instead of returning to the ship, he concludes, "it shall never be said that the son of Ulysses slept on the deck of his ship while I am alive."[2] Athenæus remarks that Xenophon, Speusippus, and Aristotle wrote treatises on hospitable entertainment. In describing the hospitality of our ancestors, each of our chivalrous writers will be found ὁμηρικώτατος, an epithet most applicable, in this respect, to the old gentlemen of France, before Richelieu had completed the work of Louis XI, in destroying or perverting them by banishment, and obliging them to reside at the court. Let us take an example. "And thenne felle there a thonder and a rayne, as heven and erth shold go to gyder. And Syr Gareth was not a lytel wery, for of all that day he had but lytel reste, neyther his horse nor he. So this Syr Gareth rode soo long in the forest, untyl the nyght came. And ever it lyghtened and thonderd as it had been wode. At the last, by fortune, he came to a castel, and there he herd the waytes upon the wallys. Thenne Syr Gareth rode unto the barbycan of the castle, and praid the porter fayr to lete hym into the castel. The porter answered ungoodely

[1] Diodorus, XIII, 83.   [2] Od. III, 358.

ageyne, and saide, thow getest no lodgyng here. Fayr syr, say not soo, for I am a knyghte of Kyng Arthur's, and pray the lord or the lady of this castel to gyve me herberow for the love of Kynge Arthur. Thenne the porter wente unto the duchesse, and told her how there was a knyghte of Kyng Arthur's wold have herberowe. Lete hym in, said the duchesse, for I wille see that knyghte. And for Kyng Arthur's sake he shalle not be herberoules. Thenne she yode up in to a toure over the gate with grete torche lyght." And after some conference with the knight, when he engaged to yield himself prisoner to her lord, the Duke de la Rouse, if he should appear and mean to do him no harm, or else to release himself with his spear and sword, "ye say wel, said the duchesse, and thenne she lete the drawe brydge doune, and soo he rode in to the halle, and there he alyghte, and his hors was ledde in to a stable, and in the halle he unarmed hym, and säide, madame, I will not oute of thys halle thys nyghte. And when it is daye lyghte lete see who wil have adoo with me, he shall fynde me redy. Thenne was he sette unto souper, and had many good dysshes; thenne Syr Gareth lyst well to ete, and knyghtely he ete his mete and egerly, there was many a fair lady by hym, and some said they never sawe a goodlyer man, nor so wel of etynge; thenne they made hym passyng good chere, and shortly when he had souped, his bedde was made there, so he rested hym al nyghte. And on the morne he herd masse, and brake his fast, and toke his leve at the duchesse, and at them al, and thanked her goodely of her lodgyng, and of his good chere, and thenne she asked hym his name. Madame, he saide, truly my name is Gareth, of Orkney, and some men call me Beaumayns. So Syr Gareth departed."[1]

[1] Morte d'Arthur, vol. I, p. 236.

The pleasure of hospitality was connected with the habits of a hardy life, which belonged equally to the host and to his guest. "Am I comfortably lodged," said Montaigne, "in a fine hall, during a dark tempestuous night? I shudder and grieve for those who are out of doors. Am I out myself, I desire no better sport."

What follows is a forest adventure from another romance of chivalry. "Than Arthur and his company rode forth, and travayled so long, til at the last they founde a strange house, and knocked so longe at the gate tyll there came to them a varlet, bare legged, redy to go to bed, for all other in the place were as than gone to theyr restes; and than this foresayde varlet demanded of theym, who it was that knocked so fast at the gate that time of night! 'Good friende,' quod Governar, 'it is a knyght that wolde fain this night have lodgyng for hym and hys company.' 'Syr,' sayd the varlet, 'if it please you to tary, I wyll go speake with my lorde and mayster, and shew hym your mynde: how be it, I think he be now at his rest, for he is olde and ancient, and hath been in his days a very good knight, and as yet he is glad to here speking of good knights, and loveth them that haunteth noble deeds of armes'; and therwith the varlet departed, and went to his master, and said, 'Syr, there is at your gates three knights armed, and are be semyng goyng to Vienne to the tornay; and they desire, by way of gentilness, this one nightes lodgyng; how saye ye, syr, shall I open to them the gates?' 'Hie thee a pace," quod the Lord, 'for I am not content that thou hast made them to tary without so long; and whan they be entered, come agayne to me, and bring me word what maner of men that they be, and what harnys and armes they bere.' Than the varlet went agayne to the gate, and set it wide open, and suffred Arthur and his company te enter; whereof they had grete nede. Than the varlet beheld Arthur, and saw wel that he was like a gentilman, being long and wel fornysshed, and mervaylously fayre above all his company. And next him he saw Hector, who was ryght fayre, hie, and wel made. And also he beheld Governar, who was in all poyntes like a man bigge, and browne of colour; and also he percyved wel how all theyr harneys wer fayre and ryche. Than was there torches brought forth, and varlets ranne for theyr horses. Than the first varlet returned agayn to his lorde, and sayd, 'Sir, sith that I was borne, I never sawe so goodlye knyghts as they be, and specially the chief of them; and as for theyr armour, it is both feyre and ryche: for I ensure you, it should seeme that they be right grete men, and comyn of a noble lygnage.' 'Well,' quod the lorde, 'loke that thou in al haste apparayle theyr lodginge; and see that they be served right honourably.' 'Well, syr,' quod the varlet, 'it shall be done incontinent.' Then the lorde sayd to the lady his wife, 'Madame, by reason of your honour and gentylness, ye should ryse and kepe companie with yonder noble knights, for I think they be some grete men; for it shall gretely annoye them, and they see not the chyef of the house to make them some chere; for as God help me, I wolde have great joy to speak with them, yf I might aryse and not hurt myself; therefore, madam, in mine absence, I pray you go and make to them the best chere that ye can.' 'Syr,' sayd the lady, 'with a right good will, syth it please you, I shall so do.' Then this lady rose, and apparayled herself ryght fresahly, who was a right fayr yonge lady, of the age of twenty-one years. And when Arthur and Hector saw her, they rose, and curteysly eche of them dyd salute other, and she sat her downe betwene them. Than Arthur sayd, 'Madame, ye haue taken a grete payne to leve the company of your lorde to come to se us.' 'Sir, it pleaseth my lord, that I shall so do; and therefore I am come to you in the stede of hym; for he wolde wyth a ryght good wyl, haue come to you hymself, yf he myght so have done; but syres, he is ancient, and it wolde sore anoye him to have broken his reste'; and so thus they talked of dyvers things. And in the mean season there was mete provided for them, and than the tables were spred and covered; and so than they washed, and sat them downe."[1]

Büsching quotes a passage from the old German poem of Swain, describing how the knight Kalogriant lost his way in a wild forest, and rode till evening, when he arrived at its extremity, and came upon a plain, where he saw a castle: "I rode up to the gate, and saw a knight standing at the outside. This was the lord of the castle; for having espied me riding at the skirts of the forest, he would not wait till I had arrived, nor oblige me to make the first salutation, but had hold of my reins and stirrup before I could address him, and then he made me a welcome, for which I have reason to thank God, for I was never before in such need of herberough. The gate was opened, and a number of fine young gentlemen and pages came out, and bid me welcome, both me and my horse; and then followed a young demoiselle, a more lovely child I never saw, and she unarmed me, and I was sorry that there were so few straps of leather to my armour, that I might not so quickly lose her charming company."

Perceforest bears testimony to the hospitable spirit of the English. "Adoncques estoit une coustume en la grant Bretaigne et fut tant que charite regna illecque, tous gentils hommes et nobles

---

[1] Arthur of Little Britain, p. 64.

dames faisoient mettre au plus hault de leur hostel ung heaulme en signe que tous gentils hommes et gentilles femmes trespassans les chemins, entrassent hardyement en leur hostel comme au leur propre; car leur biens estoient davantage à tous nobles hommes et femmes trespassans le Royaulme." Helmets used to be placed everywhere on the gates of castles, to signify to all knights who passed by, that they would meet with hospitality within. Ste. Palaye had often seen them. In Burgundy lights used to burn every night on the towers of castles, to guide persons to hospitality; a custom only omitted the night when its lord died.[1] The hospitality shown at the château de Rouvre, near Dijon, by the dukes of Burgundy, is celebrated in history. The host of these times might say, "Benedictio pereuntis super me veniat: janua mea aperta fuit omni afflicto." Describing the hospitality of the Countess of Richmond, Bishop Fisher says, "For the straungers, O mervaylous God! what payn, what labour she of her veray gentleness wolde take with them, to bere them maner and company, and entrete every person, and entertayne them, according to their degree and honour, and provyde by her own commandement, that nothynge sholde lacke, that myghte be convenyent for them, wherein she had a wonderful redy remembrance and perfect knowledge." To be able to show all reverence to worthy men, was the pride of chivalry. Thus, in the great romance of the Round Table, Sir Gallehault says, alluding to Sir Launcelot, "Jamais si grant honneur ne me avendra que jay si preudhomme en mon hostel."[2] In the Palmerin of England we read how the knight of fortune rode towards the ancient and famous city of London, desirous to see the English court, the fame whereof was blazed

---

[1] Tristan, V, 110.   [2] Tom. III, fol. xxvii.

through the whole world. After three days' travel, he arrived at the house of an ancient gentleman, which was by the roadside, two leagues from the city, and there he reposed for that night, conceiving great pleasure to confer with his host (who loved to entertain all wandering knights) about the estate of that country, with the noble adventures in old time passed, as also at that present in Great Britain. In the romance of Guerin de Montglaive, Aimeri upbraids his uncle Gerard, lord of Vienne, for his churlish and inhospitable mode of housekeeping. "Vous ne vallez rien qui ainsi faictes fermer votre palaie. La cour d'un gentilhomme doit estre deffermée à toutes gens; messagers, menestriers, heraux doivent trouver les cours ouvertes: et si y doivent manger et avoir de l'argent." The "franc manger" was a kind of pension which the possessor enjoyed on presenting himself every day at the feudal table. Foundations of this kind are still preserved in many provinces of France. But it was when the Church invited the faithful to rejoice that the magnificence of our ancestors was chiefly shewn.

> Then blazed the castle at the midnight hour
> For him whose arms had shook its firmest tower.

However, in the Nibelungen lay, the knights after mass sit down to dinner in the hall of King Etzel, every man in complete armour. Vinisauf relates how Richard I at Messina, after the difference respecting the standard had been composed, invited the king of France and his court to a grand entertainment on Christmas-day. "Voce præconaria omnem animam vocavit ad diem tantam deducendam secum cum lætitia et gaudio. Who could describe the richness of the vessels and the pomp of the attendants?" And again he records how King Richard celebrated Easter in Ascalon, on the 9th of April, 1122, and how he gave a grand feast, with plenty to eat and drink to every one that wished: he ordered tents to be placed in the suburbs, and everything to be procured that could delight his people. Froissart describes a Christmas feast in the hall of the castle of Gaston, Earl of Foix, at Ortez in Bearn, in 1388. At the upper or first table sate four bishops, then the earl, three viscounts, and an English knight belonging to the Duke of Lancaster. At another table were five abbots and two knights of Aragon; at another, several barons and knights of Gascony and Bigorre; at another, a great number of knights of Bearn; four knights were the chief stewards of the hall, and the two bastard brothers of the earl served at the high table. "The earle's two sonnes, Sir Yvan of Leschell was shewer, and Sir Gracyen bare his cuppe. And there were many mynstrelles, as well of his owne, as of straungers, and eche of them dyde their devoyre in their faculties. The same day the erle of Foix gave to haraulds and mynstrelles the somme of fyve hundred franks: and gave to the Duke of Tourayne's mynstrelles, gownes of cloth and golde furred with ermyns, valued at 200 franks. This dinner endured four hours." Holinshed says of King Henry III in 1246: "The king this year held hys Christmas at London, and had there with hym a greate number of the nobilitie of his realme which hadde bin with him in Wales, that they might be partakers of pastime, mirth, and pleasure, as they had bin participant with him in suffering the diseases of heate, colde, and other paines abroade in the fields and high mountaynes of Wales."[1]

That the custom in England of having more generous repasts on the festivals of the Church (one, by the way, which the moderns did not think

[1] Vol. II, 714.

proper to abolish) may be traced to a pagan origin, is clear from a letter of Pope Gregory to St. Augustine, in which he says, "Since the people have been accustomed to kill animals in sacrifice to devils, it may be well to permit that they slay them now on the nativity of the martyrs, in honour of God, and in order to give thanks to the Author of all things; so that, allowing them exterior pleasure, they may be brought more easily to receive interior joys: for it is impossible of a sudden to retrench everything when we have to deal with men of hardened hearts."[1]

Marchangy[2] and Strutt describe the manner of rejoicing in the northern provinces of France and in England; and Berenger furnishes a beautiful picture of a Christmas festivity in Provence, under the influence of that more genial climate.[3] The spirit and object were the same everywhere: as described in the beautiful sermon of the Pope St. Leo, which is read in the office for the night of the vigil of Christmas, "Salvator noster, dilectissimi, hodie natus est, gaudeamus. Neque enim fas est locum esse tristitiæ, ubi natalis est vitæ: nemo ab hujus alacritatis participatione secernitur. Una cunctis lætitiæ communis est ratio." Thus we find religion again presenting itself to preside over the enjoyments of men; yet, at these very seasons, when the Church seemed to invite men to a more particular gratitude, she was careful to remind them of the necessity of cultivating those general habits of a religious life, which could alone enable them to celebrate these festivals worthily. "The first of our festivals is Christmas," said holy men. "What is the object of this festival? That God appeared upon the earth and walked with men; but this is

[1] Ap. Spelman. Concil. vol. I.
[2] Tristan, ou le Voyageur en France, dans le XIV Siecle.
[3] Soirées Provençales, I, 168.

so at all times, for he saith, 'I am with you always, even till the end of the world'; therefore we can keep Christmas at all times. What does the second festival signify? We proclaim the death of Christ. That is the Paschal time; but as we can at all times celebrate the death of our Lord, so we can at all times keep the feast of the Paschal. What is the object of this day's festival? The descent of the Holy Ghost; but as the only begotten Son of God is with believers always, so also is the Holy Spirit."[1]

Notwithstanding the stately magnificence of the feudal hall, great simplicity belonged to the character of these entertainments. Men had definite wants, which were easily satisfied. Homer does not place dainty fricassees before his heroes, ἀλλ' ἀφ' ὧν εὖ ἕξειν ἔμελλον τὸ σῶμα καὶ τὴν ψυχήν.[2] Ulysses was dexterous in cooking for himself. When Publicola would reward Horatius Cocles, he procured a decree that every Roman should give him one day's provisions, and Herodotus says that the Spartan kings were served with a double portion. Our ancestors preferred the table of Cimon, which, at a moderate charge, daily nourished great numbers of poor, to that of Lucullus, which, at a vast expense, pleased the appetites of a few of the rich and voluptuous. At the supper of Seuthes, King of Thrace, the temperance of Xenophon is contrasted with the qualities of the Arcadian, who was φαγεῖν δεινόν; but it is to be feared that with the heathen chivalry, the example of Hercules was too often followed. The Emperor Charles IV is said, indeed, Esau like, to have made over Piedmont to the Duke of Anjou, in recompense of a dinner he gave him, at Villeneuve; but the poetic eye of Dante could discern no knight in the third

[1] St. Chrysostom. [2] Athenæus, lib. I, c. 8.

circle of the City of Woe. Our knights were never to go beyond the second cups of Eubulus; the first sacred to health, the second to love and friendship. To call a man drunkard, in Spain, is the very highest insult possible. The champions of the new philosophy, in the sixteenth century, deemed all this abstinence a relic of heathenism, ὥσπερ πυθαγορίζων; and Luther's knights were princes of the cup, who prided themselves in passing beyond the eight stages enumerated by the old Deipnosophist, leading to the manners of a lictor, sickness and fury. Chivalry, however, was not the advocate of lady-like delicacy. "The second day of the meeting between King Alfonso and the Cid, the king, and all they who went with him to this meeting, ate with the Cid, and so well did he prepare for them," says the chronicle, "that all were full joyful, and agreed in one thing, that they had not eaten better for three years."

The Bayeux tapestry, worked by Queen Mathilda, representing, among other exploits of the Norman knights, their first supper, after landing in England, when the cooks are presenting each of them with fowls and joints of meat on the spit, will verify what Posidonius said of the Celts, that they ate off spits; with cleanliness indeed, λεοντωδῶς δέ.[1] The old historians praise the moderation of Charlemagne, and record that at his table, excepting on extraordinary occasions, there were never more than four dishes besides the roast meat, which the hunters brought up on the spit. "Our fathers were not delicate in their choice of food," says Le Grand.[2] They used to eat the heron, crane, wild-goose, swan, cormorant, and bittern, which were served at the first tables. Liebaut calls the

---

[1] Athenæus, IV, 92.
[2] L'Hist. de la Vie Privée des François.

heron "viande royale." Gentlemen used to have heronries, and the heron, as well as the peacock, was the occasion of vows at table. To this day, the solan-goose forms the principal food of the islanders of Scotland.

The Angle-Saxons used to eat porpesses,[1] and Le Grand shews, that in France all persons who lived near the sea used to eat whales, conger-eels, the sea-dog, sea-wolf, porpesses, and seals, the last of which were served in Lent, at the first tables, and the tongue of the whale was esteemed tender and delicious. Goose, which is now banished from all but English tables, was the favourite dish of Charlemagne as of Cyrus. It is commanded in the Capitularies that there should be geese in all the emperor's country houses.

Horace did not despise the ancients for praising the rancid boar; it was the favourite meat of Duguesclin, perhaps for the same reason as the early food of Rogero, in Ariosto, had been "the marrow of the lion and the bear." "Quant est de la nourriture du corps," says the old writer of Boucicaut's life, " sa coustume est telle, que quoy qu'il soit tres largement servy, et que son hostel soit moult plantureux de tous biens, jamais à table ne mange que d'une seule viande, c'est à sçavoir de la premiere à quoy il se prend, soit bouilly ou rosty ou poulaille." It was enacted by Henry II, when preparing to set out for the Holy Land, that no more than two dishes of meat should be allowed at one meal; but yet our good countrymen and northern neighbours contrived in these wars to distinguish themselves by using a more liberal diet than their southern comrades.[2] They knew what Trygæus told the boys in the old comedy,[3] "that there was

---

[1] Turner's Hist. of Ang. Sax. III, 23.
[2] Gesta Dei per Francos, p. 1006.   [3] Aristoph. Pax, 1309.

no use in having white teeth unless they gnawed something." They understood the rules of old physicians like Hippocrates, and as for the refinement of being starved, over shadowy refections, "minims of hospitality," spread in defiance of human nature, or over a more generous board, after the manner of that dame, in eastern tale, who ate rice with a needle; they felt that the sage decided the matter justly, when he said that "old men may do it easily, but as for young men, it cannot be done, ἥκιστα μειράκια."

But let us view from another side the hospitable scenes of former times. Our ancestors did not stand in need of the researches of Persæus, who sought, in his dialogues on hospitality, ὅπως ἂν μὴ κατακοιμηθῶσιν οἱ συμπόται.[1] Conversation, music, poetry, the recital of tales, were an inexhaustible source of amusement where the custom of having holy lessons read at table, as in the houses of the Templars, and others dedicated to religion, was not observed. In the Lay of the Last Minstrel we have a faithful representation of these scenes of repose and conversation.

> The tables were drawn, it was idleness all;
> Knight, and page, and household squire
> Loitered through the lofty hall,
> Or crowded round the ample fire.
> The stag-hounds, weary with the chace,
> Lay stretched upon the rushy floor,
> And urged in dreams, the forest race
> From Teviot-stone to Eskdale-moor.

Then it was, as young Selby declares, that Friar John became dear to them; for he was—

> The needfullest among us all,
> When time hangs heavy in the hall,
> And snow comes thick at Christmas tide,
> And we can neither hunt nor ride
> A foray. ———

---

[1] Athenæus, IV, p. 131.

Thus in the description, by Henry Bradshaw, of the feast made by King Ulpher, in the hall of the abbey of Ely, when his daughter, Werburgh, took the veil in that convent, we read,

> The joyfull wordes and sweet communyacyon
> Spoken at the table, it were harde to tell;
> But the great estates spake of theyr regyons,
> Knyghts of theyr chyvalry, of craftes the comons.[1]

Sometimes the conversation would assume a solemn and religious tone. Take an instance from the annals of the Holy War.

"There was a noble hero in our army, noble by birth and by virtue, named Ausellus. He, at midday, while sleeping, saw a vision of a magnificent palace, filled with an innumerable multitude walking in stately porches. Among these he saw a companion who had lately departed from life, who came up to him and said, 'Do you know who all these noble persons are? These are they, said he, who walked in the way of God, in which you now labour, and you shall quickly mount up to them; for you have fought a good fight, and have finished your course.' Then Ausellus awoke and related his vision; confessed his sins, received the holy Eucharist, and ordered all that his men should be paid. And now intrepid, mounting on his horse he rode with other nobles round the walls, when suddenly a stone thrown from the towers smote him on his temples, and he fell dead."[2] "Once it happened," says Orderic Vitalis,[3] "that some idle knights were amusing themselves with play and conversation, in the hall of the castle of Conches, in presence of the Lady Elizabeth. One of them related a dream which he had had, in which our Saviour appeared to threaten him from the cross.

---

[1] The old English use of this word is remarkable.
[2] Gesta Tancredi, cvi.   [3] Lib. VIII.

Those who were present declared that it was an evil dream, and boded him no good adventure. Baldwin, son of Eustache, Count of Boulogne, took occasion then to declare, that he had seen himself blessed by our Saviour in a dream. The young Roger then told his mother that he too had a similar vision, and implied that our Saviour had summoned him to the joys of heaven. 'Assuredly,' he concluded, 'I affirm boldly, that he who was thus summoned has not a long time to remain in this life.' Now, the event, says the monk, was, that a short time after, the first knight had an evil end, for he died of a wound, on an expedition, without confession, and without the sacraments. Baldwin attained by degrees to the throne of Jerusalem. Roger died of a sickness that same year, and made a blessed end, and was buried in the abbey of Conches." There is a tale by Orderic most fit for the weird winter nights, but which I fear to relate in these garish days, when we " scarcely believe much more than we can see." I mean that dreadful and that edifying account of what was seen by the priest Gauchelin, of the diocese of Lisieux, as he returned through a forest one night, in the beginning of January, in 1091, from visiting a dying man at the extremity of his parish. I fear to set it down, but let all romantic readers turn to it. How much better such recitals than " the useless conversations" which Madame de Sevigné complains of in one of her letters, " which are not directed to any object: des oui, des voire, des lanternes, ou l'on ne prend aucune sorte d'interet. I prefer the Christian conversations." Gresset, in his poem, " La Chartreuse,"[1] celebrates the happiness of that society which tends to instruct the mind, and move the heart

> Loin des froids discours du vulgaire
> Et des hauts tons de la grandeur:

and the following remark of the Count de Maistre
may serve as an apology for the custom of King
Arthur's court, still, in some measure, preserved in
England. "I regret much those symposions of
which antiquity has left us some precious memorials.
Women are charming without doubt: to avoid becoming savage one must live with them. Large
assemblies have their value; it is well to consent
to them with a good grace; but when all the duties
have been discharged which are imposed by custom, I am of opinion that men would do well to
meet together; to converse even at table: I know
not why we do not imitate the ancients in this
respect."[1] Geoffrey of Monmouth, speaking of
the ancient British custom, observed in King
Arthur's court, where the queen entertained the
women and the king the knights, concludes,
"efficiebantur ergo castæ mulieres et milites amore
illarum meliores."[2] Even when a Pierre Vidal
would give to conversation the light tone of the
troubadour, who could resist the grace and interest with which the commonest incidents are
related? " Chance led me one day from Riom to
Montferrand, to the dauphin of Auvergne. If ever
there was a court full of diversion it was that.
There was no lady nor maiden, knight or page,
who was not more familiar than a little bird that
you feed with the hand. There I met brave lords
and men of wit and learning. I stopped there.
It was about Christmas, what they call 'la Ca-
lende,' in that country. When we used to rise
from table near a good fire, the knights and
jongleurs would say things 'très gaillards,' and
amuse each other well, and then, without a word,
the knights would retire to bed. One night my
lord wished still to converse with some one; so

---

[1] Soirées de St. Petersbourg.   [2] Lib. VII, 4.

perceiving the occasion favourable, I approached, and said, My lord, I had a father, who was prized in the fine world, a famous singer, and one that could give a tale well. I should like to resemble him; but hearing the favour that Henry, king of England, the valiant Marquis of Montferrat, and a great number of barons of Lombardy, Catalonia, Gascony, and France, load upon jongleurs, I resolved to follow that profession; that is why I have visited so many cities and castles."[1]

Sir John Froissart and Sir Espaenge de Lion, while on their journey together, came to the town of Tournay. "We were lodged," says Froissart, "at the sign of the Starre and toke our ease, and at supper tyme, the capitayne of Malvoysin, called Sir Raymond of Lane, came to see us and supped with us, and brought with hym four flaggons of the best wyne that I drank of in all my journey. 'I tell you trouthe,' says Sir Espaenge, in course of conversation, 'Ernalton of Spayne dyde marveylous in armes; he had an axe in his hand; whosoever he strake therwith went to the earth, for he was bygge and well made, and nat over charged with moche flesshe.' 'Ah Saynt Mary, Sir,' quod Sir John, 'is the Bourge of Spayne so bygge a man as ye speak of?' 'Yea, Sir, truely,' quod he, 'for in all Gascoyne there is none lyke hym in strength of body; therfore the erle of Foix hath hym ever in his company; it paste not a thre yeer that he dyde in a sporte a great dede as I shall shewe you. It was on a Christmas-day the erle of Foix, who used to keep the hygh feestes of the yere ever ryght solempnlie, when he made good chere to every man, helde a great feest, and a plentifull of knightes and squyers, and it was a colde day, and the erl

[1] Hist. des Troubadours, II, 28.

dyned in the hall, and with hym great company of lordes; and after dynner he departed out of the hall, and went up into a galarye of twenty-four stayres of heyght, in which galarye ther was a great chymney, wherin they made fyre whan therle was ther; and at that tyme there was but a small fyre, for the erle loved no great fyre: the same day it was a great frost and very colde, and whan the erle was in the galarye and sawe the fyre so lytell, he said to the knightes and squiers about hym, 'Sirs, this is but a small fyre, and the day so colde'; than Ernalton of Spayne went down the stayres, and beneth in the courte he sawe a great meny of asses laden with wood to serve the house; than he went and toke one of the grettest asses, with all the woode, and layed hym on his backe, and went up all the stayres into the galarye, and dyde cast down the asse with all the wood into the chymney (not into the fire), and the asse's feet upward. Wherof the erle of Foix had great joy, and so hadde all they that were there, and had merveyle of his strength; how he alone came up all the stayres, with the asse and the woode on his neck.' I toke great pleasure in this tale," adds Sir John; that is, in the display of strength. For it was in this that the knights took pleasure, as Homer, upon similar occasions, when he exclaims:

——— Μέγα ἔργον, ὃ οὐ δύο γ' ἄνδρε φέροιεν,
Οἷοι νῦν βροτοί εἰσ᾽· ὁ δέ μιν ῥέα πάλλε καὶ οἷος.

What a picture does Sir John Froissart give of the fireside, after supper, in the great castle of the Earl of Foix! "He had brought with him a book, called 'the Melyader,' conteyninge all the songes, baladdes, rundeaux, and vyrelayes, which by imagynacyon he had gathered toguyder, which book," he says, "the erl of Foix was gladde to se, and every night, after supper, I reed thereon to

hym, and whyle I reed ther was none durst speke
any worde, bycause he wolde I shulde be well un-
derstande, wherin he tooke great solace." There
was something in the dark mysterious character of
this earl, which seemed to have inspired Froissart
with great interest, and, indeed, if the tales were
true which were whispered in the castle, the knight
had reason to feel awe in the presence of his host.
Sir Espaenge, who had first informed Froissart of
the death of the earl's only son, had declined com-
plying with his repeated request to be told the
particulars of that horrible event; but, after Froissart had been some time in the castle, he succeeded
in obtaining information from "an auncient squuyor
and a notable man," whom he appears to have
never ceased importuning until he shewed him the
matter, the substance of which may be given in few
words. Young Gaston was permitted to join his
mother, sister to the King of Navarre, at his uncle's,
with whom she was then on a visit, though the
king was the deadly enemy of her husband. Upon
his return, the earl was led to a suspicion that he
had been furnished with poison by his uncle, for
the purpose of effecting his death. Immediately
he caused his son to be thrown into prison, and
would have killed him with his own hand on the
spot, but for the interference and intercession of
the knights in his castle and the people of the
country. Finally, it was determined that he should
be kept in prison "a moneth or two, and then to
send hym on some voyage for two or three yere,
tyll he might somewhat forget his yvell wyll, and
that the chylde might be of greater age and of more
knowledge. The chylde was a fyftene or sixtene
yere of age; he grewe and waxed goodly, and
resembled right well to his father. The erle of
Foyz caused his sonne to be kepte in a darke chambre, in the towre of Ortayse, a tenne dayes; lytell

dyde he eate or drinke, yet he had ynough brought hym every daye, but when he sawe it he wolde go therfro, and sette lytill therby, and some sayd that all the meate that had been brought hym stade hole and entire the day of his dethe, wherfor it was great marveyle that he lyved so longe, for dyvers reasons. The erle caused hym to be kepte in the chambre alone, withoute any company, outher to counsayle or comforte hym; and all that season the chylde laye in his clothes as he came in, and he argued in himself and was full of malencholy, and cursed the tyme that ever he was borne and engenderd to come to suche an end. The same day shat he dyed they that served hym of meate and drinke, when they came to hym they said 'Gaston, here is meate for you'; he made no care therof, and sayd 'sette it down there.' He that served hym regarded and sawe in the prison all the meat stande hole as it had been brought hym before, and so departed and closed the chambre door, and went to the erle and sayd, 'Sir, for Goddes sake have mercy on your sonne Gaston, for he is nere famyshed in prisone; there he lyeth. I thinke he never did eate any thynge syth he came into prisone, for I have sene this daye all that ever I brought hym before, lying togyder in a corner.' Of these wordes the erle was sore dyspleased, and, without any words speyking, went out of his chambre and came to the prison wher his son was, and in an yvill houre he had the same tyme a lytell knyfe in his hande, to pare withal his nayles. He opyned the prison door, came to his sonne, and had the lytell knyfe in his hande, nat an ynche out of his hande, and in great dyspleasure he thrust his hande to his sonnes throte, and the poynt of the knife a lytell entered into his throte, into a certayne vayne, and sayed, 'ah treateur, why doest nat thou eate thy meate?' and therwith the erle departed without any more doynge or saying, and went into his own chambre. The chylde was abasshed and afrayed of the comynge of his father, and also was feble of fastyng, and the poynt of the knyfe a lytell entred into a vayne of his throte and so fell downe sodaynly and dyed. The erle was scante in his chambre, but the kepar of the chylde came to hym and sayd, ' Sir, Gaston, your sonne is deed.' ' Deed,' quod the erle. ' Yea, truely, sir,' quod he. The erle wolde nat believe it, but sent thyder a squyer that was by hym, and he went and came again, and sayd ' surely he is deed.' Than the erle was sore displeased and made great complaynt for his sonne, and said, 'O Gaston, what a poore adventure is this for the and for me: in an yvell hour thou wentest to Navar to see thy mother; I shall never have the joye that I had before.' Than therle caused his barbour to shave hym and clothed himself in blacke and all his house, and with moche sore wepyng the chylde was borne to the friers in Ortaise and there buried."

This account would wring a tear from the most resolved eye: let us seek a contrast. Froissart's midnight chat with different knights and squires is truly entertaining. The very style of Sir Espaigne's stories is captivating. Thus he begins one: " Sir, aunciently, aboute a hundred yere past, there was a lorde in Bierne, called Gastone, a ryght valyant man in armes, and is buryed in the friers right solemnely at Ortaise, and there ye may see what persone he was of stature and of body, for in his lyfe tyme his pycture was made in Latyn,[1] the which is yet there." At another time he converses with a Gascon squire, called the Bastot of Maulyon. "At a tyme as we were talkyng and devysing of armes, sytting by the fyre abyding for midnight, that therle shulde go to supper, than this squire

---

[1] In metal.

began to reckon up his life, and of the dedes of
armes that he had been at, sayinge, howe he had
endured as moche loss as profite.¹ Than he demanded of me and sayd, 'Sir John, hav ye in your
historye any thyng of this matter that I speke of?'
and I answered and said, 'I coude nat tell tyll I
here them; shewe forth your mater, and I wyll
gladly here you; for paradventure I have herde
somwhat but nat all.' 'That is true,' quod the
squyer, that he began to saye thus: 'The first tyme
that I bare armur was under the Captal de Buch, at
the battle of Poytiers, and as it was my happe, I had
that day thre prisoners, a knight and two squiers,
of whom I had one with another, four hundred
thousande frankes. The next yere after I was in
France, with the erle of Foyx and the captal his
sonne, under whom I was; and at our retourne at
Meaulx, in Brye, we found the duchesse of Normandy, that was ther, and the duchesse of Orlyance,
and a great numbre of ladyes and damoselles, who
were closed in and besieged by them of the Jaquery,
and if God had nat helped them, they had been
lost, for they were of great puissance, and in nombre more than ten thousande, and the ladies were
alone. Thus, sir,' quoth the Bastot of Maulyon, 'I
have holde you with talkyng to passe awaye the
night; howbeit, sir, all that I hav said is true.'
'Sir,' quod I, 'with all my herte, I thanke you; sir,
I trust your sayinges shall not be loste; for, sir, and
God suffre me to retourne into myne owne countre,
all that I have herd you saye, and all that I have
sene and founde in my voyage, I shall put it in
remembrance in the noble cronycle that the erle of
Bloys hath set me aworke on'; then the Bourge of
Compayne, called Ernalton, began to speke, and
wolde gladly that I shulde parcyve by hym that he

¹ A trait of nature, which did not escape Shakspeare, or Sir
W. Scott.

wolde I shulde record his lyfe, and of the Bourge Englysshe, his brother, and how they had done in Auvergne, and in other places, but as than he had no leysar, for the watche of the castell sowned to assemble all men that were in the towne to come up to the castell to suppe with the erle of Foix. Than these two squyers made them redy and lyghted up torches, and so we went up to the castell, and so dyd all other knyghts and squyers that were lodged in the towne."

The portrait which he gives of the earl on these occasions seems strongly characteristic of the dark and unhappy nobleman who murdered Sir Peter Ernalton and Gaston his own child, for we are told, "at midnight, when he came out of his chamber into the hall to supper, he had ever before him twelve torches brennyng, borne by twelve varletts, standyng before his table all supper; they gave a gret light, and the hall ever full of knights and squyers, and many other tables dressed to suppe who wolde; ther was none shulde speke to hym at hys table, but if he were called; his meat was lightlye, wylde foule, the legges and wynges alonely, and in the day he dyd but lyttell eat and drinke."

During the absence of the earl, Sir John Froissart had abundant opportunity to gratify his curiosity and his passion for tales of terror. Having alluded to the murder of Sir Peter Ernalton, it may be well to give the circumstances as briefly related to Froissart by Sir Espaenge de Leon. The earl determined to gain possession of Lourdes and the castle of Malvoysin, which belonged to the King of England, and was entrusted at that time to his cousin, Sir Peter Ernalton of Bearn, to whom the earl sent a message of invitation to Ortaise. Sir Peter seems to have suspected treachery, for he protested to his brother, whom he left in command, that he would never yield up the garrison but to his own natural lord, the King of England; and he made him swear "by the faythe of his gentylness, that he should keep the castell in lyke manner. Then Sir Peter Ernalton went to Ortayse (for all thynges consydred, he wolde go, bycause in no wyse he wolde displease the erle)." So "he alyghted at the sign of the Moon, and whan he thought it was tyme, he went to the castle of Ortayse to the erle, who with great joye received hym, and made hym syt at his borde, and shewed him as great semblant of love as he coude; and after dyner he said, Cosyn Peter, I hav to speke to you of dyvers thynges." Then the third day after, the earl signified his intent and will, that the garrison of Lourdes should be yielded up to him. "Whan the knyght herde these wordes," says Froissart, "he was sore abasshed, and studied a lytell: howbeit, all thynges considered, he sayd, 'Sir, true it is, I owe to you fayth and homage, for I am a poor knyghte of your blode, and of your countrey, but as for the castell of Lourde, I wyll nat delyver it to you; ye have sent for me to do with me as ye lyst; I holde it of the Kyng of England; he sette me there, and to none other lyving wyll I delyver it.' When the Erle of Foyx herd that answer, his blode chafed for yre, and sayd, drawyng out his dagger, 'O treatour, sayest thou nay? By my heed thou hast nat sayd that for nought'; and so therwith strake the knyght that he wounded him in fyve places, and ther was no knyght nor baronne that durste steppe betwene them. Then the knyght said, 'Oh, sir, ye do me no gentylness to send for me and slee me.' And yet for all the strokes that he had with the dagger, the erle commanded to cast hym in prison, downe into a depe dyke; and so he was, and ther dyed, for his woundes were but yvell looked unto. 'Ah! Saynt Mary,' quod I to the knight, 'was not this a great crueltie?'

'Whatsoever it was,' quoth the knight, 'thus it was.'"

At other times the conversation assumed a still more awful tone. "It is a great marveyle to consyder one thynge, the which was shewed me in therle of Foix's house, at Ortayse, of hym that enfourmed me of the busyness at Juberothe: he shewed me one thyng that I have often tymes thought on sithe, and shall do so as long as I lyve." He proceeds to relate how the earl of Foix knew the event of that battle the day after it was fought, though it was not till ten days after that the tidings came. On another occasion, when he was told by a squire how Sir Peter of Bearn "hath an usage, that in the night tyme, whyle he slepeth, he wyll ryse and arme hymselfe, and drawe out his sword, and fyght all about the house, and can not tell with whom, and then goeth to bedde agayne; and when he is wakying, his servaunts do shewe hym how he dyde, and he wold saye he knewe nothynge therof, and how they lyed. Sometyme his servaunts wolde leave non armure nor sworde in his chambre, and when he wold thus ryse and fynde non armure, he wolde make such a noyse and rumoure as though all the devylles of helle had been in his chambre. 'Ah! saynt Mary,' quoth I, 'how dyde Sir Peter of Bierne take this fantasy?' 'By my faith,' quod the squyre, 'he hath ben often demaunded therof, but he saith he can not tell whereof it cometh: the first tyme that ever he dyde so was the night after that he had ben on a day of hunting in the wodes of Bisquay, and chased a marveyllous great beare, and the bear had slaine four of his houndes, and hurt dyvers, so that none durst come near him; then this Sir Peter toke a sworde of Burdeaux, and came in great yre, and assailed the bear, and fought longe with hym, and was in great perell, and tooke great payne ere he could overcome hym; finally, he slewe the beare, and then returned to his lodgyng, to the castell of Languedudon, in Bisquay, and made the beare to be brought with him. Every man had marveyle of the greatnesse of the beest, and of the hardyness of the knyght, howe he durst assayle the beare, and when the countess of Bisquay, his wyfe, saw the beare, she fell in a swone, and had great dolour, and so she was borne into her chamber." The squire goes on to relate how on the third day she asked permission of her husband to go on a pilgrimage to St. James, with her son and daughter. So she went to the king of Castile, and "ther she is yet," he says, "and wyll not return agayn. And so thus the next night that sir Peter had thus chased the bear and slayne him, while he slepte in his bedde this fantasy tooke hym: and it was said that the countess his wyfe knewe well, as sone as she saw the beare, that it was the same that her father dyde ones chase; and in his charging he herde a voyce, and sawe nothynge, that sayde to hym, 'Thou chasest me, and I wolde the no hurte, therefore thou shalt dye an yvell dethe.' Of this the lady had remembrance when she sawe the beare, by that she had herd her father saye before, and she remembered well how kynge don Peter strake of her father's heed without any cause, and in lykewise she feared her husbande, and yet she sayth and maynteyneth that he shall dye of an yvill dethe, and that he doth nothynge as yet, and that he shall do hereafter." All this will seem but rambling stuff to such readers as Sir William Temple, or his friend, who found the stories of the tale-tellers in the north of Ireland the best remedy to make him sleep, when abroad on the mountains in his wolf-hunting there; but our ancestors had another taste. Such as that of Sir Philip Sidney, who never heard "the old song of Piercy and Douglas, without finding his heart moved more than with a trumpet." The quiddity of Ens and Prima Materia, might hardly have succeeded in keeping their eyes open; nay, minstrelsy itself could not always prevail. When Sir Folker, in the Nibelungen Lay, guarded the king, and played on his instrument, as the guests retired to the large hall, where their beds were prepared,

>Sweetly from his strings resounded many a lay;
>And many thanks the heroes to the knight of fame did say.
>At first his tones resounded loudly the hall around;
>The champion's strength and art was heard in every sound;
>But sweeter lays and softer, the hero now began,
>That gently closed his eyes full many a way-tired man.

But they could not sit up till morning, like Alcinous listening to Orlando, or honest King Arthur; more awake than if they heard Ulysses himself relate his adventures.[1] The dream, the ghastly vision,

>———— et penetralia
>Sparsisse nocturno cruore
>Hospitis,

were themes that never tired,

>When glowing embers through the room
>Taught light to counterfeit a gloom.

XI. Here I find myself in a situation from which there is no escape: the tale of terror must be uttered, "sunt enim quædam adolescentium auribus danda." Without it we cannot discern all the features of the chivalrous character;—the mystery, the weakness which belonged to it; for it is not to be denied that there was superstition in those ages, though we censure the moderns for stupidly con-

---

[1] Od. XI, 374.

founding superstition with the beautiful and sublime manifestations of faith which were practised by simple Catholics. Superstitious fancies, however, like those of the moderns, there certainly were, from which the Church laboured to deliver men; and, on the other hand, there were also mysterious, and, at the same time, profound views of nature, which no real philosopher would designate by a reproachful term. Let us draw closer round the hearth, and hear some old knight or pilgrim relate what he has seen or learned beyond the sea. There sits one who is come from St. Cuthbert's holy isle; who has been to the tomb of Michael Scot, in the abbey of Melrose, who has visited the grave of Dun Scotus, in the church of the Minor Friars, at Cologne, who has travelled by night through the forests of Hainaut and Bohemia, and across the wilds of Egra.[1] One is never weary with hearing how he has wandered through the woods and swamps of the Alpine range, floated down the Danube into Hungary, how he has sat watching the setting sun from a moss-grown battlement amidst the ruins of the castle of the Hungarian kings, with the Danube below, rolling on its majestic flood through the black forests of the plain, which is bounded on one side by the Carpathian chain, and is lost in distance on the other, as it stretches out towards the shores of the Euxine. The complin bell has indeed prescribed silence to the Knight Templar,[2] and holy men [3] have even said that it is an execrable custom to disturb the sacred night, which is the season for heavenly discipline, with useless or pernicious fables; but the castle was not a cloister, and it was at the midnight hour, when

---

[1] The inhabitants tell marvellous stories of these plains. See Feller's Voyages, II, 115.
[2] Regula IX.   [3] Nieremberg, Doct. Ascet. V, VIII, 46.

the knights sat assembled in "the sounding vaulted hall, about the round, massy stone table, when the awakening storm would drive a wild snow-dust against the clattering windows, making all the doors to tremble in their casements, and the heavy bolts to rattle violently," that all were ready to exclaim with reverend Chaucer,

> God forbide but that men should believ
> Well more thing than thei hav seen with eye!

Then they were told, that in the choir of the church belonging to the convent of Santa Clara, at Valladolid, may be seen the tomb of a Castilian knight, whence groans and accents issue every time that any members of his house are to die: that there is a bell in Aragon, in a small town called Velilla, on the Ebro, which tolls of itself previous to great events; that it was heard when Alphonso V, King of Aragon, went into Italy to take possession of the kingdom of Naples; again, at the death of Charles V; that it denoted the departure of Don Sebastian, King of Portugal, for Africa: how lights used to gleam in the chapel of St. Simeon when any member of the house of Saulx was near death:[1] how, immediately before and after sunset at the windows of the castle of Voiron in Dauphiné there used to be seen women of the most ravishing beauty, who disappeared on the near approach of any one, and nothing was found there but some flowers:[2] how, in the convent of Cordova, there was a clock which struck with a particular tone whenever a monk of the house was to die. Then they were told, that in the forest of Bourgtheroulde, in Normandy, over the ruins of

---

[1] Mem. de Gaspard de Saulx Tavannes in the collection of Mem. relatifs à l'Hist. de France, t. XXIII, p. 140.
[2] Gervais de Tilsburi, Merveilles du Dauphiné.

his ancient castle, Robert-le-Diable, that converted sinner, used to be seen sometimes in a hermit's cowl:[1] that between the castle of Gisors and the tower of Neaufles there is a vast subterraneous passage, now firmly closed, and containing immense treasures, into which it is possible to penetrate on one day and one hour and one moment of the year, namely, when the priest reads the genealogy of Christ at the mass of midnight at Christmas; but woe to the man who lets the instant escape for return:[2] that on the night between the 27th and 28th of July, after the battle of Bouvines, there were heard shouts of warriors in the church of St. Denis: that in an ancient Latin book in the abbey of St. Riquier, near Amiens, written 140 years before the battle of Crecy, that battle was nevertheless foretold; nay, they knew that the Cid went to the great battle of the Navas de Tolosa after his death, if old ballads said true, " for the night before the battle was fought at the Navas de Tolosa, in the dead of the night, a mighty sound was heard in the whole city of Leon, as it were the tramp of a great army passing through; and it passed on to the royal monastery of St. Isidro, and there was a great knocking at the gate thereof, and they called to a priest who was keeping vigils in the church, and told him, that the captains of the army which he heard were the Cid Ruydiez and Count Fernan Gonzalez, and that they came there to call up King Don Fernando the Great, who lay buried in that church, that he might go with them to deliver Spain; and on the morrow that great battle of the Navas de Tolosa was fought, wherein sixty thousand of the misbelievers were slain, which was one of the greatest and noblest battles ever won over the Moors." They were re-

[1] Tristan, III, 40. [2] Ibid. III, 147.

ferred to the records of the house of Austria for proof that phantoms were seen in the Cathedral of Prague the night before the battle under the walls of that city in 1620, when the Imperialists, under the Duke of Bavaria, gained that famous victory which recovered the kingdom. They were assured, on the authority of Brugiantini of Ferrara,[1] that Count Rogero, having entered the castle of Pontier, near Mayence, and being murdered there in the night, he appeared in a dream to his wife at Montauban, and related his fate, and told her where his body lay buried at the gate of the castle. Pale were their looks when, in the old ballad, the words of the female spectre were repeated:—

"Sum meat, sum meat, ye King Henrie!
Sum meat ye give to me!"

Again, they were told how Melusina, who had married Guy de Lusignan, Count of Poictou, continued down to Brantome's time to be the protectress of her descendants, and how she was heard wailing as she sailed upon the blast round the turrets of the Castle of Lusignan the night before it was demolished: how the lady of the Castle of Espervel always left the chapel at mass before the consecration: they trembled to hear of the Nacht Lager, or midnight camp, which seemed nightly to beleaguer the walls of Prague; and how the rock of the Teufelsleiter on the Rhine bears that name from the knight who gave up his body and soul to save his mistress from the robbers' castle, and carried her off on the Satanic horse, which he dismissed so boldly, saying, "Dank für den herrlichen Ritt!" just as Viscount Dundee, whom the Covenanters called the bloody Clavers, rode a steed which they said Satan must have given him, be-

[1] Angelica innamorata.

cause it was like Pedasus, ὃς καὶ θνητὸς ἐὼν ἕπεθ' ἵπποις ἀθανάτοισιν,[1] though precipices are shown where a fox could hardly keep his feet, down which the gallant charger conveyed him safely in pursuit of the enemy. Then they heard of the famous Wilde Heer of the Rhine, who rides about at midnight with his horrid troop, amid the rattle of cannon wheels, from castle to castle, predicting war to the German Empire; having been once the haughty young Baron of Rodenstein, who broke his vows, and preferred the pleasures of battle and high adventures to the company of his gentle lady, till she died for grief, and appeared to him in the forest to proclaim the sentence which condemned him for ever to this horrid ministry;[2] how he appeared at the breaking out of the Silesian war in 1740, at the coronation of the Emperor Charles VII in 1742, at the beginning of the war with France in 1734, before the battle of Dettingen in 1743, before the Seven Years' War in 1756, after the battle of Hochkirch in 1758, and shortly before the coronation of Joseph II in 1764. Who would not tremble when he heard

—— τὸν ἁρματόκτυπον ὄτοβον, ὄτοβον,
ὅτε τε σύριγγες ἔκλαγξαν ἑλίτροχοι.[3]

Then they were told of a Count de Macon, who, while revelling in his hall with many knights, was suddenly alarmed by the entrance of a gigantic figure of a black man, mounted on a black steed; this terrible stranger, without receiving any obstruction from guard or gate, rides directly forward to the high table, and with an imperious tone orders the Count to follow him: again, how Wallace,

[1] Il. XVI, 154.
[2] There is a fine plate, Rheinische Bilder, by Vogt. Francfort, 1821.
[3] Æschyl. Sept. cont. Theb.

taking refuge in the solitary tower of Gask, was disturbed at midnight by the blast of a horn, and descending, sword in hand, was encountered at the gate of the tower by the headless spectre of Fawdoun, whom he had slain the day before; like that horrid black foul κακοδαίμων which appeared to Cassius, and so terrified the Epicurean that he had to shout out for lights and company.[1] They heard that when Orlando, dying at the entrance to the pass of Cisera, blew his horn with such force that it burst, Charles being then in Gascony, and hearing the peal distinctly, wished to return instantly to save his nephew, but was prevented by the counsels of the traitor Ganelon, who told him that the hero was only hunting for his pleasure in the forest, the sound, however, bringing to him Theodoricus, the only surviving Paladin; that at that moment Turpin, saying mass before King Charles for the souls of certain persons lately deceased, heard the songs of the angels who were conveying Orlando to heaven, and immediately announced his death to Charlemagne.

The historian as well as the minstrel, presented a mysterious side of nature to their imagination. "Ecce magnum signum!" cried Charles the Bold, struck motionless in the midst of his ardour, when the gold lion is knocked off his helmet, and falls on the saddle. King Robert Bruce, looking from the turrets of Brodrick Castle, in the island of Arran, sees across the forth of Clyde a wondrous light gleaming over the land, which encourages him to make his descent. King William the Red, dining in the castle of Malwood, is warned by a monk not to hunt that day; at whom, however, he laughs heartily, then pursues the chase, and is slain.

Men were, indeed, unwilling to let it appear that

[1] Val. Mat. I, 7.

they gave credit to such legends as that which is related in the Lady Adeline's song; of the friar whom King Henry's might could not expel from the Norman church, when yielded to the house of Amundeville:

> Say nought to him as he walks the hall,
>   And he'll say nought to you:
> He sweeps along in his dusky pall
>   As o'er the grass the dew.[1]

Or that of the eve of St. John—how

> The lady looked through the chamber fair
>   By the light of a dying flame,
> And she was aware of a knight stood there,
>   Sir Richard of Coldinghame!
>
> By Eildon-tree, for long nights three,
>   In bloody grave have I lain,
> The mass and the death-prayer are said for me,
>   But, lady, they are said in vain.
>
> Love mastered fear—her brow she crossed.
>   How, Richard, hast thou sped?
> And art thou saved, or art thou lost?
>   The vision shook his head.[2]

Or that in the piteous lay of Harold, which was sung to the guests in Branksome Hall,—how the Lady Rosabelle was lost, and how

> O'er Roslin all that dreary night
>   A wondrous blaze was seen to gleam.
>
> Seemed all on fire that chapel proud
>   Where Roslin's chiefs uncoffin'd lie,
> Each baron for a sable shroud
>   Sheathed in his iron panoply:

a light which always denoted the death of a St. Clair, and so it was then; for

> There are twenty of Roslin's barons bold
>   Lie buried within that proud chapelle,
> Each one the holy vault doth hold,
>   But the sea holds lovely Rosabelle!

---

[1] Byron.   [2] Sir Walter Scott.

And each St. Clair was buried there,
  With candle, with book, and with knell,
But the sea-caves rung, and the wild-winds sung,
  The dirge of lovely Rosabelle.

A fine romantic glow was thrown over the scenes of common life. A knight, on the cold eve of St. Agnes, rides across the fens from Ely, and coming to the river Ouse, sees by the light of the moon a small boat with a little pole. Here may be an adventure: he gives up his horse to his squire, leaps into the boat, and pushes across the black water, hoping to meet with Osbert or Albert, so famous in the bishopric.[1] They had only to leave the cheerful hearth and ride to the wold, such as Mucklestone Moor, or to the lone and melancholy tree

Whose aged branches to the midnight blast
Made solemn music.———

And who then would scorn "the Bohemian knight, the warrior in the forest of Glenmore," whose bloody hand was no merveil to a Platonist;[2] or the visions of the forest of Broceliande in Brittany, or Ralph Bulmer, or William who carried off Leonora, or the horrid phantoms which used to appear in the New Forest, manifesting the wrath of Heaven upon the sacrilegious devastation of that once populous district?[3] Who can enter the immense hall of the castle of Marienburg, which was the residence of the grand master of the Teutonic knights, and the dark vaulted chamber twenty or thirty yards below the ground, without a feeling of horror, when the tales were told which concerned the fate of this order? Time has involved in obscurity the object for which this deep, concealed, and wonderful vault was constructed. Some have thought that it was to conceal treasure, or to hold mysterious rites

[1] Gesta Romanorum, CLV.   [2] Gorgias.   [3] Ordaric Vital.

for initiation into the order. Here came Henry Reus von Plauen, with his companions, when they had heard of the fatal battle of Tannenberg, the 15th of July, 1410, when nearly the whole order was annihilated by the victorious Poles; and here he collected the few who had escaped, and was elected grand master: he died afterwards in a dark dungeon in Dantzig. Here was buried Ulrich von Jungingen, who began the war with the Poles, and who was slain at Tannenberg. The castle of Christburg, in the western parts of Prussia, belonged to the Teutonic knights. It was the scene of many heroic deeds. At the time when the war broke out with the Poles, when Ulrich von Jungingen was grand master of the order, Albert von Schwarzburg had command of this castle. In the meetings of the chapter he had used every effort to prevent the war, which he foresaw, from the strength of the Polish king, would be full of peril. When the war broke out, the legend related that, as Albert left the castle in a sorrowful and desponding mood, for the battle of Tannenberg, the chief of the choir asked him to whom he would entrust the castle during his absence, and that he answered, full of anger, "To you and the evil spirits, who have engaged the order in this war"; that the man to whom he thus spoke shuddered and died shortly, and that after his death people saw frightful spectres over the castle, and so that no one durst live within the walls. Horrid noises issued from every quarter, which obliged the person who had the command to leave it, and after his departure no one ventured to approach it. A smith of the place, three years before the battle of Tannenberg, had gone on a pilgrimage to Rome, and after an absence of five years returned home to Christburg: he returned full of sorrow, having heard that all his old masters and friends were slain at Tannenberg, and that the castle was only inhabited by evil spirits: but the smith was a brave man and had no superstitious fears, and resolved to visit the castle; he went at noon, and on the first drawbridge he saw standing an old friend, the house steward Otto Sangerwitz; he joyfully saluted him and said, "Is it you, my worthy lord? I rejoice to find that I was misinformed when it was told me that you had fallen in the battle of Tannenberg: I'll answer for it everything else that I heard of the state of this castle was equally false." The other replied, "Whether true or false, you shall see with your own eyes; come with me, fear nothing." He led the smith through the castle courts, where he shewed him many knights, some at play, some dancing, and others lying on the ground with an expression of horror. On entering the church, a priest appeared at the altar, as if about to say mass, and there were many who appeared to keep choir, but seemed as if asleep. Returning out of the castle, the smith heard dismal groans and shrieks, and he though that the figures he had seen were not living men. The house steward now charged the smith to go to the grand master at Marienburg and relate to him what he had seen; and he further desired him to relate a circumstance to the grand master, which was a profound secret, known only to himself and his trusty friends; and he warned him at the same time that the grand master would cause him to be put to death. After this the house steward disappeared; and the smith, nothing daunted, went to Marienburg on the Thursday after Pentecost of the year 1412, told the grand master, Henry Reus von Plauen, what he had seen and heard, and was immediately thrown into the river and drowned, by order of the grand master. This popular legend is found in the history by Simon Grünaw, a Franciscan monk, who lived at

Dantzig at the end of the fifteenth century, and who relates merely what was generally reported at the time: and there certainly was some foundation for this marvellous account. Some Germans have thought that the order at this period had mysteries; that a party hostile to the war had remained in the castle; that they had designedly spread the report to prevent intrusion, and that the despotic and cautious Planen had taken this cruel step to prevent the smith from telling tales.[1]

Nor were these fancies merely echoed by barbarous minstrels: such persons as were conversant with classic lore were ready to furnish tales of a similar nature; they could relate from Herodotus,[2] that before the battle of Salamis, when the army of Xerxes had laid waste Attica by fire and sword, and the country which had been before them like a garden was behind them a wilderness, Dicæus, the son of Theocydis, an Athenian exile, who was entertained in the army of the Medes, declared, that being by chance in company with Demaratus, the Lacedemonian, in the Thriascian plain, he saw a dust rising above Eleusis, such as might be raised by a host of thirty thousand men, and while he gazed and wondered whose men they might be, he heard a voice which seemed to him like the mystic cry, such as used to be heard in the celebration of the sacred mysteries: and he told Demaratus that it boded danger to the king's host, either to his land army or to his fleet, according as it should move towards Peloponnesus or towards Salamis, for that he knew it to be something divine coming from Eleusis to assist the Athenians and their allies. And Demaratus warned him on his life not to mention it to the king; and from the dust and sound there arose a cloud which ascended to the

[1] Die Vorzeit, 1820.   [2] VIII, 65.

higher regions of the air and was borne over Salamis and the camp of the Greeks: and then followed that mighty battle which saved Greece, and was the most glorious and decisive ever gained over the barbarians. They could refer to Pausanias, who affirms, four hundred years after the battle, that every night on the plain of Marathon you might hear the neighing of horses and the noise of fighting warriors; that those who stop to listen had reason to repent it, but that if you passed on your way the ghosts were not offended.[1] They could repeat what Conon told, how the Locrians used to leave a vacant place in their ranks for the ghost of Ajax their countryman to fight for them; and how in a battle with the Crotonians, Antoleon, one of the enemy, thought to avail himself of that vacancy in the line, but was wounded in the thigh by the spectre and driven back. How, again, when the Argonauts were sailing along the coast of the Euxine beyond the mouth of the Callichorus river, they beheld on the heights the tomb of Sthenelus, the son of Actor, who, returning from the war with the Amazons, in which he had assisted Hercules, was wounded to death with an arrow, and buried there; and now his ghost had supplicated and gained permission for a moment to behold men like what he was once, and on the crown of the tumulus did he stand gazing upon the vessel, and then he again put on thick darkness; but they were terrified at the sight, and ran their ship against the shore and mounted the tumulus and made libations.[2] Even the dark reveries of necromancy and magic could be traced to the most distant ages; and the muse of Euripides could be shewn as romantic as that of the Freischütz. If Santaberemus was said to have shewn to the Emperor Basilius the soul of

[1] Lib. I, 32.   [2] Apollon. Rhod. II, 913.

his son Constantine, Apollonius was thought to have raised the spectre of Achilles over his tomb, appearing twelve cubits high. Sir John Mandeville's account of the conjurers of the East equals the wildest passage of the chivalrous romance. In old Spanish books there are strange accounts of men who confessed that they had been tempted to deny the existence of the devil from his not having replied to their horrible invocations as prescribed to them by witches, though this very denial appeared to Sir Thomas Brown as the chief work of the devil. The Sire de Giac who confessed that he had procured the death of the Duke of Burgundy, affirmed also that he had sold one of his hands to the devil. By such arts the curate of Bargota, a village near Viana, in the diocese of Calahorra, while living in Navarre, was said to have been present in the famous wars of Ferdinand V, and that he never failed on the very day to announce at Logroño and Viana the victories which had been gained. In like manner Eugene Torralba was said to have seen the sack of Rome by the Imperial troops, the death of the Constable de Bourbon, the Pope retiring to the Castle of St. Angelo, and all the other events of that dreadful day, which he related at Valladolid a few hours after. Sir Thomas Brown expressed his belief that there is "a traditional magic." Shakspeare availed himself of popular notions which had moved Bede and Albertus Magnus, and which also moved Bacon and Boyle and Newton. The clergy of all degrees, from the popes and councils to single doctors and monks, Robert de Sorbona and Friar Bacon, as in the three first chapters of his epistle on the power of art and nature, condemned all trifling with unholy fancies, all use of magic, unlawful books, characters and spells. St. Augustin says,[1] that, as

[1] Lib. de Confess.

a punishment for having believed in witches and
their art, and for having withdrawn one's faith from
God, it may be ordained that the events should
take place according to their predictions, for success
and prosperity may often be the greatest of punishments. Jean-sans-Peur, the wicked Duke of Burgundy, had suspicions of danger to his person, when
he was invited to the conference with the dauphin
on the bridge of Montereau: he had at first refused
to attend; but being repeatedly urged, he at
length, early on Sunday morning the 10th of September, summoned his four astrologers, whom he
had ordered to pass the whole night in observation,
and these four men agreed in the report, "that he
might go to Montereau without danger." The
duke, relying upon this impious security, set out for
the conference, and entered the barriers without a
helmet or a cuirass, though ever since the murder
of the Duke of Orleans he had never moved a step
without taking every possible precaution to guard
his person. The result admits of an explanation,
according to the views of St. Augustin. Such arts
were contemplated with horror by all who professed
chivalry. When Arthur de Richemont, constable
of France, first saw the Maid of Orleans, "Jeanne,"
said he, "I do not know if you are from God or
not: if you are from God, I do not fear you, for
God knows my intention; if you are from the devil,
I fear you less."[1] When Pierre, Duc de Bretagne,
was dying of a disease, which, not being understood by the physicians, was ascribed by some to a
charm, certain persons offered to cure him, with the
aid of the spirit of darkness; but the duke replied,
"that he had rather die by God's hand than live
through the devil's means." Even in the famous
legend of Friar Bacon, he breaks his wonderful

[1] Vies des Capitaines François du Moyen Age, VI, 168.

glass, which had caused the death of the two young men, saying, "'Wretched Bacon, wretched in thy knowledge, in thy understanding wretched. Had I been busied in those holy things the which mine order ties me to, I had not had that time that made this wicked glass.' Then he kept his chamber, and fell into divers meditations on the vanity of the arts and sciences; and then he made a great fire, and assembled all his scholars, and preached to them, how he had unlocked the secrets of art and nature; 'and now,' he continued, 'I wish that I were ignorant, and knew nothing: for the knowledge of these things, as I have truly found, serveth not to better a man in goodness, but only to make him proud, and think too well of himself. What hath all my knowledge of nature's secrets gained me? Only this, the loss of a better knowledge, the loss of divine studies which make the immortal part of man, his soul, blessed. I have found that my knowledge has been a heavy burden, and has kept down my good thoughts.' And so he burned his books, and went into a cell, and lived an anchorite, and dug his grave with his own nayles." So likewise Cornelius Agrippa, who had studied Michael Scot, whom he calls a learned physician, and Roger Bacon, whom he calls a necromancer, knowing him more by popular report, speaks of his own volumes de Occulta Philosophia, "in quibus quidquid tunc per curiosam adolescentiam erratum est, nunc cautior hac palinodia recantatum volo." Such subjects were not to be spoken of lightly. "Sire," said Launcelot to the hermit, who had been speaking for a long time to an invisible person, "Sire, who is that who has spoken to you? His body I saw not, but his speech was so ugly and so terrible, that there is no one who would not have had fear." "Sire," replied the Preudhomme, "Paour en doit-on bien avoir. Car il n'est riens qui tant face a redoubter comme celui. Car c'est luy qui donne conseil a homme et a femme de perdre corps et ame, lors sceut bien et entendit Lancelot de quoy il parloit."[1] But "laissons le Démon," as Du Guesclin said, "et revenons à Dieu car il faut toujours finir par la."

Many of the tales which were told at the midnight hour were strongly marked with a religious feeling, and were respecting an agency which interfered not with sound faith. Examples are easily found. Peter of Cluny, surnamed the Venerable, was a man who proceeded in all affairs with much caution, not countenancing anything frivolous. Hence M. Caussin, in his Holy Court, makes use of his authority. He telleth, "that in a village of Spain, named the Star, there was a man of quality, called Peter of Engelbert, much esteemed in the world for his parts and riches; notwithstanding, the Spirit of God made him understand the vanity of all human things: being advanced in years, he went into a monastery of the order of Cluny. He often spake among the holy friars of a vision which he saw, when he was as yet in the world. This report came to the ears of venerable Peter, who being general of the order, happened to be then in Spain. So he took the pains to go into a little monastery of Navarre, where Engelbert was, and to question him in the presence of the bishops of Oleron and Osma. This was his report. 'In the time that Alphonsus the younger, heir of the great Alphonsus, warred in Castile against certain factious, he made an edict, that every family in his kingdom should be bound to furnish him with a soldier. In obedience to the king's commands, I sent into his army one of my household servants, named Sancius. The wars being ended, he returned to my house,

---

[1] Lancelot du Lac, tome III.

where he was soon seized by a sickness, which in a few days took him away into the other world. After we had buried him, and four months were past, upon a winter's night, being in my bed, thoroughly awake, I perceived a man, who, stirring up the ashes of my hearth, opened the burning coals, which made him the more easily to be seen. Although much terrified at the sight of this ghost, God gave me courage to ask him who he was. But he in a very low voice answered, "Master, fear nothing, I am your poor servant, Sancius. I go into Castile in the company of many soldiers, to expiate my sins in the same place where I committed them." He then asked my prayers and alms.'" In the year 1053, at the Easter festival, when Earl Godwin sat with the king at table, the conversation turning on Alfred's murder, for which Swein, though six years had passed since his crime, had set off to walk barefoot from Flanders to Jerusalem, the Earl denied, with many solemn appeals to Divine Providence, that he was concerned in it; when suddenly he lost his speech, and fell from his seat. Harold, and his two other sons, raising him, and conveying him to the king's chamber, where he lingered from Monday to Thursday and then expired. The great Baron spoken of by Dante,[1] the Marchese Ugo, Lieutenant of the Emperor Otho III, when hunting, strayed away from his people, and, wandering through a forest, came, or had a vision, in which he seemed to come, to an iron forge, where he saw black and deformed men tormenting others with fire and hammers, and asking the meaning of this, he was told that they were condemned souls who suffered this punishment, and that the soul of the Marquis Ugo was doomed to suffer the same, if he did not repent. Struck with horror, he sold all his pos-

---

[1] Paradise, XVI.

sessions in Germany and founded seven abbeys, in one of which his memory was celebrated, at Florence, on St. Thomas's day.

Memorable in the history of the Rhine was the deliverance of Cologne, in consequence of a vision of angels seen in the sky, at dead of night, by the Count of Cleves and his brother Stephen, which may be seen represented on the walls to this day.[1] When Henry V besieged Meaux, a hermit predicted, in his presence, that he would die in the course of the year; which was the event, for he only lived eight months.[2] That was an awful scene in the hostel, between Lord Marmion and the palmer, after the dreadful event at Whitby, when Fitz-Eustace's song seemed to Marmion as a death-peal rung:

> Such as in nunneries they toll
> For some departing sister's soul.

And to the question of that lord,

> "Say what may this portend?"
> Then first the palmer silence broke
> (The live-long day he had not spoke,)
> "The death of a dear friend."

Gertrude, the youngest daughter of St. Elizabeth, was a child, in the convent of Aldenberg, when her mother died at Marburg. She said, "I hear the passing bell at Marburg, and my dear mother is this moment departed." After some days, news came of the event as she had said.[3]

When King St. Oswin came into the dining-hall, and expressed great joy, after giving an example of humility, in assenting to the judgment of the holy bishop Aidan, that devout man appeared sorrowful,

---

[1] Rheinische Bilder, 613, Voht. III, 321.
[2] Vies des Capitaines François du Moyen Age, VI, 42.
[3] Antiquitates Monasterii Aldenbergensis.

and said to his attendants, in the Scottish language, which the king and his courtiers did not understand, that he was assured so humble and so good a king would not live long; a prediction too well verified. Another instance is the Lady Alda's dream, as in the Spanish ballad, beginning

> In Paris sits the lady that shall be Sir Rowland's bride;

and relating how she dreams an evil dream, and her damsels seek in vain to comfort her, and then it concludes—

> Woe is me for Alda! there was heard at morning hour
> A voice of lamentation within that lady's bower:
> For there had come to Paris a messenger by night,
> And his horse it was a-weary, and his visage it was white.
> And there's weeping in the chamber, and there's silence in the hall,
> For Sir Rowland has been slaughtered in the chase of Roncesval.[1]

Alda might have repeated the very words of Atossa, when she hears of the defeat of Xerxes:

> ὦ νυκτὸς ὄψις ἐμφανὴς ἐνυπνίων
> ὡς κάρτα μοι σαφῶς ἐδήλωσας κακά.[2]

In the chronicles of Robert of Brunne we read how the Pope, at Rome, knew that King Edward I was dead, in England, the same day.

> The Pope, on the morn, bifore the clergi cam
> And told tham beforn, the floure of Christendam
> Was ded and lay on bere, Edward of Ingeland.
> He said with hevy chere in spirit he it fand.

The illustrious Bishop of Lombez, brother of the Cardinal Colonna, was Petrarch's friend. After a long separation, the bishop, being at his diocese in Gascony, and Petrarch at Parma, where information had arrived of the bishop's illness, one night

---

[1] Lockhart's Spanish Ballads.   [2] Æschyl. Persæ, 524.

Petrarch saw the bishop, in a dream, crossing the brook which watered his little garden. He ran to him and asked a thousand questions: "Whence come you? where are you going so quickly? why are you alone?" The bishop, smiling, replied, "Remember the summer that you passed with me beyond the Garonne. The Gascon climate and disposition displeased you; the storms of the Pyrenees kept you in alarm: I now think with you. I have departed and bid adieu to that country, and I return to Rome." Still as he spake he walked fast, so that they were soon at the end of the garden. Petrarch wished to stop him, and begged at least that he might have the honour to accompany him. The bishop, with a gentle movement of his hand, waved him back, and, with an altered countenance and tone, said, "No, I do not wish you to come at present." Then, says Petrarch, "I looked steadfastly upon him and beheld all the features of death. The horror of the vision caused me to cry out, and I awoke. Diem signo, rem omnem et præsentibus amicis narro et absentibus scribo; post vigesimum quintum diem nuntius ad me mortis allatus est; collatis temporibus eo ipso die quo vita discesserat, sic mihi illum apparuisse comperio." Again, upon the 6th of April, A.D. 1348, Petrarch, being at Verona, early in the morning, at the first dawn, he saw Laura in a dream, angel-mild. To his inquiry whether she were alive or dead, she replied that she was alive, but that he was dead until he should leave this life. He relates the conversation which he had with her. Upon the 19th of May he received a letter from Socrates, informing him of the death of Laura on the 6th of April, at six o'clock in the morning, the precise moment when he had seen her in a dream, and the same day and hour of the same month when he had first seen her, in the season of their joy and innocence, in the church of the convent of St. Claire, near Avignon, A.D. 1327. The first of these relations is given in a letter to Joannes Andreas, professor at Bologna, whom he consulted upon the subject of dreams. Petrarch calls it a singular hazard; but he lived at a period when the opening of a new world, in the revival of classical learning, had produced a strong inclination to reject all commonly received opinions; and the romantic sentiments of nature, which the Holy Scriptures were so calculated to cherish, were uncongenial to the acquired taste of the pedantic student; yet the learning of the ancients would have rather taught men to excuse the wild fancies which prevailed in our heroic age. Æschylus makes Prometheus reckon among his gifts to men, the power of distinguishing divine dreams.[1] The solemn words of dying Patroclus to Hector,[2] and of Hector to Andromache, when he foretells the fate of Priam and of Troy, and his own fate:

Ἀλλά με τεθνειῶτα χυτὴ κατὰ γαῖα καλύπτοι,—

the prediction of Achilles,

Εὖ νύ τοι οἶδα καὶ αὐτὸς, ὅ μοι μόρος ἐνθάδ' ὀλίσθαι
Νόσφι φίλου πατρὸς καὶ μητέρος,

and that of Idmon, the companion of Jason, pronounced before their departure from Greece,[3] are in exact agreement with the belief which prevailed with our own ancestors, as in the remarkable instances of Henry IV of France and Galeazzo Sforza, Duke of Milan. It was in 1476, on St. Stephen's day, that the duke was assassinated by the conspirators, as he marched to church, between the ambassadors of of Ferrara and Mantua. He had felt such strong forebodings in the morning, that it was with

---

[1] Prom. Vinct. 493.   [2] Il. XVI, 843.
[3] Apollon. Rhod. I, 443.

difficulty he was prevailed upon to leave his palace. The statement of Aristotle respecting the death of Eudemus, as predicted by a vision, furnished occasion to Cicero for one of his most beautiful passages. Cicero himself seems constrained to admit a belief in this mysterious agency professed by Aristotle and Plato, by Sophocles and Xenophon. Celebrated were the dreams of Cyrus [1] and Decius, of Cœlius [2] and Pompey, the night before the battle of Pharsalia, when he fancied himself at Rome, in the theatre, as in his happiest days, and crowned with victory; of Calphurnia before Cæsar's death; of C. Gracchus, in which he saw his brother;[3] and the vision which appeared to Brutus, of which last Plutarch says, in defiance of the argument of Cassius the Epicurean: "If Dion and Brutus, men of firm philosophic minds, whose understandings were not affected by any constitutional infirmity, if such men could pay so much credit to the appearance of spectres as to give an account of them to their friends, I see no reason why we should depart from the opinion of the ancients."

Cicero appeals to the greatest writers of the Stoics, and asks who can despise the two dreams which they commemorate—the first of Simonides, who, finding the dead body of a stranger, had it placed in a grave, and was intending to embark on a voyage, when the man whom he had buried appeared to him, and warned him not to sail, lest he should perish in shipwreck. Simonides thereupon returned, and those who put to sea perished. The other was of two Arcadian friends, going the same journey, who came to Megara, where one

[1] Cyropæd. VIII, 7. Granting this to be a romance, at least Xenophon thought the account credible, and suited to the character of his hero.
[2] Cicero de Divin. I, 24.   [3] Val. Max. I, 7.

slept in a public-house, and the other went as a guest to a friend. During the night, he who had gone to the public-house appeared in a dream to his companion, and entreated that he would come to his assistance, as the man of the house was going to murder him. Terrified at this dream, he at first rose up, but on reflection, his mind recovered itself, the whole seemed to be a delusion, and he again lay down. Upon falling asleep the same vision appeared to him, beseeching, that since he had not come in time to find him alive, he would not suffer his murderer to remain unpunished: his dead body was at that moment, he said, thrown into a cart by the landlord, and covered with dung, and he besought him to come quickly to the door of the public-house, before the cart should leave the town. Greatly moved by this dream, the friend rose at the dawn of day, and came to the inn door, where he saw a herdsman standing with a cart. Upon demanding what it contained, the herdsman fled. The dead body was then discovered at the bottom, and the affair being disclosed, the landlord suffered due penalty.

Socrates affirmed, in his conversation with Crito, that he was summoned by a vision, Ἐδόκει τίς μοι γυνὴ προσελθοῦσα καλὴ καὶ εὐειδής, λευκὰ ἱμάτια ἔχουσα, καλέσαι με καὶ εἰπεῖν, Ὦ Σώκρατες, Ἤματί κεν τριτάτῳ Φθίην ἐρίβωλον ἵκοιο. The vision of a tall man, of a beautiful countenance, appeared to Hipparchus, just before his death, the night previous to the Panathenæa, who said to him,

τλῆθι λέων ἄτλητα παθὼν τετληότι θυμῷ.
οὐδεὶς ἀνθρώπων ἀδικῶν τίσιν οὐκ ἀποτίσει.[1]

Sophocles gives the voice which hastens Œdipus:

[1] Herodot. V, 56.

> Ὦ οὗτος, οὗτος, Οἰδίπους, τί μέλλομεν
> χωρεῖν; πάλαι δὴ τἀπὸ σοῦ βραδύνεται.[1]

Alcestes cries,[2]

> ὁρῶ δίκωπον, ὁρῶ σκάφος.

Our ancestors describe scenes of this kind, but still more affecting and sublime. Witness the last hours of Queen Catharine, in Shakspeare; and the account of the music which announced the death of Isabella, sister of Louis IX and Abbess of Longchamp, written by a sister of the convent. "Sister Clemence, of Argas, said that the night in which our holy and reverend lady and mother departed, a little before matins, she opened the casement, which was near her bed, in order to observe whether there was any one in the court, for she knew well that madame was near her end; and that she looked out at the sky, which was very beautiful and serene, and heard a sweet voice, most melodious, over the house where she lay, and that it sounded so long, that she believed no breath in this mortal life could have produced it. Sister Clemence put her head through the bars of the window, that she might discover what it could be, and then the bell tolled for matins, and some one brought her intelligence that madame, our holy mother, had just then departed. Also sister Aveline, of Hennaut, heard singing at the same time, most sweet and melodious, and sat up on her bed, but she knew not what it was. We believe firmly that it was the melody of the holy angels, who were conducting her blessed soul to the glory of heaven."

It is something to convince the despisers of our heroic age, that what excites their ridicule belongs equally to the wisest and greatest men of antiquity.

---

[1] Œd. Col. 1627. [2] Eurip. Alcest. 260.

This is not only true, but also it may be affirmed with confidence, that the most powerful minds among the moderns have furnished an apology for our simple ancestors, in subscribing to the same sentiments. There is an abject superstition which characterizes wicked men like Caligula; [1] there is a fear which Plutarch justly condemns in his treatise on Superstition, — the fear which leads men to magic and the observances of augury; not the fear of offending Heaven, but of falling victims to some blind necessity; which influenced Augustus when he trembled if he happened in the morning to put on his left shoe before the right.[2] Such were not the feelings of our heroic ancestors in their intervals of weakness. Their life of patience, temperance, wilful poverty, and contempt of death, belong not to men who are moved by a senseless charm, by a stumble or a sneeze. True, they shuddered when they heard of dead men rising from their graves and appearing unto many; at the tales of Sir George Villiers; of the Kœnigsberg professor; of Lord Tyrone; of Lord Lyttleton; of Ficinus; of the Chevalier de Saxe; of the first Sforza, whose dream the night before the passage of the river, warned him of his fate; of Lady Fanshaw, who was awakened at midnight by a ghastly scream, and saw a female form at the window, the distance from the ground excluding the possibility of its being mortal, a lady having, unknown to her, died at that hour in the castle where she lay; of the Duchess of Mazarin, and others; but do not the most eminent writers of the seventeenth century, among the moderns, attest and countenance them? With what feelings do you read of the descent of Ulysses into hell, or of the ghost in Hamlet? and how do you account for such feelings? Are you of opinion that

[1] Suetonius.   [2] Ibid.

the arguments adduced by Quintus, in the first book of Cicero's treatise De Divinatione, have been refuted in the second?

In the intellectual as well as in the political world there is a certain harmony and union between the highest and the lowest classes, founded upon principles and opinions which the intermediate ranks are either unable or unwilling to comprehend, but which, being handed down by tradition from the earliest age of antiquity, are generally popular, and being, at the same time, sanctioned by religion and true philosophy, and connected in some degree with eminent qualities of soul, are therefore held and experienced by men who are distinguished among their contemporaries by extraordinary genius and virtue. When Hannibal, upon leaving Italy, drew near to the African coast, and was anxious to determine the place where he should land, he ordered a sailor to the mast-top to examine the country, who being asked what he saw, answered, "The ruins of a tomb upon an eminence." Hannibal sailed on. "What strange ominous abodings and fears," says Bull, "do many times, on a sudden, seize upon men, of approaching evils, whereof at present there is no visible appearance! And have we not had some unquestionable instances of men, not inclined to melancholy, strongly and unalterably persuaded of the near approach of their death, so as to be able punctually to tell the very day of it, when they have been in good health, and neither themselves nor their friends could discern any present natural cause for such a persuasion, and yet the event hath proved that they were not mistaken? And although I am no doter on dreams, yet I verily believe that some dreams are monitory, above the power of fancy, and impressed on us by some superior influence. For of such dreams we have plain and undeniable instances in history, both sacred and profane, and in our own age and observation. Nor shall I so value the laughter of sceptics, and the scoffs of the Epicureans, as to be ashamed to profess that I myself have had some convincing experiments of such impressions. Now, it is no enthusiasm, but the best account that can be given of them, to ascribe these things to the ministry of the angels of God."

Tertullian believed that the soul had a certain faculty of divination independent of any particular inspiration from God. He seeks to prove the divinity of some dreams from history,[1] not having many opponents to combat in that age; for Cicero expressly says, "Unus dissentit Epicurus." After relating the dream of Wotton, and that vision which appeared to Donne at Paris, Izaac Walton observes, "This is a relation that will beget some wonder, and it well may; for most of our world are at present possessed with an opinion that visions have ceased. And though it is most certain that two lutes, being both strung and tuned to an equal pitch, and then one played upon, the other that is not touched being laid upon a table at a fit distance, will, like an echo to a trumpet, warble a faint audible harmony, in answer to the same tune: yet many will not believe there is any such thing as a sympathy of souls. I am well pleased that every reader do enjoy his own opinion."

> What, dost thou not believe, that oft in dreams
> A voice of warning speaks prophetic to us?

are the words of the Countess to Wallenstein, who replies,

> There is no doubt that there exist such voices,
> Yet I would not call them
> Voices of warning that announce to us
> Only the inevitable. As the sun,

---

[1] Lib. de Anima, 46.

> Ere it is risen, sometimes paints its image
> In the atmosphere, so often do the spirits
> Of great events stride on before the events,
> And in to-day already walks to-morrow.
> That which we read of the fourth Henry's death,
> Did ever vex and haunt me like a tale
> Of my own future destiny. The king
> Felt in his breast the phantom of the knife;
> Long ere Ravaillac arm'd himself therewith
> His quiet mind forsook him: the Phantasma
> Started him in his Louvre, chased him forth
> Into the open air; like funeral knells
> Sounded that coronation festival;
> And still with boding sense he heard the tread
> Of those feet, that ev'n then were seeking him
> Throughout the streets of Paris.[1]

Democritus and some others of the ancient atheists, less bold than their successors in this age, acknowledged the fact of certain idols or spectres εἴδωλά τινα having appeared to men, but they evaded the argument by denying that they were immortal spirits; and Cudworth endeavours to vindicate the historic truth of the phenomena of apparitions, and the ancient divination against atheists, who "obstinately denying matter of fact and history, will needs impute these things" to imagination. Isaac Barrow speaks expressly on the same side: he says, that "concerning apparitions from another world, spirits haunting persons and places, visions made unto persons of especial eminency and influence, presignifications of future events by dreams, &c. &c., he that shall affirm all such things to be mere fiction and delusion, must thereby, with exceeding immodesty and rudeness, charge the world both with extreme vanity and malignity: many, if not all, worthy historians of much inconsiderateness or fraud; most lawgivers of great silliness and rashness; most judicatories of

---

[1] Schiller's Wallenstein, by Coleridge.

high stupidity or cruelty; a vast number of witnesses of the greatest malice or madness; all which have concurred to assert these matters of fact." He concludes with this remark, "They are much mistaken who place a kind of wisdom in being very incredulous, and unwilling to assent to any testimony, how full and clear soever: for this indeed is not wisdom, but the worst kind of folly.—Compare we, I say, these two sorts of fools; the credulous fool, who yields his assent hastily, upon any slight ground, and the suspicious fool, who never will be stirred by any the strongest reason or clearest testimony; we shall find the latter, in most respects, the worse of the two; that his folly arises from worse causes, hath worse adjuncts, produceth worse effects. Credulity may spring from an airy complexion, or from a modest opinion of one's self; suspiciousness hath its birth from an earthy temper of body, or from self-conceit in the mind: that carries with it being civil and affable, and apt to correct an error; with this a man is intractable, unwilling to hear, stiff and incorrigible in his ignorance or mistake: that begets speed and alacrity in action; this renders a man heavy and dumpish, slow and tedious in his resolutions and in his proceedings: both include want of judgment; but this pretending to more thereof, becomes thereby more dangerous. Forward rashness, which is the same with that, may sometimes, like an acute disease, undo a man sooner; but stupid dotage, little differing from this, is like a chronical distemper, commonly more mischievous, and always more hard to cure." Plancus, in a letter to Cicero, went farther, " Credulitas enim error est magis quam. culpa: et quidem in optimi cujusque mentem facillime irrepit."[1] It was well said by Cicero to one

---

[1] Epist. ad Diversos, X, xxiii.

who affected an air of superior sagacity, and who had adopted the inconsequential opinions with which the scepticism of Epicurus was so often associated, " Jam mallem Cerberum metueres, quam ista tam inconsiderate diceres." [1]

But these remarks have far exceeded their due limits: it was only required to shew that our ancestors are not to be despised for having suspected, in common with the greatest men of ancient and modern times, that " there are more things in heaven and earth than are dreamt of " in the Parisian philosophy. And so I pass on and turn again to my matter.

XIII. The simplicity of the chivalrous character is an object upon which men may look back with regret. "The inhabitants of the British isles," says Diodorus, " are of simple manners, and far removed from the cunning and wickedness of the present race of men: they lead a frugal life, and at a wide distance from the luxury of those who abound in wealth." [2] Yet the ancients did not think that it was only the virtue of barbarians, for Thucydides expressly says that " simplicity is the companion of nobility "; an idea which is expressed on the shield of the Montmorencies, which bears the word ἁπλόος. " A simple and generous man," says Plato, " ἄνδρα ἁπλοῦν καὶ γενναῖον." [3] " Before the reign of Louis XIV," says Berenger, " our manners, our ideas, were purer and wiser, our desires more moderate, our cheerfulness more from the heart; there was more good sense, more truth and freedom. Our language too, alas! has lost that bonhommie, that frankness of our Joinvilles, des Comines and Charrons." [4] Open one of the old chivalrous books and a reader who is accustomed

[1] Tuscul. I, 6.   [2] Lib. V, 21.
[3] De Repub. II.   [4] Soirées Provençales, I.

to the vitiated page of a modern novel, to all its low and degrading detail of vulgar sentiment and vulgar vice in the highest rank of society, will affect extreme disgust at what he will term the grossness of the barbarous language. "All is sound to the sound," says Mdme. de Sevigné; "such reading produces good and evil effects: for my part, I think that a young man would become generous and brave in seeing my heroes, and that a young woman would become agreeable and virtuous. Some persons may abuse things, but they would not escape better if they had never read a line." In ancient times men praised this mode of speaking clearly, or ἐλευθέρως,[1] as Hercules said,

οὐκ ἐμπλέκων αἰνίγματ', ἀλλ' ἁπλῷ λόγῳ.[2]

It is a fine passage in Euripides where he proclaims the simplicity of virtue.

Ἁπλοῦς ὁ μῦθος τῆς ἀληθείας ἔφυ
Κοὐ ποικίλων δεῖ τ' ἄνδιχ' ἑρμηνευμάτων·
Ἔχει γὰρ αὐτὰ καιρόν· ὁ δ' ἄδικος λόγος
Νοσῶν ἐν αὑτῷ, φαρμάκων δεῖται σοφῶν.

"Do not fear that you will become gross because you are simple," says Fénelon, "true simplicity produces perfect politeness."— "Je retranche en ma maison," says Montaigne, "autant que je puis de la ceremonie. A quoy faire fuit-on la servitude des cours, si on l'entraine jusques en sa taniere."[3] "Comme ta vie se rend par la simplicité plus plaisante, elle s'en rend aussi plus innocente et meilleure."[4] Such were the feelings of men in these ages. Young princesses might be seen like Nausicaa washing their brothers' linen;[5] Charlemagne, or René d'Anjou, King of Sicily, like

---

[1] Euripides, Alcest. 1018. [2] Æschyl. Prom. Vinct. 630.
[3] Essai, I, 13. [4] Ibid. II, 12. [5] Od. VI, 64.

Ulysses, not distinguishable by their dress on ordinary occasions from peasants; Earl Richard, afterwards "Cœur-de-Lion," sleeping in the same bed with the King of France when on a visit at his court; the knight, like the old Roman, content to lie upon common straw,

> Et tamen ex illo venit in astra toro.

To him,

> Nectar erat palmis hausta duabus aqua.[2]

"For can a man," he would say, "quench his thirst better from the fountain which is finely paved with marble than when it swells over the green turf?"

A duke of Medina Sidonia and his duchess, who for wealth and nobility were among the greatest in Spain, made a visit in the year 1540 to our Lady's de Regla, a church of great devotion in Andalusia, and went in a cart drawn by oxen. In later times, when families of rank travelled, ladies and female attendants would sit in the carriage, while the cavaliers rode with the men-servants, all conversing familiarly together. The King of France rode on horseback to be crowned at Rheims. François de Montholon, a magistrate, lived in a small house which had only a room and a kitchen on the ground floor, and built a hospital for the sick with 200,000 francs which the king had given him for his services; princes living in immense palaces, would dine off one dish, and inhabit but one room, not like the moderns, condemning themselves to breathe the close air of some little cottage, and forsaking their ancestral hall, with its lofty tower and pointed arch and commanding terrace, objects which exalt the imagination of those who have learned to

---

[1] Ovid, Fast. III.   [2] Ibid. II.

associate them with the virtues of chivalry, and which involve their occupier in no system of ruin, so long as he retains the simplicity and virtue of his order; because their finance is not adequate to the decoration of these apartments, the splendid furniture, the gallery, the paintings and statues, the pompous liveries, the consistent equipage, the endless banquets and assemblies; "the taste for which," as Sully says justly, "will soon degenerate into a kind of madness, whence, the loss of time is the least consequent evil: prodigality, ruin, and dishonour being the ordinary result." This simplicity pervaded the whole taste and manners and life of the Catholic baron,

> —— cui Pudor, et Justitiæ soror
> Incorrupta Fides, nudaque Veritas.

On common days he was not distinguished in dress from his vassals; his son was not otherwise clad; it was enough for a father's eye if, like the young scholar Chrysostom, described by Peter the Goatherd, "he was as good-natured a soul as ever trod on shoe of leather, mighty good to the poor, a main friend to all honest people, and had a face like a blessing." In Homer's days a youth in the employment of a shepherd might be recognized, by his gait and manners, for the son of a prince:[1] it was the countenance and manner that constituted the senatorial grace which Pliny admired in his young friend, "Est ingenua totius corporis pulchritudo, et quidam senatorius decor." On Sundays, however, and the festivals, the whole chivalry of the castle would be richly attired. The little page, Jehan de Saintré, is very particular in commanding that his embroidered suit may be finished on the Saturday night. The advice of St. Louis was

[1] Od. XIII, 223.

"qu'on se doit vetir bien honnetement, afin d'etre mieux aimé de sa femme, et aussi que vos gens vous en priseront plus. C'est aussi le dire du Saige, qu'il faut se porter selon son état, de telle maniere que les prudes du monde ne puissent dire, vous en faites trop; n'aussi les jeunes gens vous en faites peu." Many men, in these ages of forgotten merit, might have been described in the words of Tacitus, where he records the simplicity of Agricola, "Cultu modicus, sermone facilis, uno aut altero amicorum comitatus."[1] Many now, as in the corrupt age of Rome, who measure great men by ambition, if they were to behold one of our chivalrous ancestors, would demand why he was admirable? few would interpret him.

If we look at his house, it is described by Sir Philip Sidney, in his Arcadia, as "built of fair and strong stone, not affecting so much any extraordinary kind of fineness, as an honourable representing of a firm stateliness. All more lasting than beautiful, but that the consideration of the exceeding lastingness made the eye believe it was exceeding beautiful." Sismondi remarks, that the character of the superb palaces of Florence, built in the fourteenth century, is strength and majesty; "the luxury of our ancestors," he adds, "had this advantage over our own, that the works which it encouraged were destined to last for a long time. The emulation of these men had always posterity in view; ours is but vain; we only seek to please our own contemporaries; and our monuments will decay as rapidly as our reputation."[2] If we view the interior, to pass over the skins and rushes of which Diodorus Siculus speaks, we find in the castle of René d'Anjou, the most magnificent prince of his age for tournaments and public entertain-

---

[1] De Vit. Agric. XL.   [2] Hist. des Repub. Ital. V, 369.

ments, a few wooden chairs or benches, and some curtains of coarse blue stuff. Montesquieu found no other furniture in the hotel of the prime minister of the Grand Duke of Florence; and in the Palazzo Doria, in Genoa, the poet Gray says, that the "furniture seemed as old as the founder of the family." It is true, some embossed silver tables proclaim, in bas-relief, his victories at sea, how he entertained the Emperor Charles V, and how he refused the sovereignty of the commonwealth when it was offered to him; but all the rest consists of some old-fashioned chairs and Gothic tapestry. Ulysses was a skilful boat-builder; he made his own bedstead; and the Emperor Maximilian used to sit in a chair which he had made himself, which may be seen to this day in Germany. Their grounds, too, were laid out for use, rather than for pleasure, for the wild woods and rocks afforded them the greatest pleasure. Charlemagne's garden could only boast of a few lilies, roses, poppies, and heliotropes.[1] In one of his capitularies he orders all surplus of his vegetables and his fowl to be sold.[2]

The Catholic spirit of sacrifice made them ever ready to neglect personal comfort, and to attend to the encouragement of the arts and of the general happiness. St. Charles Borromeo and Cardinal Federigo, of the same illustrious house, both inspired by the same spirit of religion, were simple in private, but splendid and liberal in public. They erected and restored many noble edifices, and decorated with paintings a far greater number, insomuch as to make it observed, that Milan was no less indebted to her Borromei, than Florence to her Medici, or Mantua to her Gonzagas. It might have been affirmed of our chivalry, what Cicero

---

[1] Hist. de la Vie privée des François, I, 191.
[2] De Villis, art. 39.

said of the Roman people, "Odit privatam luxuriam, publicam magnificentiam diligit"; the converse of which is so likely to be true where the modern philosophy prevails. The simple paintings of our early masters, so characteristic of their minds, are still beheld with rapture by every eye of genuine taste. True, one may smile at the taste which presided over the Mystere de Nicodeme by Jean Michel, in which Lazarus was to be represented, "habillé bien richement en estat de chevalier, et oiseau sur le poing et bravement mainera ses chiens derrière lui"; or at that of Bonamico Buffalmacco, who, as Peacham says, "drew the four patriarchs and the four evangelists; when he expressed St. Luke, with great art, blowing the ink in his pen, to make it run." Yet the admirable Greek paintings by Polygnotus, at Delphi, as described by Pausanias,[1] had all the simplicity which belongs to our early school of Christian painting. In one picture, where there were more than eighty figures, an inscription under each principal figure gave its name. "This part of the picture," says Pausanias, "represents the sea-coast, as is plain from the quantity of little pebbles and shells scattered about." On the picture were two verses by Simonides, signifying, "Polygnotus of Thasis, son of Aglaophon, made this picture." Such was the style of their inscriptions. Another picture, by the same artist, was the descent of Ulysses to hell. "First, you see a river," says Pausanias, "and in the water the figures of little fish." We may judge of the style of composition, when he says, "If you look to the top of the picture, you see there Ajax, Palamedes, and Thersites, who play at dice." But if we find the same simplicity, and as it were timidity of design in the old

---

[1] Lib. X, c. 25, 31.

masters, who were coeval with the poetry of the middle ages, how lovely and sublime were the forms which they produced. Witness St. Michael weighing the souls, in the great picture at Danzig. How awfully serene a countenance! such as might be a ministering spirit from the throne of God, and how majestic a figure! In the great cross of the old chasubles the history of each day's gospel used to be represented in embroidery, and these figures are still affecting, from their devout and majestic air. "In general," says a German writer, "our ancient artists gladly overlooked the form of expression, in attending to the spirit of their subject. Painting at first, after its invention by John of Leyden, was cultivated almost exclusively by monks in their cells. The monasteries of Vallombrosa and Camaldoli contained many painters. In the hands of these devout men, who used to perform devotional exercises previous to painting portraits of our Saviour, or of the Blessed Virgin, an account of which is given by Orlandi, painting had a peculiar charm, though removed perhaps from the perfection which appeared in the works of Dürer, Lucas von Leyden, and Raphael, who were contemporaries. Spirituality was the chief feature of these early masters, mostly unencumbered with a close correspondence of parts, or a rigid adherence to right perspective and artificial grouping, which the understanding first invented, by long comparison. These masters resigned themselves much more to the devout and inward sentiment of their souls, and desired rather to cherish and express a holy feeling, than to form a work of sensual beauty; though this is only to be understood in general, for there remain works of this age which for every kind of perfection continue to astonish the beholder. This spiritual tendency appears in the disposition of these masters to choose in their colouring, not the warm and living tints which nature exhibits; but they painted with softer, I might say, with heavenly colours. Hence many of their figures seem aërial, fragrant, and lovely, as if the artist had dipped his pencil in purity and brightness itself. The colours are like a light transparent medium, in which the corporeal almost disappears. But above all, the deep-feeling artist thought that these soft coloured forms came forth, and seemed endued with light, when they were painted on a gold ground; the eyes were not diverted by the confused and earthly nature of the surrounding parts, but the beams of gold directed them ever back to the principal figure, as their centre. Perhaps out of overflowing piety, the gold was brought as a kind of offering, which the painter thus applied. There was also an emblem in these old paintings: all the separate parts, often the most trivial and obscure, are in spiritual and mystical relation with the principal subject of the picture. These secondary ideas are indeed often deeply concealed, and many Germans who have acquired a taste for foreign arts, reject these, the meaning of which is beyond them; but those who, full of devotion and faith, turn to the arts of their fathers with zeal and love, perceive with silent delight the tender mystery which the profound soul of the old master had laid down. Many condemn these old pictures, in which the history of the principal figure is represented complete in the distance, as the heartless French critic ridicules Shakspeare for comprising a number of years in the time of his tragedy. One cannot be too cautious in approaching the old works of art, with a view to judge them. Life had then a form so different from what it has now, and art was so entwined with it. In observing the splendid robes with which the artist adorns holy persons, we should remember the intention which prompted his hand, that as the poor as well as the rich, in these times, often and gladly gave their best and most beautiful vestments to ornament altars and holy images, the painter, with similar piety, expended his utmost skill in worthily adorning those saints whom he painted and honoured with religious honour; by means of the wide and flowing drapery, it was the intention, not only to clothe the body, but also to keep it completely out of the view and thought of the observer, and to confine the attention solely to the spiritual countenances of the heavenly. He who would feel and understand what I have now attempted to describe, as belonging to our old Christian paintings, should view the great altar-piece in the Cathedral of Cologne, and he will behold a figure of Mary which deserves a heaven, an infant Jesus which will remind him of the most masterly production of Raphael, and an old worshipping king, worthy of being ranked with the masterpiece of Dominichino."[1]

"It is common," says Groote, "to censure this epoch of the arts as indicating a depraved and childish taste; but we find at this time the one great object of art clearly understood and happily pursued; it is ever the elevating of the earthly existence to its heavenly destination; it is still ever the holy land of poetry; the unearthly, the world of faith, in which the world of sin, of sorrow, and of wretchedness disappears, and is forgotten, as in a joyful dream. O happy the people who still are found in this tranquil, innocent, blessed childhood of faith and art; to them everywhere the forms of the holy and the divine are near, and they are raised from earth to heaven."

But with regard to all the ordinary objects of life, the tastes and pleasures of men were equally simple.

[1] Carove, Ansichten der Kunst des Deutschen Mittelalters. 1822.

The old allegorical engravings, designed by Breughel and others, exhibit the simple form in which the Christian virtues were practised. It followed from the same spirit that men were enabled to enjoy the sweetest hours of life; for as Pliny described the first Christians, the dawn of each day was the signal for prayer. "Know you not, O man," said St. Ambrose, " quod primitias tui cordis ac vocis quotidie Deo debeas."[1] It appears from a record, of the date of 1512, that the family of the Earl of Northumberland used to rise at six to assist at mass. The manna of heaven melted away and was lost if the people of God did not get up before the sun to gather it, "that it might be known to all men," says Solomon, "that we must precede the sun in blessing God, and worship him at the dawning of the light. O God, my God, to thee do I watch at break of day." St. Francis of Sales made it a point of virtue to keep early hours, equally serviceable to health and holiness.[2] The prince as well as the scholar, the knight as well as the page, partook of so much of the spirit of Demosthenes, that, like him, they would feel ashamed to be conquered in early rising by the mechanic who rose before light.[3]

The Abbé de Sade, relating how Petrarch used to see Laura at her window, before sunrise, when she went to church, says, "the manners of that age were different from our own. Persons are not to be seen now at their window at the rising of the sun." Emily in Chaucer

</pre>
——— That fairer was to be seen
Than is the lily upon his stalk green,
And fresher than the May, with flowers new,
Ere it was day, as she was wont to do,
She was arisen, and all ready dight.

———

[1] Psalm 118, sec. 19.   [2] Introduction to a Devout Life.
[3] Cicero, Tuscul. IV.

And the beautiful song in Cymbeline,

> Hark! hark! the lark at heaven's gate sings,

might have been employed in those simple ages without fear of injury or offence.

In France it was usual to dine at nine o'clock in the morning, and to sup at four, after which, in Louis XII's time, they used to hunt in the park. Louis XIV dined at twelve o'clock. Madame de Sevigné writes that she is dying of hunger, because dinner is not till one. How much more rational the ecclesiastical and feudal than the commercial division of the day! Even in great cities the same simplicity prevailed. Petrarch, in one of his sonnets, describes Laura sitting on a bench outside of the house. The hours of retiring to rest were early. The gate of the castle of the Percies used to be closed at nine o'clock, after which no ingress or egress was permitted. Such was the regulation of a feudal house; how often deserving the praise of Cato:

> Casta domus, luxuque carens, corruptaque numquam
> Fortuna domini, clarum et venerabile nomen
> Gentibus, et multum nostræ quod proderat urbi.[1]

Simplicity was the characteristic of all ranks in these ages. What a contrast to later times, when a philosopher might have taken up his lantern, like Diogenes, and searched for a man: the professional character superseding that of humanity; the lawyer, the merchant, the commercial nobleman, the minister, all enunciating like some brazen head of a friar Bacon, rather than expressing the sentiments of a mortal.

Plato, speaking of the happiest period of society, when men were neither rich nor poor, seems to

---

[1] Lucan, IX, 201.

describe the middle ages: ἀγαθοὶ μὲν δὴ διὰ ταῦτά τε ἦσαν καὶ διὰ τὴν λεγομένην εὐήθειαν· ἃ γὰρ ἤκουον καλὰ καὶ αἰσχρά, εὐήθεις ὄντες ἡγοῦντο ἀληθέστατα λέγεσθαι καὶ ἐπείθοντο.[1] They had made less progress in commerce and machinery, they had less skill in the multiplied arts of injury and destruction, εὐηθέστεροι δὲ καὶ ἀνδρειότεροι καὶ ἅμα σωφρονέστεροι καὶ ξύμπαντα δικαιότεροι. The state of society in these ages was precisely that which, according to Plato, produces the most generous and noble manners, γενναιότατα ἤθη.

XIV. "The journey of high honour lies not in plain ways."[2] Habits of endurance were necessary to men who had many things to lose far dearer than property or life; who had to contend with the force of material evil, and not to bend themselves to its dominion. On beholding the figure of each knight, one might say like Amphitryo, on shewing Hercules:

οὐκ ἂν ἴδοις ἕτερον
πολυμοχθότερον πολυπλαγετότερόν τε θνατῶν.[3]

Büsching quotes a saying of Tristan,—"knighthood must begin from childhood. Honour requires bodily suffering, and comfort is the ruin of honour when we indulge in it too long or too much."[4] "Let princes and great lords take heed how they breed up their children in luxury," says the Castilian Guevara.[5] "Quid non adultus concupiscet qui in purpuris repit?" said Quinctilian. A youth bred in delicacy will appear, in the voyage of life, like Æeta in his painted ship or floating island of pleasure, when the wind began to freshen.[6] Our ancestors held with the Spartan king, πολύ τε

[1] De Legibus, III.   [2] Sir Philip Sidney's Arcadia.
[3] Eurip. Hercul. 1196.
[4] Ritterzeit und Ritterwesen, I, 12.
[5] L'Horloge des Princes, lib. II, c. 33.
[6] Max. Tyr. Diss. I, 3.

διαφέρειν οὐ δεῖ νομίζειν ἄνθρωπον ἀνθρώπου, κράτιστον δὲ εἶναι ὅστις ἐν τοῖς ἀναγκαιοτάτο ς παιδεύεται.[1] Tancred, "cui nihil dulce nisi fuerit sudore conditum,"[2] is an example of our Christian chivalry, observing the plan commended by Xenophon " never to sit down to dinner πρὶν ἱδρῶσαι."[3] Plato cites Hesiod, where he says that the gods, in holding out virtue to men ἱδρῶτα προπάροιθεν ἔθηκαν.[4] The seasoning of the Lacedemonian feast was required to relish that of our ancestors, labor in venatu, sudor, cursus ad Eurotam, fames, sitis.[5] Sardanis, warning Crœsus to beware of the Persians, said that they had only leather to cover their limbs, and that they fed on not what they liked best, but what they could get.[6] Like the lad in the Anglo-Saxon colloquy, who replies to the question, what he drank, "ale, if I have it, or water, if I have it not."[7] Cæsar relates of the Suevi, the most warlike of all the German tribes, that they used no wine, thinking that it rendered men unable to bear labour and effeminate.[8]

Görres attributes the noble air which characterizes the Romans, to their habits of extreme temperance. A salad, a piece of bread, and a flask of wine constitute the nourishment of the labouring men, who are all finely made and as strong as any in the world; in fact, the human form is beheld there in its highest beauty. What William of Jumiéges relates used to be noted as a lesson to all who despised the offer of frugal fare; for he records that two monks, Baldwin and Gondouin, having come into certain vast deserts, had begun to cut down trees and force a way into the forest. William, Duke or Marquis of Normandy, when hunting

[1] Thucyd. I, 85.   [2] Gesta Tanc. XIV.
[3] Lacedæm. Respub. II. Cyropæd. VIII, 1.   [4] De Legibus, IV.
[5] Cicero, Tuscul. V.   [6] Herodot. I. 71.
[7] Turner, Hist. Angl.-Sax.   [8] IV, 2.

found them thus employed, and asked them their country and what object they proposed. They related everything to him, and concluded by offering him some of their black bread and the water of charity. The duke disdained to accept the bread or the water, and passed on through the forest. Soon an enormous boar was started, and, turning upon the dogs, rushed over them and overthrew William. Upon coming to himself, he retraced his steps to the monks and gladly accepted their charity; he also gave them the land and assisted them to make their cells habitable.[1]

It was natural that temporal chivalry should be more reconciled to privations when it beheld the virtue and dignity which accompanied the spirit of mortification in holy men. A memorable instance occurred on the preaching of St. Bernard to the Albigenses, who were inflamed with rage by the calumnies of their leaders. It was even feared that the saint might fall a victim to their blind fury; for, upon entering their country, he openly preached against their democratical principles. On one occasion, having concluded his sermon before a great multitude, at Toulouse, and while in the act of mounting his horse, one of the furious zealots came up and cried out, before all the people, "Lord abbot, do you know that the horse of our master, against whom you have been preaching, is not so fat and sleek as your own?" St. Bernard answered mildly, and with an unmoved countenance, "My friend, I do not deny what you say, but you should consider that this beast, on whose account you reprove me, is designed by nature to thrive and become sleek, and that is not what offends God; nor are we justified before Him by means of our

[1] History of the Dukes of Normandy, book III, chapter vii.

horses, but every man must stand for himself"; and with these words, he threw aside the dark flowing habit of his order, and showed his majestic form worn down and emaciated with constant labours and abstinence. So affecting a spectacle moved even these furious men. They fell on their knees and implored pardon and a blessing. In Perceforest, Sir Estonne invites Claudius to eat of his deer, of his own cooking, in the forest, saying, "Sire, quant je suis es deserts d'Ecosse dont je suis seigneur je chevaucherai huit jours ou quinze que je nentreray en chastel ne en maison, et si ne verray feu ne personne vivant fors que bestes sauvages, et de celles mangeray atournees en ceste maniere et mieulx me plaira que la viande de l'empereur." Hence the custom, which appears from Eustache Deschamps, of the page and squire being bound occasionally to help in the kitchen. To such men the commands of the Church were of easy observance. La Journée des Harengs, so called from the quantity of this fish found by the English in the convoy, which was to relieve Orleans during the memorable siege, will indicate how faithfully Lent was observed in that age, even by a besieged city. Such as contented themselves with admiring the austerities of life in the first fathers and founders of our religion, which gave rise to monasteries, cloisters, hermitages, cells, and solitary habitations, still retained a conviction that they were not exempt from obedience to ecclesiastical discipline; for in a manuscript of the king's library, at Paris, it is recorded, among the expenses of the hotel of Philippe de Valois, that he gave alms on the Thursday after St. Martin, for not having fasted the preceding Wednesday, and again, for not having fasted on the vigil of St. Andrew.[1] In these ages men did not listen

---

[1] La France sous les cinq premiers Valois, I, 386.

with such attention to lectures upon constitutional weakness. They knew, in defiance of all maxims, that among those who have attained to long lives, the greatest number have been men of abstemious and even austere habits;[1] and the old heathen physicians were aware how much they conduced to health of body and to perfection of mind. Plutarch even says that abstinence from lawful pleasures is an exercise which enables men to abstain from what is forbidden.[2] Let those only who have studied the human character condemn the sentence which Muño Gustioz, in the poem of the Cid, passes upon Asur Gonzalez, saying

You breakfast before mass, you drink before you pray,
There is no honour in your heart, nor truth in what you say.

Plato, after remarking the hardy education which Darius had received, whereas all his successors were born to the crown, and bred among women and slaves, without any one to contradict them, concludes, that from the same period no king of the Persians was great, excepting in name. οὐ γὰρ μή ποτε γένηται παῖς καὶ ἀνὴρ καὶ γέρων ἐκ ταύτης τῆς τροφῆς διαφέρων πρὸς ἀρετήν.[3] Youth was not to be guided to virtue along flowery paths, nor to knowledge by amusement. Children were not to be promised a tenderness which nature had refused to men: "instead of sweetening the edge of the cup, they were told the liquor was bitter, but that they must drink it."[4] Such was the education which had been given to the conquerors of Marathon;[5] each of whom might have said with Hercules,

ἡβῶντα, μόχθους οὓς ἔτλην τί δεῖ λέγειν;[6]

---

[1] Nieremberg, Doct. Ascet. VI, vi, 56.
[2] Plut. de Socratis genio. [3] Leges, III.
[4] Barante de la Lit. Française. [5] Aristoph. Nubes.
[6] Eurip. Hercul. 1240.

"Nothing," says Plato, "should interfere with exercising the body to labour and the soul to wisdom,"[1] according to the precept πειρῶ τὸ μὲν σῶμα εἶναι φιλόπονος, τὴν δὲ ψυχὴν φιλόσοφος. Thus Philopœmen spent his time between agriculture and the study of philosophy;[2] a mode of life which, in the middle ages, was considered as divine and religious, and conducive to the perfection of saints. The passion for glory could induce Alexander to pour the water upon the ground which his fainting soldiers had carried to him in a helmet when passing the Gedrosian desert. The spirit of sacrifice in the middle ages produced deeds equally heroic: Agesilaus held that a prince should excel ordinary men in being able to endure the summer's sun and the winter's cold.[3] This was the education to form men like the old Roman, " with a mind unconquerable, of rigid innocence, and despising riches; in abstinence and patience of labour, of an iron frame and soul: "[4] or like the Spaniard, who, as Landor says, " has the qualities of the cedar, patient of cold and heat, nourished on little, lofty and dark, unbending and incorruptible." What Lucan says of Cato when his soldiers were suffering from thirst in the deserts of Africa, " Stat, dum lixa bibat," was characteristic of our knights. The squire of chivalry had to perform the most laborious offices, and the blow which he received on admission to the order was to denote the sufferings for which he had still to prepare himself.

Büsching remarks that " the habit of obedience, the principle of which was derived from the patriarchal ages, thus learned in youth, was a noble preparation for subsequent command. The progress to knighthood was long and gradual; nothing sud-

[1] De Legibus, VII.
[2] Pausanias, lib. VIII, 49.
[3] Xen. Agesil. 5.
[4] Livy, XXXIX, 40.

den hurried the boy from an unwarlike service to the life of peril. Every one had to obey and learn, so that step by step he might become familiar with the dangers and troubles of a chivalrous life." Equally admirable were the effects of this education in regard to religion and the cultivation of the mind. The saints have shown that the way of holiness lies in obedience and observance of the most minute rules.[1] That furious ardour for bursting every restraint which possesses so many of the moderns, ends, we find, in the subjection of the soul to the passions, or in the loss of reason. No rank was then exempt from obedience. Wirnt von Gravenberg relates how his hero, Wigolais, though a king's son, was bred up like other boys, to discharge every kind of youthful service. The squire and the knight were to be able to say, like the youth in Athenæus, "If a ladder must be mounted, I am a goat; a blow endured, an anvil; for drinking water, a frog; for bearing the winter cold without shelter, a blackbird; the summer heat, a grasshopper; for walking barefoot early in the morning, a crane; for passing a sleepless night, a bat."[2]

Montaigne alludes to a mode of education which succeeded the chivalrous system, "Si j'avoy des enfans masles je leur desirasse volontiers ma fortune: le bon pere que Dieu me donna, qui n'a de moy que la réconnoisance de sa bonté, mais certes bien gaillarde, m'envoya des le berceau nourrir à un pauvre village des siens et m'y tint autant que je fus en nourrisse et encores au dela: me dressant à la plus basse et commune façon de vivre. Ne prenez jamais, et donnez encore moins à vos femmes la charge de leur nourriture; laissez les former à

[1] Euseb. Nierembery. Doct. Ascet. VI, viii, 63. Lewis of Granada, Sinner's Guide, II, 8.
[2] Lib. V. 414.

la fortune, soubs des loix populaires et naturelles : laissez à la coustume de les dresser à la frugalité et à l'austerité, qu'ils ayent plus tost a descendre de l'aspreté qu'à monter vers elle." Thus Henry IV of France used to go bareheaded on the mountains, and without shoes or stockings, like the other children of the province; Du Guesclin went barefoot in his youth; Bavo-le-brun, Governor of Hainaut, is said by Jaques de Guyse to have required all from the age of six to fifteen to go barefoot.[1] The wretched race of the Cagots of the southern provinces of France were forbidden to walk without shoes that their infected bodies might not pollute the ground.[2] Every step that removed men unnecessarily from the wisdom and beauty of nature was a punishment to our ancestors. What a lovely passage occurs in one of the books of Plato, where Phædrus meets Socrates barefooted, and they agree to wander along the banks of the Ilissus, and Phædrus congratulates himself for having no shoes, that he may follow Socrates walking through the clear water. Montaigne even objects to the education of children by their parents, because, he says, these latter are unwilling to see their son "noury grossierement comme il faut et sans delicatesse"; and he adds in conclusion, " car il n'y a remede, qui en veut faire un homme de bien, sans doute il le faut hazarder un peu en ceste jeunesse et souvent choquer les regles de la medecine." It was an education of this kind in the most savage region of the Apennines, at the castle of Pietro Mala, where deep snow covers the ground for more than half the year, that made Pietro Saccone dei Tarlati, a chief of the Ghibelins, in the fourteenth century, the terror and astonishment of the Florentines and the inhabitants of the plains of Italy. He

---

[1] Chron. du Hainault, I, 30. [2] Tristan, VI, 334.

retained the manners and customs of the ancient northern conquerors, despising the luxury and softness of the south: attached to his mountains, he seemed rather to glory in becoming the King of the Alps than to aspire at governing the fertile countries at their feet, and in resembling the eagle which soars among the Apennines from rock to rock, but rarely descends into the plains.

In the romance of Guerin de Montglaive, we read, that upon occasion of a solemn feast in the castle of this prince, Mabilette seeing at table her four sons, Arnault, Milon, Regnier, and Gerard, all splendidly apparelled, "Noble duke," she said to her husband, "do you not thank heaven with me, for having given us four such sons, the least of whom has already the air and address of a preux chevalier?" Guerin, for the first time in his life, evinced to Mabilette impatience and anger. "No, woman," he replied, "I have no pleasure in keeping them at home to lead a good-for-nothing life between balls, hunting, and feasting; such habits will never gain them praise, but only render them jovial companions." Then looking at his four sons with great fierceness, he continued, "et vous autres quatre grands gaillards, ne rougissez-vous point de perdre temps et jeunesse à banqueter comme poussins sous une mue? Par la foi que je dois à Monseigneur Saint Martin, mieux aimerois je n'avoir point lignée, que de la voir, comme la folle vigne qui ne porte point de raisins." The departure of the four youths was the consequence of this scene, and when the day arrived for them to take leave of the Duke and Duchess, Guerin, says the romance, shed no tear; on the contrary, "I envy your lot," he said to them, "and so far from being pleased with governing my vassals, I had far rather set out to seek high adventures as formerly with my two friends, the terrible giant Robastre and the

enchanter Perdrigon. Age and marriage, my
children, often diminish chivalry; behold me like
a sick lion; my friends are grown devout, Robastre
has become a hermit."

The old Lord Gray, to inure his sons for war,
would usually in the depth of winter, in frost, snow,
rain, and what weather so ever fell, cause them at
midnight to be raised out of their beds and carried
abroad a hunting till the next morning, then perhaps come wet and cold home, having for breakfast
a brown loaf and a mouldy cheese.[1] The monks of
St. Denis say that Charlemagne, during a long
winter's night, used to go to bed and get up again
four or five times, observing the Homeric lesson to
a king,

οὐ χρὴ παννύχιον εὕδειν βουληφόρον ἄνδρα.

The man in the old play, who reckons the want
of a pillow among the evils of poverty,[2] would have
amused knights like old Sir Ewan Cameron of
Lochiel, who kicked a snowball from under the
head of his grandson. Garci Fernandez Manrique,
who was famous for often surprising the Moors
during the night, had founded the convent of St.
Salvador de Palacios de Benagel for Benedictine
nuns; he used to shame his men if they ever complained of his hours by reminding them of the holy
sisters and their matin bell.

These were the habits which enabled our ancestors to rival the ancients in the vastness of their
enterprises, with whom, as Pliny said, "multum de
nocte vel ante vel post diem sumitur"; thus Cicero
dated many of his letters "ante lucem."[3] If the
Scotch mountaineer boy could say, "I can sleep
weel enough mysel out-bye beside the naig as I hae
done mony a long night on the hills," the prince

---

[1] Peacham. [2] Aristoph. Plutus, 542.
[3] Ad Quint. III, 2, 7; ad Att. XIII, 38.

could also boast that he used to sleep like Rhesus, by the side of his courser, could also repose beneath the midnight dew, and could use the words of the Spanish ballad,

> My bed is cold upon the wold,
> My lamp yon star,

or without taking his feet out of the stirrups, and only leaning on his lance, he strove to disappoint invading sleep rather than indulge it.

> Alike to him was time or tide,
> December's snow, or July's pride;
> Alike to him was tide or time,
> Moonless midnight, or matin prime.

At a moment's warning, in the dead of night, they were liable to be summoned from the cheerful hearth of the feudal hall. Then

> There was saddling and mounting in haste,
> There was pricking o'er moor and lea;
> He that was last at the trysting place,
> Was but lightly held of his gay ladye.

What a heart-stirring and poetic scene! The fears and adieus of the gentle and lovely women; the horses led out into the court looking but half awake; the moonlight streaming on the polished saddles and the steel breastplates; the knights hastily mounting; the rattle of spurs and the sound of the trumpet!

A gentleman once asked Bayard what inheritance a father was bound to leave his children. "He should leave them," he replied, "the mind that fears neither rain nor tempest, nor force of man, nor human injustice; and that is wisdom and virtue." This was the spirit of those champions, Amadis de Gaul; Palmerin of England; Tirante the White; Lisuarte of Greece; Don Belianis;

Perion of Gaul; Felixmarte of Hyrcania; Esplandian; Ciriongilio of Thrace; Rodomont; Sobrino; Rinaldus; Orlando.

> Non hic Atridæ, nec fandi fictor Ulyxes:
> Durum ab stirpe genus.——
> —— patiens operum parvoque assueta juventus.[1]

But, leaving romance, it is certain that the aspiring spirit of youth, nurtured under the influence of that generous religion which was capable of developing the whole greatness of man's nature, led on by faith and hope and courage, was ready to accommodate itself to every condition of human life, to pity rather than to covet the objects of vulgar ambition, the obstacles to virtue and honour, and to endure, with perfect content, the pressure of circumstances, which would be intolerable to men of vulgar thoughts and worldly minds. Let the coward amuse himself with living as long as he may; c'est son métier; but do not let him come to annoy us with his impertinences respecting the unhappiness of those who are not like himself.[2] True; such men must expect many adversaries, many dangers; many labours and sufferings, "sed mihi omnis oratio est cum virtute, non cum desidia, cum dignitate, non cum voluptate," with those who believed themselves born, not for sleep, and feasting, and pleasure, but for honour and justice, and the service of their brethren and of their country. Such was the language dictated by this disposition of soul. Youth was too virtuous to be influenced by the desire of selfish enjoyment and imaginary independence; to share with women the easy comforts of life without participating in its hardships and dangers, and withal it was too sharp-sighted to be deceived by the vulgar estimate that would identify rank with

---

[1] Æneid, IX. [2] De Maistre.

honour, or a title with possession. "It is to labour," said the old philosopher, "that Hercules owed his divinity. If you take away the wild beasts, and the tyrants, and the journeys above and below, and all the adversities, you do away with the virtue of Hercules. Take from the Athenians their course to Marathon, and their death there, and the hand of Cynægirus, the calamity of Polyzelus, and the wounds of Callimachus, and you leave them nothing majestic, excepting some incredible fables concerning Erechtheus and Cecrops."[1] The rights of primogeniture, coeval with the earliest records of human society, were approved of by the greatest authority in these ages; yet such was the disposition which characterized young men, that so far from envying the external privileges from which fortune might have excluded them, if the choice had been in their power, they would have preferred the spur to the label,[2] the post of personal exertion with the neglect of men who seek their own interest, to the privilege of ease, and comfort, and power, with the applause and professions of the same crowd; that is, they would have preferred the occupation and freedom, and even hardship which accompanied an inferior rank, to the enjoyments, or incentives of enjoyment, with the privileges and obligations which were attached to a more conspicuous station: they felt that it was more gratifying to extend than to receive honour, and that the generous pride of power was even surpassed by that of service. They would rather have faithfully to obey than to command with authority. These feelings and associations may have been despised by him,

[1] Max. Tyr. V, 7.
[2] Alluding to the mullet or spur rowel which is used by heralds to distinguish the third son, and the label which denotes the eldest, who inherits the estate of his house.

> Cui pulchrum fuit in medios dormire dies, et
> Ad strepitum citharæ cessantem ducere curam.

In all ages there have been persons who would have loved the manners of the Egyptians,[1] who would have urged the Greeks to follow the advice of Antileon the Thurian to sail home sleeping, like Ulysses.[2] "Look at these effeminate persons," says Sully, "who abound in our cities and at court. You see nothing of the simple, manly, and generous virtue of our ancestors; no sentiment, no solidity in the mind, an air affected, passion for play and debauchery, great attention to dress, exquisite perfume; they seek only to bear the palm from women." With them

> Not a man, for being simply man,
> Hath any honour.[3]

Would you ask such a person, "cur timet flavum Tiberim tangere?" he will reply like him in the old comedy,

> Ἰδού. θεῶ τὸ σχῆμα, καὶ σκέψαι μ' ὅτῳ
> μάλιστ' ἔοικα τὴν βάδισιν τῶν πλουσίων·[4]

but it is not the less certain that those feelings which belonged to chivalry had a deep foundation in the purest principles of our nature. Where there is health and strength, there is nothing which virtue cannot endure with cheerfulness; nay, with all the pride and ecstasy of youth. In comparison to the delight and recompense of feeling which the Creator has attached to life, and inseparably connected with the discharge of duty even in the present world, what are the choicest luxuries, the richest parade, the proudest distinctions that can be the gift of fortune or of the world? What are

---

[1] Sophocles, Œdip. Col. 337.
[2] Xen. Anab. V, 1.
[3] Shakspeare's Troil. and Cres.
[4] Aristoph. Vespæ.

they to the heart of man but disappointment and vanity? It is easy for men of worldly minds to stigmatize these sentiments as chimerical, and to boast of solid blessings as opposed to vain, imaginary pleasures, but they should be reminded that this is to be guilty of the very declamation, and to be the sport of the very imagination which they propose to censure.

Laertes thought he would cultivate peace of mind by shutting himself up for twenty years in his farm-cottage; but, as Plutarch observes, he was mistaken in his hopes, since from his country, his house, and his kingdom, he did indeed escape, τὴν δὲ λύπην μετ' ἀπραξίας καὶ κατηφείας ἀεὶ συνοικοῦσαν εἶχεν.[1] It is only religion which can sanctify retirement. What is comfort, that idol of the modern ages, which it is madness and folly and ingratitude not to worship? What is this specious object of desire, when there is no activity or excitement? No alternate succession of fear and hope? Things ought to be unmasked as well as men. Take away the mask, and what remains? It is a phantom ready to mock our bitter misery when he has perfected his scheme of deceit, and when our experience must disclose his treachery. It is a fiend that expects his evening prey. What are riches without the ability of enjoyment? What is rank without honour? But hardships and dangers not only conduced at the time to the happiness of the person who experienced them; their remembrance was a source of pleasure and a school of wisdom. "Forsan et hæc olim meminisse juvabit," was always a just prediction. As the swine-herd said to Ulysses, inviting him to sit up till a later hour, and relate his adventures, "There is no greater pleasure than to

[1] De Tranquillitate Animi.

relate what one has suffered."[1] Regner Lodbrog, imprisoned in a loathsome dungeon, solaced his mind by recollecting his past deeds of chivalry; how he delivered the beautiful Swedish princess from an impregnable fortress, restoring her to her father, and obtaining her hand in marriage for his reward. How comparatively tranquil must he have felt in the hour of danger, who could repeat the words of the Trojan hero,

> ———————— Non ulla laborum
> O virgo, nova mi facies inopinave surgit :
> Omnia præcepi, atque animo mecum ante peregi.

Theseus was moved by the memory of his own misfortunes to shew pity to those of the stranger. Œdipus ascribes his own fortitude to his long experience of suffering.[2] The chivalry of Hercules, exerted against cruel men and monsters, was ascribed by the ancients to the sufferings of his youth, serpents having conspired to destroy him in his cradle, and a wicked tyrant in his maturer age.[3] And when adversity was sanctified by the sublime faith of the Christian hero, what a source of perfection did it afford! If James I of Aragon had not learned by experience the miseries of captivity, Spain would not have enjoyed the blessing of the order of knights of our Lady of Mercy, founded by him to redeem captives. True, unassisted nature does not always derive benefit from suffering. Witness the cruel Prefect described by Tacitus: "Eo immitior quia toleraverat."[4] Yet many in every age have confessed, like Christians, that it was good for them to have been afflicted. No person who had not struggled with the world, who had not felt in his own bosom what were the

[1] Od. XV, 399. [2] Soph. Œd. Col. VII, 563.
[3] Diodor. Sic. IV, 17. [4] Annal. I, 20.

sufferings incident to a life of hardship, could have left that sentence, memorable for its instruction, and immortal in the page of poetry:

> Me quoque per multos similis fortuna labores
> Jactatam hac demum voluit consistere terra,
> Non ignara mali, miseris succurrere disco.

The conclusion from the whole might have been expressed in the words of the admiral of France to the barons and knights who complained of their sufferings in Scotland: "We can not be alwayes at Parys or Dygeon, at Beaune or at Chalons; it behoveth them that wyll lyve in this worlde, thynkynge to have honoure to suffre sometyme as well povertie as welth."[1]

When the physicians warned Vespasian, in his last illness, that his exertions in transacting public affairs were increasing his disorder—"Well," said he, "imperatorem stantem mori oportet." The Romans, in the statues which they erected to their deceased emperors, made them sitting; in order to signify, that all the felicity of this world could not bestow true rest, which could only be enjoyed in another life. "We are born for action," says Montaigne; "and not only an emperor, but every gallant man ought to die standing." The good Earl of Derby hoped that it might be his fate to be shriven in his helmet, like William de Ramsey, who died in his presence. Siward, the great Earl of Northumberland in the reign of King Edward the Confessor, when he perceived that the hour of death was at hand, caused himself to be put in armour and to be set up in his chair, affirming that a knight and a man of honour should die in that manner rather than lying on a couch like a feeble and faint-hearted creature; and so, sitting upright

---

[1] Froissart, II, c. 3.

in his chair, armed at all pieces, he ended his course, and was buried in the monastery of St. Mary at York.[1] When Arthur de Richemont, Duke of Bretagne, perceived that his last hours were come, he refused to keep his bed any longer; so, rising up, and leaning on the arms of his knights, he walked out into the great hall of his castle at Nantes. It was Christmas-eve, and he went to confession; thence to the mass of midnight; the next day his devotion edified every person who beheld him. On the 26th he expired, sitting in the same ducal chair from which he used to administer justice to his subjects. It was with similar views that Montaigne expressed his wish that death might take him in the act of pursuing his rural occupations; and it was the pride of Bayard, even in the article of death, that he died in the exercise of duty. But it will be asked, were not such notions inconsistent with the duty of self-preservation? Without doubt men often fell victims to this daring spirit in the spring of life: thus—

> Arcite is doom'd to die in all his pride,
> Must leave his youth and yield his beauteous bride.

The startling steed, the remorseless billow, these, and a thousand accidents incidental to human life, often accomplished, in an unlooked-for hour, the deed of separation. As Boccaccio says of the Florentines, "How many accomplished young men, whom not their fellows only, but Galen, Hippocrates, and Esculapius himself, would have pronounced in perfect health, have dined with their parents and companions in the morning, and been in the evening of the same day with their ancestors in another world." Cardan and Gauricus had foretold verdant and happy old age to Henry II, who was so miser-

[1] Brompton Chron.

ably slain in the flower of his youth. Early life was on many accounts more subject to sudden destruction than maturity and age.

> Tho', in the visions of romantic youth,
> What years of endless bliss are yet to flow!
> But mortal pleasure, what art thou in truth,
> The torrent's smoothness, ere it dash below!

Cicero remarks that youth is more liable to accidents and death than age. Lord Bacon has objected to the doctrine of the philosophers, that it has rather increased the fear of death in offering to cure it; and perhaps it may be allowable to condemn those monuments like that of the landgrave William III, in the church of St. Elizabeth, at Marburg, or that of Louis XII and Anne of Bretagne, in the Abbey of St. Denis, where the deformity of the dead carcase is shewn in horrible similitude. The tombs of men in the middle ages reminded men of heaven, or of the oratory, not of the grave. Sir Thomas Brown says "that he felt ashamed of death; the very disgrace and ignominy of our natures, that in a moment can so disfigure us, that our nearest friends stand afraid and start at us." Not to notice the error of language in speaking of the body without the soul as still the man, it may be affirmed that even this disgrace and ignominy belong not of necessity to the mortal remains. The ancients, indeed, expressed their concern at the death of a man when his form is yet in perfect symmetry, and fresh with the sweetness and the bloom of youth; saying, "How could poison pass these lips, and yet retain its venom?"[1] And yet how beautiful is the description of the death of young Simois in Homer! and with what grace does Virgil represent the dead body of Evander's youthful son. When Ajax had

---

[1] Moschus, Id. II.

slain Archilochus, he called out to Polydamas to remark the noble form of his lifeless foe.[1] And Priam, in affecting terms, compares the misery of an old man like himself being slain and trampled upon, to the fate of a young warrior who falls in battle, and everything becomes him even in death.

πάντα δὲ καλὰ θανόντι περ, ὅττι φανήῃ.[2]

There was something agreeable to the delicate mind of our ancestors in the idea that death might be stripped of its deformity.

——— E morte in sì bel viso è bella,

said an Italian poet, and Sir Philip Sidney, in his Arcadia, speaks of drawing up a young man of well-pleasing favour, that one would think death had in him a lovely countenance. If men were cut off in youth by a violent death, did it follow that they had increase of suffering? πορφύρεος θάνατος may be a less evil to the animal part of nature than many of the remedies with which men try to ward off fate.

What youthful bosom does not sympathize with those feelings so piteously expressed by the Chevalier Bayard, when he lay on the bed of sickness, dying, as he thought, by a gradual and inglorious decay, like a woman, crying out, like dying Hercules, "O dear arms, are you those with which I once slew the Nemean lion, and conquered the mighty force of the Hydra?"[3] True it was religion not to despise one's self in sickness;[4] and there was much to admire in the condition of the gentle and resigned sufferers, unlike the barbarous Cimbrians and Celtiberians, who used to weep like women in

---

[1] Il. XIV, 472. [2] Il. XXI, 73.
[3] Sophocles, Trachiniæ. [4] Eccl. 38.

their diseases, though they would rejoice in battle like giants. Nevertheless it was not necessary that every man should look attentively at all the circumstances of death, such as are often so horribly described, since, as the holy Caussin remarks, there are many to whom they will never happen. No one could be certain that he would have to encounter the wondering eyes, tears of pity, and swoonings, and the lecture, "quantum mutatus ab illo!" Montaigne might therefore be indulged in his mode of regarding death, of which he says, "Je la gourmande en bloc : par le menu, elle me pille."[1] Euchenor, however, who deliberately chose to receive death in battle rather than wait for it through the gradual course of sickness, was a heathen.[2] It is one thing to desire an event; it is another to be prepared for it, and to confess that it may have some advantages.

The young were cut off by a violent and cruel death! But how sweet was it to think of those who sincerely lamented them! for

> Ill bore the sex a youthful lover's fate.

How sweet to think of that soft hour when their names and hard fortune would be told to weeping maidens—

> While lisping children, touch'd with infant fear,
> With wonder gaze, and drop th' unconscious tear.

The epicureans of our age may ridicule the idea; but with our ancestors this life, which awaited the young and generous, in the heart and recollection of those whom they loved, was an enviable protraction of existence.

Again, if they reflected upon the uncertainty of all human happiness, how often in braving danger

---

[1] III, 4. [2] II. XIII, 670.

might it have been wisdom to exclaim with Evander—

Nunc, O nunc liceat crudelem abrumpere vitam
Dum curæ ambiguæ, dum spes incerta futuri.

If Pompey had fallen by the chance of war in the plains of Pharsalia, in the defence of his country's liberty, how glorious would have been his death! But what a result awaited him! " He who a few days before commanded kings and consuls, and all the noblest of Rome, was sentenced to die by a council of slaves, murdered by a base deserter, cast out naked and headless on the Egyptian strand, and when the whole earth," as Velleius says, " had scarcely been sufficient for his victories, could not find a spot upon it for a grave!"

True, to Christians, sudden death was terrible; and they prayed to be delivered from it; but that was not a reason why they should be always trembling like the heroes or even the gods of Homer, lest they should suffer $\dot{v}\pi\grave{\epsilon}\rho$ $\mu\acute{o}\rho o\nu$. And, besides, is not that also sudden, and even unforeseen, which occurs in the thousand ordinary cases when the sufferer, after a protracted illness, is unconscious of danger to the last, and resolved to disbelieve the warnings of friends and the misgivings of his own heart, and all is dead but hope? Buffon appeals for the truth of this statement to the testimony of physicians and clergymen, who are in the habit of witnessing the last hours of men. But even if the sick were conscious of approaching death, and had lived a life of wickedness, men were warned not to place much reliance upon tears and groans in that hour.

The penance and conversion of a dying man is but little esteemed by divines, who, however, leave it to God's secret judgment. Father Parsons quotes a learned man of his time, who says, "The subject brings with it more fear than matter of doubt"; as if he would say, that there is little or no doubt at all, for the danger is lest it is not true conversion, but only sorrow to leave the world, and fear of punishment. He shews, that St. Augustine, Hugo de S. Victore, St. Isidore, and all the school divines, do all fear that such late conversions are vain, for God created us not to live forgetful of him, and then lament our sins on our death-bed; but as the Holy Ghost, by the mouth of Zachary, uttered, " That being delivered from the hand of our enemies, we may serve him without fear, in holiness and justice before him, all our days." St. Cyprian went so far as to decree, that such penitents were debarred from all hope of communion and peace; but Pope Leo, and also Cœlestine, have deemed that too hard, and have appointed that absolution and communion be not denied them at the hour of death, leaving the rest to God's secret judgment. St. Augustine's words are, "The penance which is demanded by a sick man, is sick and weak also of itself; but that which is demanded by him who lies a-dying, I am afraid lest it die in like manner with him"; and again, "A faithful man that has lived well, goes away securely; he that dies the same hour he was baptized, goes hence securely; he that is reconciled in his health, and does penance, and afterwards lives well, goes hence securely. But he that is reconciled, and does penance at the last end, I am not so sure that he goes hence securely. Where I am secure, I do tell you, and do give security; and when I am not secure, I may give penance, but I can give no security. What say I then, that this man shall be damned? I do not say so. What then, do I say he shall be saved? No. What then do I say? I say, I know not, I presume not, I promise not."

In the middle ages the sentence of theology was

often anticipated by the honesty and good sense of men of honour. Xenophon complained to his army, that the soldiers who were when in safety the most intemperate and petulant, had been the most helpless and despairing during the danger of the retreat, and he pointed out an instance of a man who had committed some shameful act of violence, who had before appeared too feeble to carry his shield. The transition is sometimes sudden, from open presumption and impiety to a great shew of religion. Jocasta, when terrified at the condition of Œdipus, enters the stage with boughs of supplication in her hand, and goes with every expression of humility to the temples of those very gods whose oracles she had just before treated with contempt. Thus Livy says of Tullus, " Tunc adeo fracti simul cum corpore sunt spiritus illi feroces, ut, qui nihil ante ratus esset minus regium quam sacris dedere animum, repente omnibus magnis parvisque superstitionibus obnoxius degeret, religionibusque etiam populum impleret." And the messenger in the Persæ relates, that when the army came to the river Strymon, on the ice of which they had to pass, although it had begun to thaw,

———————Θεούς δέ τις
Τὸ πρὶν νομίζων οὐδαμοῦ, τότ' ηὔχετο
Λιταῖσι, γαῖαν οὐρανόν τε προσκυνῶν.

Many of the French sophists, on finding themselves afloat, have acted the famous part of Bacchus to Xanthias.[1] But in the middle ages men carried their principles of honour into their religion; and who but a base sycophant would despise and forsake a king during the period of a rebellion, and then cringe and fawn upon him when he came in his power and great glory? Man, indeed, as Sir

[1] Aristoph. Ranæ.

Philip Sidney said before a battle, "may for a moment forget his God, and yet hope that his God may not forget him"; but it was not the part of a man of honour to provoke and forsake God in the world, and to call upon him with tears in death. There was no danger from this sentiment of chivalry, "Qu'y a-t-il plus monstrueux," says Charron, "que d'estre brave à l'endroict de Dieu!" True, but then he adds, "Et coüard à l'endroict des hommes": a wise sentence, for the man of real valour must have been animated by a sense of religion, which would have convinced him of the necessity of being always ready. Merlin laughed at the young man for purchasing a pair of shoes, when he was not to reach his own gate alive; and yet it did not follow that the youth, however ignorant of the precise hour of his summons, was therefore unprepared for it, and a fit object of the magician's ridicule.

It is for the rich man, trusting in his riches, to cry out—

> Miser! O Miser!—omnia ademit
> Una dies infesta mihi tot præmia vitæ.

It is for the worldly-minded politician to sigh his soul away, like Mazarin, saying, with his last breath, "Il faut quitter tout cela!" Nay, let us not be surprised to hear the philosopher, as he is termed, gravely argue,

> Ἅπαντα μᾶλλον, ἢ θανεῖν
> Ἑτοῖμος ὢν ὑπουργεῖν.

But it was with quite different views that the chivalrous youth of Christian ages were taught to regard death. A monk who observed me shrink back from approaching the dead body of a young man who had been killed in the garden of his monastery, drew me near him, and the few simple words which he addressed to me, accompanied with a peculiar air and countenance, which expressed his soul, left an impression which no time or distraction has ever been able to diminish. It is such men who can teach us to understand the thoughts of our ancestors; they had not those strait ligaments or narrow obligations to the world as to dote on life, or be convulsed at the name of death. "Not that they were insensible of the dread and horror thereof, or by raking into the bowels of the deceased, continual sight of anatomies, skeletons, or cadaverous remains, like vespilloes or grave-makers, had become stupid, or had forgot the apprehension of mortality, but that, marshalling all the horrors and contemplating the extremities thereof, they found not anything therein able to daunt the courage of a man, much less a well-resolved Christian." Cheerful obedience was their spirit. Like the page and esquire of chivalry, they were always armed and ready to follow orders; ready, ay ready, was their cry. Whatever was the suffering or the danger, they knew that the issue was in the hands of God, and they felt the sweet peace and the glorious freedom which arose from an entire resignation to his will. No acquisition of riches, or authority, or connection unduly attaching them to life, could ever have compensated for the loss of that spirit which was the joy and the glory of their nature.

XV. The brilliant amusements of chivalry have been made so familiar to this age by various admirable writers, that I shall endeavour rather to shew the spirit which in general directed them, than to imitate descriptions which are so easily found in the pages of Ste. Palaye, Büsching, La Colombiere and Scott. The Homeric games resembled the tournaments of later chivalry; men of a certain rank only engaged in them, but a concourse of all orders attended as spectators. Sylla held a tournament of boys, or the game of Troy, said to have been invented by Ascanius, of which there is a description in Virgil.[1] The French seem to have been the first to have instituted the regular tournament, and Geoffroi de Preuilli, who died in 1066, is considered as having first established the laws which were observed respecting them. René d'Anjou, Comte de Provence, and King of Naples, painted with his own hand various representations of these games, and described the rules which were to guide those who engaged in them.[2] It was in the reign of Henry the Fowler that tournaments were first held in Germany.[3] The emperor sent commissioners to England, to make a report of the tournaments there. It was King Stephen, in the first half of the twelfth century, who first introduced tournaments into England; then the Italians adopted them; and, after the crusades, the Greek emperors held them at Constantinople, and the Comneni distinguished themselves by their address in the τορνέμενον. The clergy, however, lamented the prevalence of these dangerous diversions. The author of the Life of St. Bernard says, on one occasion, "A large company of noble warriors came to Clairvaux when the time of Lent was near beginning; they were almost all youths devoted to secular warfare, seeking those execrable vanities, which are commonly called tournaments." When the young Bayard addressed his cousin, the Abbot of Ainay, whom he met in the meadow near the Rhone, and requested that he would give him a little money to supply his expense for his first tournament,—"On my faith," replied the good man, who loved him as a son, "you must seek elsewhere for some one to assist you in this affair; the goods of this abbey have been destined by its pious

---

[1] Æneid, V, 545.
[2] Les Tournois du Roi René d'après le manuscrit de la Bibliothèque Royale. Paris, 1827.
[3] Favin, Theatre d'Honneur et de Chevalerie, X, p. 1744.

founders for the service of God, and not to be dissipated in jousts and tournaments."[1]

The number of deaths at tournaments was very great. At Cologne, on one occasion, the lists resembled a field of battle; moreover, it was said that they prevented the nobles from assisting Europe against the Turks in the East. On these accounts the church prohibited them, and at length ecclesiastical burial was refused to all who fell in tournaments.[2] The hatred of the clergy against them may be instanced in the monk of St. Denis, who, describing the hanging of a certain proud knight, says that the executioner cried, "Laissez aller"; the expression of the heralds, to signify the commencement of these games. A scene from the chivalry of Spain must be sufficient for this place. During the rejoicings which took place in the city of Granada, on the coronation of the Moorish king Boabdil, Don Rodrigo Tellez Giron, master of the order of Calatrava, scouring the Vega with a body of horse, desired to know whether there were any knights in Granada who would venture to meet him, hand to hand; so he sent his squire with the following letter to the king:—"Illustrious Sire, may your Majesty enjoy the new crown your virtue has acquired, as long as your heart can wish! For my part I rejoice, though our faith is different; but I trust, ere long, that the Almighty will open your Majesty's eyes, and bring you and your house to the knowledge of his blessed Son Jesus, and to the friendship of the Christians. Hearing that there are fetes, in honour of your coronation, it seems to be just that the knights of your court should try their valour in tilts and tournaments with the troops

[1] Hist. de Bayart par Alfred de Terrebasse.
[2] Vide Concil. Remens. an. 1157, ap. Martene, VII; Concil. Lateran. an. 1177, 30; Ducange, Glossar. voc. Jousta, Tournamenta.

under my command. I have been scouring the Vega; and if there be any knight in Granada willing to meet me, hand to hand, with your Majesty's consent, I shall expect him on the morrow beneath the large oak, near the city, giving you my word of honour, that none of my people shall advance but myself, or an equal number only to those who may sally from Granada. The Master, Rodrigo Tellez Giron."

The king, having read the letter, looked round the court, and found every one equally disposed to accept the challenge. It was determined that twelve knights should be chosen, and each day one was to leave the city. The queen drew the lots, and it fell to Muza to be the first combatant. The king immediately sent an answer to the master, informing him of the event, and saying that the ladies of the court would view the battle from the towers of the Alhambra.

The next morning the grand master, after taking every precaution lest the Moors should break the truce, galloped forward to meet Muza. Meanwhile the expected combat had thrown the ladies of the court into great agitation; but the lovely Fatima, who secretly loved Muza, was more grieved than the rest, knowing Don Rodrigo's fame. During the night, as Muza was preparing for the combat, she sent him, by a page, a green and purple banner for his lance, embroidered with gold, which Muza received with a good grace, although he paid his court to Daraxa, from whom he would rather have received it. The morning had scarce dawned, when Muza, completely armed, sent to the king, who immediately arose, and ordered the trumpets to sound, whereupon a vast concourse of knights assembled. The king dressed himself very magnificently, in a garment of gold brocade, covered with pearls and precious stones, and he left the city just as the rays of the sun began to gild the towers of Granada. Muza rode by his side with two hundred cavaliers, and as they approached the master and his fifty attendants, the trumpets sounded. Muza rode forward, and the master advanced to meet him. The master wore a vest of blue velvet over his armour, embroidered with gold; his shield bore a red cross; a second cross he also wore upon his breast; his horse was a beautiful dapple grey. His lance was adorned with a banneret, and a cross upon it, with the motto, "For this and for my king." His whole air was so noble, that the king remarked, it was not without reason he enjoyed such glorious fame. The two knights, after a short but courteous salutation, retired to a short distance. The queen and the ladies had ascended the towers of the Alhambra to view the combat. The king ordered the clarionets to sound, and immediately the knights rushed upon each other with great fury, but neither was unhorsed. They continued skirmishing for some time, making frequent evolutions with their steeds. The master being badly mounted, flung his lance, and wounded by accident the horse of his opponent. Muza leaped from his back, and advanced to meet Don Rodrigo, who leaping from his horse, drew his sword, and flew to meet Muza. The knights now fought on foot, and gave each other many dreadful blows, and at length the master clove away the crest from Muza's helmet, who was stunned, but soon recovering, raised his sabre, and with a dreadful stroke wounded the master on the arm, who repaid him with a back stroke on the thigh. Fatima perceiving the wound of Muza, could no longer endure this cruel spectacle, but fell back on the ground, and was borne away. The combat was now very fierce, but the master had evidently the advantage, and Muza grew weaker and weaker every moment; which

Don Rodrigo observing, wished to see him converted, and therefore resolved not to continue the battle any longer. Retiring, therefore, a few steps backward, he addressed him in the gentlest manner. 'Noble Muza, it strikes me that combats so bloody little coincide with the hour of rejoicing, let us therefore, if you please, desist. You are so worthy a knight, that I cannot help soliciting your friendship, rather than the continuance of the combat.' Muza replied, 'Most evidently do I perceive, illustrious master, that your motive for desiring thus amicably to end the conflict, is because my wounds have thrown me into such a situation, that death alone can ensue from prosecuting it, and that you would fain grant me life. I certainly acknowledge it a great favour, nevertheless I am ready to continue the fight till death; but if, as you are kindly pleased to say, you indeed covet my friendship, with my whole heart I thank you.' Both knights returned their swords to the scabbard, and then parted with lasting sentiments of esteem for each other."[1]

The bull-fights were another exercise of courage and activity, which was most ardently pursued by the chivalry of Spain. The church, however, expressly condemned them as wicked and inhuman. Pope Pius V prohibited them on pain of excommunication; but Gregory XIII was induced to withdraw this sentence, provided they were not held on festival days; but all in orders were forbidden to be present at any time.[2] Still the clergy strained every nerve to counteract this cruel passion,

[1] The Civil Wars of Granada, and the History of the Factions of the Zegries and Abencerrages, to the final Conquest of that City by Ferdinand and Isabella. Translated from the Arabic, by Gines Perez de Hita, of Murcia, and from the Spanish by Thomas Rodd. London: 1803.
[2] Thomassin, II, lib. I, c. 2.

by extending indulgences to all who frequented the churches during the time of a combat.[1] Not that the clergy were ever opposed to harmless recreations and useful exercise. Muratori relates that the holy fathers of the Company of Jesus used to sanction certain tournaments among their innocent and happy Indians, as a recreation and trial of skill.

It is important to remark the spirit with which even the most objectionable of these recreations were pursued. The Egyptians told the Elian ambassador, that the custom of allowing Elian and foreign knights to engage in their games was most unjust: for that it was not possible that fair play should be the result, or that the strangers could meet with justice contending with Elians.[2] How astonishing and disgraceful would such suspicions have appeared to our Christian chivalry, when men invited their bitterest enemies to enter the lists with them during the intervals of a truce?

Xerxes having asked what was the reward of the victor in the Olympic games, was told that it was a crown of olive. Tritantæchmes, the son of Artabanus, when he heard that it was an olive wreath, and not money, expressed his astonishment before the assembled host, Παπαί, Μαρδόνιε, κοίους ἐπ' ἄνδρας ἤγαγες μαχησομένους ἡμέας, οἳ οὐ περὶ χρημάτων τὸν ἀγῶνα ποιεῦνται, ἀλλὰ περὶ ἀρετῆς ![3] Yet Pausanias relates how often the combatants in the Olympic games were bribed to suffer themselves to be vanquished, and that the fines paid by similar offenders had been sufficient to erect several statues:[4] but the tournaments of chivalry were never made the instrument of a sordid passion. It is a great error to compare these brilliant games, which could

---

[1] Countess d'Aulnoy's Travels in Spain. [2] Herodot. II, 160.
[3] Herod. VIII, 26. [4] Lib. V, c. 21.

furnish employment to the noblest artists, and a subject even for the muse, with the ferocious combats of greedy barbarians. What was the prize which excited those who engaged in the exercises of chivalry? Let us hear Froissart. "After dyner knyghtes and squyers were armed to just, and so they justed in the markette place, xi knyghtes of the one side; the yonge Kyng Charles justed with a knyght of Heynalt, called Sir Nycholas Espinoy; so these justes were nobly contynued, and a yonge knyght of Heynalt had the prise—this knyght justed greatly to the pleasure of the lordes and ladyes: he had for his prise, a gyrdell gyven by the Duchesse of Bourgoyne, from her own wast." The knight might have said with Entellus, in the Æneid—

Haud equidem pretio induotus pulchroque juvenco
Venissem: nec dona moror.[1]

The savage spectacles which pretend to no grace or refinement, but merely to exhibit the ferocity and cunning of a brute nature, may have attractions when a taste for blood has once entered into the heart. It was thus that St. Augustin describes Alipius,[2] who beheld the combat of the circus against his will, but who could not afterwards turn away his eyes from it; having in a manner drunk blood and becoming intoxicated with the sanguinary pleasure. Such sports may indeed be traced to the amusement of the suitors of Penelope, when Antinous excited the two beggars to a pugilistic combat, proposing a prize for the conqueror, and exulting in the sight of blood;[3] or to the shooting of the devoted dove over the grave of Patroclus,[4] or to the gladiatorial scenes, where the persons

[1] Lib. V, 397.   [2] Confess. VI, 8.
[3] Od. XVIII.   [4] Il. XXIII.

engaged were so despised, that when Cicero had exhausted all the terms of reproach, he concludes by calling Catiline a gladiator;[1] but no shadow of likeness do they offer to the gay and generous contests which assembled the chivalry of Europe, in the courts of Windsor, or under the towers of the Alhambra. It is not strange that there were men who regretted the old amusements of the nobility, when they beheld it ruined by the extravagant expense of the carousals, or corrupted and debased by the introduction of games which were made the instruments of avarice, or the pretences for effeminate inactivity.[2] "In these ages," says Muratori, "the young nobility were exercised in tournament and hunting, and in trials of strength and activity. Men then understood better what are the proper amusements which became them. Many are not capable of applying themselves to philosophy or letters, but they can exercise their bodies in a becoming manner."[3] Other games for the young man, πειρώμενος ἥβης, were quoits, ball, prisoners-base, shooting at the popinjay, pierre de faix, or trying who could throw a heavy stone farthest, hazel wand or rose garland, tilting with hollow canes, running at the quintain. But, above all, the joyful hour was when

> To chase the stag with hound and horn
> Earl Percy took his way.[4]

After the battle of Poitiers, Edward III traversed France, having with him boats of boiled leather, to

[1] Orat. I in Cat. 12.
[2] In 1784, a French nobleman published "Recherches sur les Carrousels, suivies d'un Projet de Jeux équestres à l'imitation des Tournoys de l'Ancienne Chevalerie, dans lequel on démontre l'utilité que la noblesse retireroit du rétablissement de ces jeux, autrefois l'école de l'adresse et de la valour."
[3] Treatise of the Public Happiness.
[4] See the Mémoires Historiques sur la Chasse par Ste. Palaye.

fish in the rivers, thirty falconers on horseback, with their birds, sixty couple of greyhounds, and as many harriers; and many of the lords also had their own dogs and hawks with the army.[1] Gaston Count of Foix had dogs from all parts of Europe to the number of 1,600; and Le Grand, on the authority of Gace-de-la-Vigne, who flourished under King John, says that there were then in France more than 20,000 persons who kept hounds. A white dog, Souillard, was given as a great present to Louis XI.

The old romance of Gérard de Roussillon reckons among the hunting equipage of Charlemagne, lions and bears dressed; and Le Grand justly thinks that the passage proves the custom to have existed at the time the romance was written, brought into France by the crusaders. The monk of St. Denis, author of the life of Charles VI, and Mathieu de Coucy, testify that Galeazzo Visconti, duke of Milan, had leopards for the same purpose. The emperor Frederick, in his book, "De Arte Venandi," speaks of animalia agrestia; scilicet modos leopardorum, canum, lincos, lincas, furectos, &c.: and among the printed letters of Louis XII there is one of Jean Calier to Marguerite of Austria, daughter of Maximilian, in which a description is given of a chase of this kind.[2] Gaston Phœbus, Count of Foix, hunted in Sweden and Norway.

King John of France, while a prisoner in England, used to hunt in Windsor Park, and he composed a treatise on "Fauconnerie et Vénerie." Gasse de la Vigne, who drew it up, says, speaking of the jovial meetings and adventurous stories after the chase, "that the worst in the chase are not the most laconic in their account of it." To the Emperor Frederick II's treatise, "De Arte Venandi

---

[1] Froissart. [2] Vie privée des François, tom. I, p. 422.

cum avibus," King Manfred made additions. In the Weiss Kunig, it is related how the young Maximilian learned to shoot with the cross-bow and the English bow, to hunt with falcons, and to pursue mountain game, to chase stags, wild goats, chamois, wild boars, marmots, and hares. There is an engraving representing savage rocks and precipices; the young prince having crossed a torrent and shot a chamois, while two attendants are left on the other side in astonishment at his boldness. Near Innsbruck, I have seen the cleft in the side of the rock, nearly perpendicular, on which he is said to have stood, unable to get forwards or backwards, so that he was obliged to descend by the aid of a rope, which was let down to him from above. The noble spirit of chivalry required that the animals pursued should be worthy of attack, and not a timid prey. Thus Gaston de Foix says of the wild boar, "c'est une orgueilleuse bête." It was also necessary that even wild beasts should be attacked with a certain regard to honour. Le Grand quotes Télincourt, saying, that in Germany and Italy nets were used by gentlemen in hunting, but that in France and England, according to the sentiments of the Counts of Foix, of Fouilloux, Salnove, and all other noble hunters, on chassoit plus noblement, and that only base people used nets.[1]

At the magnificent entry of the Constable, Anne de Montmorency, into London, he was preceded by twenty-six gentlemen of the first houses of France, each carrying a falcon on his fist. The best gerfalcons were from Norway and Russia, the best vultures from Armenia and Persia; and the author of the " Deduits de la Chase, par le Roi Modus," regarded the falcons of Sardinia as "les plus hardis du monde." D'Esparon speaks of a kind of falcon,

[1] Vie privée des François, tom. I, p. 378.

which being let fly from Fontainebleau, was taken the following day at Malta, a distance of five hundred leagues. Their strength of wing will explain why a hunter was said to be "maistre de son cheval, compagnon de son chien et valet de son oyseau." Of the fidelity of his dog there are many romantic instances, such as that in the German ballad of Adolfseck, where the hound of the Emperor Adolf returns from the battle to his mistress, and conducts her to the bloody field of Oppenheim, to the spot where she found the emperor's body among the slain. In the Bibliotheca Patrum, there is a long and devout letter from King Æthelbert to St. Boniface, in Germany, which concludes by begging that he will send him two falcons expert at flying at cranes, for the king says such falcons are very scarce in England; and then, led away by his favourite passion, he gives the holy man, as if he were a brother hunter, a long account of the faults of his own falcons.[1] St. Boniface, amidst his holy labours as a missionary, writing to King Ethelbald, sends him a hawk and two falcons, two shields and two lances, "pro signo veri amoris et devotæ amicitiæ," and then bids him farewell in Christ. These insatiable hunters endeavoured to propose certain religious and moral ends, which their passion might be directed to further. Xenophon advised young men to cultivate a taste for all such violent amusements, adding, "Others who avoid such labours shew themselves to be of the basest natural disposition; they do not conform either to good laws or to good principles; for, from not labouring, they do not discover how a man should be good, so that they can neither be devout nor wise."[2] The Count of Foix held the same doctrine in his manuscript treatise on hunting, which he

---

[1] Vol. XIII, Epist. XL, p. 86. [2] De Venatione, c. I.

sent as a present to the Duke of Burgundy. It begins with the most solemn invocation. "Au nome et en honneur de Dieu Createur et Seigneur de toutes choses et du benoist son fils Jhu Christ et du Saint Esprit, de toute la Sainte Trinite, et de la Vierge Marie et de tous les saints et saintes qui sont en la grace de Dieu." He declares that he is not competent to teach the science of arms and chivalry, nor of gallantry, for there are many better knights and more worthy lovers than himself, but that on hunting he may presume to discourse. He first shews that the hunter must be a good man, and that he must take heed not to lose the knowledge and service of God, from whom all good is derived, even the success of recreation. "Or te prouueray comment bon veneour ne puet avoir par raison nul des sept pechiez mortels: Premier tu sces bien que oiseusete est cause de tous les sept pechiez mortelz. Quar quant on est ocieus et negligent sans travail et ne se occupe en fere aucune chose et demeurer en son lit ou en sa chambre c'est une chose qui tue a ymaginations du plaisir de la char. Quar il na autre fors que de demeurer en un lieu et penser en orgueille ou en avarice ou en yre ou en paresse ou en goule ou en luxure ou en envie, or te prouverai comment ymagination est seigneur et mestresse de toutes œuvres bonnes ou mauvaises que on fet et de tout le corps et membres de l'omme." A beautiful description follows of the joy of the hunter's life; how being risen with the small birds, he can hear them sing at morning lauds.

> Sole fere radiis feriente cacumina primis,
> Venatum in silvas juveniliter ire solebam.[1]

In the heat of the day he has shelter under the green boughs, and at night, being full weary, he

---

[1] Ovid, Met. VII, 28.

can only desire the rest of sleep: hence he lives the best, the happiest, and the longest of all men. "Et on desire en cest monde vivre longuement et sain et en joie et appres la fin la salvation de l'ame. Et veneurs ont tout cela, dont soyez tous venours."[1] The avoidance of sloth and its attendant vices was constantly represented as the end of hunting.[2]

Holy men endeavoured to turn this taste to a good purpose in their books of spiritual instruction. In 1516 was printed the work of Guillaume Michel: "Foret de conscience, contenant les chasses spirituelles": a title which must have had a powerful attraction. On the other hand, the good hunters cited on their side St. Hubert, "Qui étoit veneur, ainsi que St. Eustache, dont est à conjecturer que les bons veneurs les ensuyvront en Paradis avec la grace de Dieu." St. Hubert abolished the worship of idols in the forest of Ardennes. The order of the Knights of St. Hubert was instituted by Gerard V, duke of Cleves. The knights wore a gold collar ornamented with hunting-horns, and sustaining a medal with an image of St. Hubert. The hunting-lodge of the dukes of Savoy was adorned with moral and religious emblems furnished by the chase.[3] Men wished even to shew that it was not injurious to their intellectual cultivation, and so Mattea Maria Bojardo, a feudal lord and knight, declared that he conceived some of the happiest thoughts in his poem of Orlando Innamorato, while hunting in a wood near Scandiano; and on these occasions he would hasten back at full gallop to his castle. Certainly the woods and the hunting-castle of Moritzburg, in Saxony, with its vast hall, adorned with the horns

---

[1] MSS. du Bibliotheque du Roi.
[2] Livre du Roy Modus et de la Royne Ratio.
[3] Le Pere Menestrier, l'Art des Emblemes, 105.

and skins and portraits of various animals, appeared to me most fruitful in subjects for sweet debate.

Pliny says, in his epistle to Tacitus, that he had taken three boars, and had meditated much as he sat watching the nets; and then he adds, "There is no reason to despise this kind of study. It is wonderful how the mind is excited by the agitation and movement of the body. The wood on all sides, and the solitude, and even that silence which belongs to hunting, are great incitements to thought. You will find that Minerva wanders among the mountains not less than Diana."

Yet it must not be denied, the passion of hunting led to the most criminal excesses. The clergy loudly complained. The old Legende du Braconnier, describing the joy of the poor fellow when he sees the blue water of the Oder, hoping to swim across it, and then his cruel death by the hounds and hunters, who come up before he can reach the bank, presents a revolting example of occasional ferocity.[1] The dukes of the house of Farnese were in other respects, as Muratori observes, good princes; but their wood of Colorno, with its herd of wild boars infesting the outskirts, where no one dared to kill them, was a monstrous injury. It must be remembered that the Knights Templars were not allowed to hawk or to shoot with a bow, or even to accompany any one to such diversion, unless when in the East, for the purpose of guarding his person. Such amusements their rule pronounced to be unbecoming the character of religious men.[2]

The love for horses was characteristic of chivalry.

> Sir Walter Blunt, new lighted from his horse,
> Stain'd with the variation of each soil;[3]

---

[1] Ballades Fabliaux et Traditions du Moyen Age.
[2] Sec. XLVII.   [3] Shakspeare, Hen. IV, I, 1.

or the knight, like Masistius, mounted on his Persian charger, glittering with gold;[1] were equally objects of envy to every garçon troteur. Even when not pursuing the chase, to ride across the country, like Ischomachus, stopping at nothing,[2] was a favourite diversion. Charles VI of France was said to have injured his health by too great fatigue in riding day and night: he had engaged in a trial to discover whether he or his brother could ride in the shortest time from Montpelier to Paris. Xenophon ridicules the degeneracy of the Persians, covering their horses with carpets, desiring rather to sit softly than to ride on horseback, and fearing as much to fall off as the enemy.[3] Not so our knights. The Duke of Orgoule's horse, named Assille, "was suche, that there was none that could mount on him but al only the duke and the varlet that kepte hym, and both daye and night he was ever tied with foure grete chaynes of yren;[4] like the mayster Stephen's great and myghty black horse, with rede eyen sparkelyng as fyre."

After the death of Scanderbeg his war-horse would never suffer any one to mount his back, but died unmanageable, at the end of a few weeks,[5] though it is not said that he could shed tears like Æthon.[6] When the king of France had signified his pleasure to see Bayard on his little horse, the young page was as happy as if he had been given the city of Lyons: he immediately went to Piron de Chevas, the groom of the duke of Savoy, and said "My friend, I hear the king has told my lord that he wishes to see my horse after dinner, and me on his back: I beseech you, let him be prepared in the best condition, and I will give you my short

---

[1] Herodot. IX, 20.   [2] Xenoph. Œconom. c. XI.
[3] Anab. III, 2.   [4] Arthur of Little Britain, p. 113.
[5] Sismondi refers to Marinus Barletius, III, 370.
[6] Æneid, XI, 90.

dagger with all my heart." "Bayard, my friend, keep your baston; I do not want it: do you go and make yourself smart, for your horse shall be in good order." "When Arthur had the Sowdan's good horse," says the old romance, "he was more gladder of the horse than he would have been of all the treasure in France": "Hoc decus illi, hoc solamen erat."[1] "Je ne demonte pas volontiers quand je suis à cheval," says Montaigne, "car c'est l'assiette en laquelle je me trouve le mieux et sain et malade."

Sir Philip Sidney says, that when at the emperor's court, he learned horsemanship of Gio. Pietro Pugliano, "one that with great commendation had the place of an esquire in his stable; and he, according to the fertileness of the Italian wit, did not only afford us the demonstration of his practice, but sought to enrich our minds with the contemplation therein, which he thought most precious. Skill of government was but a pedanteria in comparison of being a good horseman. Then would he add certain praises, by telling what a peerless beast the horse was, the only serviceable courtier without flattery, the beast of most beauty, fathfulness, courage, and such more, that if I had not been a piece of a logician before I came to him, I ihink he would have persuaded me to have wished myself a horse." The Duke of Newcastle, whom M. de la Gueriniere pronounces to have been "the most learned horseman of his time,"[2] dedicating his great work on horsemanship to King Charles II, beseeches him to love horses, and to learn the maxims of mild government from them: he declares, in defiance of Socrates,[3] that it is easier to make a good philosopher than a good horseman: that in general a scholar and a horse are a mutual

---

[1] Æneid, X, 858.   [2] Ecole dé Cavalerie, 61.   [3] Plato, Meno.

trouble to each other, which the youth in the old comedy seems to have understood when he refuses to apply to study, and become so sickly, that he would be ashamed to look his horse in the face.[1] Our ancestors, like Xenophon, loved to see the horse in his natural beauty, with long flowing tail and mane,[2] such as the gods and heroes of old used to mount. They had a great affection for them. Hector talks to his Xanthos and Podargos, Æthon and Lampos, as if they were old companions, and as precious as himself to Andromache; like the border hero, who says,

> Dear to me is my bonny white steed,
> Oft has he helped me at pinch of need.

This affection appeared in the regret of Xenophon, when obliged to part with his favourite at Byzantium, of Godfrey of Bouillon, on losing his horse, and of the Cid, when in his last will he orders that they should place his body in complete armour upon Bavieca, and so conduct him to the church of San Pedro de Cardeña, and then directing them, when they bury Bavieca, to dig deep, lest he should be eaten by dogs. A tomb was erected in the gardens of Navarre, to La Pie, the mare which Turenne used to ride in battle. Who has not heard of Favel and Lyard, which King Richard brought from Cyprus? All the world knows the affection of Alexander for Bucephalus, of Orlando for Brigliadoro, of Rinaldo for Bayard, of Rogero for Frontin, of Rodrigo, the last King of Spain of the Gothic race, for Orelia, which he bestrode that unfortunate day when he lost the battle, the kingdom, and his life.

The education of chivalry, as of the heroic times, trained each knight to take care of his own horse.

---

[1] Aristoph. Nubes, 119.   [2] Xen. de re Equestr. IV.

Xenophon requires, that the stable should be so near the house that the master can often see his horse. In taking care of his horse, he says, he takes care of his own body, which in danger is part of his horse.[1] Hence his care to provide for the horses of his friends.[2] He quotes the saying of a barbarian to a king, that it is the eye of the master which can alone keep a horse in good condition.[3] When Nausicaa returns to her father's house, it is her royal brothers who unharness the mules; and King Priam orders his own sons to put the mules to the chariot;[4] and when Achilles receives Priam, two of his dearest companions unharness the horses.[5] In like manner, when the knight of the savage man, having lost his squire Silviam, arrived at the house of an ancient knight, who was accustomed to entertain all strange knights, seeing him without a squire, he came and took his horse himself, and afterwards helped to unarm him. And the knight of La Mancha, going into the stable of the inn where he lodged, after the adventure of Montesino's cave, offered to help the man with the lances to serve his mule, which he did accordingly, cleansing the manger and sifting the barley. After the death of the Cid, Gil Diaz took great delight in tending Bavieca; so that there were few days in which he did not lead him to water, and bring him back with his own hand. The people did not think it strange, when they saw Osmond, governor of the young prisoner, Richard duke of Normandy, carrying on his back a great truss of hay, to feed his favourite horse, as they supposed, when this brave man was in reality carrying off his pupil concealed within the truss, while the King of France and the inhabitants of Laon were at supper; in which enter-

---

[1] De Re Equestr. IV.   [2] Anab. I, 9.   [3] Œconom. XII.
[4] Il. XXIV, 189.   [5] Id. 573.

prise he succeeded, and by pressing his horse, had lodged him safely in Coucy about midnight.

In that interesting account which Sir John Froissart gives of his riding in company with Sir Espayne de Lyon, he does not disdain to relate how upon arriving at Tarbe, they took their lodging at the Star, and that "it was a town of great easement bothe for man and horse, with good hay and otes, and a fayre ryver"; nor does he forget, amidst the splendour of the Earl of Foix's castle, where he resided for more than twelve weeks, that his "horse was well entreated."

Swimming was a favourite exercise of the middle ages, when men would have fully entered into the feeling of the Egyptians, who used to say, that man was a water animal, judging from the smoothness of his form, and the property of his nature, which was more liable to thirst than hunger.[1] Charlemagne established a place for swimming, at Aix-la-Chapelle; and he was himself so well skilled, that Eginhart says, "no man surpassed him." The young prince of Urbino, in the time of Tasso, when at Castel Durante, is described as taking the diversion of swimming in its noble lakes, and hunting in the forests. Beltenebroso, riding in the forest, came to a little river, winding among the trees, into which he plunged, to refresh himself after the heat of battle. When Orlando had wandered into the forest of Arden, he alighted from Brigliadoro, near a fountain; stooping to drink, he sees a crystal palace at the bottom, through the walls of which he beholds a brilliant assembly; full of delight at the adventure, armed as he is, he plunges into the fountain.[2]

In the battle of Anthon, in 1430, the Prince of Orange, in complete armour, to escape being made

---

[1] Diodorus, lib. I, 43.   [2] Orlando Innam. II.

prisoner, threw himself, with his horse, into the Rhone, and the horse passed it, swimming across, and landing him safely; but Sertorius wounded, swam across the Rhone in his cuirass. The ancients relate great exploits in swimming. Scyllias, the Macedonian, according to Herodotus, swam eighty stadia through the sea, to bear news to the Greeks. Josephus, after shipwreck, swam for nearly a whole night. Pyrrhus is said to have swum from sun-set to sun-rise. Homer must himself have been a diver, shewing such a passion for the simile: yet Achilles expresses a most unworthy fear of the Scamander, complaining that he is likely to be swept away by a great river, like some shepherd lad perishing in a wintry torrent.[1] Even Alexander the Great, before Nysa, had to exclaim, "Wretch that I am, that I did not learn to swim." The Romans had a proverb to express their contempt for persons who were neither scholars, nor skilled in bodily accomplishments:

Neque natare, neque literas novit.

Nor was it mere caprice that dictated this alternative, since, as the poet has well remarked,

———————— The same Roman arm
That rose victorious o'er the conquer'd earth
First learn'd, while tender, to subdue the wave.

In 1627, a French soldier swam across the arm of the sea, between the Isle de Ré and the continent, with a letter for the king: he was much torn by fish. When Vienna was besieged by the Turks in 1683, a messenger swam across the four arms of the Danube, with intelligence of succour to the garrison from the Duke of Lorraine. Jason, on his journey to Iolcus, was stopped by an inundation of the river Evenus; not like young Lochinvar,

[1] Il. XXI, 281.

Who staid not for brake, who staid not for stone,
Who crossed the Eske river where ford there was none.

Yet the history of the middle ages abounds with dismal events resulting from the neglect of this admirable art: witness the brook at Towton, the Oglio, the Ticino, the Gusciana, the Pescara, so fatal to good King Henry's host, to the troops of Cremona, to the Swiss who fled after the battle of Pavia, to the Florentines, and to the brave Sforza di Cotignola, who sank in the flood while his horse swam to shore; twice was the warrior seen raising his iron gauntlet out of the water! he was swept away, one of the most enterprising and intrepid men that Italy ever produced. Socrates asks a sophist whether the art of swimming seems to him an excellent thing. "Μὰ Δί' οὐκ ἔμοιγε,"[1] was the reply: to such persons Thomson's advice seems insane,

Nor when cold winter keens the brightening flood,
Would I weak, shivering, linger on the brink—

though it may have been sanctioned by the practice of the old senators, as Pliny bears witness. To be convicted of swimming daily three times across the Tiber, in winter, is sufficient ground, in their estimation, to send any man to Anticyra; yet the pleasure and the advantage resulting from such habits did not merely exist in the poet's imagination, as men in these ages knew from experience; though the knight, like Cicero's friend Trebatius, studiosissimus homo natandi, might have found his hand more able to furnish him with the pleasure than to prove its excellence to others.

Ah quanto mallem quam scriberet illa nataret
Meque per assuetas sedula ferret aquas!

---

[1] Plat. Gorgias.

Thevenot says[1] that Sir Everard Digby was one of the first who wrote upon the art of swimming. The ποταμῶν ἱεροὶ ῥόοι, where the limpid waters laved the green sward, or the

> Well-known pool, whose crystal depth
> A sandy bottom shews,

furnished one of life's prime pleasures to him who loved every stream as though it had been that river on whose wave the gentle King Larbino and many other knights gazed till they expired; or that river of laughter, where Orlando remained a willing prisoner at the bottom till Rogero, Gradasso, Bradamant, and Flordelis followed him.

> Flumina amem silvasque inglorius.

Ajax, before he kills himself, bids farewell to the fountains and rivers which were familiar to him;[2] yet, however familiar, always presenting fresh pleasure, verifying the saying of Heraclitus, that you cannot bathe twice in the same river;[3] at one time gently flowing, transpicuous, clear, each stone at the bottom glittering in the morning sun, with violets shedding a sweet perfume from enamelled banks and lilies growing out of the water; and at another leaving its ancient channel, you are borne along over the invaded meadow

> Exspatiata ruunt per apertos flumina campos.[4]

Thomson feels that

> Even from the body's purity, the mind
> Receives a secret sympathetic aid.

It is something that one comes out from the river, like Telemachus from the bath, δέμας ἀθανάτοισιν

---

[1] L'Art de Nager. Paris, 1782.   [2] Soph. Ajax, 862.
[3] Plat. Cratylus.   [4] Ovid, Met. I.

ὅμοιος. It was the dictate of nature which kept back Æneas from approaching sacred rites till he had washed in the living stream.[1] In the middle ages people bathed before communion: a feeling of delicacy sanctified by the Church in the asperges of her holy rites.

What noble independence of character was the result of these habits! Lord Bernard's little foot page cares not for broken bridges; Malcolm Græme, leaving the island, is offered a boat;

> "Tell Roderick Dhu I owed him nought,
> Not the poor service of a boat
> To waft me to yon mountain side."
> Then plunged he in the flashing tide.

The muse of Schiller deigned to sing the courage of the diver,[2] and what nourishment for the imagination awaited him

> Eximius animam servare sub undis;

whether visiting the blue abyss of the Leman lake, where, perhaps under a clouded atmosphere you enjoy the deep azure of the Italian sky; or deeper still, moving along through the "luce carentia regna," arriving perhaps at a world like that seen by Orlando, when he had sunk in the water of the enchanted lake, after falling from the bridge with the churl who defended it, whom he slew at the bottom; or receiving such a welcome as Mandricardo met with when he jumped into a river to escape the flames; or seeking through the salt sea the dwelling of the Nereids,

> ———— under the caves,
> Where the shadowy waves
> Are as green as the forest's night.

---

[1] Æneid, II, 716.   [2] Gedicht des Tauchers.

What a joyful soul was theirs when swimming in the sea, at a distance from the shore, cheered by the presence of familiar faces, riding over the billows in the midst of gulls and other fowl τῇσίντε θαλάσσια ἔργα μέμηλεν, who only rise for a moment to skim the surface of the green abyss, or gliding over the gentle wave, when

> Adspirant auræ in noctem, nec candida cursus
> Luna negat; splendet tremulo sub lumine pontus.

While wandering thus over the watery waste, man was restored as it were to a state of wildness and natural liberty, in which his proud heart triumphed; nay, there was a rapture even in braving the horrors and confusion of a tempest,

> Quum medio celeres revolant ex æquore mergi
> Clamoremque ferunt ad litora ———

when the sight was darkened, and the only knowledge they retained of a faithful comrade was derived from hearing between the intervals of roaring billows

> ——————— The bubbling cry
> Of a strong swimmer in his agony.

But in a moment even this would cease; and they would recover from some rude shock of rushing waters to see him in the distance drifted towards the shore, leaving them alone.

> ——— Venti volvunt mare, magnaque surgunt
> Æquora; dispersi jactamur gurgite vasto.

But it was the approach to shore that presented the greatest scene of terror, and here the stoutest hearts might for a moment fail, and justify the groans of Ulysses.

―――― Ubi alterno procurrens gurgite pontus
Nunc ruit ad terras, scopulosque superjacit undam
Spumans, extremamque sinu perfundit arenam:
Nunc rapidus retro, atque aestu revoluta resorbens
Saxa, fugit, litusque vado labente relinquit.

Rowing was another favourite exercise when men loved simple and laborious amusements,

Nec crimen duras esset habere manus.

To manage dexterously the oar was the Norman's boast. Ariosto describes Orlando an hour before sunrise rowing a skiff to the coast of Ireland. Harold the Bold boasts of skill in this exercise as one of his most estimable qualifications. The Loire, the Rhine, and the Thames have borne many a crew of adventurous knights, sub luce maligna,

Νύκτα δι' ὀρφναίην, ὅτε θ' εὔδουσι βροτοὶ ἄλλοι,

not as gentle as the Tiber was to Æneas, which stopped its current for a time "remo ut luctamen abesset,"[1] but requiring all the strength and silence which Phormio told the Athenians were requisite in such exercises,[2] and which the Argonauts had to practise in the memorable adventure when they rowed between the Cyanean rocks while they were closing upon them.[3] The winged charger, as Homer would say, not like the enchanted bark of Partenopex and Gugemar, of Rinaldo and the Fairy Queen,

Sulcat aquas, juvenum sudantibus acta lacertis,

while the sleepy Palinurus and the "dura sedilia" revive the images of Virgil: πᾶς ἀνὴρ κώπης ἄναξ alludes to a happy society, in which the object of

[1] Æneid, VIII, 89. [2] Thucyd. II, 89.
[3] Apollon. Rhod. II, 590.

ambition was not who should make the best oration, or become the most able sycophant, ἀλλ' ὃς ἂν ἐρέτης ἔσοιτ' ἄριστος.¹ Happy ambition! which could not conceive a higher dignity than to be elected king over the oars, like Jason, ἀνὰ τραφερήν τε καὶ ὑγρήν.²

The passion for chess and tables, like that which Tacitus ascribes to the Germans, led to sad disasters. In the romance of Ogier le Danois, Charlot, the degenerate son of Charlemagne, incensed at losing two games to the young Baldwin, kills him with the massive chess-board. In the Book of Heroes the chess-men are as large as life. In Galien le Restauré another scene of violence occurs. In Froissart we read how the poor French governor of Evreux was tempted to admit within the gate Sir William de Granville, through the hope of seeing a most goodly set of chess-men, and of playing a game with him for a cup of wine, whereby he lost his fortress and his life. Patroclus killed his friend, the son of Amphidamas, in his sudden fury upon losing a cross game at tables.³ But in general the habits of the middle ages were inconsistent with such games. Castiglione says that "a moderate skill in chess is more commendable than an exact one."⁴ Boccacio censures it as destructive of conversation, of which our ancestors were so fond, as Burton shews in his Anatomy of Melancholy. It might suit the lazy suitors of Penelope,⁵ or a miserable Claudius, who used to play at dice in his chariot; but it was this which excited the rage of Charlemagne against his son-in-law:

> Now Gayferos the live-long day,
> Oh arrant shame, at draughts does play.

---

[1] Aristoph. Vespæ, 1093.   [2] Orphei Argonautica, 300.
[3] Il. XXIII, 87.   [4] The Courtier, II, 155.   [5] Od. I, 107.

It was an evil day for Rome when the ingenuous youth forsook the dusty plain and the Tiber for dice and tables.[1] Men in the ages of which we write were not infected with avarice, and they had no deficiency of stimulus. When they played at such games it was always the dignified part to lose.[2]

Gaming was forbidden by the canons of the church, and also by the civil and imperial law. Aristotle[3] places gamesters in the same class with highwaymen and plunderers. St. Bernardine of Sienna[4] says they are worse than robbers, because more treacherous, and covering their rapine under seducing glosses.

Of such games Gilles de Rome says, in his Mirror of Example, "Ils sont plains de mensonges, de parjuremens, de blasphemes, de inutiles et viles parolles et oultre sont deffendus de nostre mere saincte eglise":—And it happens by means of these that many who are of noble lineage and of great parentage degenerate "et sont plus vilains en faicts et en meurs que austres moyns nobles."

Among the amusements of the great in the middle ages painting should not be omitted,—that enchanting art, "the daughter of peace and contemplation," as Lanzi says, "which shuns not only the sound but the very rumour of war." Even among the ancient Romans the Fabii boasted of the skill of their founder in this sublime art. René d'Anjou, Francis the First, and innumerable nobles were celebrated as painters. Under the fostering influence of the church all the arts which pertain to genius afforded an employment which was esteemed worthy of nobility.

But to return to exercises of the body. Games

---

[1] Horace, Ode III, 24.
[2] Hist. des François par Monteil. II, 231.   [3] Ethics, I.
[4] Serm. 38, Domin. 5, Quadrag. t. 4.

representing the feats of chivalry are described as
having been pursued by Du Guesclin, Boucicaut,
Maximilian, and Götz von Berlichingen. Livy
mentions a similar exercise between the Macedonian
youths, wherein Demetrius and Perseus commanded
the opposite ranks,[1] and Perseus having been
beaten, cherished resentment against Demetrius, of
which meanness Richard Cœur de Lion was guilty
after his tilt with William de Barres in the suburbs
of Messina, whom he only forgave for having vanquished him, on the intercession of the whole army.
But in the courts of chivalry, as in the courts of the
college, the spirit of religion entered to moderate
the passions and to guide the diversions of youth.
Thus one section of many books of instruction, like
the Libellus Precum of the Jesuits, was entitled
" Modus gerendi se in lusu "; for the clergy of
the middle age, unlike our commercial sophists,
encouraged the diversions of youth. A little reflection will convince men that they acted wisely.

> Cernis ut ignavum corrumpant otia corpus
> Ut capiant vitium ni moveantur aquæ.[2]

There are times when it is better to hear the quoit
than the philosopher. " προσήκει μάλιστ' ἐλευθέρῳ
τοῦτό τε τὸ γυμνάσιον καὶ ἡ ἱππική," says Plato.[3]
" Recreation is necessary," said the most indefatigable and laborious of men.[4] A fondness for
juvenile sports distinguished Socrates, Agesilaus,
Archytas the Tarentine, Scipio, and Lælius, who
used all to play with children and with slaves.[5]

Νέων δὲ μέριμναι, σὺν πόνοις ἑλισσόμεναι, δόξαν εὑρίσκουσι.[6]

---

[1] Lib. XL, 6.   [2] Ovid, Epist. ex Pont. I, v.
[3] Laches.   [4] Aristotle, Ethics, IV, 8.
[5] Ælian, Var. Hist. XII, 49; Cicero de Orat. II, 6.
[6] Pindar.

Theophrastus, we are told, wrote, among his innumerable treatises, one περὶ ἱδρῶτος; and while the philosopher in his study was vainly contemplating the phenomena, the thoughtless lover of the Stadium,

> Multa tulit fecitque puer; sudavit et alsit,

or the youths like Helymnus and Panopes in Virgil, assueti silvis, were accomplishing the design, and profiting by the provision of nature. Chivalry guided by religion pointed out the line which separates base from laudable recreation; "unum illiberale, petulans, flagitiosum, obscœnum; alterum, elegans, urbanum, ingeniosum, facetum." "In what manner am I to suppose you employ your leisure?" says Horace to Tibullus,

> An tacitum silvas inter reptare salubres
> Curantem quicquid dignum sapiente bonoque est.

Socrates speaks of the vilest of men, "τὰς πόρνας ἀγαπῶντα μᾶλλον ἢ τοὺς ἑταίρους."[1] How much more forcibly were such lessons impressed upon the minds of the young, when accompanied with all the generous motives employed by the Catholic religion in recommending her pure morality? that religion which disdained not to preside over the innocent pleasures

> Of many a youth and many a maid,
> Dancing in the chequer'd shade,
> When young and old came forth to play,
> On a sun-shine holiday.

Nature in every form furnished delight to men in these simple ages.

> Whom call we gay? That honour has been long
> The boast of mere pretenders to the name.
> The innocent are gay—the lark is gay,
> That dries his feathers, saturate with dew,
> Beneath the rosy cloud. ———

---

[1] Xen. Mem. II, c. 5.

Every youth and gentle squire too

>——— a hearer of his song,
> Himself a songster, is as gay as he.

How is he described by Chaucer?

> Singing he was or floyting alle the day,
> He was as freshe as is the moneth of May.

Such was young Wilfried in Rokeby,

> Who loved the quiet joys that wake
> By lonely stream and silent lake.

When the Cid travelled from Valencia to the Cortes at Toledo, there went with him five hundred esquires on foot, all hidalgos, besides those who were bred in his household. The Paladin, in Ariosto, on foot

> ——— More lightly through the forest hies
> Than half-clothed churl to win the cloth of red.

Albert[1] relates that many of the most noble knights in the crusade, having lost their horses, continued to serve on foot. Here again was an exercise, replete with pleasure, for those who were in that short but precious moment of life, when young, vigorous, full of health, of security, of confidence in themselves and in others, an expansive fulness extended as it were their being through all their sensations, and embellished to their eyes the whole of nature with the charm of their existence. They too would have confessed that when they travelled on foot, "en guise de garcons trotereaulx," as Lancelot and Mordrec, in the strange forest,[2] it was in their happiest days; wandering over the snow tracts which compose the higher Alps, the icy deserts of Grindenwald and the Grimsel, the Ghemmi

---

[1] Gesta Dei per Francos, 257.   [2] Lancelot du Lac, III, p. 20.

and the Jochberg, or the wild and stormy tops of the
Pilatus. Here again man left behind him the earth
and its infections. Like the chamois he breathed
the liberal air, and triumphed in his liberty. All
these amusements contributed to the instruction
and enlargement of the mind, by enabling it to
appreciate the beauty of history and romance. As
Major Rennell well observes, "how can closet critics
enter into the spirit of the Anabasis, or feel for the
Greeks in the plains of Babylon, on the crags of
Caucasus, or amidst the snows of Armenia? How
can they comprehend the sufferings of Stanislaus,
King of Poland, in effecting his escape across the
marshes and washes of Dantzic?" To them the
adventures of chivalry and the song of the minstrel
can be little more than an insipid narration of what
concerns them not; nay, who but a swimmer can
understand Homer and Orpheus, when they speak
of the broad Hellespont; or who that has not passed
nights among dismal fens, such as those of which
Tacitus says "fennis mira feritas," can enjoy the
account of that night-heron which Minerva sends
as an omen to Ulysses and Diomede, which they
cannot see from the darkness, ἀλλὰ κλάγξαντος
ἄκουσαν?[1] None should presume to criticise the
deeds and adventures of chivalry, unless those "qui
decus istud sudore et factis adsequebantur." These
amusements, which the Egyptians condemned as
dangerous and injurious to the duration of strength,[2]
Xenophon justly affirmed afforded health and
sharpened the senses, and kept off old age; nay,
even tended to the acquisition of temperance and
justice.[3] "You have only to retain the mind which
can enjoy these youthful sports," would the knight
have said—

[1] Il. X, 276.   [2] Diodor. Sicul. I, 81.
[3] De Venatione, XII.

Et tibi, crede mihi, tempora veris erunt.

Those who such simple joys have known,
Are taught to prize them when they're gone.

They were beyond comparison superior to the more artificial and expensive amusements which belong to riches and rank, in which there is nothing gaillard or folastre, as Montaigne would say. According to the simple view, the untutored heart of our ancestors, to exchange them for such a formal mockery of nature would be

Flat treason 'gainst the kingly state of youth.[1]

It was with sorrow and shame that the old Roman contrasted his recreations with those of youth. "Sibi arma, sibi equos, sibi hastas, sibi clavam, sibi pilam, sibi natationes et cursus habeant: nobis senibus talos relinquant et tesseras."[2] They who regarded such an exchange as desirable, might indeed have given an instant answer to the question of the poet,

Quæ tibi summa boni est?

but they would have been sure to hear a bitter reproof

Expecta: haud aliter respondeat hæc anus.

"The exercises of chivalry," says Caxton, "are not used and honoured as they were in ancient time, when the noble acts of the knights of England that used chivalry were renowned through the universal world. O, ye knights of England, where is the custom and usage of noble chivalry? What do ye now but go to the bains and play at dice?

---

[1] Shakspeare, Love's Labour Lost, IV, 3.
[2] Cicero de Senectute.

Alas! what do ye but sleep and take ease, and are all disordered from chivalry? Leave this, leave it, and read the noble volumes of St. Graal, of Launcelot, of Tristrem, of Galaod, of Perceval, of Perceforest, of Gawayn, and many more; there shall ye see manhood, courtesy, and gentilness."[1]

[1] Of the Order of Chyvalry and Knyghthood.

END OF PART 1.

www.ingramcontent.com/pod-product-compliance
Lightning Source LLC
Chambersburg PA
CBHW022122290426
44112CB00008B/774